Georgia State Literary Studies

10

CHAUCER'S FRENCH CONTEMPORARIES
The Poetry/Poetics of Self and Tradition

GEORGIA STATE LITERARY STUDIES SERIES: NO. 10

General Editor: Victor A. Kramer

ISSN 0884-8696

Other Titles in this Series:

1. Jack I. Biles, ed. *British Novelists Since 1900.*
2. Victor A. Kramer, ed. *The Harlem Renaissance Re-examined.*
3. R. Barton Palmer, ed. *The Cinematic Text: Methods and Approaches.*
4. Christine Gallant, ed. *Coleridge's Theory of Imagination Today.*
5. William A. Sessions, ed. *Francis Bacon's Legacy of Texts: "The Art of Discovery Grows with Discovery."*
6. Ted R. Spivey and Arthur Waterman, eds. *Conrad Aiken: A Priest of Consciousness.*
7. Hugh T. Keenan, ed. *Typology and English Medieval Literature.*
8. Carl R. Kropf, ed. *Reader Entrapment in Eighteenth-Century Literature.*
9. Matthew Charles Roudané, ed. *Public Issues, Private Tensions: Contemporary American Drama.*
10. R. Barton Palmer, ed. *Chaucer's French Contemporaries: The Poetry/Poetics of Self and Tradition.*
11. Eugene Hollahan, ed. *Gerard Manley Hopkins and Critical Discourse.*
12. Eugene Hollahan, ed. *Saul Bellow and the Struggle at the Center.*

CHAUCER'S FRENCH CONTEMPORARIES

THE POETRY/POETICS OF SELF AND TRADITION

Edited by

R. BARTON PALMER

AMS PRESS
New York

Library of Congress Cataloging-in-Publication Data

Chaucer's French contemporaries: the poetry/poetics of self and
  tradition/edited by R. Barton Palmer.
    (Georgia State literary studies; 10)
    Includes bibliographical references and index.
    ISBN 0-404-63210-6 (hardcover: acid-free paper)
    1. French poetry—To 1500—History and criticism. 2. Guillaume,
de Machaut, ca. 1300-1377—Criticism and interpretation.
3. Chaucer, Geoffrey, d. 1400—Contemporaries. 4. Influence
(Literary, artistic, etc.) 5. Aesthetics, Medieval. 6. Self in
literature. 7. Poetics. I. Palmer, R. Barton, 1946-
II. Series: Georgia State literary studies; v. 10.
PQ192.C482 1999
841'.109—dc20   91-58148
                                                                CIP

All AMS Books are printed on acid-free paper that meets the guidelines
for performance and durability of the Committee on Production Guidelines for Book Longevity of the Council on Library Resources.

Copyright © 1999 by AMS Press, Inc.
All rights reserved.

AMS Press, Inc.
56 East 13th Street
New York, N.Y. 10003

MANUFACTURED IN THE UNITED STATES OF AMERICA

CONTENTS

Prefatory Note
   Victor A. Kramer   vii

Notes on Contributors   ix

Introduction
   R. Barton Palmer   xiii

The Genius of the Patron: The Prince, the Poet, and
   Fourteenth-Century Invention
   Douglas Kelly   1

Machaut's Legacy: The Chaucerian Inheritance
   Reconsidered
   William Calin   29

Reliving the *Roman de la Rose*: Allegory and Irony in
   Machaut's *Voir-Dit*
   Sylvia Huot   47

The Metafictional Machaut: Reflexivity in the
   Judgment Poems
   R. Barton Palmer   71

Machaut's Text and the Question of His Personal
   Supervision
   William W. Kibler and James I. Wimsatt   93

Machaut and the *Octosyllabe*
   Steven R. Guthrie   111

Only Connect: Machaut's Book of Morpheus and the
    Powers of the Weak
    Margaret J. Ehrhart   137

Falconry and Fantasy in Guillaume de Machaut's *Dit
    de L'Alerion*
    Constance B. Hieatt   163

Poets, Peace, the Passion, and the Prince: Eustache
    Deschamps' "Ballade to Chaucer"
    Murray Brown   187

"Trop peu en scay": The Reluctant Narrator in
    Christine de Pizan's Works on Love
    Barbara K. Altmann   217

The "Marquerite": A Distinctive Signature
    Claire Nouvet   251

Tradition, Dream Literature, and Poetic Craft in *Le
    Paradis d'amour* of Jean Froissart
    Peter F. Dembowski   277

Reg(u)arding the Text: The Role of Vision in the
    Chansons of Charles d'Orléans
    Sarah Spence   293

Author, Editor, and the Use of Illustrations in the
    Early Imprints of Villon's Works: "Ung Chascun
    n'est maistre du scien"
    Cynthia J. Brown   315

Select Bibliography
    R. Barton Palmer and David Weems   349

Index   357

PREFATORY NOTE

This expansion of a subject that was first treated in a limited way in an issue of *Studies in the Literary Imagination* in 1987 brings to maturity one phase of an investigation which this volume's editor has been shepherding for over a decade. As a translator of Machaut, and as someone intimately involved in the pursuit of the ongoing development of scholarly investigations which provide connections between British and French culture and texts, Professor Palmer has recruited a wide range of scholars to flesh out his original examination of this topic. Along with the earlier group of six essays, now revised, eight more newly commissioned articles have been written which thereby justify the present book-length investigation of a complex inter-textual topic. We believe this will lead to further study of this topic.

Framed by diverse studies that investigate the "genius of the patron" and the shaping role of the editor at this early moment in literary history, these articles about French and English texts serve as models of how to study particular authors or specific texts, and as well as paradigms for future investigations. As with all good art we are reminded that more study and re-reading makes it possible to see myriads of connections.

And as with the other books in the Georgia State Literary Studies series, we believe that this collection serves to bring together some of the very best scholarship of the present moment and that this gathering, like the series as a whole, will assist scholars all over the world to make still more valuable connections.

This series could not exist without the generous commitments of the faculty editors who are primarily responsible for gathering the books' contributors and the generosity of the scholars who have responded to requests to write for the series. Just as we are thankful for the continuing support that the College of Arts and Sciences and the Department of English provide in the form of graduate research assistance and limited released time for individual faculty editors, we also are extremely thankful for the assistance which the many contributing scholars far beyond Georgia State University have provided by their direct support of this endeavor.

Victor A. Kramer
General Editor
Georgia State Literary Studies Series
Georgia State University

NOTES ON CONTRIBUTORS

BARBARA K. ALTMANN is currently assistant professor of French at the University of Oregon. She has also taught at Dartmouth College. Her publications include studies of Machaut and Christine.

CYNTHIA J. BROWN is professor and chair of the Department of French and Italian at the University of California (Santa Barbara). Her books include *The Shaping of History and Poetry in Late Medieval France, Poet, Patrons, and Printers: Crisis of Authority in Late Medieval France,* and a critical edition of Andre de la Vigne's *La Ressource de la Chrestienté.*

MURRAY L. BROWN received his Ph.D. from the University of Nebraska–Lincoln, and he is now assistant professor of English at Georgia State University. He has published articles in *Studies in Iconography, Manuscripts,* and *Mediaevalia.*

WILLIAM CALIN is Graduate Research Professor at the University of Florida; he has taught previously at Dartmouth, Stanford, Oregon, and the University of Poitiers, and has been Visiting Fellow, Clare Hall, Cambridge. He has published nine books and sixty articles on French and Occitan literature. His most recent volumes are *A Muse for Heroes: Nine Centuries of the Epic in France, In Defense of French Poetry: An Essay in Revaluation,* and *The French Tradition and The Literature of Medieval England.*

PETER F. DEMBOWSKI is Distinguished Service Professor of French at the University of Chicago. Among his many publications are *La Chronique de Robert de Clari; Étude de la langue et du style, Jean Froissart and his Meliador*, and several critical editions such as Froissart's *Paradis d'Amours*. He has prepared a new edition and translation into modern French of *Erec et Enide*.

MARGARET J. EHRHART is professor of English at Edward Williams College of Fairleigh Dickinson University. She is the author of *The Judgment of the Trojan Prince Paris in Medieval Literature* and several articles on Guillaume de Machaut. She is currently studying Machaut's reception of the *Roman de la Rose*.

STEVEN R. GUTHRIE is an associate professor of English at Agnes Scott College. He has published in various places on the Middle English lyric and on language and meter in the Continental-English tradition. His current studies include the effects of a polyglot tradition on vernacular meters and the attempts of late medieval poets to explore the concept of personal privacy.

CONSTANCE B. HIEATT is professor emeritus of English at the University of Western Ontario. While she is best known for work on Old English poetry and medieval culinary recipes, she has also published books and articles on Middle English poetry and Old Norse sagas—among other things. Her most recent book is *Guillaume de Machaut: The Tale of the Alerion*, ed. and trans. with Minnette Gaudet.

SYLVIA HUOT teaches French at Cambridge University. She is the author of *From Song to Book; The Poetics of Writing in Old French and Lyrical Narrative Poetry*, and *The "Romance of the Rose" and its Medieval Readers*, and co-editor, with Kevin Brownlee, of *Rethinking the "Romance of the Rose": Text, Image, Reception*. She has published articles on medieval French, Provencal, and Italian literature, and is writing a book, *Allegorical Play*, on the old French Motet.

DOUGLAS KELLY is professor of French and Italian at the University of Wisconsin–Madison. Author of many articles on medieval French literature, Kelly has written such well-known books as *Medieval Imagination, The Art of Medieval French Romance,* and *The Arts of Poetry and Prose.*

WILLIAM W. KIBLER is the Superior Oil-Linward Shivers Centennial Professor of Medieval Studies at the University of Texas, where he has taught since 1969. In addition to many articles on medieval French literature, he has recently published his Penguin Classics translation of *Chrétien de Troyes: Arthurian Romances*. He is also the author of *An Introduction to Old French*. With James Wimsatt he has published *Guillaume de Machaut's Jugement du roy de Behaigne and Remede de Fortune* in the Chaucer Library.

CLAIRE NOUVET is associate professor of French and Italian at Emory University. She has published articles on Froissart, Abelard and Heloise, *The Romance of the Rose*, and Ovid's Narcissus. She has completed a book entitled *An Open Book: The Romance of the Rose*, forthcoming. She is also the special editor of the *Yale French Studies* issue entitled "Literature and the Ethical Question." She is currently working on a book devoted to Abelard and Heloise's correspondence.

R. BARTON PALMER is Calhoun Lemon Professor of Literature at Clemson University and Executive Director of the South Atlantic Modern Language Association. Author of many articles on literary/film theory and medieval literature, Palmer is the editor/translator of four volumes devoted to the narrative poetry of Guillaume de Machaut. He is currently working on a number of studies devoted to the influence of Machaut on Chaucer, and, with Daniel Leech-Wilkinson, is preparing an edition and English translation of Machaut's *Voir-Dit*. His most recent book is *Hollywood's Dark Cinema: The American Film Noir.*

SARAH SPENCE is associate professor of classics at the University of Georgia. She is the editor/translator of *The French Chansons of Charles d'Orléans* and the author of *Rhetorics of Reason and Desire: Vergil, Augustine, and the Troubadours*. At present she is finishing a study of the self in the twelfth century.

DAVID WEEMS, now deceased, was a graduate student at Georgia State University whose major interest was medieval literature.

JAMES WIMSATT is Temple Centennial Professor emeritus of English Literature at the University of Texas at Austin. He has published extensively on Chaucer and the French poets, often in collaboration with William Kibler. The University of Toronto Press has recently published his comprehensive *Chaucer and His French Contemporaries: Natural Music in the Fourteenth Century*.

INTRODUCTION

When the issue of *Studies in the Literary Imagination* that is the point of origin for this present volume was published in 1987, I felt as editor some justification was needed for a scholarly focus on texts and authors that had suffered disdain and, more often, neglect at the hands of specialists. The nineteen-seventies and early eighties, to be sure, had witnessed the appearance of important work by Daniel Poirion, Jacqueline Cerquiglini, James Wimsatt, Douglas Kelly, William Calin, and Kevin Brownlee, among others; this scholarship successfully urged a re-evaluation of the fourteenth-century French poets who were both Chaucer's contemporaries and an important source of inspiration for him. In many cases this criticism built on and extended what had been discovered by earlier generations of philologists, students of French and English literature who had begun the recovery of a tradition nearly forgotten since the late Middle Ages.

Ironically, philological studies had traced the connections of writers like Guillaume de Machaut and Jean Froissart to earlier poetry (especially the *Roman de la Rose* and the *Ovide moralisé*) only to supply the rationale for the aesthetic dismissal of works and authors alike. The reason for this is simple. The canons of post-Romanticism demanded that writers who revised or rewrote instead of creating in the modern sense could not be taken seriously. What Paul Zumthor has termed the principle of textual *mouvance* was unappreciated by Neogrammarian critics.[1] As is well known, the supposed trajectory of Chaucer's career provided the model against which his contemporaries' inferior capacities of invention could be measured. Here was a genius who escaped the domination of tradition by fleeing his library for a social pageant that, like a modern novelist, he could faithfully represent. Authors such as Machaut, Eustache Deschamps, Christine de Pizan, Froissart, and Charles d'Orléans could be the objects of historically oriented inquiry; but they could not be accommodated easily to then dominant notions of "literature."

During the last quarter century, these judgments have been largely discredited, especially by the demonstration that originality is an inappropriate criterion whose application can only distort our understanding of medieval literary production, including that of Chaucer. Within the last six or seven years, however, what is truly distinctive about the productions of Chaucer's French contemporaries has begun to emerge. In this regard, the essays contained in the 1987 issue of *Studies in the Literary Imagination* were very much *dans le vent* of critical change, even as, in part, they confirmed the continuing productivity of more traditional approaches. In the lead essay of that issue, William Calin wrote: "indeed, the greatest gift Machaut offers Chaucer is the notion of a poet writing poetry about the writing of poetry by a poet" (p. 35 in this volume). Calin maintains that the blind spot in earlier scholarly studies is not only a matter of teleology (the first authors considered better than the last). It also relates to formal values, especially what we would now term poetic self-consciousness and intertextuality (aspects of structure summed up, for Chaucerians like the Victorian George Lyman Kittredge, in the dismissive term "conventionalism"). In a recent book, Robert S. Sturges argues that such textual features create "ambiguous relations with the reader, balancing literary convention with potential 'truth' and inviting the reader's ironic participation in the literary work as game."[2] Like some of the scholars whose work is included here, Sturges views these emerging literary forms as indices of an altered intellectual climate, one in which problems of knowledge and value have been foregrounded. This shift in the reading of texts, Sturges argues, alters not only the consumption of late medieval poetry, but its form and content as well.

Even more than the original collection, the essays in this book exemplify a deep interest in the somewhat unexplored poetics of late medieval French literature, in the form and rhetoric that inscribe a historical mode of production (the courtly system determined by the relationship between patron and poet) and construct its fictional effects, importantly conditioned by the court as a site of reading. Unlike earlier romance and dream vision, the texts of the fourteenth- and fifteenth-century masters are often poems whose subject matter is, in some sense, poetry itself. Within this international context, Chaucer's much-discussed play with narration and narrators comes to seem less original and more a part of a thriving trans-Channel tradition. The customary matter of this tradition is not poetry in the narrowly formalist sense of a group of texts, but rather of a "making" around which other activities are organized, notably interpretation and evaluation. Interesting in such a context is the fact that the works in this tradition are often deliberately and overtly intertextual; that is, they invite, indeed depend upon a reading through the "givens" of valued earlier texts, through the informing matrix of the already written, the already read. As Sylvia Huot, for example, here demonstrates, it is not the case that Machaut was unable to escape the influence of the *Roman de la Rose*, but rather that he recalls some of the noteworthy elements of that still then controversial text only ironically to renew and replace them. Thus in the *Voir-Dit* the dialectic between self and tradition provides both the opportunity for the writing of poetry and its material as well.

This book is organized to emphasize the determining material effects of the courtly mode of production. It thus begins with a wide-ranging examination of the patron's role in the generation of courtly poetry and ends with a consideration of the impact another emerging figure—the editor—had on both the writer, now not necessarily a figure tied to the court, and the form of poetry. The eight new essays also permit a more thorough coverage of writers other than Machaut and Froissart; Eustache Deschamps, Christine de Pizan, Charles d'Orléans, and François Villon are now given the attention they deserve.

In the lead essay Douglas Kelly demonstrates the extent to which the courtly mode of literary production, especially the relationship between prince and poet, finds its reflex in the poetical texts of Machaut and Froissart. As Kelly argues, the notion of the patron's "genius" can be understood and represented in five ways within the texts themselves: the patron as the donor who commissions, and in some sense pays for a literary work; the patron as a poet who can contribute verse to the author he supports and protects; the patron as feudal master, as the idealized image of various virtues which the poet celebrates; the patron as pupil, as someone in need of the poet's instruction and help; finally the patron as the object of affection whose existence and encouragement generate the text. Within the poems themselves these roles intriguingly interchange. In Machaut's *Jugement dou Roy de Behaingne*, for example, the patron is represented primarily as master, for it is Charles of Navarre who judges the debate; and yet the patron is also represented as a demanding lady love, as the figure of Good Fortune who objects to the poet's inattentiveness and to his production of a supposedly antifeminist work.

Kelly's categories further our understanding of the ways in which late fourteenth century texts embody, in what I'd term a metafictional way, the extratextual relationship(s) of poet to patron. Kelly points out that this level of meaning "complicates the analyses of the author-in-the-work and of the narrator" (p. 19). For we must ask to what extent the poetry in each case has its origin (either fictionally or existentially) in what he terms the genius of the patron. Such a perspective similarly complicates our notion of "the art of invention as the technique was conceived in the Middle Ages" (p. 19). Clearly post-Romantic assumptions about authorship are not adequate to this type of creative practice. Instead, as Kelly concludes, echoing Zumthor's theory of *mouvance*, we must view the genius of the poet as "putting together anew," and the genius of his/her patron as that "light which gives life to the poetic inventions" (p. 22). In any case, this body of texts testifies eloquently to the complex spectrum of practices which engendered them; they constitute, in many ways, our best evidence for the underlying assumptions of late-fourteenth-century French literary practice.

This literary culture exerted a strong influence on writers associated with the English court. Building on Kittredge's early studies of Machaut's influence on Chaucer, William Calin makes a strong case in his revised essay that the *Book of the Duchess* derives its overall structure from Machaut's *Dit de la fonteinne amoureuse* even though many of the English poem's details (as James Wimsatt demonstrated long ago in his *Chaucer and the French Love Poets*) come from a variety of other sources. Calin uses the narratological concept of the *mise-en-abyme* to demonstrate how both poems are more reflexive than previously thought. If Chaucer's dreamer is reading Machaut's poem (rather than the *Ovide moralisé* or in the original Latin text), then "Machaut would offer a complete intertextual matrix for Chaucer, his book as pre-text included in Chaucer's intertext" (p. 33–34). Calin also argues that Machaut's *Jugement dou Roy de Navarre* provided Chaucer with the model for his two versions of the Prologue to *The Legend of Good Women*. The parallels between the two works are indeed striking, even though this fact has not been recognized by most Chaucerians (who are unfamiliar not only with the longer Machaut work but also with his Marguerite poems, and these may have inspired the Prologue's concern with the myth of the daisy).

Once again the resemblance between the two narrative poems is based on reflexivity since both narrators are called to account for poetry they have composed that, apparently antifeminist, has injured their reputations and calls for retribution (in both cases, the production of more texts, this time with the correct doctrine.) Chaucer and Machaut, Calin shows, equally disagree with the charges and manage to suggest, subtly and indirectly, that they are innocent. Both use their narrators, here and elsewhere, to create a distance between the poet and his textual production, as well as to offer a meditation on the vagaries and discontents associated with the making of such poetry. The influence of Machaut, Calin argues, does not end with the so-called early period. "*Troilus*," he suggests, building on the work of James Wimsatt, "can indeed be thought of as Boccaccio medievalized, that is filtered through Machaut" (p. 39). Furthermore, according to Calin, Machaut's creation of a narrator limited in vision and understanding of his own experience in the *Voir-Dit* may have influenced the conception of *The Canterbury Tales* and its model of narration. Calin concludes by suggesting that the *Manciple's Tale* and, especially, the *Merchant's Tale* manifest the continuing influence of Machaut on Chaucer's imagination, and he calls for a re-evaluation both of that influence and of the sophisticated artistry of late medieval French poetry.

Sylvia Huot's analysis of the *Voir-Dit* depends on the theory of intertextuality first popularized by Julia Kristeva (drawing on the work of M. M. Bakhtin). For it is the "presence of the *Rose* in the *Voir-Dit*" which indexes Machaut's originality, "reveals both his understanding of this complex poem and his concept of his own poetic work" (pp. 47–48). Machaut re-presents the famous erotic imagery in the earlier poem, but such re-presentation has a double effect: on the one hand it invests the new fiction with the deeper meanings that have concretized around the older, but on the other it opens up an "ironic disjunction between the experience that is being portrayed and the character of its participants, and the language and literary models with which it is evoked" (p. 48). As Huot sees it, the result is a poem which explores the textual production of meaning by offering a "critique, both humorous and enlightening, of the conflicting poetic registers operating in the *Rose*" (p. 48). In addition, Machaut makes his "true poem" an intertextual matrix full of references to other works in the varied tradition of love poetry. Casting himself in the role of Lancelot, for example, the poet lover, as Huot puts it, "has little understanding of just what he is in for, of the potential obstacles and dangers inherent in the experience of passionate love" (p. 50). One of those obstacles is dealing with the erotic, an aspect of the love experience which Machaut has ordinarily been thought to neglect. Huot challenges that received opinion by demonstrating that the poet engages with the two scenes, the episodes of the leaf and the kiss, which in the *Rose* are most highly charged with *double entendre*. But his success as an artist appropriating the requisite models is ironically undercut by the fact that "in his role as lover, he has finally proved incapable of transposing art into life" (p. 59). Yet Huot does not think such a failure is simply ironic. For "if the bedazzled Guillaume is ultimately caught in the intricate web of metaphor, Machaut the poet has succeeded in orchestrating a poetic *tour de force* that rivals the *Rose* itself" (p. 66).

Like Calin and Huot, I argue that Machaut's texts, contrary to the older view, are deliberately reflexive and overtly intertextual; the judgment poems construct their own web of references and presences, thereby attaining a hitherto unimagined degree of reflexivity and self-containment. This "spatial form," however, constitutes a historical/critical problem, although this is more apparent than real. The insights of modern critical theory, particularly narratology, have not often been used to illuminate the structures of medieval texts because medieval scholarship has been dominated by historicist approaches, especially philology and Robertsonianism. A truly historicist approach, however, is impossible; critics must recognize that the objects of their interest are shaped by the irreducible presentness of their inquiries. I argue that, perhaps surprisingly, this is no disability, but in some respects an advantage, because the postmodern critic is uniquely situated to recognize aspects of structure not considered within the literary theorizing of the Middle Ages themselves.[3] Such an approach will "hardly produce a science of these texts, but it should be capable of a knowledge that is not only engaging (with the concerns/interests of its own historical moment) but also revealing (of a past incapable in some ways of knowing itself)" (p. 75). To the post-modern critic, Machaut's two judgment poems are metafictional in the sense that much contemporary fiction is: that is, Machaut offers a self-enclosed imaginative world and, at the same time, a commentary that in its consciousness of literary production dispels the illusions of that world. For Machaut, metafictionality is the means by which he can represent himself as a poet within the poem, even as he continues to write the kind of poems required by tradition. In the *Jugement dou Roy de Behaingne*, Machaut dramatizes the discontents associated with poetic subjectivity; for the poet is both the servant of his betters and the source of their emotional enlightenment. In the companion piece *Jugement dou Roy de Navarre*, Machaut goes much further, making his fictional persona (a poet named Guillaume de Machaut) the principal character. Here the narrator is called to account for supposedly producing an antifeminist text and must defend himself in a debate against the allegorical personage Good Fortune (who represents not only the poet's traditional beloved, but also the patron and, to a lesser degree, literary tradition itself). In this work Machaut explores the contradiction between the poet's imaginative freedom (it is he who, extratextually, chooses to provoke his textual counterpart) and artistic constraints (like his real-life reflex, the narrator must please the court and not transgress the rules governing poetry devoted to *fin'amors*). In many ways, the *Navarre* is a unique text because it is so centrally concerned with the poet's situation. Chaucer's imitation in the prologue of *The Legend of Good Women*, by way of contrast, is not so daring because the English poet focuses on the stories which the narrator must tell as penance, not on the attack against and his defense of previous poetic accomplishments.

The next two essays demonstrate that the texts of Machaut and his followers still need the kind of attention which earlier generations of philologists paid them: issues of editing, metrics, and literary history have in no way been finally resolved. In the case of Machaut, one reason for this is that the MS tradition of his *oeuvre* (as well as the strictly linguistic aspects of his poetry) never received, during the first flourishing of philology, the attention accorded to the more valued texts of the High French Middle Ages. Ernest Hoepffner's edition of most of the narrative *dits*, for example, is based on a preliminary examination of the MS filiation whose final version never appeared (even as his editing of this corpus of poems was not completed). This gap was never filled by other studies (and it is shameful that Machaut's most celebrated poem, the *Voir-Dit*, has at this moment still not been republished in an edition conforming to modern critical standards). The imposing presence of the beautifully illustrated omnibus MS of Machaut's works (BN 1584, usually termed A), along with the fact that this MS contains a table of contents that attests, in some vague sense, to the poet's personal supervision of its execution, led Hoepffner and others to accept it as the best codex. It may indeed represent in some way Machaut's last word on the texts of his collected poetry and music. François Avril, an expert on MS illumination of this period, suggests that the art work may have been done in Reims where Machaut was then permanently resident. But is it the best basis for modern editions of the poetry? William Kibler and James Wimsatt have cast at least partial doubt on the authority of BN 1584. Their comparison of MSS, especially BN 1586 or C, which represent earlier versions of the *Jugement dou Roy de Behaingne* and the *Remede de Fortune*, with the texts in A makes a strong case for the greater reliability of C. Wimsatt and Kibler support this view by examining the details of the excision of four passages from the *Behaingne* in the tradition represented by A and by evaluating the relative merits of passages with disputed readings. The importance of their findings, however, is not limited to editorial policy. As they point out, the emerging portrait of Machaut in the last fifteen years or so has been that of a poet intimately involved with the codification, copying, and transmission of his collected works. Their conclusion entails a significant though hardly total modification of that portrait: "in the case of both poems, little indicates that the transmission of the text was accompanied by the poet's correction, emendation, or revision." They go on: "though Machaut obviously was concerned with the general aspects of the presentation of his *oeuvre*, as with other poets of the time he left textual details largely to the scribes, whose standards of accuracy were hardly modern" (p. 106).

Steven Guthrie's study of Machaut's use of the *octosyllabe* similarly re-opens an area of inquiry which, somewhat neglected since the decline of philology, has been invigorated in recent years by the use of methods and approaches derived from linguistics. As Guthrie suggests, the octosyllabe has never been studied in depth, particularly in regard to rhythmic structure. Guthrie's method is to focus on three principal issues: poetic meter; spoken performance; and the relationship, in song, between poetic meter and musical rhythm. Studies of the octosyllabe in its earlier stages of use reveal a regularity which in later periods is broken in a number of ways. The usual explanation for this development is that later poets wanted to avoid monotony. Guthrie's statistical study of line types from the twelfth century through to Machaut's practice in the fourteenth, however, uncovers a number of complex factors influencing this development. Starting from the assumption that "the metrical unit is the halfline, whose ideal embodiment is a major linguistic phrase in an overall rising rhythm," Guthrie traces the evolution of the octosyllabe as it is influenced by linguistic change, music practice, and poetic desire for rhythmic complexity. But the process of change is itself constrained by poetic tradition, attesting to the influence of older texts (in some fashion) on Machaut's practice: "Machaut's narrative line, then, is much more abstract than that of the *Gormont* poet, both in terms of binary recurrence and in terms of the concrete enforcement of the caesura, but the two belong to the same essential metrical line, and Machaut's practice is an extension of the *Gormont* poet's practice" (p. 123). This means, Guthrie argues, that traditional views of poetic performance (based on the assumption of a strong binary pulse in recitation) should be modified to account for the statistically supported facts of rhythmic variation and complexity.

Poetry in this tradition, however, cannot be understood from formalist and philological perspectives alone; these texts also responded to their social and intellectual environment, as the next three essays demonstrate. Machaut and his followers (up to and including François Villon) lived in a turbulent political climate. Machaut was a young man when the last of the Capetians died, and he lived to witness not only the beginning of a new dynasty—the Valois—but a dispute over their succession which was to disturb the peace of France for more than three generations. For some time Machaut was personally involved in this dispute at the highest levels; from 1349 to at least 1357, possibly even to 1361 he gratefully received the patronage of Charles of Navarre, mortal enemy of the Valois, though he kept up good relations at the same time with the royal house, benefitting, apparently, from the favor of both the dauphin (the future Charles V) and his influential brother, Jean, Duc de Berry. Machaut's *Confort d'ami*, addressed to the king of Navarre as he lay imprisoned by John the Good, and *Prise d'Alexandrie*, an epic chronicle dedicated to the exploits of Pierre of Lusignan, each manifest an interest in politics; the former text quite explicitly takes up issues championed by the reformers of 1357, who wished for a *renovatio* of the government and its head. And yet Machaut has not often been considered as political a writer as his contemporaries and followers: Eustache Deschamps, Christine de Pizan, and Alain Chartier.

Margaret Ehrhart challenges that received opinion here, arguing that the "*Dit de la fonteinne amoureuse* is Machaut's response to the political turmoil that characterized fourteenth-century France" (p. 135). Traditionally thought of as an occasional love vision poem, the *Fonteinne amoureuse*, Ehrhart argues, belongs also to the *speculum principum* or "mirror for princes" genre. The poem, she goes on to suggest, develops the "portrait of a realm whose leadership has failed it" (p.   ).

But this would be impossible to say directly, for Machaut was dependent on the goodwill of the very class which he criticizes. Using the obliqueness of the dream vision and depending on meanings associated with classical myth, Machaut instead developed "themes that resonate with the political situation in contemporary France" (p. 136). Such reticence finds a formal reflex in the poem itself, for Machaut very deliberately characterizes his own narrating self as a clerk who can only follow the powerful, whose station does not allow him to deal directly with the problems they face. But verbal play in the work's prologue hints that it is the reader's job to supply the meanings he cannot speak directly, to pick up on the many dark hints which, Ehrhart thinks, Machaut develops in his seemingly optimistic and traditional love vision. For example, the three dreams referred to in the poem all prove true in some disastrous sense. Her husband Ceyx has perished at sea, Alcyone learns. Hecuba's dream of Troy's destruction is prophetic, and the dream shared by the Roman senators makes known the inevitable destruction of the empire. Even the poem's emphasis on love's sorrow and its amelioration (furnished by the dream that Venus allows both the narrator and his grieving, noble companion) has its dark side. For Paris's success in love ultimately means the destruction of his home and family. As Ehrhart puts it, "Paris was his country's torch" (p. 151). Her close reading of the poem's web of allusions and implications suggests that the work "situates late fourteenth-century France in a context of dynastic rise and fall" (p. 153).

In her study of Machaut's *Dit de l'alerion*, Constance B. Hieatt makes a case that this work is the first "making an extensive comparison between the arts of falconry and love" (p. 162). This poem, Hieatt suggests, finds its reflex in Chaucer's occasional use of falconry terms as metaphors for various aspects of the love experience, a tradition that finds its most precious and complex embodiment in Shakespeare's *The Taming of the Shrew*. Intriguingly, Hieatt's close analysis of Machaut's use of falconry terminology and practice in the *Alerion* demonstrates that much of the poet's knowledge likely came not from practice, but from the many popular books on the subject well read by the nobility of the period. The term "alerion" itself is not even mentioned by most of these works (Machaut's ultimate source may have been, Hieatt demonstrates, either Vincent of Beauvais or Thomas of Cantimpré). Of further interest to Machaudistes is Hieatt's complex and convincing analysis of how the poet develops the beloved/bird analogy, leaving out that information about falconry which might not fit its transference to a courtly love context. For example, while the narrator mentions the careful feeding of his bird, as prescribed by the falconry manuals, he never admits to withholding food or keeping the bird awake for days at a time, techniques then used in taming and obedience work; no lady could be treated in these ways (though Shakespeare's Kate proves a more fitting object for such attention). Hieatt's detailed treatment of Machaut's use of both learned and more popular (hence somewhat fantastic) source material is too complex to be summarized adequately here. Her essay provides yet another demonstration, however, of the extent to which Machaut's works depend on intertextual ties, for the courtly reader is certainly asked to examine and apply his own knowledge of falconry in decoding what is undoubtedly one of the most unusual treatments of love in fourteenth-century poetry.

The relationship between Chaucer and his French contemporaries is largely an indirect one, a matter of poetry prompting other poems, of authors reading and then writing within a vaguely conceived framework of the contemporary and fashionable. Murray Brown's discussion of the cultural context of Eustache Deschamps's "Ballade to Chaucer" illuminates what may be a most interesting exception to this general rule. The date and occasion of this remarkable poem are unknown as matters of fact, but Brown argues that it likely was composed at the time of Sir Lewis Clifford's mission to the French court in 1391. An understanding of this context, he suggests, explains Deschamps's effusive praise of the English poet and the kind or rhetoric he employs. Contextual study, moreover, importantly "addresses the relationship between the two poets and the several patron-prince-pupils" (p. 187) who were involved.

Deschamps praises Chaucer for having translated the *Rose*, an act of cultural *translatio* which would furnish the grounds for political reconciliation (an aim, Brown argues, that Deschamps would only have pursued had it been that of the nobles upon whom he depended). While Deschamps likely became acquainted with Chaucer during the latter's captivity in Reims (early 1360), it was their later association with The Order of the Passion of Jesus Christ (an organization which provided some of the basis for an eventual cessation of hostilities between the two countries) that provided the immediate reason for the poem's composition and its particular form of praise. In fact, the ballade was likely "part of a cultural exchange, an informal dialogue between the two courts . . . and as the conferences approached and hopes for peace became greater, so did the gifts attending them" (p. 192). As such it represents a distinct change in Deschamps's politics. His earlier poetry manifests a hope for "a complete and bloody vanquishing of the English, literally demanding their total destruction" (p. 198). Later he came to believe that the English were not the sole cause of continuing hostilities; he hoped for a peace which would remove the need for destruction. Under the influence of Philippe de Mézières, Deschamps embraced the ideals of the Order most strongly. This led eventually to a break with his patron, Louis of Flanders, who had much to gain from an ongoing war. In supporting the peace program of the Order, however, "Deschamps placed himself with a distinguished group of poets and literary figures: Chaucer, Mézières, Boucicaut (Marshal of France), Granson and Clifford, to name only a few" (p. 207). The ballade he wrote to his English counterpart is the best evidence we have of their joint political hopes and efforts.

Brown demonstrates the extent to which the political and the poetical could be experienced jointly by men. But are the same "voices" available to a woman? Christine de Pizan's treatment of gender and politics forcefully poses this issue. Barbara Altmann's analysis of the "reluctant narrator" in the works of Christine devoted to love demonstrates both the indebtedness of this remarkable writer to her predecessors (especially Machaut) and her original use of inherited conventions. Altmann finds that this narratological "construct" is "portrayed with remarkable consistency from the earliest to the latest writings in Christine's literary production" (p. 216). Bearing a resemblance to the writer we have come to know from manuscript miniatures, this textual self is present in Christine's writings from the very beginning, even in those "which conform more closely in subject matter to popular courtly models" (p. 216). The most important convention here is the "je" or "I" which seems to be speaking from personal experience in lyric forms (the "I" in narrative forms, as we have seen, can speak the experience of others). While Christine follows Machaut in creating a narrator who is a conflation of experiencing self and professional writer, she breaks from tradition in two important ways: her narrator is a woman who is not in Love's service.

The result, as others have recognized, is a voice outside the ordinary courtly economy of desire and emotionality who is yet, as author, powerful enough to comment on that economy. Though the *Cent Ballades*, for example, largely take love as their subject, Altmann demonstrates that Christine's skillful manipulation of the narrating/lyrical "I" allows her to distance herself from love as a poetic "matter." Unlike Machaut, Christine offers herself as "a poet figure who considers love a convenient and

Introduction   xxvii

pleasing subject matter for poetry, one topic among others, however privileged it may be" (p. 222). Altmann discovers that in all six other works by Christine about love, some of the same mechanisms of disavowal (associated with the narrator figure) are present to some degree. Perhaps the most important of these are Christine's repeated hints that the subject matter she deals with has been imposed on her by the wishes of a patron; thus writing about love becomes part of the writer's duty. An extension of this is that Christine also suggests that writing about love is itself a form of entertainment; an index of this ludic impulse is that, following Machaut, Christine ends some of her works with an anagram designed to reveal her name. If Machaut's *Voir-Dit* reveals the impossibility of reconciling the experiencing and producing "I's," for the act of composition cannot be the act of love, then "in Christine the social tension is replaced by a personal and professional one: must she play court poet and write the love stories that are so well-received or can she devote herself to the more studious pursuits suitable to a woman of high intelligence and thorough education" (p. 241).

For Claire Nouvet, Jean Froissart's poetry is also connected directly to the emerging literary economy of the late fourteenth century: "a commissioned and remunerative narrative, the text inscribes the social constraints presiding over its composition; it becomes the story of its own production" (p. 249). Nouvet argues that it is Froissart's *Prison amoureuse* which, modeled on Machaut's *Voir-Dit*, best exemplifies the later author's desire to produce self-reflexive poetry. The *Prison* is in many ways an even more "writerly" text than its source, for though "at first an advisor in matters of love, the Protagonist of the *Prison amoureuse* soon becomes an advisor on the subject of courtly writing, before finally assuming the role of professional poet when Rose asks him to collect their correspondence into a volume" (p. 250). This result is a radically different representation of poetic identity, one connected directly to the poet's adoption of "a pseudonym as well as a signet, a specific figure, a seal, which functions as his signature" (p. 250). Nouvet's discussion of these structural features is too complex to be explained briefly here, but I should note that her analysis, like that of many other contributors to this volume, depends heavily on the deliberate (that is, rhetorical) intertextuality of the *Prison*, a fascinating poem. Such spatial form means that the poet writes himself into the text and "does not therefore transcribe an already constituted self" (p. 269). The narrative, "is designed to avoid any recognition of this status" (pp. 269–70). Yet a symptomatic reading of the text reveals the disappearing self. "If the lyric 'I' exemplifies the 'dying' inherent in the very constitution of the self in and as an image, the emergence of the professional writer 'echoes' this original disappearance" (p. 273).

As Peter Dembowski reminds us, Froissart's *Paradis d'amour* has been long recognized as an important influence on Chaucer's early poetry. It is itself a complex reworking of themes and structures popularized by Machaut. Only in the last fifteen years has this poem, along with a number of other important Froissart works, been published in an edition conforming to modern standards. Editor of the *Paradis*, Dembowski provides here the first full-scale critical analysis of this important text. His essay touches on many of the issues raised by the other contributors: the reworking of the traditional features of the dream vision; the metafictional representation of the poet's self and *oeuvre* within the text itself; the fictionalizing of the poet's attempts to make a place for himself within the structures of literary tradition, even as he expresses his gratitude for the gift of poetry and the opportunity to compose it. It is this last aspect of the *Paradis* which Dembowski ultimately finds the most intriguing and significant: "the poet thanks the gods not only for the gift of an expanding and comforting experience, but also, and explicitly, for having received the gift of poetry writing. . . . It is mostly then that we can catch a glimpse of the real self of this extraordinarily dedicated and proud maker of traditional poetry" (pp. 284–85). As Dembowski implies, much more work needs to be done in the exploration of this dynamic and creative encounter between self and tradition, an encounter that involves not only poetic fiction but the poetics which are its ground of being.

Sarah Spence's discussion of vision in the poetry of Charles d'Orléans depends on the notion that "subjectivity and the self are ... progressively valorized through the course of the high Middle Ages" (p. 292) and that this is the intellectual climate "from which Charles is trying to emerge" (p. 292). Specifically, his writing depends on the effort to "escape from or deny any necessary dependence on the world as known through the senses" (p. 293). Overturning the notion that the lyrics are simple, Spence argues instead that "the simplicity is more a sleight a hand" and that they depend on "one of the darkest concepts in poetry, *nonchaloir*" (p. 293). In this regard, Charles denies the reader one of his most fundamental points of attachment, the assumption that his relationship to the text is "based on the structure of the self" (p. 293). In the later chansons, for example, "space and time both disappear; there is little sense of a definite past or future" (p. 298). Thus the "internal persona" is not only unrevealed, "it does not need to see to exist" (p. 300). In fact, the textual space this persona comes to occupy is defined by the numbness implicit in the concept of *nonchaloir*; for Spence this space is not a "synonym for the abyss" but rather Charles's attempt to signal "the existence of a voice that has no direct connection to the world" (p. 301). Here is a voice, in other words, that indexes the textual, denies the referential. Spence locates this feature of Charles's poetry in the changing intellectual climate of the High Middle Ages. Unlike the other writers discussed here, however, Charles does not make his poems webs of intertextual references; this is part of his general refusal "to make reference to anything that he could not have known first hand" (p. 304). Like Froissart and Christine, Charles is thus a writer interested in the ludic possibilities of reading. "When textual desire is reduced to mere play we have entered a realm of anti-hermeneutics and an area that threatens to expose the fragility—even the denial—of our selfhood" (p. 308).

The text becomes a problematic object in the equally problematic exchange between the emerging professional writer and his readers (both courtly and otherwise); behind this exchange, of course, stands the figure of the patron, who may assume a diegetic as well as an extratextual presence. The increasing use of printing in the century following Chaucer's death added yet another figure to this mode of literary production: the editor.

Textual instability (and the author's corresponding lack of control over his texts) remained a feature of this new economic/cultural relationship, as Cynthia Brown demonstrates in her discussion of the early printed versions of François Villon's poetry. Brown focuses particularly on "the use of rubrics and illustrations in the early printed editions of Villon's works as a form of editorial intervention" (p. 314). Recognizing, as Villon himself did, that an author is "not the master of his own," Brown raises a not-easily answered question about the meaning of the resulting text, an artifact whose possibilities of interpretation are affected by what the editor contributes. This term, as Brown recognizes, is somewhat unstable, referring both to printers, who in the early days of printing had "primary control" over the form of the resulting book, and booksellers, "who came to share and even assume some of the functions of a modern editor as the bookmaking process grew more complicated" (p. 315). In order to increase the attractiveness of their offerings, early editors often included illustrations. One of the effects of this alteration is to reinforce the presence of the author in the text, "for Villon's image and name are repeatedly displayed" (p. 318) in the early edition of Levet. At the same time, "contradictions between word and image, between editorial and authorial voices, arise" (p. 318). In Marot's edition, for example, a dedicatory verse addressed by the editor to François I and a letter to readers explaining editorial practice both index Marot's presence and partial reappropriation of Villon's words. As Brown concludes, "*mouvance* . . . didn't entirely disappear with the advent of print . . . the more conspicuous manifestations of *mouvance* began to shift to the periphery or margins of a printed work" (p. 334). The poetics of self and tradition which defined the production of Chaucer and his French contemporaries would themselves have to change, given the new realities of writing and reading. As the "postmodernism" of this tradition attests, however, many of the problematics (perhaps especially the relationship between authorship and authority) which defined this literary era are still with us.

NOTES

1. *Essai de poètique medievale* (Paris: Seuil, 1972).
2. *Medieval Interpretation: Models of Reading in Literary Narrative, 1100-1500* (Carbondale: Southern Illinois Univ. Press, 1991), p. 77.
3. Postmodern approaches of this kind are, of course, becoming increasingly popular among critics, although most of the studies that have appeared so far have been more concerned with hermeneutical than with either formal or narratological issues. See, for example, R. Howard Bloch, *Etymologies and Genealogies: A Literary Anthropology of the French Middle Ages* (Chicago: Univ. of Chicago Press, 1983) and Gerald Bruns, *Inventions: Writing, Textuality, and Understanding in Literary Theory* (New Haven: Yale Univ. Press, 1982).

Douglas Kelly

The Genius of the Patron: The Prince, The Poet, and Fourteenth-Century Invention

> Si que je pris mon escriptoire
> Qui est entaillie d'ivoire,
> Et tous mes outils pour escrire
> La complainte qu'i voloit dire.
> Si commença piteusement
> Et je l'escri joieusement.
>
> (*FA* 229–34)[1]

The *Fontaine amoureuse* reflects a division of labor that is not unusual in medieval writing. The poet makes of his or her mind a scribe to record the thoughts and sentiments of the prince. This fits the model more elaborately represented by the patron, architect, and artisans that E. Panofsky discerned in the construction of Saint-Denis.² The patron commands, the architect plans, the artist executes. This commonplace model better illustrates the medieval conception of invention than does that of the artist's genius as the only one that mattered.³ The Romantic and post-Romantic tendency to exalt the artist's and, today, the performer's genius neglects what so many pre-Romantic dedications proclaim: the patron as the one who inaugurates the work to be written, who conceives of it before providing for its redaction by a scribe. The presumed superiority of aristocratic genius to that of others implicit in this model is a relatively unexplored aspect of medieval alterity. Is the current commonplace that flattery alone inspired praise of the patron and his or her contribution to the invention of the work adequate to medieval conceptions of the patron's genius and its place in artistic invention? Is laudation always flattery? How committed were patrons to what they commissioned? How involved were they in its realization?

Recent studies in a variety of disciplines have shown the influence of the milieu the writer wrote for on his or her conception of the work to be written.⁴ Wace and Benoît de Sainte-Maure did not complete their chronicles on the Anglo-Norman dynasty because Henry II disapproved of their accomplishments or progress, in striking contrast to the *Brut* and the *Troie*, which they did complete. Chrétien de Troyes asserts that he received a book about the grail, the best story ever told, from the greatest source of bounty the world had known. The best illustration of the patron—architect—artist paradigm is surely found in the Prologue and Epilogue to the *Chevalier de la charrette*. However one reads this romance, and whatever quibbles may still be heard about its qualities and intentions, the author/narrator explicitly attributes its conception to Marie de Champagne, its plan (*antancion*) to Chrétien, and its execution to both Chrétien and, on the evidence of the Epilogue, Godefroi de Leigni. That the patron could serve as source and model for a work, and that scribes could continue and complete what others had begun, is abundantly illustrated elsewhere, down to the end of the Middle Ages.⁵

Daniel Poirion has shown that poets in the later Middle Ages took their place under the aegis and guidance of great princes and contributed to the realization of extensive projects that bore witness to the prince's majesty and to his or her conception of literature and literary and social ideals. One such prince was Jean de Berry,[6] whose lamentations Machaut copies in careful *ordonnance* as the Complainte at the beginning of the *FA* (cf. 1513–16). The Dit itself is based on the young prince's departure for England as hostage in 1360, shortly after his marriage to Jeanne d'Armagnac. If the Dit does not reproduce in detail the circumstances of the departure, it does evoke an *état d'âme*, offering both an analysis and consolation. The patron appears in this work alongside the poet, who transcribes and communicates the former's sentiments to a loved one. And the patron rewards the poet's service. This in no way precludes his influence on the kind of work to be written and the place it will have in his life. The *matière* and *sens* of the patron schematize the Dit's biographical circumstances and define its context. In other words, the patron determines the poet's *ordonnance*. In an initial digression recalling Jean de Luxembourg, Machaut's first major patron (*FA* 101-88), the poet recalls the distinctive roles of prince and poet, revealing how the latter complements the former, keeping as close to him as possible in moments of danger and distress, which anticipates the union of heads, hearts, and minds that occurs when the prince and the poet have the same dream beside the Fountain of Narcisse (*FA* 1543-68). The prince's love becomes a model of right thinking and feeling and, congruently, for good writing. The patron as *patron*—as model—epitomizes and topically illustrates the model. His mind is the source of the Dit, for "c'estoit cil/Qui avoit l'engin si soutil" (*FA* 1513-14). Poetic transformations of the model in the metamorphoses of the Dit's literal and figurative narratives, the identities, comparisons, and contrasts established in the examples of Ceys and Alcyone, the Apple of Discord and Fall of Troy, and the memory of Narcisse and Pymalion, and, finally, the consolation offered by the dream lady, allow Machaut to restate that model within the Boethian framework that marks his later Dits, most notably the *RF* and the *CA*.[7] In the latter work, the patron as pupil learns who he is from examples based on his ideal self. Machaut's prince, as patron, is represented as generous donor; as source, planner, and architect of artistic productions; as pupil sitting at the feet of his sagacious mentor; and as *patron* or model and pattern for conduct. Whatever the actual organization of the prince's court may have been, Machaut represents its majesty as the expression of princely genius, to which the poet gives praise and expression.

It is difficult, without documentation, to define more precisely the real role of the prince in the choice and elaboration of the works he commissioned, that were commissioned for him, or that were written to gain his favor. Aristocratic *sens*, as wit, was the standard referent in works written for the nobility, and had been so since the origins of vernacular literature.[8] That *sens* is the genius of the patron. As a preliminary inquiry into its intended role in the composition of the literary work, we shall consider here five aspects of that genius in the works of Machaut and Froissart. In doing so it will be evident that the personae or roles of the patron complement those of the author and artist. Kevin Brownlee has studied the persona of the latter in the Dits.[9] Here, we shall consider briefly the former. The five aspects are: 1. the patron as donor; 2. the patron as poet, whom the author/narrator may serve as amanuensis, messenger, or glossator; 3. the patron as master who instructs, corrects, or even reprimands his poet; 4. the patron as pupil who heeds the poet's counsel; 5. the patron as lady or loved one who invites, encourages, and responds to the poet's writings.

THE PATRON AS DONOR

Here we may be brief. The patron who commissioned a work or manuscript, or for whom the latter were prepared and presented, is well known and documented. The poets themselves seem to have eagerly accepted such commands,[10] even when the patrons imposed constraints on them.[11] Froissart's discomfort at having to rise at midnight to read *Meliador* to Gaston de Foix, or Christine de Pizan's disinclination to write about love when more serious subjects awaited her attention, did not prevent either from accepting the tasks asked of them, and sometimes even enjoying them as pastimes or diversions.[12] The fact that these writers were in the employ of the patrons made them agents of their master's will. If that will changed, the work stopped.[13]

THE PATRON AS POET

The troubadours and trouvères included members of the aristocracy, from Guilhem IX, Ebles II of Ventadorn, and Jaufre Rudel, through, in French-speaking courts, Conon de Béthune, the Châtelain de Couci, and Guilhem's descendant, Thibaut de Champagne, king of Navarre—himself an ancestor of Charles the Bad, Machaut's patron in several Dits. Aspiring poets, some of them aristocrats, inspired or commissioned the redaction of the arts of the Second Rhetoric.[14] Nobles' names appear among the later poets, many of whom are accomplished by the standards of the times: Jean de Garencières, Othon de Grandson, and, of course, Charles d'Orléans and René d'Anjou (who also learned to paint from Jan van Eyck[15]). The *Cent ballades* of Jean le Sénéchal contains many examples of prince- and chevalier-poets, notably Jean de Berry, the patron whose words Machaut captured in verse and rhyme in the *FA*. Another author-patron is Wenceslas de Brabant, whose lyrics are the source for *Meliador*.

Now, Wenceslas contributed more than his poems to Froissart's romance. Peter F. Dembowski sees in this prince "the primary model" for its heroes. Indeed, not only Wenceslas himself, but "the attitudes of Froissart's benefactors during the 1360's, 70's and 80's have been undeniably imprinted upon his work."[16] The romance gives voice to the aspirations of the world Froissart wrote for, an aristocratic milieu that provided the context in which it was written. Thus it stands in the same relation to its audience as Froissart's disquisitions on *prouesse* in the Prologues of the *Chroniques* to the events which they relate. In *Meliador* the insertion of the lyrics into the narrative is coherent and intelligent: "The *rondeau* fits the moment and the moment excuses the *rondeau*."[17] This is true, within the narrative context. But in the context of the invention of the romance, the reverse obtains. Froissart as author made the moment fit the *rondeau*; the *rondeau* excuses, that is, gives significance to the moment. The entire *Meliador* is an Arthurian, or pseudo-Arthurian, elaboration of the narrative potential of the lyric pieces that, historically, antedate the romance and are by a different author. The poet-patron models the narrative his artist writes, and *Meliador* conforms to the patron-architect-artist paradigm. Wenceslas provided Froissart with *sens*; indeed, he invented the abstract expression of that *sens* in his lyrics. Froissart for his part elaborated a chivalric narrative from Arthurian *matière* and commonplaces, giving content and intention to the scattered poems of Wenceslas.[18] The procedure was not new. Jean Renart had shown the way, and the authors of medieval Dits not infrequently incorporated earlier lyric pieces into more elaborate narratives or treatises.[19]

One step removed from the patron as actual poet is the patron as ideal poet. Medieval hierarchies gave precedence to theory over practice. Knowledge of the arts of rhetoric and grammar was deemed superior to the practice of those arts. In this context, Chrétien de Troyes's flattery is credible when he states that Marie de Champagne provided the most important contribution to the *Charrette*, its *matière* and *sens*, whereas he only put these into writing:

> Mialz oevre
> ses comandemanz an ceste oevre
> que sans ne painne que g'i mete. (21–23)[20]

His "sans ne painne" are reduced to the actual composition of the work. For, as Chrétien concludes, "gueres n'i met/fors sa painne et s'antancïon" (28–29)—he is little more than hired craftsman! An interesting and complex instance of the patron as poet and as donor occurs in the *Voir-dit*, where Péronne[21] presents her poems for the master's approval, requests the composition of the Dit, and judges the performance of her servant as both lover and poet.

One step ahead of the actual composition of the poem stands the patron as the source of its *status archetypus*, its *sens* and *matière*. This image of the relation between poet and patron appears in the *FA* and in Froissart's *Bleu chevalier*. Each poem is a message the poet is to bear to an anonymous love. But the message is in verse, "Qu'il y avoit, dont j'eus merveilles,/Cent rimes toutes despareilles" (*FA* 1051–52). Anticipating the patron's request, Machaut presents him later with the copied Complainte, offering to serve as intermediary after the former has departed for prison. Similarly, in the *Bleu chevalier* the poet is invited to record the words of a patron so that a lady may hear of and know his fidelity.

> Je vous requier
> Que vous voilliés ordonner .I. dittier
> Com d'aventure avés, et sans cerchier,
> Dedens ce bois trouvé un chevalier
>   De bleu vesti
> (Et de la dame ordonnés ent aussi),
> Dont vous avés hui maint regret oÿ. (*BC* 424–30)[22]

Froissart and Machaut assume the role of the poet as "registre" or historiograph, as in the *Chroniques* or the *Prise d'Alexandrie*. The "registrar" also appears in the *Joli buisson de jonece*.

The purpose of registering the words and deeds of others is praise (*JBJ* 395)[23]—recording, preserving, and communicating who is praiseworthy among the great, who, by their life, serve as patrons and as *patrons* for those who come after them. What, indeed, would we know of what they exemplify

> Se ce ne fuissent li registre
> Qui yauls et leurs fes aministre?
> Et ossi li aministreur
> Qui en ont esté registreur
> En font moult a recommender. (*JBJ* 409–13)

The *œuvre de commande* becomes the exemplary expression of a patron's words and deeds. It communicates him or her to the private or public reader. Froissart precedes these reflections by the laudation of all his former and present patrons and benefactors (*JBJ* 226–373).

Such laudation supposes that the patrons were capable of recognizing and supporting talent, while employing it in the service of the ideas the patrons were believed to represent and to foster. Talent serves to articulate the nobility of the patrons—nobility founded in these writings less on blood than on mind, a quality of mind (*sens*) that determines a standard of taste in arms, love, and verse. There is implicit in this scheme a model of invention wherein the patron is in the favored place: he or she conceives the work.

THE PATRON AS MASTER

Our authors acknowledge the authority of the patron's mind. Machaut accedes to the judgment of Jean de Luxembourg, his most cherished patron, in the *JB*, and, in the later *JN*, accepts Charles the Bad's correction of his thought. In each case, the patron assembles a number of "counsellors" to aid him in arriving at a decision. The source of contention in both Dits is a typical courtly *cas*, the "legal" implications of which go beyond the circumstances peculiar to it. Since I have discussed this "case" elsewhere,[24] I shall confine myself here to describing how the patron fits into it.

Each work presents the "courtroom" and decision that results from the arguments advanced by different personifications. In the *JB*, the château of Durbuy (*JB* 1379) radiates the qualities of its lord, as the porters Honneur and Courtoisie receive the litigants and the poet, and the person of the king is accompanied by additional abstract qualities personified: Hardiesse, Prouesse, Largesse, Richesse, Amour, Beauté, Loyauté, Liesse, Désir, Penser, Volanté, Noblesse, Franchise, Honneur and Courtoisie again, and Jeunesse (*JB* 1476–83). These constitute an array of characteristics that fuse in the ideal self of the prince. As Machaut says of the personifications associated with lady Bonneürté in the *JN*,

> Mais aussi com pluseurs rivieres
> Arrousent, et pluseurs lumieres
> Radient et leur clarté rendent

> En tous lieus ou elles s'estendent,
> Ces douse nobles damoiselles[25]
> Qui de tous biens furent ancelles,
> Chascune selonc sa nature,
> En meurs, en maintieng, en figure,
> Embellissoient ceste dame
> De cuer, de corps, d'onneur et d'ame.
> Car tant estoit d'elles parée,
> Arrousée et enluminée,
> Ou chascune l'embelissoit
> De quanque de li bel issoit,
> Et chascune la repartoit
> De la vertu qu'elle portoit. (*JN* 1305–20)

The King of Bohemia elects Loyauté, Amour, Jeunesse, and Raison[26] to assist him in passing judgment (*JB* 1620–22), whereas the king of Navarre chooses Congnoissance, Avis, Raison, and Mesure as counsellors (*JN* 1583–1602).

The decision in *JN* follows a debate among three agents, each of whom expresses a different point of view in the mind of the king as judge: Machaut, Bonneurté and her companions, and the king. The princely patron is arbiter. His authority is founded on qualities like finesse, discretion, intuition, love, reason, and a sense of moderation or propriety—all of which are projected in the *JN* into *bonneurté* as the quintessence of felicity and nobility. There is scorn for lesser minds, as the lady reveals in identifying the Machaut figure.

> Vez la Guillaume de Machaut.
> C'est uns homs a cui il ne chaut
> A tort ou a droit soustenir. (*JN* 1499–1501)

Does this not imply that the poet is a mere agent of the patron, ready and willing to take up whatever task the patron wishes? If so, it suggests that outside the context of the immediate debate, the mind of the patron is paramount in the conception of the work.[27] That mind is a pattern—a *patron*—of right thinking (*sens*), when it is arrayed and adorned with qualities like those personified in the two *Jugements*.

The lady Machaut debates with in the *JN* is not a "real person" in the sense that Machaut and the king of Navarre were.

She is, as indicated, "Bonneürté" (*JN* 3851). She manifests herself in the world to dissipate melancholy like that in the images that begin the Dit, and countermand the effects of Fortune. The right-minded person will perceive her bounty and order his or her thinking according to her wishes. The Machaut figure lacks this vision at the beginning of the Dit, but the king of Navarre, who relies on Bonneurté and the attributes that accompany her as personifications, sets the poet straight and establishes proper thought. By its Boethian character, this vision corresponds to universal order and establishes felicity in all contexts: prosperity, friendship, love, chivalry and knighthood, honor and courtesy, nobility, science and wisdom—in short, in all species of the active and contemplative life, whatever may be the particular circumstances in historical reality.

> Dont au monde n'a grant signeur
> Ne dame, tant aient d'onneur,
> Qu'il ne leur fust et bel et gent,
> S'estre pooient de sa gent. (*JN* 3961-64)

The vision of the world evinced in Machaut's later poetry is made in the *JN* to emanate from the patron to the poet. That vision rests upon the principle of *bonneurté*, a Boethian principle of universal order and felicity.

Abstraction and discrimination tend to stylize the patron as the summation of ideal qualities he or she represents. The patron may even metamorphose into a rainbow of qualities so profoundly idealized as to eliminate the ego in favor of a more general abstraction or image. In Froissart's *Temple d'honneur*, which celebrates, according to Fourrier's convincing demonstration, the marriage of Humphrey X de Bohun and Jeanne d'Arundel,[28] the couple ascend to the virtual deification of the qualities they represent by their union.

> Honneurs si marie au jour d'ui,
> Ense com enfourmés j'en sui,
> Un sien fil que Desir on nomme
> . . . .
> Et li donne Plaisance a fame,

Fille Courtoisie le sage. (*TH* 117–19, 122–23)

The identification of abstractions corresponds to the assimilation of the person and the image, but as a sublimation in a flower, a beast, a temple, or a clock (all of these *matières* are used by Machaut or Froissart in their Dits). In such imagination, the individual de-personalizes and generalizes to such an extent that the narrator can become any appropriate *destinateur*, just as the loved one may be assimilated to the desired or hoped for *destinataire*. The poem may be first person; the reality of the patron/poet relation acknowledges that the speaker is assimilable. "Il parle à la première personne, mais au nom de son commettant," concludes Fourrier regarding the *Dit du cerf blanc*, which—rightly, I think—he attributes to Machaut.[29] The poet as both *commettant* and as messenger appears as well for Pierre de Lusignan in Machaut's *Dit de la marguerite* and, perhaps, his *Dit de la rose*.[30] If in fact the *CB* was written for Wenceslas de Brabant, its inclusion in a manuscript made for Robert d'Alençon would illustrate the assimilation of the narrative *je* to a third particular.[31] The procedure is analogous to the poet's use of the same poem for different patrons and circumstances.

The rhetorical stance of the poem's narrator is eminently illustrated in medieval lyric production, at least within the contexts of *fin'amours* and of moral and religious poetry. Elocution is meant to convince. The specific patron employs the poet much as he or she would a scribe, or as a politician would engage a speech-writer today. The writer puts into words the patron's thoughts or sentiments, and directs these toward an audience. The poet as messenger can, accordingly, assume all shapes, like Morphée or Enclimpostair, to whom he is assimilated.[32] He can enter the mind of the patron and share, in great proximity and even intimacy, the latter's thoughts, feelings, experiences, and imaginings. In the *FA* (1543–54), the patron rests his head in the poet's lap, and the poet his head on the patron's, and both dream the same dream: "tous deus un songe songames" (2520). The image is construed, however, by reference to the qualities that constitute noble *bonté*, as both goodness and bounty (*largesse*). "Por che fet bon les bons hanter" (*TH* 1055). Machaut would agree,[33] insisting moreover on the importance of firm will and fidelity—the "ferme arrestance" he desires for the stag representing another patron (*CB* 552): "Fay de ton cerf tant qu'il ne se desvoie./Se tu le fais, honneur avras et joie" (*CB* 690–91). This is the purpose of the *TH* as well (1035–46).

The poet-narrator is a changeable figure, ever as the patron wishes. He may even be reduced to a sort of buffoon in need of correction. Correction of his ineptitude or misapprehensions occurs in one way or the other in the *RF*, the *JN*, the *DA*, and the *VD*. The correction takes place in the context of greater or lesser nobility. It behooves the poet, as cleric, to stay close to his patron, following him wherever he may lead:

> ... mieus vaut les bons ensuïr
> Souvent que morir ou fuïr.
> Qui se vuet mirer, si se mire. (*FA* 129–31)

In short, the patron should show the way: "Ne fai pas clers tes consaus d'armes" (*CA* 3105).

THE PATRON AS PUPIL

The *consaus d'armes* is, nonetheless, very much present in the clerical poet:

> Qui de ces quatre poins se garde
> En fort ville assise, il n'a garde,
> S'elle est de bonne gent garnie,
> D'engiens et d'autre artillerie.
> Se de ce y avoit defaut,
> On la porroit penre d'assaut. (*CA* 3387–92)

In the light of the foregoing, is it not just as preposterous for Machaut to appear to advise his lord and patron on how to wage war as it is for the cleric, in the *JN*, to debate with him, that is, with the universal principles he represents and that express his thought and mind through the personifications that accompany Bonneurté?

The question is a modern one. It evinces preoccupation with the very "real" referred to on occasion above, rather than with the ideal with which medieval literature concerns itself. The ideal is inaccessible to the senses by themselves, which are limited to the immediate and changeable, like Machaut in the *JN*, before the correction given by Bonneurté. The poet, like Morphée, has the chameleon's ability to take on the colors appropriate to the milieu he or she is located in. In poetry of the imagination, the milieu is the context. The context in Machaut tends to emphasize noble love, or, more broadly in the *CA* and the *Prise*, nobility in love and other activities deemed characteristic of the noble life.

> Einsi est il certeinnement
> De vray humein entendement
> Qui est ables a recevoir
> Tout ce qu'on vuet et concevoir
> Puet tout ç'a quoy on le vuet mettre,
> Armes, amours, autre art ou lettre. (*RF* 35–40)

For noble patrons of this time, secular poetry confined itself to "l'estat d'amours et d'armes" (*TH* 277). These two constitute the milieu and thus the context of the *CA* and the *Prise*; they also find their place in Froissart's *PA*, *JBJ*, and *Meliador*.

Conventional images can cite the cleric as foolish, or as a source of counsel for the lord. These roles are assumed according to circumstances. A cleric may be a bad counsellor in arms, especially on the field of battle, as Machaut suggests in his description of clerical cowardice in the *FA* (92–188). But he can also represent wisdom and offer sage advice. The complete passage containing the recommendation on clerical *consaus d'armes* bears this out.

> Ne fai pas clers tes consaus d'armes,
> Qui doivent prier pour les ames
> Et doivent compter et escrire
> Et chanter leur messes ou lire
> Et *consillier les jugemens*
> *Aus consaus et aus parlemens.*
> Si que tien chascun *en son ordre*
> Si bien qu'il n'i ait que remordre. (*CA* 3105–12; emphasis mine)

The clerical persona advises in private counsel, thus assuming the role of master, as in the *PA* or the *CA*, or that of companion, as in the *FA*. He may, like the patron, be doubled and abstracted to a personification like Esperance in the *RF*[34] or Morphée in the *FA*. The numerous representations of the poet according to diverse topical schemes, the diverse mythographic inventions used to portray him, justify using Morphée and Enclimpostair as protean images of the figure who, in the last analysis, adopts the shape and persona demanded by both patron and *patron*. The poet changes to fit the patron's thought.

A good example of this kind of poet is Flos in Froissart's *PA*. The Dit is about service. The poet presents himself as counsellor about love, love being assimilated to service and functioning as an allegorical representation of it (*PA* 11–16). The poet retains his general referentiality—Flos is a generic name—so as to speak for all flowers to Rose, the patron who has identified himself with the flower in the name of his love because "la rose est souverainne sur toutes flours" (Letter I.35–36). The reason for rejecting any single flower in favor of the generic Flos is:

> de leurs noms ne voel point
> Par maniere de desparel,
> Quoi qu'a yauls ne me fai parel. (*PA* 881–83)

He declines to elaborate further (891–94). However, he *illustrates* the genus, not by an *Urpflanze*, but by the daisy, a flower known to refer to a conventional or real Marguerite in Froissart's life.[35]

The choice of the name Flos is susceptible of several interpretations. First, the letter *F* initials Froissart's own name. The image of Flos as daisy reinforces this suggestion of the person within the genus, yet does not undermine Rose's choice of the sovereign flower for his sovereign lady. The daisy is small; nonetheless, as the flower that represents Flower/Flos, Froissart's love is assimilable to Rose's through their common genus. Finally, the movement between Flos and Rose on the one hand, Flos and "Marguerite" on the other, and, also, between Flos and the other flowers represented in the genus, fits the poet's role in relation to patron and *patron*. First, he is counsellor in love, as Rose wishes:

> Pour ce vous escrips fiablement, com chils qui moult desire a acquerre l'amour et compagnie de vous et consel d'une tres grief maladie que ma tres souverainne dame et amours me font a present souffrir et porter; car en la discretion de vous et de vostre avis sont pluiseurs ymaginations propisces pour ent respondre et consellier, se mestier fet. (Letter 1.6–12)

The cleric can counsel in different *matieres* by images that conform to a pattern of truth. This is Flos's service to Rose, unidentified by name in the Dit, but recognizable as Wenceslas de Brabant.[36] Friendship and esteem between Rose and Flos bind master and servant. Froissart's alias Flos's service is counsel on love. As Flos he comprehends all specific loves (Letter II.29–32) as the genus flower does all species of flower. The *PA* interlaces the adventures of the two lovers, counterpointing the one love by the other, yet referring each to a common ideal of noble and estimable love as a source of joy and worth, a source the two share as if by elective affinities: "les meurs et conditions de vous," affirms Rose, "s'acordent asses as miens" (Letter I.4–6). The generic suggests the adaptability of the flower to whatever *manière* is appropriate. The poet as Morphée or Enclimpostair assumes the shape and guise (*patron*) appropriate to the truth he or she may imagine and enunciate in service to another by whom he is, by the goodness of the other, received into service. The diversity of functions parallels the array of distinctions we observed for the persona of the patron.

It follows that the patron, like the poet, may not yet (as, for example, at the beginning of many romances) realize the qualities he or she represents. In such cases it is necessary to counsel or comfort the patron, guiding him or her towards what is desirable in arms and love. Machaut's Boethian model is useful for the nobleman in disgrace. Like Boethius, he requires counsel to bear misfortune, to overcome past sins and misdeeds, and see the world aright. However, there is one major difference between Boethius and Machaut: Philosophia is represented by the poet.

And the poet, by providing counsel, is in the service of the patron, and therefore subservient.

Four major categories of the model of service define the relation of poet and patron in the context of counsel:

1. *Author: patron*. This is the first and most obvious image of the relation. It comprehends the individual who employs the poet for a specific task. The latter may write something new, or refurbish a "product" which is removed from the shelf and reused.

2. *Servant: master*. The artist in the service of a lord fits the more general relation between servant and master: each must accept reciprocal obligations and responsibilities.

3. *Master: disciple*. In this image, the social hierarchy reflected in the two preceding species of relation fades into a kind of awkward equality,[38] as the poet seeks to discern the ethical, social, or chivalric persona the patron should seek to realize and shows him or her the way. The demonstration may take various forms: *chastoiement* (*CA*); dialogue or exchange of messages (*VD, PA*); correlation of dreams, Ovidian mythographs, or personifications (*JN, DA, FA, PA, JBJ*); treatise (*TH, RF*[39]).

4. *Ami: Ami(e)*. The most intimate image is based on affinity, friendship, or love between patron and poet. The sentiments that unite them are presented as sincere, profound, and mutually respectful:

> Sire, et se je t'apelle amy,
> N'en aies pieur cuer a my;
> Car bien sçay que tu es mes sires,
> Et je des mieudres ne des pires
> Ne suis, mais sans riens retenir
> Sui tiens, quoy qu'il doie avenir. (*CA* 21–26)

The patron can respond in kind: "Chiers amis, a fin que vostre affection soit plus encline a ma plaisance, en avant je ne vous voel riens celer, mais tous mes secres amoureus segnefiier et escrire . . ." (*PA* Letter I.42–45). That both Froissart and Machaut correlate love service with service in general allows us to include the lady as patron as well as disciple, as, for example, in the *VD*.

The fixed star in these configurations is the patron. He or she realizes and represents the *patron*, or should do so. This is to say that he or she projects the configuration or array of qualities that constellate about and delineate the idea of which he or she is the actual or potential incarnation. The poet clings to this figure, seeking by such proximity to do whatever he can by counsel and reflection to express praise, or to counsel the thoughts, character, or aspirations of his lord. The lord, in asking counsel, is also the final judge of the worth of the poet's craft. Humility is incumbent upon the latter: "uns ignorans poet alefois dire tel parole qui est entendue en milleur maniere qu'il ne le vaille; ce ne fait mie li biens de li, mais des escoutans" (*PA* Letter II.9–12). The *PA* elaborates upon an array of images, topically glossed in the context of love and service, so as to reveal how poetic and patronal wit come together to produce a statement—a *dit*—on love and service. The loved one herself intervenes at one point to request a supplement on a matter the poet-counsellor overlooked in his gloss of the mythographs, dream, and personifications of the Dit (Letter XI.15–43).

THE PATRON AS LADY/LOVE.

Love is the supreme master of both poet and patron. Froissart's equation of service and love permits him to establish service to love as image for himself and his patron. Now, love may manifest itself in a number of manners and modes. As a personification—the god of love—it becomes the ultimate patron,

> Qui est mon signeur et mon pestre,
> Mon dieu mondain et mon chier mestre,
> Dont toute ma joie me vient! (*PA* 651–53)

Love may also appear as the lady, the object of love who, by her presence, solicits the poet's writing. A person fits an image, then specializes or generalizes through the image. This allows for the curious "law of substitution" or "law of reversibility" by which different loves may show forth the ideal image.[40] In this way, the same poem may be addressed to different individuals, and new patrons and new loves take the place of former ones. Both phenomena appear in the *VD*. The substitution does not, of course, preclude differences, in images like those in the debates about the best flower (analogous to the contests as to the best poem in the puys which are decided by a "Prince" and rewarded with a flower), about the lover who suffers most in the *JB* and *JN*, or the best bird in the *DA*; most dramatic perhaps is the substitution of the Virgin Mary for the lady in the *JBJ*. The lady, like the patron, presents an array of attributes, prismatically distinguished by description, but blending in the image of the individual as that individual achieves typicality. Just as the poet imbues his mind with the qualities of the patron in order to learn from and instruct that patron, so the poet as lover seeks to mirror in himself the qualities of the lady who

> M'estoit miroir et exemplaire
> De tous biens desirer et faire.
> Et pour le bien qu'en li vëoie,
> De tout bien faire me penoie
> Et me gardoie de mesprendre,
> Si qu'on ne me peüst reprendre,
> A mon pooir, car sa bonté
> M'en donnoit cuer et volenté. (*RF* 171–78)

The constituents of the *bonté* are displayed in full array as the "doctrine" the poet is to acquire and then express in his writings (327–56). The lady, like the lord, serves as inspiration and as source for inventive genius.

The lady love for Machaut is, accordingly, the lady as patron and *patron*. She assumes the various roles Machaut and Froissart assign the patron: instructor in the *RF*; patron who requests a work and instruction on love and poetry in the *VD*; source of direct instruction which the poet communicates, as for Rose's lady in the *PA* or the lion's lady in the *DL*.

It is not possible to discuss here all the features of the lady in the works of Machaut and Froissart. The friendship that unites the patron and poet is considerably complicated by the interposition of love when the patron is a woman, just as it is when gender enters into the use of personifications. For example, many have noted the curious ambiguity between Esperance and the lady in the *RF* or the confusion—the blending—of lover and patron that occurs for the shared dream in the *FA*, of the lion and lover as well as the lady and the old knight in the *DL*, or the amalgamation and topical interfacing in the *PA* of Flos's Ovidian invention, Rose's dream, and the lady's request for a gloss on the Phaeton myth. The contextual reversals and substitutions in the *JBJ*—youth and age, lady and Virgin Mary, Jeunesse as philosopher, Philosophie as defender of poetry and love, the bush as, alternately, desire, the seven ages of Man, and Christ—eloquently bespeak the ambiguities of existence which the Dits try to sort out by clear and convenient distinctions. Poetic genius, as we noted at the outset and have attempted to demonstrate in the special cases of Machaut and Froissart, is susceptible of diverse explications. In our two authors, certain factors are always present: love, the patron, the poet. The extent to which they blend and the ways by which they are differentiated, vary from work to work, and may indeed comport several senses in the same works. For example, Machaut's "livre ou je met toutes *mes* choses" contains works that belong to others.[41] Similarly, the *Prologue* that introduces the complete works and sets forth the constituents of the poet's genius—Nature and Love—does not preclude the reception of that genius from others: God, the lady, the patron. Ultimately, all images conform to the *patron*[42]—that *sensus archetypus* from which poetry, like architecture and the other arts, derives its meaning and *imprimatur*. The poet is an array of parts: patrons, loved one, architect, artisan.

CONCLUSION: LATE MEDIEVAL GENIUS

The genius of the patron poses a problem on two critical fronts. For historical criticism, it complicates the art of invention as the technique was conceived in the Middle Ages. To what extent were others involved in and responsible for the conception of the work of literary art? For more modern critical presuppositions, it complicates the analyses of the author-in-the-work and of the narrator. What is the place of the patron-in-the-work and how does he or she figure as narrator? The problem is perplexing and intriguing, especially because it opens the way for experimentation and reinterpretations within a new paradigm of artistic genius. It is therefore on the same plane as the problem of Lollius in Chaucer's *Troilus* and *House of Fame*, Kyot in Wolfram's *Parzival*, Guillaume de Lorris and Jean de Meun in the *Roman de la rose*, or Godefroi de Laigni in Chrétien's *Charrette*.[43] There are in each instance various possible explanations for these "authors," just as there are for the "patrons" in Machaut and Froissart and works like, as noted, Chrétien's *Charrette* and *Conte du graal*—that is, explanations ranging from major intervention by the patron or other authority to authorial play on a received, commonplace paradigm for invention and elaboration of a literary work of art. In any case, between intervention and play, the actual range of possibilities precludes opting unreflectively for only one possibility. As Machaut insists in the *JN*, medieval distinctions blend into a whole in real life, but with variable constituents and proportions. Only the *status archetypus* is one and unmixed.

Under these circumstances, the appropriate critical stance seems to me to be dictated by the notion of genius itself. Genius in its various antique and medieval manifestations and connotations realizes eminently that rich confusion of meanings that flow together in the word, like the qualities of Charles the Bad that for Machaut blend in the prince's person.[44] We cannot begin here to delineate such genius. We can however note a few features of the medieval genius that help clarify the relation between the author's genius and the patron's genius. First, it bears repeating that the medieval notion of genius has little in common with modern Romantic or post-Romantic definitions. Second, the word does embrace literally and figuratively the art of writing, both as mental conception of the work and as copy. The foregoing discussion shows that the copying tends to reside with the artist, who, as scribe, puts the plan or patron's *sens* into words. Machaut's *Prologue* evinces this scheme in the two figures of the poet as David and Orphée, the former a prophet (126) calming the anger of God, the latter a poet (138) transforming the order of nature by sweet song. Machaut as poet is in the service of two "patrons", Nature and Love. They provide him with *sens* and *matière*, which I take to be sources of invention and the context of the work.[45] They are his genius. He is their scribe. That is, his hand writes what his mind dictates. But who are Nature and Love?

A poet corresponding to Orphée appears in Froissart's pseudo-Ovidian invention, Pynoteus. Like Orphée, Pynoteus is a poet. He is able to shape the forms of things as images in matter. But life derives from a higher instance—in the mythograph, from Phebus Apollo.[46] The poet prays for that divine spark, and his prayer is answered.

> Car lumiere en la foelle vint,
> Et li poëtes, qui le tint
> Toute ardant, le mist a le bouce
> Del ymage et, lors qu'elle y touce,
> Elle sali sus, toute otele
> Comme une aultre femme mortele. (*PA* 1920–25)

We recall that this substitution of the image for the dead beloved came at the request of Rose, Froissart's, that is, Flos's, patron. The absence of the patron/Phebus Apollo is dramatized in Pynoteus's prayer, which rehearses the disastrous ride of Phaeton, who took his father's chariot without being able to control it, and was finally destroyed by Jupiter's thunderbolt. The poet without patron can write little of worth, and do much harm.[47] But the patron him- or herself requires a poet as scribe to develop and set forth what he or she is. Rose reports his dream to Flos so that the latter may make something of it. "Si vous pri, chiers amis, anchois qu'il soit noient veüs ne escandelisiés, que vous le voelliés lire de cief en cor, et parfaitement viseter et examiner, et ce qui necessaire n'i est oster, et ce qui y besongne mettre et adjouster, et ma rudece escuser, car je ne sui pas mestres pour ordonner si mestrieusement que pour estre nommés ne recommendés entre les ouvriers de cel art. Et pour ce que vostres sens est grans et ymaginatis [the poet's genius!] et abuvrés en tels oevres, je vous pri que vous voelliés sus mon songe mettre aucune exposition nouvelle, ensi que la matere le requiert" (*PA* Letter VIII.15–25). What the patron dreams is his own life, seen in a dream. He requests a book about it (Letter

X.10–15). The genius of the poet, "abuvrés en tels oevres," resides in putting together anew, whether as a Pynoteus combining earth and water to recreate the image of Neptisphelé, or Froissart himself combining various images in a book, as Machaut made a *livre* of all his "things," many of which, like Rose's dream in the *PA*, belong to another. The genius of the patron is light which gives life to poetic inventions. In the case of Wenceslas de Brabant, such a *patron* may be his own poems, with which Froissart invented *Meliador*, or his life, out of which the poet made a book.

NOTES

1. Unless otherwise indicated, quotations and other references are from E. Hoepffner, ed., *Œuvres de Guillaume de Machaut*, SATF 57, 3 vols. (Paris: Firmin-Didot, 1908–11, E. Champion, 1921). Sigla for Dits referred to in this paper: Vol. I—*P*: "Prologue," *JB: Le jugement dou Roy de Behaingne, JN: Le jugement dou roy de Navarre;* Vol. II—*RF: Remede de Fortune, DL: Le Dit dou lyon, DA: Le dit de l'alerion;* Vol. III—*CA: Le confort d'ami, FA: La fonteinne amoureuse.* References to *VD: Le livre du voir-dit*, ed. P. Paris (Paris: Société des bibliophiles françois, 1875).
2. "Abbot Suger of St.-Denis," in his *Meaning in the Visual Arts* (Garden City, N.Y.: Doubleday, 1955), pp. 108–45. The practice was common, even in apparently everyday matters like letter-writing; see G. Constable, *Letters and Letter-Collections*, Typologie des sources du moyen âge occidental, 17 (Turnhout: Brepols, 1976), pp. 42–55.
3. J. Bumke, *Mäzene im Mittelalter: die Gönner und Auftraggeber in der höfischen Literatur in Deutschland 1150–1300* (Munich: C. H. Beck, 1979), pp. 9–10.
4. Besides J. Bumke, *Mäzene*, see the collection he edited, *Literarisches Mäzenatentum: ausgewählte Forschungen zur Rolle des Gönners und Auftraggebers in der mittelalterlichen Literatur*, Wege der Forschung, 598 (Darmstadt: Wissenschaftliche Buchgesellschaft, 1982), which contains an excellent critical *état présent* with bibliography (pp. 1–31); P. Gallais, "Recherches sur la mentalité des romanciers français du moyen âge," *Cahiers de civilisation médiévale*, 7 (1964), 479–93; 13 (1970), 333–47, especially pp.

333–38; T. H. Elwert, "Il 'committente' nella letteratura medievale," in *Orbis mediaevalis: mélanges de langue et de littérature médiévales offerts à Reto Raduolf Bezzola* (Bern: Francke, 1978), pp. 113–26. On this problem, see the paper by R. Schnell, "Kirche, Hof und Liebe: zum Freiraum mittelalterlicher Dichtung," and that by H. U. Gumbrecht, "Auf gemeinsamer Suche nach der 'höfischen Kultur' des Mittelalters? Antworten (und Fragen) an R. Schnell," especially pp. 93–108 and 116–18, in E. Ruhe and R. Behrens, eds., *Mittelalterbilder aus neuer Perspektive: Diskussionsanstösse zu amour courtois, Subjektivität in der Dichtung und Strategien des Erzählens,* Beiträge zur romanischen Philologie des Mittelalters, 14 (Munich: W. Fink, 1985). For Machaut and Froissart, treated here, consult D. Poirion, *Le poète et le prince: l'evolution du lyrisme courtois de Guillaume de Machaut à Charles d'Orléans* (Paris: PUF, 1965); P. F. Dembowski, *Jean Froissart and His "Meliador": Context, Craft, and Sense,* The Edward C. Armstrong Monographs on Medieval Literature, 2 (Lexington, Ky.: French Forum, 1983), pp. 25–59. See also P. Zumthor, *Le masque et la lumière: la poétique des Grands Rhétoriqueurs* (Paris: Seuil, 1978), pp. 39–55.

5. See, for example, E. Kleinschmidt, *Herrscherdarstellung: zur Disposition mittelalterlichen Aussageverhaltens, untersucht an Texten über Rudolf I. von Habsburg,* Bibliotheca Germanica, 17 (Bern, Munich: Francke, 1974); B. Schmolke-Hasselmann, *Der arthurische Versroman von Chrestien bis Froissart: zur Geschichte einer Gattung,* Beihefte zur Zeitschrift für romanische Philologie, 177 (Tübingen: Niemeyer, 1980), pp. 184–248. The prose romances, Arthurian and non-Arthurian, are also pertinent illustrations. See my "Le patron et l'auteur dans l'invention romanesque," in *Théories et pratiques de l'écriture au moyen âge,* eds. E. Baumgartner and C. Marchello-Nizia, Littérales, 4 (1988), 25–39.
6. D. Poirion, *Poète,* pp. 29–31; E. Hoepffner, *Œuvres,* III, xxvi-xxviii.
7. See my *Medieval Imagination: Rhetoric and the Poetry of Courtly Love* (Madison: Univ. of Wisconsin Press, 1978), pp. 130–44; and "Assimilation et montage dans l'amplification descriptive: la démarche du poète dans le Dit du XIVe siècle," in *Mittelalterbilder,* pp. 292–93.
8. As in "en tous lius si le faisoit/Qu'as autres examplaire estoit/De sens et de cevalerie,/D'ensegnement, de courtoisie,/Et de francise

et de largece... ," 1419–23 in *Amadas et Ydoine*, ed. J. R. Reinhard, CFMA 51 (Paris: Champion, 1974). These matters are discussed more at length in my *The Art of Medieval French Romance*, (Madison: University of Wisconsin Pr., 1992), ch. 3.

9. *Poetic Identity in Guillaume de Machaut* (Madison: Univ. of Wisconsin Press, 1984).
10. On the social status and precarious existence of writers, cf. J. Bumke, *Mäzene*, pp. 13–21, 68–72; P. Zumthor, *Masque*, pp. 47–48.
11. As in *Claris et Laris*, ed. J. Alton, Bibliothek des litterarischen Vereins in Stuttgart, 169 (Tübingen: Laupp, 1884), 83–88; *L'histoire de Guillaume le maréchal, comte de Striguil et de Pembroke*, ed. P. Meyer, 3 vols. (Paris: Renouard, 1891–1901), 5143–48.
12. B. J. Whiting, "Froissart as Poet," *Mediaeval Studies*, 8 (1946), 207; C. C. Willard, "Christine de Pizan's *Cent Ballades d'amant et de dame*: Criticism of Courtly Love," in G. S. Burgess, ed., *Court and Poet*, Selected Proceedings of the Third Congress of the International Courtly Literature Society (Liverpool: 1980), ARCA: Classical and Medieval Texts, Papers and Monographs, 5 (Liverpool: F. Cairns, 1981), pp. 357–64. Cf. J. Cerquiglini, "*Un engin si soutil*": *Guillaume de Machaut et l'écriture au XIVe siècle*, Bibliothèque du XVe siécle, 47 (Paris: Champion, 1985), pp. 139–41.
13. J. Bumke, *Mäzene*, pp. 14–21.
14. Cf. E. Langlois, *Recueil d'arts de Seconde Rhétorique* (Paris: Imprimerie Nationale, 1902), pp. vi–vii, xii. For examples of aristocratic relations with puys, see the references in R. Berger, *Littérature et société arrageoises au XIIIe siècle: les chansons et dits artésiens*, Mémoires de la Commission Départementale des Monuments Historiques du Pas-de-Calais, 21 (Arras: Imprimerie Centrale de l'Artois, 1981). In general, see P. Zumthor, *Masque*, pp. 39–47.
15. D. Poirion, *Poète*, p. 53.
16. P. F. Dembowski, *Jean Froissart*, p. 59.
17. P. F. Dembowski, *Jean Froissart*, p. 94.
18. In addition, contemporary events appear to inform the romance, much as they do in Froissart's *Prison amoureuse*, which reflects Wenceslas de Brabant's defeat in and imprisonment after the Battle of Bastweiler. See A. H. Diverres, "The Geography of Britain in Froissart's *Meliador*," in *Medieval Miscellany Presented to Eugène Vinaver* (Manchester: Manchester Univ. Press, 1965), pp. 97–112, "Froissart's *Méliador* and Edward III's Policy towards Scotland,"

in *Mélanges Rita Lejeune* (Gembloux: Duculot, 1969), II, 1399–1409, and "The Irish Adventures in Froissart's *Meliador*," in *Mélanges Jean Frappier* (Geneva: Droz, 1970), I, 235–51; as well as B. Schmolke-Hasselmann, *Versroman*, pp. 228–32; A. Fourrier, ed., *La prison amoureuse* [= *PA*] (Paris: Klincksieck, 1974), pp. 20–28.
19. J. Cerquiglini, *"Engin,"* pp. 32–49; S. J. Williams, "An Author's Role in Fourteenth Century Book Production: Guillaume de Machaut's 'Livre ou je met toutes mes choses'," *Romania*, 90 (1969), 452–53. Cf. M. Zink, *Roman rose et rose rouge: le Roman de la rose ou de Guillaume de Dole* (Paris: Nizet, 1979), pp. 26–44.
20. *Le chevalier de la charrete*, ed. M. Roques, CFMA 86 (Paris: Champion, 1958).
21. Who can no longer be identified with Péronne d'Armentières; see J. Cerquiglini, *"Engin,"* pp. 223–43.
22. *BC* = Jean Froissart, "Le dit du Bleu chevalier," in *"Dits" et "débats," avec en appendice quelques poèmes de Guillaume de Machaut*, ed. A. Fourrier, TLF 274 (Geneva: Droz, 1979), pp. 155–70; see also *PA* Letter XII.21–25.
23. *JBJ* = *Le joli buisson de jonece*, ed A. Fourrier, TLF 222 (Geneva: Droz, 1975).
24. *Medieval Imagination*, pp. 137–44.
25. Machaut's grouping of personifications identifies twelve, but many are accompanied or led by others. There are eighteen in all: Raison, Largesse, Congnoissance, Avis, Attemprance, Pais, Concorde, Foy, Constance, Charité, Honnesté, Prudence, Sapience, Doubtance de meffaire, Honte, Peur, Souffissance, Mesure; see my *Medieval Imagination*, p. 139. These qualities, be it noted, belong to the patron and judge in the debate; the comedy in the poet's comportment stems from his failure to grasp the thought of his patron.
26. Added to the others *JB* 1491, she corrects what is wrong.
27. Hence, the patron "punishes" the poet by having him write poetry that extols good love (*JN* 4181–89).
28. A. Fourrier, ed., *"Dits,"* pp. 23–27; *TH* = *Temple d'honneur* is on pp. 91–127. See also P. F. Dembowski, "Li orloge amoureus de Froissart," *L'Esprit Créateur*, 18 (1978), 19–31.
29. A. Fourrier, ed., *"Dits,"* p. 83; see also pp. 79–86. *CB* = "Dit du cerf blanc" is on pp. 302–29.
30. A. Fourrier, ed., *"Dits,"* pp. 72–75; cf. pp. 83–84.
31. A. Fourrier, ed., *"Dits,"* pp. 76–84.

32. D. Kelly, "Assimilation," pp. 293–94, 296–97.
33. In the "Plaidoirie de la rose et de la violette" (A. Fourrier, ed., "*Dits*," pp. 191–203), Froissart appeals to the King of France to resolve a similar debate. Cf. Machaut's "Dit de la fleur de lis et de la marguerite" (A. Fourrier, ed., "*Dits*," pp. 289–301), in which the lady is assimilated to both the lily and the violet. On this, see J. I. Wimsatt, *The Marguerite Poetry of Guillaume de Machaut*, University of North Carolina Studies in the Romance Languages and Literatures, 87 (Chapel Hill: Univ. of North Carolina Press, 1970), p. 27; Wimsatt also gives an edition of this Dit (pp. 15–26).
34. On the gender ambiguities such personifications suggest, see J. Cerquiglini, "*Engin*," pp. 141–55; on the possible moral significance of such ambiguities, see my "Image et imagination dans les inventions des poètes: miroir et réceptivité dans les dits allégoriques," in *L'image au moyen âge*, Actes du Colloque d'Amiens du 19 au 23 mars 1986 (Göppingen: Kümmerle), pp. 137–49.
35. B. J. Whiting, "Froissart," pp. 197 and 206.
36. B. J. Whiting, "Froissart," p. 199; A. Fourrier, *PA*, p. 27.
37. On this word, see my "La spécialité dans l'invention des topiques," in *Archéologie du sigue*, eds. L. Brind'Amour and E. Vance (Toronto: Pontifical Institute, 1983), pp. 101–25.
38. *CA* 21–26, *FA* 1239–70, *PA* Letter III.5–11.
39. On the link to *CA*, see my *Medieval Imagination*, pp. 124–25; on *traitie*, see A. Fourrier, ed., "*Dits*," pp. 12–22; J. Cerquiglini, "Le clerc et l'écriture: le *Voir Dit* de Guillaume de Machaut et la définition du *dit*," in *Literatur in der Gesellschaft des Spätmittelalters*, ed. H.-U. Gumbrecht, Begleitreihe zum Grundriss der romanischen Literaturen des Mittelalters, 1 (Heidelberg: C. Winter, 1980), pp. 151–68; D. Kelly, "Assimilation."
40. A. Leupin, "The Powerlessness of Writing: Guillaume de Machaut, the Gorgon, and *Ordenance*," *Yale French Studies*, 70 (1986), p. 131.
41. Belong in the sense that they were written for and given to others.
42. *Patronus* in medieval Latin signifies, among other things, "master of unfree dependents," "feudal lord," "ward of women or persons under age," "pattern, standard, model," according to the *Mediae latinitatis lexicon minus*, comp. J. F. Niermeyer (Leiden: Brill, 1984), p. 776. For analogous French meanings, see W. von Wartburg, *FEW*, VIII, 25–27; Tobler-Lommatzsch, VII, 490–91.
43. Cf. the provocative (in the best sense of the word) articles by R. Dragonetti, "Pygmalion ou les pièges de la fiction dans le *Roman*

de la rose," in *Orbis mediaevalis*, pp. 89–111; D. F. Hult, "Author/Narrator/Speaker: The Voice of Authority in Chrétien's *Charrete*", in *Discourses of Authority in Medieval and Renaissance Literature*, eds. K. Brownlee and W. Stephens (Hanover, NH, London: Univ. Pr. of New England, 1989), pp. 76–96, 267–69. The validity of their hypotheses depends, of course, on the historical facts.

44. The use of the word and its derivatives is far from being clear. But see for now J. C. Nitzsche, *The Genius Figure in Antiquity and the Middle Ages* (New York, London: Columbia Univ. Press, 1975), for a good general orientation.
45. See my "Image et imagination."
46. The reference anticipates Froissart's relation to another patron, Gaston Phebus de Foix, whose handsome features caused contemporaries to liken him to the sun god; see R. F. Dembowski, *Jean Froissart*, p. 54.
47. On the love allegory complementing the allegory of service and of imprisonment, see my *Medieval Imagination*, pp. 163–69.

William Calin

Machaut's Legacy: The Chaucerian Inheritance Reconsidered

Machaut's legacy in England, and specifically his influence on Chaucer, leads to the scrutiny of some of the more fascinating aspects of literary criticism and the history of medieval scholarship. The first generation of modern Chaucer scholars—Kittredge and Lowes—were knowledgeable in medieval French. They read almost all the texts and, at this early date, made almost all the appropriate textual analogies.[1] Of course, they were scholars and philologists, not literary critics in our sense of the term. This means that, after citing so many examples of borrowing or of translation, they occasionally missed major structural similarities—themes, patterns, *topoi*—that were not of a specifically textual or stylistic nature. This also means that, even though Kittredge was an extraordinarily sensitive reader of poems, he made no effort to appreciate Machaut and Froissart in esthetic terms or to question the place these late medieval Frenchmen held in the canon. In any event, the next two or three generations of Anglicists gave to the world a quality and quantity of criticism far superior to anything comparable in French studies during the same period. However, they were not always people who read Old French. As a result, the foundations laid by Kittredge, Lowes, and their contemporaries were not built upon as much as they could have been. Major books of Chaucer criticism, exemplary in all other respects and which discuss thoroughly, say, the presence of Ovid in *The Legend of Good Women* and Boccaccio in *Troilus and Criseyde*, do not treat with comparable seriousness the Machaldian legacy, indeed scarcely mention the canon of Rheims. They ignore Machaut and ignore Wimsatt, who, among the scholars of the fourth generation, has done the most to fill this gap in Chaucer studies.[2] And even when Jean de Meun, Machaut, and Froissart are recognized, the esthetic problem remains, a tendency to assume that the Frenchmen had less to contribute than Ovid, Boccaccio, and Petrarch, therefore that Chaucer borrowed less from them and that, whatever he took and whenever he took it, Gallic lead was automatically transmuted into the gold of Albion.

The most Gallic and most derivative of Chaucer's major texts, aside from his translations, would be *The Book of the Duchess*[3] where, as Wimsatt has forcefully demonstrated, approximately one-half of the poem is adapted directly from *Le Roman de la Rose*, Machaut, and Froissart. Scholars have generally assumed that the book that most influenced the *Duchess* was Machaut's *Jugement dou Roy de Behaingne*.[4] In a sense this is true. More lines were translated from the *Behaingne* than from any other text; and it is in the *Behaingne* that Chaucer found a seminal motif: a bereaved Knight mourning the death of his beloved, overheard by a Narrator. Clemen and others compare the *Duchess* to the *Behaingne*, pointing out the ways that Chaucer has changed his source and improved on it.[5] The point, of course, is that Dan Geoffrey had several models by Guillaume to work from. In my opinion, the most important of these models, the one which inspired him the most, in theme and motif, in structure and tone, was not the *Behaingne* but Machaut's *La Fonteinne amoureuse*.[6] True, in the *Fonteinne* no one is dead: the Knight has merely been separated from his beloved, forced into exile. This said, in the *Fonteinne* Machaut provides the following increments, which Chaucer adopted with gusto.

1. A story in which one allegedly unhappy lover dreams of another unhappy lover. In the frame the Narrator claims to be enamoured, suffering from melancholia, and in need of consolation. In the story proper he offers consolation to a lover still more wretched than himself. Thus, in both the *Fonteinne* and the *Duchess* the Narrator witnesses the Other's misery but also plays an active, obtrusive role in the plot. In both texts the hero-lover can be considered, to a certain degree, the Narrator's double, an alter ego on whom he has projected his own wretchedness. By rendering the Knight even more miserable than himself, the Narrator lightens his own burden. And by consoling the Knight, he creates a measure of hope. Thus the Narrator indulges in wish-fulfillment and releases tension in a fantasy world of dreams.

2. In the frame of both texts the Narrator, suffering from insomnia and from love sickness, hears of or reads Ovid's myth of Ceyx and Alcyone, a tragic story of love and sleep. Praying for sleep, he dreams of the tragic love of his prince. In Machaut and later in Chaucer we find the themes of sleeplessness, melancholia, and Eros in the frame linked to the same themes in the story proper. *La Fonteinne* and the *Duchess* tell of myth, dream, and reality, of a story from the Classics related to concrete experience and to the realm of Morpheus.

3. Chaucer also learned from Machaut what scholars have called modern dream psychology. In the *Fonteinne* dream Venus recounts the wedding of Peleus and Thetis, the Apple of Discord, and the Judgment of Paris, and she refers to the Fall of Troy; then she and the Lady comfort the Lover. This manifest dream content is derived from the dreamers' day residue, including their obsession with love and their respective ladies, the fact that they fall asleep near a fountain on which are carved images of the Abduction of Helen and the Trojan War, and that they talk of the pagan gods, including Venus, who built the fountain.

The power of Morpheus, God of Dreams, and the power of the dream as revery, adventure, and initiation are key structural motifs that grant unity to *La Fonteinne amoureuse*; Chaucer adopts them for his own first book.

4. Both poets, however, by creating believable dream psychology, undermine the dream's authority since, for the medievals, a dream derived from the subject's personal anxieties and reflecting his day residue, is an *insomnium* or *somnium animale*, of subjective and, therefore, limited value. Machaut and Chaucer choose to interpret their fictional dreams objectively and in psychological, subjective, specifically human terms, to treat the dream vision seriously and to poke fun at it at the same time. Hence Machaut, followed by Chaucer, in a humorous passage undercuts his own Morpheus myth by having the Speaker promise offerings, including a glorious feather bed, if only the Greek god answers his prayer:

> Et pour ç'au dieu qui moult scet et moult vaut,
> Pour mieus dormir, un chapiau de pavaut
> Et un mol lit de plume de gerfaut
>   Promés et dong. (807–10)

> Yif he wol make me slepe a lyte,
> Of down of pure dowves white
> I wil yive hym a fether-bed,
> Rayed with gold and ryght wel cled
> In fyn blak satyn doutremer,
> And many a pilowe, and every ber
> Of cloth of Reynes, to slepe softe—
> Hym thar not nede to turnen ofte. (249–56)

Therefore, although their respective Narrators and Lovers, as literary characters, more or less believe in the reality of what they experience, the poets as creators know better. For they know that their own narrating personae are an illusion and their dream world is no more and no less fictional than the waking one.

5. It is in the *Fonteinne* that Chaucer found a Narrator-Witness who mingles with the high aristocracy, is received as a friend, becomes the Knight's sympathetic confidant, helps the

latter to express himself, and succeeds in providing comfort, consolation, and understanding. At the bottom of the scale, a *povre homme* (1263), he nonetheless participates in courtly doings as a maker of verse, a user of words, in part because his patron and master also composes verse. The tact, the refinement, the subtle, elegant human interaction between prince and poet are not Chaucerian inventions but borrowing from his illustrious predecessor.

6. Chaucer also took from the *Fonteinne* the notion that the Witness overhearing the Knight's lyrical complaint by accident could later, upon meeting the hero, pretend not to know the reason for the latter's misfortune. This carefully motivated increment in Machaut—the Narrator overheard his Prince's lamentation the previous evening, and, after a short delay, he confesses that he overheard it—becomes more problematic and less coherent in the *Book of the Duchess*.

7. Finally, as an artistic *mise en abyme*, frescos from *Le Roman de la Rose* and stained glass recounting the story of Troy in the Chaucerian Narrator's chamber correspond to and no doubt derive from the stories of Paris and Helen and of the Trojan War chiseled on the Machaldian Fountain. The fountain of love is a beautiful artifact, constructed out of marble, ivory, and gold, the central image in a pattern of gold imagery, a perfectly symmetrical artifact that corresponds to and reflects the symmetrical ring structure of the *dit* as a whole, and a work of art that recounts Ovidian myth narrated elsewhere in the text. It is a *mise en abyme*, an artistic entity that reflects, comments on, and symbolizes the narrative structure that contains it. Following up on this line, it would be a delightful touch were the *romaunce* (48), the *bok* containing *written fables* (52), that Chaucer's Narrator reads, telling of Ceyx and Alcyone, to have been not Ovid, not the *Ovide moralisé*, but Machaut's own *Fonteinne amoureuse* or a compendium Machaut manuscript. The written text would then have provided as much day residue for the Chaucerian Narrator's subsequent dream as the Knight's verbal, lyrical complaint (in fact by Machaut himself) did for Machaut's Narrator. Machaut would then offer a complete intertextual matrix for Chaucer, his book as a pre-text included in

Chaucer's intertext, in dream and waking reality, in much the same way that Machaut included Ovid, for that matter his own Ovidian *complainte*, in *La Fonteinne*.[7]

A roughly comparable situation exists for the Prologue to *The Legend of Good Women*.[8] Chaucerians, including Frank and Kiser,[9] who have written excellent books on the *Legend*, are familiar with the French "Marguerite poems," although the Marguerite texts were to become readily available only in recent editions by Wimsatt and Fourrier.[10] Chaucer's Myth of the Daisy was inspired by a pattern of court encomium and court play derived from Machaut, Froissart, Deschamps, and their world. A number of specialists are less conscious of the fact that the core of the Prologue is taken from Machaut's *Jugement dou Roy de Navarre*.[11] In the *Navarre* Machaut's narrating persona recounts how in springtime, following upon a harsh winter, he was accused before a court of love (the authority figures are one man and one woman) of having defamed ladies and *fin' amor* in a previous book: *Le Jugement dou Roy de Behaingne*. After a mock defense in a mock trial, in which the hero appears to have the worst of it ("sa cause est mal plaidoïe," 3646; "vous aviez mespris/Contre les dames de haut pris," 3797–98; "Mais vous avez si mal prouvé," 3985) but which in fact shows the plaintiff's charges to be absurd, he is condemned—to write more poetry of love. All this is taken over into the Prologue. As for the legends themselves, significantly four of the five exempla recounted by the Machaldian Narrator's accusers, bookish stories from Antiquity told by feminine allegories in defense of woman, reeappear among Chaucer's legends in defense of Good Women. They are the myths of Dido, Ariadne, Medea, and Thisbe. It is by no means unlikely that the impulse for the legends and the reference to "olde bokes" (25), "olde stories" (98), and "these olde appreved stories" (21) concern Machaut as much as they do Virgil and Ovid.

That Machaut's and Chaucer's Narrator as a literary character defends himself badly or fails to defend himself at all does not ipso facto repudiate his cause. A valid thesis can be defended ineptly without its being discredited on its own terms. Machaut and Chaucer have chosen to have their personae as Narrator describe how he as Litigant lost the trial, committing minor errors in procedure or through inept or non-existent defense, while the main question remains unanswered. After all, it is the poet—Guillaume de Machaut or Geoffrey Chaucer—who prepares the speeches on both sides. He chooses to lose, and his choice is a literary one, contributing to a literary structure. It is obvious that, for both poets, guilt ultimately is based upon a simple tautology: to undermine *fin' amor* results in the undermining of *fin' amor* and is surely a crime in a value system based upon the sanctity of *fin' amor*. And to be "forfais" vis-à-vis ladies and *fin' amor* means that one is equally guilty before the God of Love—Amor—the symbolic guardian of the cult. Unfortunately, the poet and at least a section of his public may adhere to a different system with different rules and different icons. Meanwhile, subtly, indirectly, the Narrator proclaims his right to tell the truth as he sees it. Even the Chaucerian persona, who assumes a more passive role than his predecessor, declares:

> Ne a trewe lover oght me not to blame
> Thogh that I speke a fals lovere som shame...
> Algate, God woot, yt was myn entente
> To forthren trouthe in love and yt cheryce... (466–67, 471–72)

Thus the poet, while he gives the impression of recanting his earlier works, in fact defends them and his own function as artist with brio.

Indeed, the greatest gift Machaut offers Chaucer is the notion of a poet writing poetry about the writing of poetry by a poet. The Litigant is accused, condemned, and allowed to repent not as a man, in his alleged function of lover, but as an implied author, in his real function of maker of texts. Both the Champenois and the Londoner depict an unusually sophisticated view of the writer: the "clerkly poetic narrator,"[12] author of books, proud of his artistic achievement yet at the same time capable of mocking himself both as a poet and lover. The Narrating poet-persona appears to be inept and loses his case, yet at the same time Machaut and Chaucer mock the artificial code of *fin' amor* and the hypocrisy of a rigid, aristocratic court; in fact, they undermine the orthodox courtly world while appearing to yield to its decrees. Thus Machaut provides Chaucer with a highly sophisticated narrative technique, homodiegetic narrative with an actorial rather than authorial focalization. For the Machaldian and Chaucerian "I" is the center of consciousness and single focus for the narrative. The world of the text is his world, filtered through him. What he says is to be given credence; he participates actively in the story as hero. Indeed, since the mode of the *dit amoureux* is relatively dramatic—the Narrator shows rather than tells; his technique is scenic rather than panoramic; and there is no interference from other, delegated voices, as in *Le Roman de la Rose*—Machaut and Chaucer succeed in creating, up to a point, the illusion of objectivity and impartiality. However, for this very reason the focalization is external to the Narrator's deepest feelings and sentiments. Like Jean de Meun's protagonist, we recognize him to be obtuse and naïve, too close to himself as hero, not aware of all the comic overtones in what he says. Specifically, this inept, obtuse, comic narrator as a narrating voice is reliable enough in his recounting of events yet totally unreliable in that, in spite of what appears to be his conscious intention, the picture he paints, one of defeat, veils yet at the same time reveals the vision of victory, a poet writing poetry in answer to criticism of his poetry, elaborated by the real author.[13]

Thus Machaut and Chaucer, even though they identify with their Narrators, erect a barrier between themselves and their all too human literary creation. They are more sophisticated than their Narrators and their Litigants. From this situation emerges distance and control: the unself-conscious, unobtrusive Narrator separated from the moderately self-conscious and obtrusive Litigant; yet both *erlebendes ich* and *erzählendes ich* are unaware of the true meaning of their story and are separated from the implied author behind the scenes, who provides support and correction, sympathy for and criticism of, the Narrator and Litigant as hero(es). It then becomes the reader or audience's duty to interpret meaning and to interpret texts, indeed to judge character, much as the authorities do within the fiction of the book, hopefully in a more sophisticated manner and with better results. And the modern reader will find such highly self-conscious texts, metatexts concerned with the nature of writing, concerned with their own textual creation, especially pertinent.

Generations of scholars assumed that the Chaucerian persona—the naïve, inept, timid, cowardly witness-narrator and naïve, inept, timid, cowardly lover who is also a highly self-conscious, bookish, clerkly author—is a Chaucerian creation, one mark of his originality. In fact, it was largely invented by Machaut, who took some hints from Jean de Meun, then was elaborated by Froissart. The artist—a real or metaphoric cleric—seeks to establish a bond with his secular aristocratic master, the *miles dominans*, through flattery and self-denigration, thus to achieve through rhetorical manipulation that synthesis of *fortitudo et sapientia*, Mars and Apollo, *chevalerie et clergie*, which served as a courtly ideal. The speaker thus is admitted into the company of the high nobility and, because of his tact and wisdom, and their graciousness, permitted to become their friend. This stance of Horatian friendship extends from the late Middle Ages to the fall of the ancien régime: [14] from Machaut to Voltaire and, transferred across the Channel, from Chaucer to Pope.

Similarly, the book-experience-dream sequence claimed to be distinctly Chaucerian is also borrowed from the French, the chief difference being that Machaut's tales include as intertextual *mises en abyme* the author's own lyrical or narrative creations, self-referential autotexts—in *Remede de Fortune* the Narrator's *lai*; in *La Fonteinne amoureuse* a *complainte* attributed to the princely lover; in *Le Jugement dou Roy de Navarre* the implied author's own previous *Jugement dou Roy de Behaingne*; in *Le Voir Dit* the implied author's entire previous corpus—whereas, until the *Legend of Good Women*, Chaucer uses works by Cicero, Ovid, Virgil, and Machaut. Writing in English not French, Chaucer assumes a modesty-topos: his persona reads other people's books, and he claims to be a mere translator; his persona lacks Machaut's joyful self-assurance. The nature of the persona means that, in this respect as in others, Chaucer innovates, in English, by imitating, illustrating, and partaking of a continental French convention, also shaping it to fit his own social, linguistic, and esthetic situation in England.

The nature of the persona also tells us something about the alleged reality of the Chaucerian self-portrait and the alleged restraints imposed upon him by oral performance. Bronson challenged the modern, "new critical" analyses of the persona elaborated by Bethurum, Donaldson, and Kane, among others.[15] According to Bronson, because Chaucer himself read his texts to the court, the likeness between the persona and Chaucer the writer had to be close and any divergences relatively minor. In essence, Bronson claims that the "I" telling the story in the *Duchess*, the *House of Fame*, the *Legend*, and the *Canterbury Tales* is not a persona but the real Geoffrey Chaucer and should be so designated.

In my opinion, Bronson and his followers err with regard to the nature of orality in the Middle Ages. All medieval literature was meant to be delivered orally, to be sung, chanted, or read aloud. Yet most medieval texts, whether heterodiegetic (chansons de geste, romances, and fabliaux) or homodiegetic (courtly lyrics, allegories of love) are largely conventional in mode and told by a conventional, archetypal narrator. Secondly, the fact of Chaucer's semi-retirement away from London in his later years indicates that Geoffrey himself could not have habitually recited his own works at court or anywhere else and that, more often than not, others read the master's texts. Finally, since, as I have indicated, the persona is conventional and of French provenance, the extent to which it corresponds to the historical London government functionary had to be to a large extent fortuitous. By no means fortuitous, of course, was the ironic tension felt between the persona and the real Chaucer or between both of them and the reader of the day, one aspect of medieval audience response which we will never be able to capture in its essence. We can, however, take it for granted that the more cultivated among the audience were aware of the nature of the Chaucerian Speaker. Ever since the dissemination of the first Machaldian texts, the horizon of expectations of the courtly medieval public had been enlarged to include the new persona. Hearing him speak English, hearing him designated as "Geoffrey" would presumably have elicited a shock of recognition and of pleasure from those who indeed had ears to hear.

The old cliché, of Chaucer drifting away from French influence in his later "periods," is now fortunately defunct. Wimsatt has shown the pervasive textual presence of Machaut, as an authority on *fin' amor* and on Boethian *fortuna*, where we would ordinarily least expect it: in *Troilus and Criseyde*.[16] *Troilus* can indeed be thought of as Boccaccio medievalized, that is filtered through Machaut. In the *Canterbury Tales*, the French presence is, of course, enormous. Twenty-one out of twenty-four tales have literary associations with France.[17] It is true that, in his masterpiece, Chaucer primarily looks elsewhere than in the direction of the dominant contemporary French courtly mode embodied in Machaut and Froissart. (By the 1390s, Machaut was no longer contemporary.) For the extraordinary range of style and subject-matter in the *Tales*, Chaucer sought inspiration in fabliaux, *Le Roman de Renart*, and the more satirical, earthy sections of *Le Roman de la Rose*; also in chronicles, saints' lives, and moral and penitential treatises.

Yet Guillaume does not disappear from Geoffrey's purview. A case can be made that one of Chaucer's triumphs in the *Canterbury Tales* lies in the realm of narrative technique, for he imagined a work of art focused on a community of unself-conscious narrators, including himself, each with his own narrow vision and absence of lucidity, telling stories whose interest for us derives in part from the fact that they reflect their tellers' limited insight and imperfect self-knowledge. For such a conception of narrative, one appropriate inspiration would be Machaut's masterpiece, *Le Voir Dit*, the first I-narrative in modern literature constructed on and grounded in the limited, restricted point of view of the narrator-hero. *Le Voir Dit* also has a direct tie with the *Manciple's Tale*.[18]

The *Manciple's Tale*, however, is not the only place where one can detect a direct, textual Machaldian legacy. Let us consider the *Merchant's Tale*,[19] recognized by all as a masterpiece constructed in the French fabliau tradition and utilizing a variety of French material, borrowing heavily from *Le Roman de la*

Rose and Deschamps's *Miroir de mariage*. The Merchant's obscene *hortus conclusus*, the locus of January's cuckolding and spiritual blinding, had been assimilated to the Garden of Delight in *Le Roman de la Rose* and to sundry biblical gardens cited by the typological critics. In my opinion, in addition to these, Chaucer also had in mind the park in *La Fonteinne amoureuse*. The *Fonteinne amoureuse* alone will account for why Greek gods are associated with the fairies in regard to January's garden. Machaut says that his garden was Cupid's *demours* (1381), and that Venus, Jupiter, nymphs, and fays came there regularly to take their pleasure. Indeed, it and more particularly the Fountain of Love at its center, the artistic *mise en abyme* alluded to above, were constructed by Cupid and by Pygmalion, under Venus's orders and at Jupiter's instigation:

> Et adont il me prist a dire
> Que ce fu jadis li demours
> De Cupido, le dieu d'amours,
> Et que Jupiter et Venus
> Y sont par maintes fois venus
> Pour eaus deduire et solacier,
> Pour acoler, pour embracier,
> Et pour le deduit ou nature
> Mist plus son entente et sa cure,
> Pour avoir plaisence et solas,
> Comment qu'on en soit de po las—
> Car aucune fois il anuie
> Plus qu'après biau temps longue pluie—
> Et que Jupiter l'ordonna
> Qui de ce serpent l'or donna,
> Et Venus le marbre et l'ivoire
> Fist entaillier, c'est chose voire,
> Par Pymalion qui bien ouevre,
> Qui escheva toute ceste ouevre—
> Cupido fist le remenant
> Qui est bel et bien avenant—
> Et que les nimphes et les fees
> Y faisoient leurs assamblees
> Et qu'encor souvent y venoient
> Et leur parlement y tenoient,
> Leurs gieus, leurs festes, leurs caroles
> Et leurs amoureuses escoles . . . (1380–406)

The Machaldian Narrator and his Knight fall asleep and dream of a visit from Venus, who provides consolation and comfort to the victimized Knight and who, in recounting the Wedding of Peleus and Thetis, recalls her interest in the figure of Priapus:

> Moult bonnement s'i esbatoient...
> Jovis Preapus o sa perche
> Qui sa robe lieve et reverche
> —De ma main ma face couvri,
> Quant je le vis, mais j'entrouvri
> Mes dois pour la mieus aviser
> Et pour mieus celle part viser,
> Car si volentiers le vëoie
> Qu'au vëoir trop me delitoie,
> Et les autres le maudissoient,
> Nompourguant elles en rioient— ... (1667, 1675–84; cf. also 2591–602)

Chaucer's Merchant also tells of a garden and well. His is made by January, so beautiful that Priapus could not describe its beauty, where Pluto, Proserpine, and "al hire fayerye" come to take their pleasure:

> So fair a gardyn woot I nowher noon.
> For, out of doute, I verraily suppose
> That he that wroot the Romance of the Rose
> Ne koude of it the beautee wel devyse;
> Ne Priapus ne myghte nat suffise,
> Though he be god of gardyns, for to telle
> The beautee of the gardyn and the welle
> That stood under a laurer alwey grene.
> Ful ofte tyme he Pluto and his queene,
> Proserpina, and al hire fayerye,
> Disporten hem and maken melodye
> Aboute that welle, and daunced, as men tolde. (IV 2030–41)

Like Machaut's Venus, Pluto and Proserpine intervene in the narrative: Pluto literally opens January's eyes as to the behavior of his wife, but Proserpine helps May find the appropriate explanation that will comfort her husband and exculpate herself. No need for me to develop the subtle ironies involved in Chaucer's use of the *Fonteinne* and his mastery of intertextuality in incorporating pieces of Machaut's *dit* in his own text, undermining Machaut's characters and his own characters by setting them off against Machaut's. On the one hand, Machaut's *fonteinne delitable* (1422) is a work of high art situated in a locus of high courtly love, created by Pygmalion, which used to be presided over by celestial deities; on the other hand, referring back to and mocking it, Chaucer's Merchant's phallic pear tree is planted in a plot of degenerate lust, created by the senile January, now presided over by the lord and lady of Hades. Since Machaut had evoked Jupiter, Juno, Venus, and Cupid, associated with fairies, it is an elegant touch on Chaucer's part to bring in the gods of the nether world, their antipodes, promoted to king and queen of the fairies, in this anticourtly text redolent of "the material bodily lower stratum."[20] And what a contrast between Venus and the Lady's *Confort*, so pure, so idealized, transmitted through and in a world of dreams, and the corrosive, cynical, demystifying truth and countertruth revealed to January, in concrete actuality, which leads to his utter befuddlement in a private, subjective fantasy-existence. Chaucer's direct horticultural models are French not biblical, and it is the *fin' amor* of Guillaume de Lorris and Guillaume de Machaut that is mocked not the *caritas* of Solomon and St. John. The typological hermeneuticists of the Robertsonian school deepen our understanding of the *Tale*, add overtones and enrich its literary reality. However, they perceive only the bark. The kernel lies elsewhere.

I should like to conclude by raising an issue touched on earlier: that of value judgment. Since the generation of Kittredge and Lowes, in theory we are scholars, philologists, men of science, and we do not indulge in subjective, impressionistic valuations of the texts we study. In fact, traditionally Chaucerians investigate how their author uses, changes, or adapts his sources, with the implicit esthetic presupposition that he is a giant of world literature whereas his sources are not, therefore that inevitably he improves upon them. This turns out to be the situation for all of Chaucer's predecessors, with the possible exception of Dante. The same "great books approach," the same "superiority complex" applies to Ovid, Petrarch, and Boccaccio, as well as to Jean de Meun, Machaut, and Froissart.²¹ It would be possible to quote a dozen books on Chaucer that allude to the artificiality of French verse, the thin, conventional, inartistic French sources, their empty formalism, exaggeration, over-refinement, and over-subtlety, their pretty, topical, surface elegance, their artificial, conventional, pedantic sameness, their stiff conventions, modishly elegant and mechanical, based on dull, arbitrary, and inept artifice.²²

To be fair, these Anglicists simply echoed the verdict on later medieval French literature disseminated within French departments both in Paris and abroad. Generations of romance philologists, under the influence of German romanticism, were fascinated by the oldest, earliest texts, purportedly the "simplest" and most "naïve," thus favored chanson de geste, *roman courtois*, and the troubadour *canso*, whereas they consciously, willfully disdained the more civilized, refined muse of the fourteenth and fifteenth centuries. Since the mid-1950s, however, a revolution has occurred in Old French studies: the introduction and practice of modern criticism, and the reception into the canon of writing from the turn of the twelfth century up to Villon. Specifically concerning Machaut, four full-length studies and a host of articles have put the Canon of Rheims on the map and in the very front rank of medieval poets.²³

The new generation of Chaucerians and the new generation of *romanistes* have no superiority or inferiority complexes, are no longer enslaved to the great books approach or to questions of national pre-eminence. We can all deal with the fourteenth-century creators—Petrarch, Boccaccio, Machaut, Froissart, Christine, Juan Ruiz, Juan Manuel, Chaucer, and Gower—see how they evolve, how they react to each other, how they have created one of the most exciting moments, a truly European moment, in the history of world culture.

NOTES

1. G. L. Kittredge, "Chauceriana, I: The *Book of the Duchess* and Guillaume de Machaut," *Modern Philology* 7 (1909–10): 465–71;

"Chauceriana, II: 'Make the metres of hem as thee leste,'" *Modern Philology* 7 (1909–10): 471–74; "Chaucer's *Troilus* and Guillaume de Machaut," *Modern Language Notes* 30 (1915): 69; "Guillaume de Machaut and *The Book of the Duchess*," *PMLA* 30 (1915): 1–24. John L. Lowes, "Chaucer and the *Ovide moralisé*," *PMLA* 33 (1918): 302–25; "The Prologue to the *Legend of Good Women* as related to the French *Marguerite* Poems and the *Filostrato*," *PMLA* 19 (1904): 593–683.

2. James Wimsatt, *Chaucer and the French Love Poets: The Literary Background of the "Book of the Duchess"* (Chapel Hill: University of North Carolina Press, 1968); *The Marguerite Poetry of Guillaume de Machaut* (Chapel Hill: Univ. of North Carolina Press, 1970); *Chaucer and the Poems of "Ch" in University of Pennsylvania MS French 15* (Cambridge: Brewer, and Totowa, N.J.: Rowman & Littlefield, 1982); and a series of important articles. Prior to Wimsatt, Charles Muscatine's epoch-making *Chaucer and the French Tradition: A Study in Style and Meaning* (Berkeley: Univ. of California Press, 1957), which concerns French writers of the earlier centuries.

3. *The Riverside Chaucer*, 3rd ed., gen. ed. Larry D. Benson (Boston: Houghton Mifflin, 1987): 330–46.

4. *Œuvres de Guillaume de Machaut*, ed. Ernest Hoepffner, Société des Anciens Textes Français, vol. 1 (Paris: Firmin-Didot, 1908): 57–135.

5. Wolfgang Clemen, *Chaucer's Early Poetry* (New York: Barnes & Noble, 1964): chap. 1.

6. *Œuvres de Guillaume de Machaut*, vol. 3 (Paris: Champion, 1921): 143–244.

7. Unresolved, of course, is the question to what extent the *Duchess* differs from *La Fonteinne*. Our answer to the question will depend on our reading of the *Duchess*; a quasi-infinite number of readings have been made. A challenging one, which emphasizes Chaucer's transformation, even rejection, of Machaut, is by R. Barton Palmer, *"The Book of the Duchess* and *Fonteinne Amoureuse*: Chaucer and Machaut Reconsidered," *Canadian Review of Comparative Literature* 7 (1980): 380–93.

8. *The Riverside Chaucer*: 588–603, Text F.

9. Robert Worth Frank, Jr., *Chaucer and "The Legend of Good Women"* (Cambridge, Mass.: Harvard Univ. Press, 1972); Lisa J. Kiser, *Telling Classical Tales: Chaucer and the "Legend of Good Women"* (Ithaca: Cornell Univ. Press, 1983).

10. Wimsatt, *The Marguerite Poetry of Guillaume de Machaut*; Jean Froissart, *"Dits" et "Débats"; Avec en appendice quelques poèmes de Guillaume de Machaut*, ed. Anthime Fourrier, Textes Littéraires Français (Geneva: Droz, 1979).
11. *Œuvres de Guillaume de Machaut*, vol. 1: 137–282.
12. I borrow the term from Karl D. Uitti's suggestive essays "The Clerkly Narrator Figure in Old French Hagiography and Romance," *Medioevo Romanzo* 2 (1975): 394–408, and "From *Clerc* to *Poète*: The Relevance of the *Romance of the Rose* to Machaut's World," in *Machaut's World: Science and Art in the Fourteenth Century*, ed. Madeleine Pelner Cosman and Bruce Chandler (New York: New York Academy of Sciences, 1978): 209–16.
13. I touch on such questions of narrative technique in *Le Roman de la Rose* and Machaut, in *A Muse for Heroes: Nine Centuries of the Epic in France* (Toronto: Univ. of Toronto Press, 1983): chaps. 5 and 6.
14. See my *In Defense of French Poetry: An Essay in Revaluation* (University Park: Pennsylvania State Univ. Press, 1987): chap. 6.
15. Bertrand H. Bronson, "*The Book of the Duchess* Re-opened," *PMLA* 67 (1952): 863–81, and *In Search of Chaucer* (Toronto: Univ. of Toronto Press, 1960).
16. Wimsatt, "Guillaume de Machaut and Chaucer's *Troilus and Criseyde*," *Medium Aevum* 45 (1976): 277–93.
17. The figures cited by Haldeen Braddy, "The French Influence on Chaucer," in *Companion to Chaucer Studies*, ed. Beryl Rowland, rev. ed. (New York: Oxford Univ. Press, 1979): 153.
18. *Le Livre du Voir Dit de Guillaume de Machaut*, ed. Paulin Paris (Paris: La Société des Bibliophiles François, 1875); *The Riverside Chaucer*: 283–86.
19. *The Riverside Chaucer*: 154–68.
20. The term is from Mikhail Bakhtin, *Rabelais and His World* (Cambridge, Mass.: MIT Press, 1968).
21. For a revisionist attack on "Whig literary history," Lee Patterson, *Negotiating the Past: The Historical Understanding of Medieval Literature* (Madison: Univ. of Wisconsin Press, 1987).
22. The words are direct quotes. There is no need to identify the sources.
23. The books: Daniel Poirion, *Le Poète et le prince: L'évolution du lyrisme courtois de Guillaume de Machaut à Charles d'Orléans* (Paris: Presses Universitaires de France, 1965); William Calin, *A Poet at the Fountain: Essays on the Narrative Verse of Guillaume*

de Machaut (Lexington: Univ. Press of Kentucky, 1974); Kevin Brownlee, *Poetic Identity in Guillaume de Machaut* (Madison: Univ. of Wisconsin Press, 1984); Jacqueline Cerquiglini, *"Un engin si soutil": Guillaume de Machaut et l'écriture au XIVe siècle* (Geneva: Slatkine, 1985). One article, by a distinguished Anglicist, proclaims Machaut's inherent esthetic worth vis-à-vis Chaucer: Constance B. Hieatt, *"Un autre fourme"*: Guillaume de Machaut and the Dream Vision Form, *Chaucer Review* 14 (1979–80): 97–115.

Sylvia Huot

Reliving the *Roman de la Rose*: Allegory and Irony in Machaut's *Voir Dit*

The *Voir Dit* was Machaut's last major *dit amoureux*, and can be seen as the culmination of his long and illustrious career as a love poet.[1] In this highly self-reflexive *dit*, Machaut goes farther than ever before in the explicit representation of himself as poet, composer, and compiler of books. Modern critics have offered various readings, often quite illuminating, of the *Voir Dit* as a self-conscious reflection on Machaut's role as love poet and on the paradoxes inherent in the adoption of this role by an aging clerk.[2] Largely absent from these readings, however, is a consideration of the relationship between the *Voir Dit* and the *Roman de la Rose*, one of Machaut's most important vernacular sources. The present study examines the presence of the *Rose* in the *Voir Dit*, and suggests ways that Machaut's use of the

Rose reveals both his understanding of this complex poem and his concept of his own poetic work.

In the *Voir Dit* Machaut draws on the *Rose* as a source of imagery for the love experience. Allusions to the *Rose* heighten the eroticism of the love story; at the same time, the use of a sacralizing language suggests an attempt to infuse the love relationship with a deeper meaning. But there always remains an ironic disjunction between the experience that is being portrayed and the character of its participants, and the language and literary models with which it is evoked. Guillaume, Machaut's persona in the *Voir Dit*, casts his love in terms of both sacred and erotic allegory, as myth, as chivalric romance; in the end, these models are proved to be effective only in the imaginative space of the literary work. The *Voir Dit* offers a critique, both humorous and enlightening, of the conflicting poetic registers operating in the *Rose*.

The tendency to transfigure the love relationship is initiated at the beginning of the story, when Guillaume, delighted at having received Toute Belle's first rondeau, declares:

> Or faisons une trinité
> Et une amiable unité;
> Que ce soit uns corps & une ame,
> D'Amours, de moy & de ma dame.
>   (ed. Paris, vv. 252–55)
>
> Now let us make up a trinity and a loving union; may it be one body and one soul, consisting of Love, myself, and my lady.

The rhyme pair *trinité / unité* unmistakably points to the triune God of Christianity; these rhymes appear, for example, in Nature's discussion of the Trinity in the *Rose* (vv. 19111–12). No sooner does the love affair begin, in other words, than the possibility arises of its allegorization: the configuration of the wise poet, the wilful and strangely powerful lady, and the love that binds them reflects the conjoining of divine wisdom, power and love. The allegory never quite comes into focus, but the impulse to recast the love for Toute Belle in sacred terms informs the rhetoric of both the narrative and the letters. Toute Belle is capable of performing "belles miracles" [beautiful miracles (*VD*, v. 814)]; indeed her curative powers surpass those of the saints, for "onques nul miracle ne vi/Si grant com d'un amant ravi" [never did I see a miracle as great as that of a ravished lover (*VD*, vv. 819–20)]. She is described in terms evocative of the Virgin: she is the carbuncle, the diamond that bestows grace, the ruby that cures all ills, the pole star (*VD*, vv. 95–106).[3] The initial list of Toute Belle's attributes culminates in an image that perfectly unites the registers of erotic and sacred allegory: "Briefment, c'est la rose vermeille / Qui n'a seconde ne pareille" [in short, she is the red rose, unique and without peer (*VD*, vv. 107–8)].

As the amorous correspondence gets underway, the interplay of sacred and erotic registers and the appropriation of literary models continues. In the tenth letter in Paulin Paris' edition, Guillaume assures Toute Belle that he will love and serve her forever, not only in the chivalric manner of romance heroes such as Lancelot and Tristan, but also as a deity: "& aourray comme Dieu terrien & comme la plus precieuse & glorieuse relique que je véysse onques en lieu où je fuisse" [and I will worship (you) as an earthly god, and as the most precious and glorious relic that I ever saw anywhere (*VD*, p. 68)]. The sacred and chivalric dimensions of the love relationship are equally present in Guillaume's promise, a few lines later, to visit Toute Belle by Pentecost. Pentecost, starting point of so many Arthurian adventures, will provide the time frame for the initiation of Guillaume's amorous quest; at the same time, the meeting will be a holy visitation, a descent of poetic inspiration, a loosening of the tongue—or at least of the pen—in preparation for the poetic undertaking to follow.

Let us consider the dense clustering of highly charged terminology and literary allusions in this letter. Lancelot and Tristan, to begin with, are ambiguous models at best. Both loved with an unwavering and whole-hearted devotion, it is true; and both were paragons of chivalry. Both compensated for the absence of the beloved lady through art: Tristan by composing and performing *lais*, Lancelot by writing and painting the story of his love for Guinevere on the walls of his chamber.[4] As a pair, Tristan and Lancelot thus reflect both Guillaume's poetico-musical activity on behalf of Toute Belle, and his fascination with her portrait, enshrined at his bedside. Nonetheless, Tristan and Lancelot are not wholly positive models, for both were involved in adulterous love affairs that brought dishonor on both themselves and their ladies, and ultimately brought about serious disruption of the social order; and however one may wish to interpret the moral tone of the prose romances from which Machaut would have known these stories, it must at the very least be agreed that love is shown to have fierce and powerful enemies, and that these enemies can sometimes get the upper hand. A similar ambiguity clings to the third example mentioned along with Tristan and Lancelot in one of Guillaume's earlier letters (ed. Paris, no. 2): the love of Paris for Helen, the disastrous consequences of which are all too well known. As Jacqueline Cerquiglini has shown in such detail, the *Voir Dit* is, on one level, the story of the clerk who would be a knight; by associating himself with Paris, in particular, Guillaume blurs the distinction, so carefully drawn in the *Fonteinne amoureuse* through the very example of the Judgment of Paris, between chivalric lovers and clerkly love poets.[5] In his eagerness to cast himself as the hero of a romance, Guillaume ignores the problematical aspects of his literary models. One might well say that he has little understanding of just what he is in for, of the potential obstacles and dangers inherent in the experience of passionate love and its commemoration in art and verse.

Moving from knightly models to the promise to worship Toute Belle as god and relic, Guillaume attempts to transpose this chivalric model into a sacred register. Yet here too, the undercurrents of his words work against the overt message. Not only is the precise meaning of "earthly god" somewhat unclear; but the various meanings of the term "relics" are, shall we say, all too clear. The word does have undeniable significance in the context of religious worship; but in the context of love poetry, it has a rather different sense, one illustrated nowhere more vividly than in the *Rose*. In fact, Guillaume's letter clearly echoes the Lover's final approach to the Rose, cast in terms of a great desire to "aourer / le biau saintuaire honourable" [worship the beautiful, honorable sanctuary (*Rose*, vv. 21562–63)] and to approach the sexual "relics" contained therein.

The Lover's conquest of the Rose is also described rather elaborately as a pilgrimage; and so is Guillaume's approach to Toute Belle. The pretext for the lovers' first meeting is Toute Belle's presence in an area to which Guillaume can go on pilgrimage; and the space of sacred devotion quickly becomes a context for amorous devotion as well:

> Si alay à l'église: mais
> Tantost com le piet mis dedens,
> Je fis un veu entre mes dens,
> Que tant comme laiens seroie,
> Tous les jours de nouvel feroie,
> Pour l'amour de ma dame douce.
> (*VD*, vv. 1514–19)

> Thus I went to the church; but as soon as I set foot inside, I made a vow under my breath that as long as I was there, I would compose new poetry every day for the love of my sweet lady.

The ballade that follows duly reiterates Guillaume's veneration of Toute Belle: "Mon Dieu terrien est & fu & sera" [she is, always was, and will continue to be my earthly god (*VD*, v. 1546)]. At a later point, the two lovers actually meet in a church, where the Mass provides the occasion for a surreptitious kiss:

> Mais trop richement m'echéy,
> Que quant on dist: *Agnus dei*,
> Foy que je doy à saint Crapais,
> Doucement me donna la pais,
> Entre .ii. pilers du moustier.
> (*VD*, vv. 2663–67)

> But what happened to me was truly wonderful: at the *Agnus dei*, by the faith of Saint Caprais, she sweetly gave me the kiss of peace, between two pillars of the church.

In this brief image, Machaut truly outdoes himself. For in this Holy Mass that is really an amorous tryst, we can recognize the conclusion of the *Rose*, as Guillaume replays the Lover's worshipful approach to the erotic sanctuary. In the detail that the kiss—at once chaste and erotic, contributing to both religious ritual and seduction—took place "entre .ii. pilers," Machaut links this moment to that in the *Rose* when the Lover, an eager pilgrim, kneels down "entre les .II. biaus pilerez" [between the two beautiful pillars (*Rose*, v. 21559)] that support the "sanctuary." As the elements of the scene take on their allegorical significance, we even begin to wonder about the Mass itself—could Genius be the priest officiating? Is the *Agnus dei* not the figure designated by Genius as the one who will lead Love's followers into the Heavenly Park?

Allusions to the *Rose* in fact characterize Guillaume's every meeting with his lady. When he sees Toute Belle for the first time, he finds her wearing a hood embroidered with a design of parakeets—a distant echo of the Garden of Delight filled with birds, and even of the God of Love himself, described in the initial encounter as "toz covers d'oisiaus" [completely covered with birds (*Rose*, v. 899)]. And later, seated in a lush garden, he gazes longingly at Toute Belle's lips as she sleeps in his lap; the secretary, covering her lips with a leaf, tempts Guillaume to kiss the leaf, then removes it as the trembling lover bends down. Awakening, Toute Belle teasingly accuses her lover of being "outrageus" [overly bold (*VD*, v. 2289)]. In the red lips partially covered by the leaf, one cannot help seeing the *rose vermeille*, itself surrounded by leaves. And in the ruse employed to bring about the lovers' first kiss, one is reminded that Bel Acueil's first gift to the Lover was in fact a leaf, plucked from beside the rosebud; and that it was upon receiving this leaf that the Lover was emboldened to ask for the Rose itself, a request that frightened Bel Acueil and resulted in the first appearance of Dangier. Nonetheless, it was not long after the acquisition of the leaf that the Lover managed to kiss the Rose. Machaut has conflated the two episodes of leaf and kiss, heightening the erotic resonances of the scene.

Who would have thought that Machaut, generally credited with a non-erotic representation of love, would have drawn on precisely the most erotic, and even the most audacious, moments in the *Rose*? Who would imagine that this aging would-be lover, shy and fumbling, might be modelled on the young and virile character who holds nothing back in his repeated attempts on the Rose? Yet it is so. Let us consider another important passage in the *Voir Dit*, the arrival of Toute Belle's portrait. One obvious source for this scene is the Pygmalion episode in the *Rose*, as will be discussed below. Aside from its associations with the Pygmalion story, the scene in which Guillaume receives the portrait acquires a highly charged eroticism from its echoes of the closing section of the *Rose*. The very word *ymage* recalls the final avatar of the lady in the *Rose*, the feminine image supported by the infamous two pillars, at whom Venus fires her burning arrow, and whose chief function appears to be as a vehicle for the erotic "sanctuary":

> Cil pilerez d'argent estoient,
> mout gent, et d'argent soutenoient
> une ymage en leu de chaasse
> . . . . .
> mes plus oulanz que pome d'ambre
> avoit dedanz un saintuaire,
> couvert d'un precieus suaire.
> (*Rose*, vv. 20767–69, 20776–78)

> These pillars were of silver, very lovely, and they supported a silver image used as a reliquary . . . but more aromatic than an apple of amber was the sanctuary within, covered with a precious cloth.

It is this figure that occasions the digression about Pygmalion. The "ymage" recurs as the Lover approaches the "relics"; and this passage is an important intertext for the portrait scene. First, Guillaume unwraps the portrait:

> Je pris ceste ymage jolie,
> Qui trop bien fu entortillie
> Des cuevrechiés ma douce amour,
> Si la desliay sans demour.
> (*VD*, vv. 1358–61)

> I took that pretty image, which was thoroughly wrapped with the kerchiefs of my sweet love; so I untied it without delay.

The Lover of the *Rose* similarly unveils the object of his desire:

> Trés an sus un po la courtine
> qui les reliques ancourtine;
> de l'ymage lors m'apressai
> que du saintuaire pres sai.
> (*Rose*, vv. 21569–72)

> I lifted the curtain a little, that shielded the relics; then I approached the image, drawing near to the sanctuary.

Guillaume then renders homage to the portrait, "A genous & à jointes mains" [on bended knee and with clasped hands (*VD*, vv. 1368)]; the Lover of the *Rose* similarly tells us that "m'agenoilli san demourer" [I got down on my knees without delay (*Rose*, vv. 21561)]. Just as the Lover of the *Rose* adopts a worshipful attitude toward the image and relics before him, so Guillaume vows to adore his image "Com ma souveraine déesse" [as my sovereign goddess (*VD*, vv. 1376)]. And Jean's Lover expresses his desire "au reliques touchier" [to touch the relics (*Rose*, vv. 21555)]; Guillaume places the precious portrait beside his bed, "Pour li véoir & atouchier, / A mon lever & au couchier" [to see and touch it upon rising and upon going to bed (*VD*, vv. 1390–91)]. It is clear on even a first reading of the *Voir Dit* that Guillaume's religious veneration of the portrait is decidedly and comically idolatrous; a reading of the passage in tandem with the *Rose* brings out the covert eroticism of the scene, preparing for the amorous pilgrimage to follow.

The centrality of the portrait in the *Voir Dit* has obvious parallels with the story of Pygmalion. Guillaume, like Pygmalion — especially Jean's Pygmalion — dresses and ornaments his image: "Je la vesti, je la paray" (*VD*, vv. 1392). At a much later point, he describes a dream in which the image speaks to him, and at the end of which he expresses amazement at the idea of a talking image, which he knows can only have been an illusion. We recall that it was when his image spoke that Jean's Pygmalion knew she was truly alive. Similarly, Guillaume's dream of a talking portrait marks the extent to which his image has taken on a life of its own, to such an extent that it now complains of having been punished for Toute Belle's offenses—as if the portrait was somehow utterly independent of the person it supposedly represents. The portrait indeed displaces Toute Belle from Guillaume's life: his relationship is less and less with Toute Belle herself, more and more with her image in portrait, letters, and songs.

A similar series of allusions to the closing section of the *Rose* marks the culminating episode in the erotic dalliance of Guillaume and Toute Belle, the encounter in the scented cloud of Venus. The occasion is, once again, a pilgrimage, arranged expressly so that the lovers can be together. When it is time to separate, Guillaume goes to the room where Toute Belle is sleeping and opens a small window (*fenestrelle, VD*, v. 3674). Already the alert reader may recall the *archiere* of the *Rose*: that small opening, at once architectural and anatomical, at which Venus aimed her arrow and into which the Lover, with some effort, inserted his staff. True to his model, Guillaume then unveils the opening: "Si tiray un po la cortine" [then I pulled aside the curtain a little (*VD*, v. 3676; cf. *Rose*, v. 21569)]. Like the Rose, which is accompanied by Bel Acueil, Toute Belle is not alone; she is accompanied by the *pucellette* who, Machaut reminds us, had previously been gathering flowers in the garden: "Qui, el vergier vert & feuilli, / Les fleurs dou chapelet cueilli" [who, in the green and leafy garden, gathered flowers for a garland (*VD*, vv. 3680–81)]. This seemingly gratuitous comment, remarkably enough, enables Machaut to introduce a crucial rhyme pair that occurs both at the end of the *Rose* and at the midpoint, in the God of Love's prophetic citation of the end:

> jusqu'a tant qu'il avra coillie
> seur la branche vert et foillie
> la tres bele rose vermeille
> (*Rose*, vv. 10569–71)

> until he will have gathered the beautiful red rose on the green and leafy branch;

and

> par grant joliveté cueilli
> la fleur du biau rosier fueilli.
> Ainsint oi la rose vermeille.
> (*Rose*, vv. 21747–49)

> With great joy I gathered the blossom of the beautiful leafy rosebush. Thus I had the red rose.

The double association of this rhyme pair with the climax of dream and poem alike greatly strengthens its power to evoke the moment of erotic and poetic consummation. This, coupled with a repeated insistence on Toute Belle's red lips—in which *vermeille*, then *vermillette* appear in rhyme position (*VD*, vv. 3704, 3707)—unmistakably identifies Guillaume's encounter with Toute Belle as a living out of the allegory of the *Rose*. Even the time of day is appropriate: daybreak, at the moment of waking.

It is at this point that, like the Lover of the *Rose*, Guillaume gets down on his knees (*VD*, v. 3709; *Rose*, v. 21561). Curiously, however, his purpose is to deliver a prayer to Venus; and here he takes on aspects of Pygmalion, praying to Venus that she help him consummate his love for the statue. The appearance of the cloud is hailed three times in rapid succession—Guillaume is an excitable narrator—as a "miracle," thereby recalling the vivification of Pygmalion's statue, described by Jean de Meun as "miracles apertes" [manifest miracle (*Rose*, vv. 21130)]. Its perfumed aroma in turn recalls the odour of the Rose that infused the Lover on the occasion of the kiss; while its darkness, assuring that "riens goute n'i véoit" [nothing whatsoever could be seen (*VD*, v. 3793)], is a distant echo of the Lover's much more lascivious allusion to the usefulness of his staff for feeling about "es fosses ou je ne voi goute" [in ditches where I can see nothing (*Rose*, v. 21372)]. On the surface, it is unclear just what takes place inside the cloud; indeed, one cannot help suspecting that Guillaume may have concentrated chiefly on the composition of a virelai.[6] But the subtext of the *Rose*—the gathering of the bud, Pygmalion's consummated desires—imbues the scene with a subtle but pronounced eroticism; if we are not shown precisely what Guillaume and Toute Belle do, at least we are reminded of what he would like to think they are doing.

Guillaume's repeated insistence on the "miracle si apertes" [such a manifest miracle (*VD*, v. 712)] of his resuscitation as a result of Toute Belle's attentions likewise recalls the central event in the story of Pygmalion. Yet here we encounter a curious reversal, since in the *Voir Dit* it is not the woman but the man who is miraculously given life; and this reversal alerts us to the complex network of mythological allusions that Machaut has created.

In some versions of the *Rose*, the story of Pygmalion is not the only place that "miracle" occurs. An important interpolation, dating from the late thirteenth century and appearing in a significant number of fourteenth-century manuscripts—hence very possibly known to Machaut—adds the story of Medusa and Perseus to the *Rose*. This interpolation immediately precedes the Pygmalion story, and is occasioned by the same motif of the tower image, whose curative powers are contrasted with the lethal effects of Medusa; and it opens with an allusion to miracle:

> Tel ymage n'ot mais en tour;
> Plus avienent miracle entour
> Qu'onc n'avint entour Medusa.
>   (ed. Langlois, vv. 1–3)

> No tower ever had such an image; more miracles take place around it than ever took place around Medusa.

The "miracles" effected by the feminine tower image are, specifically, the restoration of life to those who have been turned to stone, the resuscitation of the dead, and the restoration of sanity, or "droit sen" (v. 44). These curative transformations are remarkably similar to those that Guillaume ascribes to Toute Belle. as he states it in an early letter (ed. Paris, no. 4):

> Je estoie assourdis, arrudis, mus, impotens, par quoy joie m'avoit de tous poins guerpi & mis en oubli; mais vos douces escriptures me font oÿr & parler, venir & aler, & m'ont rendu joie.
>   (p. 41)
> I was deaf, rough, mute, impotent, whereby joy had completely

abandoned and forgotten me; but your sweet writings make me hear and speak, come and go, and have restored my joy.

From Guillaume's description of his previous state, one might well say that he had, metaphorically, been turned to stone, and that he had lost his senses. His repeated claims that Toute Belle "resuscitated" him similarly echo the assertion in the Medusa interpolation, with regard to the tower image, that "ceste resouscite" [this one resuscitates (ed. Langlois, v. 36)]. The language with which Guillaume describes his malady and cure further recalls the characterization of works of art in the *Rose*. Jean stresses the immobility and muteness of art, stating that no art works could ever "par eus aler, / vivre, mouvoir, santir, paler" [go by themselves, live, move, feel, speak (*Rose*, vv. 16034–35)]. And Pygmalion reflects sadly that "J'aime une ymage sourde et mue, / qui ne se crole ne semue" [I love a deaf and mute image that neither shifts nor moves (*Rose*, vv. 20821–22)].

The deafness, muteness, and immobility with which Guillaume characterizes his life before Toute Belle, and the ability to hear, speak, and move about that he has gained from corresponding with her, thus have roots in both of the mythological exempla tied to the appearance of the "ymage" in the *Rose*. The dangers associated with these myths also invade Guillaume's life. At a later, less idyllic stage of the affair, as Guillaume pours forth poetry and songs for a distant and curiously unresponsive Toute Belle, he begins to resemble Pygmalion, singing and dancing for his lifeless statue; or again, as Toute Belle's behavior finally reduces Guillaume to silence and stasis, making him afraid to visit her and unable to write, there is a suggestion of the effects of Medusa on those who behold her.[7] In all cases Toute Belle is the agent of miraculous or lethal power, Guillaume the recipient. Through her he acquires once again a poetic voice, an ear for music; the joyous disposition needed for the pursuit of his craft; the energy to launch himself into an imagined knightly adventure in which human love will take on a sacred aura, or, in turn, to embark on a pilgrimage that he hopes to infuse with eroticism. Through her he is reduced to despair, the fate of so many literary lovers.

Insofar as Toute Belle's acquaintance has given Guillaume a new life, we may say that this life is itself a revival, an incarnation, of literary models, and in that sense, a bringing to life of art. At the same time, it is through the ultimate failure of these models—the resolutely non-allegorical nature of his pilgrimage, the non-mythic status of the portrait he adores—that Guillaume is forced finally to abandon his amorous and heroic pretentions. In his role as the image of Machaut the poet, Guillaume is supremely successful at transposing life into art; but in his role as lover, he has finally proved incapable of transposing art into life. He is, in fact, no Pygmalion; Toute Belle is no saint sent by Heaven. When near the end of the book he receives a visitor, it is no Genius, fresh from the tearful confession of Nature herself, armed with an extravagant vision of the sanctity of erotic love: no, it is only an ordinary human priest, confessor of Toute Belle, bearing a reproachful letter soaked in her tears. The priest does deliver a flowery sermon complete with an elaborately worked out allegory that responds, point by point, to Guillaume's own earlier poem; its purpose, however, is not to empower Guillaume to perpetuate the species, but rather to remind him of his failings. Indeed, the priest chides Guillaume for having "maniere de fame" [a feminine manner (*VD*, v. 8743)], as though he were one of the *escoilliez* who, according to Genius, have "meurs femenins" [feminine traits (*Rose*, v. 20030)]. In the end the literary models that Guillaume had hoped to live out have turned against him.

We have seen that earlier, there was a decisive dissociation of Toute Belle herself from the portrait that inspires Guillaume and haunts his dreams. By the end of the book, the disjunction between life and art has become even greater. As people in the "real world," Guillaume and Toute Belle can continue an affectionate exchange of poems and letters. But the allegorical and mythical dimensions of their love, the miracles, the erotic encounters within scented clouds, the sacred and secret love of the romance knight and lady: all of this is recognized to be a literary construct, viable only in the space of the book. It is part of the genius of the *Voir Dit*—and a principal reason why so many readers at least since Paulin Paris have ascribed to it an autobiographical veracity—that it contains within itself this distinction between the real event and its literary recasting. The very failure of the story to adhere to the literary models in which it is cast seems to confirm its truth. Is it not a marvel when a fictional character can be forced to abandon his own pretentions to literariness?

In this strange work written near the end of his career, Machaut plays with and undercuts literary language at the same time that he demonstrates its power to create an enduring work of fiction. Jean de Meun had already created a text in which allegory is taken to an extreme, indeed allowed to run wild. He gave us an amorous hero who fancies that the entire divinely ordained natural order somehow depends on the success of his own erotic foray, who manages to seduce and even impregnate a metaphor, and who conceives of his sexual conquest as a replay of Hercules' conquest of Cacus. While writing a type of poetry that is in many ways very different from the *Rose*, Machaut nonetheless learned a great deal from his study of Jean's poetic strategies, which he appropriated, suitably transformed, into his own frequently humorous poetry.

But is the *Voir Dit* a purely comic work? Does Machaut draw on the *Rose* only for ironic purposes? The attempt to experience human love as an allegory for divine love, in effect to live out the *Song of Songs*, might even be seen as a noble effort; certainly it makes for interesting poetry. Part of Guillaume's problem may be that he does not know whether the allegory in which he casts himself should be the *Song of Songs* or the *Romance of the Rose*: will he have erotic adventures with a spiritual significance, or spiritual and aesthetic adventures with an erotic significance? This ambivalence can be traced back to that moment in the *Rose* where erotic and sacred registers are most problematically juxtaposed: the discourse of Genius, which medieval readers alternatively saw as serious moral teaching—surely not without at least some appreciation of its humor as well—or as sacrilege. As attentive a reader, as great a poet as Machaut must have been aware of these different possibilities, and may even have felt himself torn between them. Let us then turn to an examination of Machaut's relationship to Jean de Meun's enigmatic priest of Nature.

Machaut's reception of Genius was twofold. On the one hand, Genius can be seen as the final poet figure in the *Rose*.[8] He reads, and rewrites, Guillaume de Lorris' allegory; more generally, he stands for the very process of writing as the supreme creative act. In his praise of procreation, Genius elaborates an extended metaphor of fruitful sexual coupling as an act of writing; at the same time, as priest of Nature, he engages in a form of writing himself that sustains—one might say "underwrites"—the great chain of being. In this respect Genius is a potent model for the figure of the writer, and for writing as a creative process that mediates between the sacred and the erotic. Yet this last point also accounts for what is problematic in Genius: his vision of an absolute concordance of the natural and the divine, his strange equation of sexual fulfillment and spiritual salvation. Here I will first examine Machaut's use of Genius as a writer figure, and then turn to his treatment of love as a meeting ground for the sacred, the natural, the erotic.

Machaut most explicitly presents himself as poet in the *Prologue* that appears in the later manuscripts of his collected works, and the stance that he adopts is in many ways related to the figure of Genius in the *Rose*. He portrays himself, first, as specially selected by Nature to compose love poetry: the opening rubric explains that Nature wished to "reveler et faire essaucier les biens et honneurs qui sont en Amours" [reveal and exalt the benefits and honours that are in Love (ed. Hoepffner, *Pr.*, p. 1)], while in the opening ballade, Nature expressly commands Guillaume to make "Nouviaus dis amoureus plaisans" [pleasant new love poems (*Pr.*, v. 5)]. Nature explains that she who presided over Machaut's birth has endowed him with special skills: intellect, rhetoric, and music. In this respect, Machaut casts himself in the guise of Genius, also sent as Nature's emissary to address the amourous: "Genyus, li bien anpalez, / en l'ost au dieu d'Amours alez" [Genius, the well-spoken, go to the hosts of the God of Love (*Rose*, vv. 19305–6)], and again: "Alez, amis, au dieu d'Amors / porter mes plainz et mes clamors" [go, friend;

bear my plaint and my lamentation to the God of Love (vv. 19339–40)].

In the second pair of ballades, Machaut portrays himself as receiving subject matter from the God of Love. It is noteworthy that Cupid's participation here is not to inflame the poet with amorous desire, as at the beginning of Ovid's *Amores*, but rather to provide him with hopeful and pleasant thoughts: as the rubric states, "pour lui donner matere a faire ce que Nature li a enchargié" [to give him material to do what Nature commanded (*Pr.*, pp. 3–4)]. Machaut claims to write under the dual auspices of Nature and Love, but by no means necessarily as a lover in his own right. Similarly, Jean's Genius is welcomed by the God of Love and crowned as a bishop: although he is hardly in a position to fall in love, Genius' sermon is nonetheless partially authorized by Cupid. Of course the relationship of Genius or Nature to Cupid cannot be exactly the same as that of a human poet; and Machaut also models his persona on that of Jean de Meun. The scene of poetic election is based in part on the midpoint passage of the *Rose*, where Jean's birth is assured by Lucina, a Natura figure, and his poetic inspiration provided by the God of Love. But by having Nature take the initiative in his own formation as a poet, Machaut reverses the priorities established by Jean, and strengthens the parallel between himself and Genius.

An important aspect of Machaut's strategy in placing Nature as the highest authority behind his poetic and musical compositions is the implied analogy between natural and artistic creation. The first three ballades make repeated use of the words *fourmer* (and its derivatives *enfourmer, confourmer*), *ordener*, and *faire* to refer alternately to the creation of the world through Nature, to Nature's special creation and endowment of Machaut the poet, and to Machaut's own literary and musical creativity.[9] Thus poetry and music participate actively in the formative processes fundamental to the natural order. Indeed, by operating in the service of both Nature and Love, *rhetorique* and *musique* provide an interface between natural creative processes and the affective realm of desire. Through poetry and music, as Machaut elaborates in the remainder of the *Prologue*, dark passions are tamed, spirits raised; desire is intellectualized, sublimated; love bears fruit in the form of poetic and musical composition.

The association of love with the creation of poetry and song, if particularly powerful in the works of Machaut, is nothing new in the Old French tradition. But although Machaut could have had any number of sources for this idea, I would argue that the figure of Genius in the *Rose* is one of the most important. Writing is fundamental to Genius' identity. In both the *Rose* and *De planctu Naturae*, it is he who inscribes the ever-changing natural world in a mysterious book:

> en audiance recordait
> les figures representables
> de toutes choses corrumpables
> qu'il ot escrites en son livre,
> si con Nature les li livre.
> (*Rose*, vv. 16250–54)

> In [Nature's] presence he recorded the representations of all corruptible things, which he had written in his book, as Nature transmitted them to him.

The natural world, then, is a metaphorical book, written by Genius in collaboration with Nature. When at the end of her "confession," Nature asks Genius to communicate to the followers of Love the rules "qui sunt escrites an mon livre" [that are written in my book (*Rose*, v. 19354)], we must assume that it is in this same book, this written record of natural creation and procreation, that Nature's "rules" are encoded; and that these rules cover both the avoidance of sin and the imperative to increase and multiply. Genius also assumes the role of scribe in recording Nature's message for Love's troops: "Lors escrit cil, et cele dite" [then he wrote and she dictated (*Rose*, v. 19376)]. Finally, it is in his address to Love's barons that Genius elaborates his extended metaphor of the phallus as pen, the female body as tablets on which to write. To engage in the act of procreation is to participate in writing the great book of nature. Machaut has appropriated this metaphor and literalized it: he participates in the work of nature by writing actual books—and Machaut makes it amply clear that he is a writer, very much involved in book production—explicitly about the "rules" and effects of love.[10]

Machaut also addresses the divine nature of music in his *Prologue*, commenting that this "science" is not only an important aspect of the divine offices, but is even practiced in Heaven, by "li angles, / Li saint, les saintes, les archangles" [the angels, the male and female saints, the archangels (*Pr.*, vv. 115–16)]. The poet-musician thus not only participates in the work of Nature, but also imitates that of the angels. Music can soothe the spirits of humans and of God alike: it spreads joy, comforts the sorrowful, and was used by David to appease the wrath of God. Machaut attributes miraculous, resuscitative powers to music, asserting that Orpheus—identified as a *poetes* (*Pr.*, v. 138)—removed Eurydice from Hell, "Par sa harpe et par son dous chant" [with his harp and his sweet singing (*Pr.*, v. 137)]. Machaut does not mention Orpheus' ultimate failure. By focusing exclusively on the moment of Orpheus' triumph, Machaut exalts poetry and music to the level of "miracles apertes" [manifest miracle (*Pr.*, v. 145)]. What is more, he presents the amorous poet-musician in the image of Christ as Harrower of Hell—a standard interpretation of Orpheus in the medieval mythographic tradition—and leaves out those parts of the story that would make Orpheus a figure for human depravity. For Machaut, poetry and music are not only the interface between Eros and Nature, but also between Eros, Nature, and God.

This three-way mediation between the sacred, the natural, and the erotic is fundamental to the figure of Genius. As priest of Nature, Genius presides over the joining of soul and body—the collaboration of God and Nature—in the moment of conception. In *De planctu naturae*, Alain de Lille's Genius chastises those who have veered too far in the direction of erotic pleasure for its own sake, recalling them to the rightful purpose for which sex was intended. Natural procreation does provide the matrix within which sexual activity can be legitimized and even blessed by the sacrament of marriage. Nonetheless, the balance is always a delicate one, since excessive erotic desire violates the marriage sacrament and can, if pursued for its own sake, equally violate the principle of procreation; procreation in itself does not legitimize fornication; and nothing can ever sanctify sexuality to the point where it equals chastity. The very act whereby a new soul is conjoined to a new body also constitutes the transmission of Original Sin.

It is this last point that is conveniently overlooked in the *Rose*, not by Jean de Meun himself but by his characters. For Genius, procreation is sufficient to sanctify sexuality in an absolute sense, allowing for the transposition of erotic love from the Garden of Delight—a figure for desire, for the postponement of sexual consummation, hence for death—to the Heavenly Park, a figure for the fulfillment of desire and for eternal life. Machaut recasts the three-way meeting of the sacred, the natural, and the erotic through a transformation of the elaborate metaphoric construct. Procreation—the realization of natural creativity—is replaced by poetic creation, in a literalization of Genius' exhortation, "greffes avez, pansez d'escrire" [you have pens, remember to write (*Rose*, v. 19763)]. It is thus through the power of poetry that eros can be sanctified: that a language can be forged capable of mediating directly between the registers of nature, eros, and divinity—indeed, capable of expressing any one in terms of any other.

The *Voir Dit* is in many ways a rewriting of Machaut's earlier *Remede de Fortune*. In both poems Machaut portrays himself as an anxious lover plagued by uncertainty who learns—or attempts to learn—that his love can survive and flourish only when it is free of erotic desire; in both, his persona composes lyric poetry, including a lament about Fortune that is subsequently responded to by an admonitory figure; in both, he receives instruction about the nature of love; in both, he encounters the personification of Hope. In both poems Machaut draws on the *Rose* as a source for the narrative setting, and in both cases his persona is modelled to a certain extent on the Lover of the *Rose*. In the *Voir Dit*, however, Machaut treats his persona with an even greater degree of irony: it is now an ailing cleric in his sixties who emulates the twenty-year-old hero—himself a comic figure—of an erotic allegory. Moreover, Machaut's portrayal of Guillaume suggests that the latter does not fully grasp the literary conventions that he wishes to enact. Guillaume, filled with a longing that he can name only as *Desir*, hopefully and even obsessively writes, embarks on pilgrimages, thinks about relics, dresses up an image; he expectantly watches for miracles, declares himself "resuscitated"; he attempts to inscribe his love for Toute Belle in the context of sacred devotion, earthly paradise, eternity. In the end, he experiences everything except the one thing he wanted, the one thing that all of these activities are meant to be figures for: a fully consummated sexual relationship. It is as though the proliferation of metaphors in the *Rose* has clouded his understanding of what is really at stake. The sexual desire that spurs him on blocks any possibility of a true sacralization of his love for Toute Belle, at the same time that his inability to decode the allegory prevents him from experiencing true erotic fulfilment.[11]

But if the bedazzled Guillaume is ultimately caught in the intricate web of metaphor, Machaut the poet has succeeded in orchestrating a poetic *tour de force* that rivals the *Rose* itself. Both the power and the limitations of poetic language are masterfully demonstrated in the *Voir Dit*. Poetry cannot transform erotic love into divine Grace—cannot, to return to the language of the *Rose*, turn genitals into sacred relics, or relics into genitals, simply by a transfer of names. Machaut's ironic use of the *Rose* in the *Voir Dit* shows that he appreciated the comedy and the audacity of Jean's erotic allegory, his brilliant distortions of such authors as Boethius and Alain de Lille, his merciless lampooning of the pretentions of courtly diction. At the same time, the very success of such an enterprise, the real force of the literary parody, is bound up in the fact that, in a different sense, poetry *can* transform the erotic into the sacred, through the power of allegory. In the *Voir Dit*, as in the *Remede de Fortune* and the *Prologue*, Machaut affirms the potency of writing, of poetic discourse, to create a literary space for the interplay and mutual glossing of the many registers—sacred and erotic, chivalric and clerkly, mythic and historic—of language and experience.

NOTES

This essay is part of a larger study that I am preparing of the reception and manuscript tradition of the *Roman de la Rose* in the fourteenth century. I would like to thank the John Simon Guggenheim Memorial Foundation for a fellowship that supported work on this project.

1. The following editions have been used: Guillaume de Machaut, *Le Livre du Voir Dit*, ed. Paulin Paris (Paris: Société des Bibliophiles François, 1875); Machaut, *Prologue*, in *Oeuvres de Guillaume de Machaut*, ed. Ernest Hoepffner, Société des Anciens Textes Français, vol. 1 (Paris: Firmin-Didot, 1908); Guillaume de Lorris and Jean de Meun, *Roman de la Rose*, ed. Félix Lecoy, Classiques Français du Moyen Age (Paris: Champion, 1973–75). The Medusa interpolation in the *Rose* is cited from Ernest Langlois, ed., *Roman de la Rose*, 5 vols., Société des Anciens Textes Français (Paris: Firmin-Didot, 1924), note to vv. 20810–11.
2. Some important studies are Sarah Jane Williams, "An Author's Role in Fourteenth-Century Book Production: Guillaume de Machaut's 'livre ou je met toutes mes choses'," *Romania* 90 (1969): 433–54; William Calin, *A Poet at the Fountain: Essays on the Narrative Verse of Guillaume de Machaut* (Lexington: Univ. of Kentucky Press, 1974); Kevin Brownlee, *Poetic Identity in Guillaume de Machaut* (Madison: Univ. of Wisconsin Press, 1984), pp. 94–156; Jacqueline Cerquiglini, *"Un Engin si soutil": Guillaume de Machaut et l'écriture au XIVe siècle*, Bibliothèque du XVe Siècle (Paris: Champion, 1985).
3. Jacqueline Cerquiglini comments on the use of imagery associated with the Virgin Mary in the descriptions of Toute Belle, in *"Un Engin si soutil"*, pp. 80–82.
4. Lancelot's murals, accompanied by written captions, are described in *Le Livre de Lancelot del Lac*, part 3, *The Vulgate Version of the Arthurian Romances*, vol. 5, ed. H. Oskar Sommer (1912; rpt. New York: AMS Press, 1969), pp. 217–18; and *La Mort le roi Artu*, ed. Jean Frappier, Textes Littéraires Français (Geneva: Droz, 1964), pp. 61, 64. In Thomas's version of the *Roman de Tristan*, Tristan compensates for Iseut's absence during his marriage to Iseut aux Blanches Mains by making statues of Iseut and Brangain that are so lifelike that they can scarcely be distinguished from the real

thing. But this episode does not appear in the prose *Tristan*, which was most likely Machaut's source for the story. The prose *Tristan* does, however, contain a number of Tristan's *lais* as lyric insertions.
5. See Cerquiglini, *"Un Engin si soutil"*, pp. 107–38. The failure of the poet's attempt to cast himself as a noble lover is also discussed by Daniel Poirion, *Le Poète et le prince: L'Évolution du lyrisme courtois de Guillaume de Machaut à Charles d'Orléans* (Paris: Presses Universitaires de France, 1965), and is an important theme in Brownlee's detailed analysis of the *Voir Dit* in *Poetic Identity*. In *Poet at the Fountain*, Calin notes Guillaume's "inability to conform to Arthurian romance in a post-Jean de Meun world" (p. 181). The Judgment of Paris in the *Fonteinne amoureuse* has been discussed by Calin, *Poet at the Fountain*, pp. 146–66 *passim.*; Margaret Ehrhart, *The Judgment of the Trojan Prince Paris in Medieval Literature* (Philadelphia: University of Pennsylvania Press, 1987), pp. 130–41; Brownlee, *Poetic Identity*, pp. 201–2; Cerquiglini, *"Un Engin si soutil"*, pp. 124–25. In a *complainte*, Guillaume claims that Toute Belle affords a resolution of the Judgment of Paris conflict by subsuming the attributes of the three rival goddesses and transcending all of them: Venus, Juno, and Pallas, he says, will serve her (*VD*, vv. 5867–71).
6. I argue that Machaut portrays Guillaume as having occupied himself within the scented cloud of Venus by composing a virelai in *From Song to Book: The Poetics of Writing in Old French Lyric and Lyrical Narrative Poetry* (Ithaca: Cornell Univ. Press, 1987), pp. 285–86. Calin, following a different line of argument, shows that Machaut strongly implies that Guillaume did not actually consummate his relationship with Toute Belle; see *Poet at the Fountain*, pp. 190–91.
7. Indeed, Guillaume is sometimes reduced to silence and immobility by Toute Belle's presence as well. For reflections on the possible analogies between Toute Belle and Medusa, see Alexandre Leupin, "The Powerlessness of Writing: Guillaume de Machaut, the Gorgon, and *Ordenance,*" *Yale French Studies* 70 (1986), pp. 144–46.
8. See Kevin Brownlee, "Jean de Meun and the Limits of Romance: Genius as Rewriter of Guillaume de Lorris," in *Romance: Generic Transformation from Chrétien de Troyes to Cervantes*, ed. Kevin Brownlee and Marina Scordilis Brownlee (Hanover: Univ. Press of New England, 1985): 114–34.

9. I have noted Machaut's emphasis on form and order in natural and creative processes in *From Song to Book*, p. 237. See also Shirley Lukitsch, "The Poetics of the 'Prologue': Machaut's Conception of the Purpose of His Art," *Medium Aevum* 52 (1983): 258–71.
10. I have discussed Machaut's self-presentation as writer and author of books, as opposed to singer or simple maker of poems, in *From Song to Book*, pp. 232–38, 242–301. As I show there, writing is fundamental to Machaut's concept of himself as a poet, especially by the time he wrote the *Voir Dit* or the *Prologue*.
11. For a discussion of Chaucer's somewhat similar treatment of the *Rose* and the conventions of courtly poetry as an obstacle to sexual fulfilment, see Winthrop Wetherbee, *Chaucer and the Poets: An Essay on Troilus and Criseyde* (Ithaca: Cornell Univ. Press, 1984), pp. 53–86. Commenting on the *Troilus* and the *Rose*, Wetherbee states: "In both cases a combination of genuine innocence, sexual timidity, and the deceptive euphemisms of courtly rhetoric creates a barrier, verbal and psychological, that prevents any open acknowledgment of the physical realities of the quest" (p. 69). While one could debate the innocence of the *Rose* protagonist, Wetherbee nonetheless articulates an important insight that is equally applicable to the *Voir Dit*.

R. Barton Palmer

The Metafictional Machaut: Reflexivity In The Judgment Poems

Since its beginning with the philological inquiry of the nineteenth century, criticism of medieval literature has set itself the impossible task of closing the gap between the pastness of ancient texts and the modern context of their reading and analysis. The historicism of the philologist, of course, was largely untheorized. It rested on the unstated assumption that both editorial methods (designed to restore texts to their "original" states) and background research (to explain allusions and illuminate an intertextual web of sources and analogues) would somehow place the modern reader in the position of his medieval counterpart. Concerned with textual and literary reconstruction, nineteenth-century philologists ignored the reader's role in the "performance" of remote works. This approach bypassed the cognitive problems facing the modern critic, who would understand, interpret, and judge (often unconsciously) according to his own horizons, values, and expectations. But, as phenomenology has taught us, the past is inevitably a construction of the present, exists only insofar as the present, by an act of will and apprehension, calls it into existence. The past cannot be hypostatized through the physical and intellectual restoration of various documents; thus the act of reading itself must be transformed, not only what is read.

It is this difficulty which has been addressed by Robertsonianism, the most strident of medieval historicisms. Robertsonianism purports to historicize the act of reading by constructing a code from the contexts of medieval literature which enforces a single-minded and orthodox interpretation of what these often puzzling texts offer. In this way Robertsonianism prevents the modern reader from being led astray into constructing meanings that are not original and intended. What is repressed within this methodology, however, is its origin in a preliminary act of reading (of ancillary materials, which are still texts) that cannot by definition be itself historicized.[1] Hence the circularity of this approach, whose insights are hardly science in the Marxist sense but rather deeply inflected by the various factors (intellectual, academic, and other) which have produced them in the present (and not in the past, to which they can only appeal). For example, Robertsonianism valorizes the notion of original intention as the goal of reading (and postulates, for reasons of doctrinal necessity, the same intention for all medieval works). In so doing, it utilizes, but without theoretical justification, a particular brand of academic hermeneuticism that must been seen within its own historical context (especially now that it has come under vigorous attack from other critical positions). Furthermore, medieval literary practice itself offers strong evidence that such a view of textual meaning was hardly then so universal; as Karl Uitti has shown, the notion of *translatio studii* affects deeply the literary production of the twelfth century and after, and this concept both venerates the existence of a textual tradition and authorizes the creation of new meanings for old works through an intellectual recontextualization.² In any case, we must conclude that the criticism of medieval literature proceeds from the phenomenal encounter of contemporary reader with ancient text; the experience of meaning therefore must always be in some important senses a "present" one, for what we discover corresponds to our own interests and predilections.

The necessary failure of historicism to reconstruct an objectively discovered past, however, is not a disability. In fact, I will argue here that the critic's historical situation—his distance intellectually, socially, and literarily from the objects of his analysis—offers an important advantage, may produce unexpected insights. By this I do not invoke the view that what matters are readings or understandings occasioned by the text but then seen as separable from its pastness; such a view pays more attention to the historical circumstances into which these readings are ultimately inserted than to those which produced the text. If historicisms like Robertsonianism isolate the text from the process of its performance by different classes of readers (evoking a univocal meaning which becomes strangely timeless after it historically emerges), then this writerly view of the reader's role conversely marks as historically irrelevant those textual features which make possible (even if they do not determine) the meaning which readers construe. I would not underestimate the important role that readings of ancient texts have played in modern culture (one only has to think of the ways that certain views of Chaucer and Shakespeare were used in nineteenth-century Britain to bolster official forms of nationalism). More to the point, a pervasive New Critical formalism (to which Robertsonianism is a violent reaction) has produced in the American academy an understanding of medieval literature which is largely apolitical and ahistorical, leaving unread a whole body of "engaged" literature that does not fit its model of textual self-containment.³ These are important issues, and I would not slight them. However, it seems to me that the text itself still has an interest for us of an historical object even as it evokes a past we cannot hope to grasp securely. We must attend to textual otherness however much the passage of time problematizes this process. And, intriguingly, though remote from the works that interest him, the twentieth century medievalist is provided by his historical situation with an important perspective, one that will allow him to recognize and analyze textual features whose existence and significance were a blind spot within the literary theorizing of the later Middle Ages.

In his influential *Theory of the Avant-Garde*, Peter Bürger has argued that "in bourgeois society, it is only with aestheticism that the full unfolding of the phenomenon of art becomes a fact, and it is to aestheticism that the historical avant-garde movements respond." This development has important consequences for both the artist and literary critic, as Bürger goes on to suggest:

> Artistic means is undoubtedly the most general category by which works of art can be described. But that the various techniques and procedures can be *recognized* as artistic means has been possible only since the historical avant-garde movements.... What is acknowledged is simply that the possibilities of cognition are limited by the real (historical) unfolding of the object.[4]

Bürger's observations hold an important truth for students of medieval literature: that as critics we should not limit ourselves to approaches or categories that are in some way authorized either by the rhetorical tradition that provided medieval writers with models and understandings of their craft or by the religious orthodoxy within which literary production was justified. A revealing case in point is mimeticism. Unlike classical literary theory, medieval rhetoric never theorized literary texts as, in any sense, imitations of reality; certainly the even more complex doctrines of nineteenth century realism, particularly the concept of *vraisemblance* so central to the understanding of what has been called the "reality effect," were never remotely anticipated in medieval aesthetical treatises. And yet this does not mean that medieval works are not mimetic or even realist to some important degree and that these aspects of their textual construction should not be investigated. Indeed, as Bürger argues, it is inevitable that certain aspects of ancient literary works were unnoticed or ignored because the total "unfolding of the (literary) object" had not yet occurred. If this is true, then the postmodern student of medieval literature possesses a potentially greater ability to understand the whole constellation of textual features in the objects of his study than the reader who was contemporary with their production. Such a critical analysis, of course, will hardly produce a science of these texts, but it should be capable of a knowledge that is not only engaging (with the concerns/interests of its own historical moment) but also revealing (of a past incapable in some ways of knowing itself).

In this essay, I will be concerned with two of the longer narrative *dits* of Guillaume de Machaut insofar as they contain (and indeed are structured by) features which we are most accustomed to discover in postmodernist fiction. The *Judgment of the King of Bohemia (Jugement dou Roy de Behaingne)* and the *Judgment of the King of Navarre (Jugement dou Roy de Navarre)* equally exemplify the love debate poetry so popular in the later Middle Ages and the literary address which works of that age often make to their makers' patrons. In other words, these poems not only create a fiction (in which the questions posed by the love poetry genre can be represented through both the experience of human characters and the individual truths of allegorical personages); they are also, in somewhat different senses, poems about the artistic/social fact of composing poetry. These two works, then, are metafictional in the sense which Patricia Waugh suggests much modernist and postmodern fiction is: offering both a created world with which the reader is meant to engage as a second reality and the commentary/interpretation/ironic undermining that calls attention to that created world as the product of certain rhetorical strategies.[5] In John Fowles's *The French Lieutenant's Woman*, for example, the reader is presented with a narrative that purports, in the style of Thomas Hardy, to be a "Victorian novel," but is addressed, in some chapters, by a narrator who points out the difficulties of such a project and, indeed, of fictional fabulation in general.

In the judgment poems Machaut's aim, of course, differs substantially from that of Fowles, who is playing with, or perhaps attacking, the tradition of realist fiction, one of whose cardinal features is an illusionism that effaces the act of telling upon which narrative fiction is based. Postmodern metafiction is determinedly intertextual, a self-conscious reflection on the idea and forms of the realist novel (and, occasionally, an engagement with the ideological assumptions that underpin this literary tradition). For Machaut no such tradition existed to be attacked or exposed by a partial refusal, itself in literary form. What we might call the metafictional impulse in Machaut's *oeuvre* derives from other sources, chiefly the poet's need and desire to call attention to his role in the production of love poetry as well as his intention to mediate the reception of his works by establishing the particular intertextual network within which they were to be read. Reflexivity and self-mediation in the judgment poems are to an important degree related features. Kevin Brownlee has most convincingly demonstrated that Machaut, unlike the major authors of the twelfth and thirteenth centuries, conceived of himself as a *poète*, as the creator of a corpus of works that manifested his own identity and experience (particularly with the emotional turbulence of love) even as they served the rhetorical/professional requirements of poetic composition.[6] Machaut was demonstrably concerned with the copying, codification, and distribution of his poems; he even composed a prologue for collected versions of them that contains, as Shirley Lukitsch shows, a remarkably well-developed and insightful aesthetic whose obvious purpose is to guide the reader's interpretation of the poetry that follows.[7] We should not be surprised, therefore, that authorial self-consciousness should be linked to the poet's desire for his works to be read within the proper literary context. In any case, this "interpretive" level of the two judgment poems, when given its proper place within the works as a whole, does much to explain their particular structure and meaning; for we will see that these two *dits* are quite unlike earlier works in the love poetry tradition because they are not only about the doctrine and experiences of *fin' amors*, but also about the poet's attitudes toward the making of poetry with such themes.

 This is hardly a radical new insight—much that I say here has been anticipated, in one way or another, by both Kevin

Brownlee and Douglas Kelly.[8] Neither of these two critics, however, emphasizes the metafictionality of the judgment poems; thus the later *Voir Dit* (the aptly named *True Story* which fictionalizes, but not completely, the love correspondence between the aging poet and his younger beloved) appears to be a somewhat shocking departure for a writer who suddenly breaks the spell of fiction to write about his own presence. Actually, the *Jugement dou Roy de Navarre* strikingly anticipates this complex misture of "real" experience and poetic conventions, suggesting in the process that an illusion-breaking reflexivity is an effect toward which Machaut worked during his career as a whole. Indeed, even the much earlier *Jugement dou Roy de Behaingne* often plays slyly with a metafictional perspective; for example, in that poem different characters twice refer to dramatically presented speeches as being contained "above" in the text itself.[9]

Machaut's obvious indebtedness to the *Roman de la Rose* in the *Behaingne* has often been pointed out. In fact, as I have argued elsewhere, the references to that classic text in the courtly love tradition are so many and obtrusive, particularly at the outset, that the reader is being challenged to read Machaut's work in reference to its illustrious predecessor.[10] The springtime setting, replete with all the traditional features of the *locus amoenus*, and the lover-narrator who recounts his solitary experiences there deliberately recall the framing fiction of Guillaume de Lorris's section of the *Rose*. Mediating the reception of his poem in this fashion, Machaut, however, hardly produces what we might call a slavish imitation. The *Dit dou Vergier*, apparently Machaut's first narrative love poem, follows the *Rose* in having its narrator-lover character fall asleep in the springtime garden where he has a vision of the God of Love. In the *Behaingne*, on the contrary, the opening raises false expectations which are soon shattered when the narrator's subjectivity is abandoned as the principal focus. Contemplating the beautiful song of a bird, the narrator suddenly witnesses the arrival of a noblewoman and a knight, who begin to talk after she does not respond to his greeting. Both, it turns our, are suffering from pain caused by love; her lover has died, and his beloved has proved faithless. They disagree over which one suffers more and enter into a full-scale debate on the question.

At first the narrator's solitude indexes both the importance of his subjectivity (potential source of a meditation on the love experience) and his openness to instruction or enlightenment, which conventionally comes in the dream that attends this figure's falling asleep in the springtime setting. The dramatic interchange between the knight and lady, however, means that his solitude comes to indicate his sudden displacement from the narrative, his conversion into an unseen and eavesdropping witness. In effect, the narrator becomes a more recognizable figure; no longer the anonymous consciousness in which the story of love unfolds, he is now the very image of Guillaume the courtly poet, observing the noble personages, actions, and thoughts which he, making use of his clerkly powers, will convert into poetry. In the *Dit de la fonteinne amoureuse*, composed a few years after the *Navarre*, Machaut in fact reprises this scene, giving us a somewhat more foolish clerk who listens at night to a nobleman's complaint, copying it as a text which, the next day, he has the honor to present to him.

Kevin Brownlee suggests that one of the features of Machaut's conception of himself as a *poète* is a collapsing of the distance between the subjective "I" (direct source of the love experience) and the compositional "I" (indication of the narrator's more artistic/learned attitude toward his *matière*). And indeed it is true that, at least in general, "for Machaut, love service and poetic service are conflated in such a way as to present the poète's fundamental 'lyric' experience as the activity of poetic composition."[11] I would argue, though, that Machaut sometimes plays with or deconstructs this conflation, collapsing it into its two somewhat irreconcilable halves (for the clerkly poet writing for the socially distant members of the noble court is by definition largely separate from the emotional experiences of the class he writes about and for). Here the *Behaingne* offers us just such a moment in which the poet's function as servant is emphasized. Their debate at an impasse, the two lovers agree to find a judge to settle the dispute, but seem unable to decide who will have this choice. At this moment, the lady's dog discovers the narrator in the bushes, and this gives him the opportunity to offer himself as a guide to the nearby castle of Durbuy where, he avers, the famous King of Bohemia will willingly render a judgment. They accept his offer, and the narrator guides them to the king, who turns the matter over to his courtiers (all of whom are allegorical personages) for discussion and a decision. The poem ends with their judgment that the man suffers more, one with which the King and the narrator (at least implicitly) agree. The narrator's own experiences with love are thus put into question at the very beginning, but then permanently displaced in favor of those of the class he serves (for the narrator, we learn, is like Machaut himself, a member of King John's household, a clerk similar to the unnamed functionary, or perhaps poet, who is entertaining the assembled court when the visitors suddenly arrive in search of assistance).

In the *Behaingne*, then, the identification of love and poetic services is effectively deconstructed, foregrounding the narrator's function as something related to but distinct from the experiences of noble hearts. One way to read the poem is to see it as an exploration of Machaut's uncertainties about (or, perhaps in some sense, dissatisfaction with) the position of a clerk assigned by literary tradition the lyric "I" but prevented from unproblematically assuming that assignment by the social necessities of his role as servant to the court. Granted access to the direct experience of exalted emotion, he discovers that the goal of that access is to write for his patrons, whose subjectivity must matter more than his own (listening from his hiding place to the debate between lady and knight, the narrator displays no further inclination to attend to his own emotional transport). What is interesting here, of course, is that the narrator is not completely displaced from the drama of love (conceived here, interestingly enough, in a rather clerkly fashion, as an issue, or rather series of issues, to be debated to a conclusion). He is not only a witness to the event (this a chance surveillance which allows him to compose this work), but plays an important, if subservient, role in its resolution. Giving way to the concerns of the class he serves, the narrator does not wish to remain silent, serving a narrating function that effaces itself behind the mimesis of the poem's dramatic discourse. The role he fulfills is a larger one, for the narrator, and by implication the author as well, is also a guide (a traditional rhetorical stance Machaut exploits most in the *Confort d'ami*, a didactic work composed for Charles of Navarre).

Thus if his experience of love is denied the privilege of narrative focus (must, indeed, be demonstrated to lead away from subjectivity, for the narrator discovers the debating pair as he follows the singing bird), his duties as teacher and intellectual guide cannot be so easily laid aside. That the *Behaingne* is deliberately about the anomalous position of its maker is supported by the other metafictional aspects of the poem. Not only is its fictional nature twice undermined by references to the status of the work as written text, but the device of the little dog, so clearly derived from the well-known romance *Châtelaine de Vergy*, establishes the indebtedness of this text to others. Similarly, the mixture of "real" and fictional elements in the depiction of John's court incongruously joins a continuation of the allegorical disputation made popular by the *Roman de la Rose* to a representation of the contemporary reality so pointedly excluded by that literary tradition. As a result, the poem locates a conventional idealism in the world of individual, historical experience, testifying to the power of its author to remake—for the double purposes of play and edification—the courtly setting to which the poem is itself addressed. Indeed, throughout the *Behaingne* Machaut refuses a clear separation between the poem as rhetorical fiction and its function as a text to entertain John's court; the work, in short, represents the conflation of art and experience, establishing their unbreakable connections for the maker who must live in and write for the royal court.[12] The metafictionality of this poetry, then, may be seen to stem from the fact that the subject matter of love poetry for Machaut inevitably involves his own subjectivity as poet, as he testifies himself. The *Prologue* to the collected works represents the poet receiving the "call" to write and compose from Nature, who gives him the gifts of Meaning, Rhetoric, and Music. These, it turns out, are not really sufficient to the task, for Love then appears to give him Sweet Thought, Pleasure, and Hope—gifts for the lover and not just the chronicler of love. And yet the poet's soul is not "noble," cannot therefore furnish his poetry with all its *matière*; he is still the servant of those who are noble, and his poetry must represent that service. The *Behaingne* embodies one way of working out this contradiction even (and, of course, necessarily) as it provides us with the appropriate and conventional poetic text.

The *Behaingne* displays its indebtedness to the *Roman de la Rose* in order to mediate its reception as one of both sameness and difference; here the concern with a love question leads not only to a debate between allegorical characters (most prominently *Raison*) but to a representation of the central contradiction which defines the clerkly poet's role (a subject never raised by the two authors of the *Rose*). The *Navarre*, composed perhaps as much as a decade later and for a different patron, Charles the Bad of Navarre, similarly mediates its reception through a series of references to the *Rose*. Like Jean de Meun's continuation of Guillaume de Lorris's allegorical narrative, the *Navarre* features a lively, occasionally raucous debate about male and female experiences of love, a debate that raises the issue of antifeminism; furthermore, the debaters frequently use *exempla* (of different kinds) to make their points, though these are not usually developed as fully as the similar ones in Jean's part of the *Rose*.

There is, however, a more important structural resemblance between the two works. The *Navarre* is the only text in the Machaut corpus which explicitly takes a previous poem, the *Behaingne*, as its subject matter. After a long opening section that deals with the poet/narrator's melancholy reflections on the miserable state of his world (including his experiences with the plague of 1348–49), the poem traces how the narrator, enjoying a hare-hunting expedition now that the confinement enforced by the epidemic has come to an end, is accosted by the lady he serves (whose name turns out much later to be Good Fortune) and is accused of defaming noble women in his earlier judgment poem. Guillaume de Machaut, the lady argues, is guilty of a most uncourtly bias against women. Guillaume protests his innocence, and the two decide to debate the issue and leave the decision to the well-qualified King Charles of Navarre and his advisors for the occasion (the allegorical personages who make up Good Fortune's court). It seems likely that Machaut's decision to re-open the debate apparently settled in the earlier work and problematize its discussion in somewhat unexpected ways (especially by introducing the spectre of anti-feminism) was greatly influenced by (if not in fact derived from) Jean's continuation of the *Rose*. Like Jean, in fact, Machaut takes another poem as not only content but also as a structure to be exploited, producing a work that is much more reflexive (for here the issue of the poet's attitudes and social function is foregrounded). In the *Prologue*, Guillaume is enjoined by Love not to do anything that would injure the reputation of women:

> Mais garde bien, sur tout ne t'enhardi
> A faire chose ou il ait villenie,
> N'aucunement des dames ne mesdi;
> Mais en tous cas les loe et magnefie. (III, lines 21–24)[13]

> Take care especially that you are not emboldened
> To compose anything in bad taste,
> And never slander ladies;
> Rather always praise and exalt them.

Good Fortune's charge, then, strikes right to the heart of Guillaume's self-announced poetic mission. If he has indeed composed a work full of *villenie* that also injures the reputation of ladies, then he has failed to live up to the charges of Nature and Love. Furthermore, both the MS tradition of Machaut's poetry and the sincere flattery of imitation (by poets as notable as Christine de Pizan and Geoffrey Chaucer) suggest that the *Behaingne* was certainly, even at the time the *Navarre* was written, the most popular and successful of his narrative poems. It was a bold move for him to suggest (however lightheartedly) that the work constituted an inappropriate text in a long-standing and revered tradition. Thus the *Navarre* is not only a response to (and ultimately a reversal of) the love judgment rendered in the *Behaingne*; it is also, and more important, a fictional space in which Machaut's poetic career is carefully scrutinized, problematized, and vindicated in the very act of condemnation.

If the *Behaingne* metafictionally explores the contradictions of the poet's artistic/social position, the *Navarre* concerns itself with his paradoxical subservience to but command of the love experience. This paradox is announced by the fictional/rhetorical structure of the *Prologue*. Within the fiction, the reader is asked to believe in the process by which Guillaume is made subject to forces beyond his control; the character who bears his name not only is given the resources to speak (and thus achieve a linguistic subjectivity within the tradition of love poetry) but is bound firmly by the regulations which are to control what he writes and composes. Extratextually, of course, the *Prologue* is a statement of poetic intentions, an explication of the "rules" that the poet has set for himself. Or, to formulate it in current theoretical terms, he announces that what he will write will also write him; artistic freedom and homage to literary institutions are inextricably mixed, with the result that the poet finds his manner controlling him even as his rhetorical inspiration produces the poem. Interestingly, the *Behaingne* hints at this aspect of the poet's condition. When the debate between the sorrowing lady and grieving knight is brought to John's court, the original question—who suffers more?—is turned toward a deeper, underlying issue: the possibility of reconciling emotional release, represented by the abstraction Youth, to understanding, represented by the character Reason. The debate ends with this issue unresolved, and such lack of closure suggests how the love experience cannot easily be contained by the poem's rhetorical structure, but rather overflows into both digression and unresolved opposition (even though the announced project of the debate is to provide reconciliation through an unequivocal answer to the love question with which it begins). But Guillaume, as Good Fortune maintains, is responsible for what is contained in his various works; the doctrine, she implies, is his own or, at least, must be accounted for by him.

In the *Behaingne* the levels of fiction and comment are kept distinct; the exploration of the poet's role is not foregrounded, but literally occurs at the margins of the text. In the *Navarre*, these levels are merged; the fiction becomes the examination of the poet's performance as poet. Happily riding after his hares, the narrator in the later work is "called" from his enjoyment to a meeting with a beautiful and otherworldy lady (a motif that recalls the typical structure of the Breton lay; the reminiscence of Marie de France's *Lanval* is particularly striking). Unlike the *Behaingne*, the narrator here is no mere witness; he is called upon to debate an issue, one that relates centrally to his performance as court poet in the world outside the text. We have already seen this mixture of the "real" and the "literary" in Machaut's earlier judgment poem; but the *Behaingne* is largely a poetic fiction. The references to King John and his castle at Durbuy do ground the abstraction of the allegorical debate in the historical and specific (providing a local interest for the original audience even as they argue against a complete separation between ideal and individual emotional experience). But the typicality of the narrator and of the debating pair means that the poem does not break sharply from tradition in making room for contemporary reference. The *Navarre*, from the outset, offers a different kind of literary experience. The poem opens with the narrator's description of his feelings of melancholy on the ninth of November, 1349; these reflect both the conventional millenarianism of the *mundus senescet* topos (a world grown old and falling into disorder and ruin) and a genuine apprehension at recent events such as heavenly prognostications, widespread civil disturbance, earthquakes, the outbreak of plague, the conspiracy of the Jews, and the appearance of wandering troops of flagellants. The narrator goes on, in a very personal vein, to chronicle his own reactions to the epidemic and, then, to its passing. The obstrusive presence in the poem of these "real" elements has long troubled Machaut's critics who have either faulted him for a failure of artistry (notably Charles Muscatine) or struggled to find some thematic link between them and the more conventional "poetic" fiction that follows (most successfully William Calin and David Lanoue).[14]

The problem, I would argue, is more apparent than real and proceeds from the expectation that this poem, like the *Behaingne*, is really "about" the allegorical interchanges of love debate poetry. Can we be so sure, however, that the opening sections, in which the narrator's subjectivity is the main focus (exterior events are all related, in some way, to his melancholy state, are described because they inform and affect how he feels and acts), are somehow extraneous to the real artistic matter at hand? Both parts of the *Navarre*, on the contrary, suggest that the subject here is the poet himself, first viewed, with great seriousness, as a historical person caught up in a tumult of events beyond his control, and then examined, rather humorously, as a bumbling versifier who slandered ladies in the very attempt to exalt them. The link between the two sections of the poem is the poet's melancholy: the state of the world saddens him and then, with the end of the plague, allows him pleasure again; but his hare-hunting is interrupted by the "call" from Good Fortune, who sinks him back into a melancholy from which he is somewhat rescued by the lightheartedness of the debate's conclusion. In fact, the lady's enjoyment in making her accusations derives, at least in part, from the melancholy into which she puts her poet-servant:

> Si le me voloit prononcier
> Pour li deduire et soulacier
> Et moy mettre en merencolie.
> A ce point ne failli je mie,
> Car je fui de li galiez,
> Ramposnez et contraliez,
> Aussi com se j'eusse fait
> Encontre li un grant meffait. (lines 589–96)

> (And she wished to bring it to my attention
> In order to delight and entertain herself
> And sink me into melancholy.
> I did not fail to do so,
> For I was mocked by her,
> Reproached and contradicted,
> Just as if I had sinned
> Quite grievously against her.)

Unlike the *weltschmerz* that so affects him at the work's beginning, this melancholy can be (and is) overcome by Guillaume's gracious acceptance of the judgment against him and his agreement to do appropriate penance (which is the composition of three lyrical pieces in fixed forms with the "correct" doctrine).

The passivity of the historical subject (who must suffer what God ordains) gives way to the activity of the poet, who is responsible for the meaning of his poems even as he continues to write, in important senses, what tradition demands. Good Fortune, in effect, accuses him of losing track of what good poetry should promote and falling into a willful individuality that mars, as well, his performance in the role of good lover (like Love in the *Prologue*, Good Fortune not only represents the court Machaut must serve but the love object, service to whom will make it possible for him to discover the correct matter for his verse):

> Je croy que vous estes trop sages
> Devenuz, ou trop alentis,
> Mausoingneus, et mautalentis,
> De vos deduis apetisiez,
> Ou trop po les dames prisiez. (lines 764–68)
>
> (I think you've become
> Too wise or too backward,
> Inattentive and disagreeable,
> Eager for your sport,
> Or else you value ladies too little.)

Learning that what has angered his lady is the judgment rendered in the *Behaingne*, Guillaume, however, disagrees that he has erred. Interestingly, the debate revolves around the question of the connection of that poem to the world; Good Fortune declares that what Guillaume has written is untrue, not that the poetry itself is aesthetically deficient. This accounts for the shape that the proceedings take; in this trial, evidence is adduced, chiefly from *exempla* whose historical or truth value varies, to prove that either men or women suffer more in love. Actually, as Jean-Louis Picherit has shown in detail, Guillaume's evidence is far inferior to that of his adversaries, thus "il ressort que Guillaume est avant tout condamné pour sa piètre performance pendant la contestation, et non pas pour la doctrine qu'il défend."[15] And, in fact, William Calin may be correct in suggesting that Guillaume intended for his audience to understand that the verdict against him resulted not from any "incorrectness" in his original judgment but rather from his failings as a defense attorney.[16]

But we must, I think, discriminate between the seriousness of Guillaume the character, who deeply resents the accusations and loses his composure as the trial begins to slip away from him (actually mouthing the very anti-feminist sentiments he declared himself innocent of at the outset), and that of Guillaume de Machaut the poet, who with remarkable *sprezzatura* puts his own poetry on trial in a poem whose evident control and *finesse* testify to his commanding talent. That is, we must read the poem metafictionally, as offering both a fiction (the trial and its outcome) and a comment on fiction-making (expressed by the distance between the character Guillaume and his wiser, more sophisticated "real" counterpart). What Kevin Brownlee calls Machaut's "poetic identity" is here defined by the complex relations between these two selves.

Within the diegesis, concern about the "real" world is soon abandoned; Guillaume need no longer be a melancholy chronicler when the plague abates and he can seek out those solitary pleasures which often lead, conventionally, to a love adventure. The love experience that "discovers" him, however, offers a problematized return to real life (since it questions his career as poet) and to real life emotions (the melancholy whose original cause was the deplorable state of the world). The character Guillaume must struggle valiantly to defend his artistic judgment and ultimately loses, though the fact that he is assigned the task of writing further poems as penance (but, perhaps significantly, these are lyrics and not another narrative *dit*!) suggests the court still has confidence in his abilities. As a text, the *Navarre* functions rather differently; there is no evidence, for example, to suggest that Guillaume's reputation needed any vindication or apology. Instead, it is much more likely that the poem is intended as a playful treatment of the court poet's relationship not only with his patrons but with the tradition of love poetry itself. This double address is appropriately indexed by the character of Good Fortune who, it seems, not only has an interest in the production of appropriately moralized texts but in the careers of those she favors; she seems, therefore, to be both patron and teacher, an intriguing representation of Machaut's continued interest in and reworking of the dialogic framework of the

Consolation of Philosophy, a development which reaches its culmination, as Douglas Kelly has shown, in the *Remede de Fortune*.

Like the instructress figures of many medieval dream vision poems (Machaut's own *Dit de la fonteinne amoureuse* is a classic example), Good Fortune advises and corrects a mortal subject who is in need of guidance. But Good Fortune also appears to be a representation of the patron displeased with the poet's work; the fact that Machaut's real-life patron, Charles the Bad, sits as judge for the proceedings reinforces this aspect of her position. The joke, of course, is that standing behind the struggle between his bedeviled fictional self and his allegorical antagonist is Machaut's powerful authorial presence, within whose command of textual "making" the poem's dialogue is subsumed. In a sense, Guillaume is his own provoker, the real source of the troubles he relates in the *Navarre*; he is called to account only because such a matter makes interesting poetry, affords the real Guillaume the opportunity once again to please the court and advance his own reputation. At the same time, the distance between his intra-and extratextual selves embodies a larger truth about the position of court poet, who is both the subject of (the speaking "I," the creative self, the authenticating presence of) the poems he writes even as he is subject to (especially insofar as he must submit to the "anxiety of influence" from) the tradition within which he writes. In short, he has both immense control and yet no control at all over his *oeuvre*; he is both teacher and servant, source of doctrine and an entertainer dependent, even as his reputation increases, on the favor of those in the class above. The double-edged nature of his subjectivity (the conflation of poetic and love service so tellingly discussed by Kevin Brownlee) is embodied in the figure of Good Fortune, who is both his lady, hence source of emotional truth, and a "higher" knowledge that would correct his poetry. But, ultimately of course, she is not "real," only an aspect of that consciousness of artistic purpose which allows Guillaume to write and which he makes the most important subject of the *Judgment of the King of Navarre*.

The current re-evaluation of Machaut's literary accomplishments, with its basis equally in narratological theory and the concept of intertextuality, is effectively erasing the negative judgments of past critics, who faulted the great master of fourteenth-century French poetry for being "tradition-bound" and failing to write poetry that was more "about life." This recent criticism has begun to suggest, in fact, the affinities between Machaut's narrative poems and much modernist/postmodernist writing, texts which, like those of the medieval master, are more structural and rhetorical than mimetic. In this essay I hope to have demonstrated that the concept of metafictionality can reveal much about Machaut's methods and concerns. For the *Navarre*, I would argue, is unlike any other medieval text in its complex exploration of the poetics of authorship, in its meditations on and comic reduction of the difficulties posed by a literary tradition and its underlying ideology to the creative author. Only Chaucer, especially in the early poetry so heavily influenced by Machaut, manifests a similar concern with thematizing the artist's difficulties. The two prologues to the *Legend of Good Women*, much indebted to the general subject and plan of the *Navarre*, similarly treat the poet's "failure," his being called to account by the court/the tradition of love poetry, and his being required to write more poetry, this time with the appropriate doctrine, as a penance. And yet these two works are only intended as introductions to a collection of tales; Chaucer does not, in the manner of Machaut, make his own situation as creative artist the center of a text. What model may we suggest for the greater audacity of the *Navarre*? One way of understanding Machaut's accomplishment here involves recourse to the notion of "novelization" developed by Mikhail Bakhtin.[16] As a literary tradition begins to assert less authority on those who write within it, the presentness of the writer's situation, Bakhtin suggests, calls more insistently for its own representation. At the same time, the process of writing itself becomes problematic, for the certainties of conventional subject matter and sanctioned methods or attitudes for the writer fall away. One way of looking at Machaut's metafictionality therefore would be to characterize the reflexive and personal elements of his narrative poetry as motivated by the breakdown and loosening of literary tradition, even as this tradition insistently (and successfully) still calls for its own space within the poem. For Machaut, the final result is the paradoxical resolution of the *Voir-Dit*, the poem which can also (more importantly?) be "true," that is, offer not only the abstractions and idealizations of tradition but the vagaries and inconclusiveness of individual—and authorial—experience. The analysis of the metafictional elements in the judgment poems eases our understanding of Machaut's later intentions and accomplishments. In the *Behaingne* we witness the ways in which the poet's situation calls for representation within the traditional debating and allegorical structures of the poem; here, significantly enough, is a poetic presence still willing to efface its own demands for centrality, to be eliminated from narrative focus and, in the process, assume the burden of supporting the emotional life of the class above. But in the *Navarre* the poet becomes his own subject even as the conventional elements of debate poetry—particularly the use of *exempla* drawn from various sources—are now marshalled not to examine some point of love doctrine so much as to scrutinize playfully the success or failure of literary creation itself.

NOTES

1. As Lee Patterson puts it, "... in dispensing with the humanist hermeneutics of depth Exegeticism is unable to apply its interpretive attention to the explanation context itself, which remains wholly exempt from interpretation." *Negotiating the Past: The Historical Understanding of Medieval Literature* (Madison: Univ. of Wisconsin Press, 1987), p. 35.
2. "Remarks on Old French Narrative: Courtly Love and Poetic Form (1)," *Romance Philology* 26 (1972–3), 77–93; and "Remarks on Old French Narrative: Courtly Love and Poetic Form (II)," *Romance Philology* 28 (1974–5), 190–199. For a somewhat different interpretation of *translatio studii* see Douglas J. Kelly, "*Translatio Studii*: Translation, Adaptation, and Allegory in Medieval French Literature," *Philological Quarterly* 57 (1978), 287–310.

3. This literature is discussed by Janet Coleman in her *Medieval Readers and Writers* (London: Hutchinson & Co., 1981). American Formalist Medievalism, in its characteristic refusal of history, is obviously closely related to similar attitudes about American literature, whose political/academic implications are intriguingly discussed by Russell Reising in *The Unusable Past: Theory and The Study of American Literature* (London: Methuen, 1986).
4. Translated by Michael Shaw (Minneapolis: Univ. of Minnesota Press, 1984), pp. 18–19.
5. *Metafiction: The Theory and Practice of Self-Conscious Fiction* (New York: Methuen, 1984).
6. *Poetic Identity in Guillaume de Machaut* (Madison: The Univ. of Wisconsin Press, 1984).
7. "The Poetics of the *Prologue*: Machaut's Conception of the Purpose of His Art," *Medium Aevum* 52 no. 2 (1983), 258–71.
8. Brownlee, *op. cit.*, and Douglas J. Kelly, *Medieval Imagination* (Madison: The Univ. of Wisconsin Press, 1978), especially pp. 121–54.
9.   Car longuement
Avoit duré de nous le parlement,
Et si aviens fait meint arguement,
Si comme il est escript plus pleinnement
    Ici dessus. (Lines 1592–1596)
    (For our discussion
Had lasted a long time,
And we had made many arguments,
Just as it is written more fully
    Here above.)

      Et, a mon gré,
Cils chevaliers en a moult bien parlé,
Car en escript l'ay ci dessus trouvé,
Et par raison s'entention prouvé.
    Ce m'est avis. (Lines 1780–1784)
(And, to my satisfaction,
This knight has spoken of them very well,
Since I have found it all in writing here above,
And by reasoning has proved his contention.
    Such is my opinion.)
Text and translation are from R. Barton Palmer, *Guillaume de Machaut: The Judgment of the King of Bohemia (Le Jugement dou Roy de Behaingne)* (New York: Garland Publishing, 1984).

10. Palmer, *op. cit.*, pp. xxix–xxxvii.
11. Brownlee, p. 15.
12. This theme is foregrounded in the later *Dit de la fonteinne amoureuse.* See my article "*The Book of Duchess* and *Fonteinne Amoureuse:* Chaucer and Machaut Reconsidered," *Canadian Review of Comparative Literature* 7 (1980), 380–93 for further discussion on this point.
13. Text and translation of the *Prologue* are from R. Barton Palmer, *Guillaume de Machaut: La Fonteinne amoureuse (The Fountain of Love) and Two Other Love Vision Poems* (New York: Garland, 1993). All reference to the *Navarre* is to Palmer, ed. and trans., *Guillaume de Machaut: The Judgment of the King of Navarre* (New York: Garland, 1989).
14. Charles Muscatine, *Chaucer and the French Tradition* (Berkeley: University of California Press, 1957; William Calin, *A Poet at the Fountain: Essays on the Narrative Verse of Guillaume de Machaut* (Lexington: Kentucky Univ. Press, 1974); and David Lanoue, "History as Apocalypse: The 'Prologue' of Machaut's *Jugement dou Roy de Navarre,*" *Philological Quarterly* 60 no. 1 (Winter 1981), 1–12.
15. "Les Exemples dans le *Jugement dou Roy de Navarre* de Guillaume de Machaut," *Lettres Romanes* 36 no. 2 (May 1982), p. 115.
16. Calin, p. 112.
17. See particularly "Epic and Novel" in *The Dialogic Imagination,* translated by Caryl Emerson and Michael Holquist (Austin: Univ. of Texas Press, 1981), pp. 3–4. The larger implications of this issue are discussed further in my "Transtextuality and the Producing-I in Guillaume de Machaut's Judgment Series," *Exemplaria,* 5, no. 2 (1993), 283–304.

William W. Kibler
James I. Wimsatt

Machaut's Text And The Question of his Personal Supervision

The extant manuscripts of Guillaume de Machaut's works are exceptional among those of medieval poets in their quality and in the number that originated during the writer's lifetime. Perhaps no poet of the epoch was so blessed as Machaut in seeing his own work beautifully produced and adorned, and surely the work of none survives to our day in so rich a set of contemporary codices. These circumstances of quality and survival, together with other indications, have contributed to some scholarly assumptions about Machaut's active part in the composition and oversight of the manuscripts, assumptions that our recent work on the Machaut textual tradition calls into question.

In preparing his edition of the works of Guillaume de Machaut for the Société des anciens textes français series, Ernest Hoepffner relied heavily on two manuscript collections in the Bibliothèque Nationale in Paris. They are traditionally referred to by the sigla A (fonds français 1584) and F-G (fonds français 22545–46). Both A and F-G can be assigned to the second half of the fourteenth century, and Hoepffner thought it likely that both were copied under the personal supervision of the poet himself. He writes, in justification of his methodology: "Pour la constitution du texte, il faut . . . s'attacher aux manuscrits les plus complets, qui contiennent en quelque sorte la dernière rédaction des oeuvres de Machaut, la forme définitive que l'auteur voulait leur donner: ce sont A et F-G."[1]

Hoepffner's notion that certain collections were put together under the personal supervision of Machaut himself has been developed and elaborated in recent years. In 1969 Sarah Jane Williams, in a seminal article in *Romania*,[2] called attention to a statement immediately preceding the index to manuscript 1584 (ms. A) that suggests authorial oversight. It reads, "Vesci l'ordenance que. G. de Machau wet quil ait en son livre" ["Here is the arrangement that G. de Machaut wishes for his book"]. Building on this declaration and on statements about his manuscripts found in the *Voir Dit*, Williams posited that the poet was closely involved with the fabrication of the several manuscripts that contained his collected works, and that these manuscript collections were copied from a personal exemplar maintained and constantly updated by Machaut himself.

In her *Romania* article Williams finally drew only the guarded conclusion, "There is evidence in the manuscripts as well as in the *Voir Dit* of Machaut's supervision of the publication of his works and of his concern for their arrangement."[3] She did not at that time discuss how exceptional such indications of authorial concern are in medieval manuscripts; it often seems, indeed, that once the typical medieval author consigned his text to the scribe he cared but little for its subsequent fortunes. Eventually, though, Williams and others found broader implications in the manuscript evidence, claiming that Machaut was the first "poëte" in the modern sense of the term. In papers presented to a 1977 conference on *Machaut's World: Science and Art in the Fourteenth Century*, Williams and Kevin Brownlee and, to a lesser extent, Karl Uitti and William Calin, claim a new concept of poetic identity for Machaut.[4] For Brownlee, Machaut is "the poëte figure: acutely aware of the dignity of his calling, highly conscious of technical expertise, glorying in the breadth and diversity of his artistic production."[5] This new concept of poetic identity leads, according to Brownlee, to a new conception of the poetic artifact—which is in effect a terminologically updated version of Hoepffner's original point: that Machaut took special care in revising and overseeing his poetic *oeuvre*.

These modern views of Machaut as the self-aware poet polishing and perfecting his poetic artifacts ultimately rely on the unchallenged assumption, dating back to Hoepffner, that manuscripts A and F–G contain the "definitive form" of Machaut's poems. Our recent work on manuscript C (Bibliothèque Nationale fonds français 1586) and related manuscripts in preparing editions of Machaut's *Jugement du roy de Behaigne* and *Remede de Fortune* for the Chaucer Library[6] has led, however, to a different view of the matter, particularly as regards the *Jugement*. C, like A and F–G, is a collective manuscript, but it contains only works composed prior to the *Jugement du roy de Navarre* in 1349. As such, it probably represents the earliest stage in the assembling of Machaut's "collected works."

Although both Hoepffner and Williams recognized the unique character of C, they assigned the manuscript to the fifteenth century,[7] which in their eyes diminished its value as a witness to the poetic and musical *oeuvre* it contained. Moreover, because of his Darwinian view of the development of Machaut's poetic skills, Hoepffner naturally gave little authority to the "early" text of C. However, recent art historical research by François Avril has convincingly placed the date of C back into the 1350s, and our own work on the texts shows the versions of *Jugement du roy de Behaigne* and *Remede de Fortune* found in the later manuscripts are by no means improvements on the early versions. In the case of the *Jugement*, indeed, they are markedly inferior. While not impugning Machaut's poetic preeminence, our research calls into question the contention that he carefully oversaw the production of the manuscripts of his collected works, as well as the notion that he held a concept of himself as a "poet" in anything like the modern sense of the term.

In classifying the manuscripts containing Machaut's works, it is usual to distinguish between those that collect a considerable number, or most, of his works together, and those that contain only isolated pieces. The collective manuscripts are listed below; the dates in the third column are the latest and most authoritative assigned, generally as found in the editions of Friedrich Ludwig, or as updated by Avril.[8]

A	Paris, Bibliothèque Nationale, f.fr. 1584	(1370–77)
B	Paris, Bibliothèque Nationale, f.fr. 1585	(1370–72)
C	Paris, Bibliothèque Nationale, f.fr. 1586	(1350–56)
D	Paris, Bibliothèque Nationale, f.fr. 1587	(c. 1430)
E	Paris, Bibliothèque Nationale, f.fr. 9221	(1390s)
F–G	Paris, Bibliothèque Nationale, f.fr. 22545–46	(1390s)
J	Paris, Arsenal 5203	(1371)
K	Bern, Burgerbibliothek 218	(1371
M	Paris, Bibliothèque Nationale, f.fr. 843	(15th c.)
Pm	New York, Pierpont Morgan M. 396	(1425–30)
Vg	Vogüé	(1371–75)

The *Jugement du roy de Behaigne* is found not only in all of the collections, but also as the only long poem by Machaut in the following manuscripts:

Ar	Arras, Bibliothèque municipale 897	(14th c.)
Kr	New York, H. P. Krauss	(14th c.)
P	Paris, Bibliothèque Nationale, f.fr. 2166	(15th c.)
Pc	Paris, Bibliothèque Nationale, f.fr. 1149	(14th c.)
R	Paris, Bibliothèque Nationale, f.fr. 2230	(15th c.)
Ra	Paris, Bibliothèque Nationale, f.fr. 20026	(15th c.)
St	Stockholm, Kungliga Biblioteket Vu 22	(15th c.)
Ys	Paris, Bibliothèque Nationale, f.fr. 1595	(14th c.)

No other *dit amoureux* by Machaut exists independently of the other works in nearly so many manuscripts as *Jugement*.

Remede de Fortune is found in all of the collective manuscripts (except D, which is only a partial collection) and in one other manuscript (Cambridge, Magdalene College, Bibliotheca Pepysiana 1594) in which it and an anonymous work comprise the sole contents. The *Dit dou Lyon* and *Dit de la Harpe* are each found in one manuscript outside the collections, while the *Confort d'Ami* exists in three.[9] Williams and others have suggested that most of Machaut's works circulated independently before being gathered into the collective manuscripts, but *Jugement* is the only poem for which we have extensive evidence of this prior circulation, and the witness it brings to bear on Machaut's concern for the text of his works is unique.

In preparing his edition of Machaut's *oeuvres*, Hoepffner consulted all of the collections except Pm and Vg, but knew only P and R among the individual manuscripts containing *Jugement*. On the basis of eleven texts he constructed a tripartite stemma, for which, apparently, he never published the supporting details.[10]

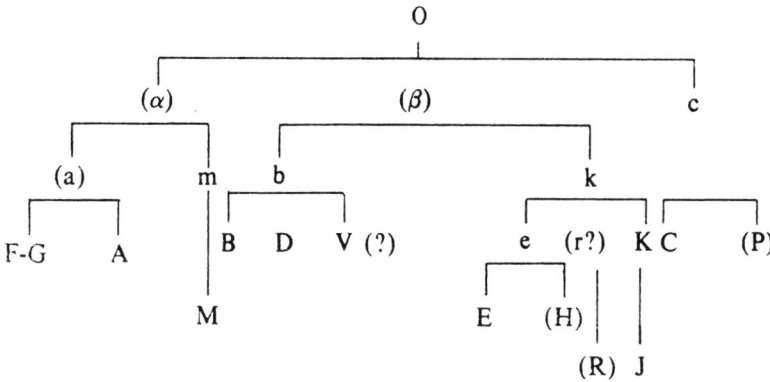

However, our study of the complete manuscript tradition of both *Jugement* and *Remede* indicates that Hoepffner's three-part division of the manuscripts does not hold for either poem, although groupings that he suggested can be maintained with modifications.

The manuscript groups differ somewhat for the two poems. For *Jugement*, instead of Hoepffner's tripartite system, we discern a binary separation in which his middle (beta) group is split between his original first and third branches. Our first group is composed of C, the earliest of the collections; E, J, and K, "secondary" collections with inferior texts; and the eight independent texts of the poem: Ar, Kr, P, Pc, R, Ra, St, and Ys. The other set is formed by the seven closely related collections which have been presumed to represent Machaut's text as it developed after 1360 under his supervision: A, B, D, F–G, M, Pm, and Vg. Because of the relationship of all of the texts in the first group to C, and despite the lateness of several of its manuscripts, we identify that group as the "early text tradition." The other set, then, makes up the "late text tradition."

	Early-Text Tradition	Late-Text Tradition
Jugement:	C / EJK / ArKrPPcRRaStYs	ABDF–GPmVg
Remede:	CEPe –JK–	ABF–GMPmVg

For the text of *Remede*, as with *Jugement*, Hoepffner's three-part stemma is not satisfactory. In place of the stemma we suggest a three-part grouping that is very similar to the two-part division just outlined for *Jugement*. Again there is an early-text group, composed of manuscripts related to C, the earliest Machaut collection; but this time the group includes but two others: E, a "secondary" collection; and Pe, the only independent text of the poem. With *Jugement* the early-text tradition similarly included C, E, and all independent texts of the work. There is likewise for *Remede* a later-text group, composed of six quite full Machaut collections, A, B, F–G, M, Pm, and Vg, all included in the similar grouping of seven *Jugement* manuscripts. (Manuscript D does not contain *Remede*). The main difference in the categories for *Remede* is that J and K are no longer closely allied to the early manuscripts, but together form a third, intermediate group. Nevertheless, we include them in our edition because of the many readings they share with the early texts.

As noted earlier, Hoepffner and critics since his time have assumed that the "late-text" collections were copied rather directly from an exemplar that the author kept with him and which he presumably perfected over the years. The production of manuscript A was thought to have been personally overseen by the poet himself, so it was natural for Hoepffner to select A as the base manuscript for his edition, and to rely secondarily upon the closely-related F–G (which has now been shown to have been created considerably after the poet's death[11]). However, the changes that the text of *Jugement*, at least, underwent from C and its related manuscripts to the late-tradition texts do not support the established view of authorial supervision which other considerations have seemed to invite. Indeed, the best exemplars of *Jugement* are found in C and in the still-better independent versions of P and Pc.

Arguments to substantiate this view are essentially of two kinds: the presence of significant lacunae in the late-tradition manuscripts, and the study of alternate phrasings. The lacunae offer the clearer, cut-and-dried evidence. The evidence from alternate phrasings is not strong in single examples, since an element of subjective judgment is generally involved, but cumulatively the testimony of individual readings can be quite impressive.

The manuscripts of the early tradition of *Jugement* are most obviously distinguished by having four passages that are consistently omitted from the late-tradition texts: lines 980–83, 1000–1047, 1816–19, and 1861–84 (The last of these is also omitted in C and P). Hoepffner's edition, although based on A, F–G and the other late-tradition manuscripts that do not have these passages, includes them without commentary among the numbered lines of the poem. Thus, only by his documenting the deletions in the list of variants does he reveal their absence from all of the manuscripts upon which his edition is supposedly based.

In each of the four cases the omission seems unplanned and deleterious. We suggest that the lacunae could hardly have gone unnoticed by Machaut had he been carefully supervising the production of the collective manuscripts, and they most certainly would not have occurred in any "autograph" manuscript he might have maintained in his possession.

Let us consider the first omission in context. The lover is speaking:

> Dame, il est voirs que j'aim tres loyaument
> Ce qui me het, c'est ma dame au corps gent,

> Qui est ma mort et mon destruiement.
> > *Quant je li voy* 980
> Autrui amer, et n'a cure de moy
> Qu'elle deüst amer en bonne foy,
> Si qu'a paine que tout ne me marvoy
> > De ceste amour;
> Car, s'elle amast ma vie, ne m'onnour, 985
> En la dolour ou je vif et demour
> Ne me lessast languir l'eure d'un jour
> Pour tout le monde.

The omission of lines 980–83 leaves line 984, "De ceste amour," dangling without a logical antecedent for the prepositional phrase. Moreover, it fails to introduce the situation that requires the subjunctives in lines 985 and 987: it is because he sees her giving her love to another instead of to himself, whom she should love, that the contrary-to-fact conditions of lines 985–88 are set up: if she loved him truly she would not let him languish, but she does allow him to suffer because she gives her love to another.

The loss of lines 1000–1047 in all of the late-tradition collective manuscripts destroys the logic of the lover's response to the lady. She had just argued (lines 881–929) that she was the more unfortunate of the two, because the Lover still had Desir, Esperance, Souvenir, and Pensee. In his reply the Lover first summarizes her points, mentioning specifically Desir, Esperance, and Souvenir, and alluding directly to Pensee:

> Et puiz que j'aim il faut qu'aie Desir
> Qui ne se puet deporter ne souffrir
> De Esperance; et si ai Souvenir
> > Qui esmouvoir
> Me fait souvent et maint penser avoir. (941–45)

He then promises to respond to her charges point by point:

> > Si respondrai
> A ces raisons au mieux que je porrai,
> Et sur chascune .i. poy m'arresterai. (972–74)

The omission is clearly detrimental, for not only are the entire sections on Esperance and Souvenir omitted, but the transition from Souvenir to Pensee in lines 1048–49 is destroyed:

>   Et se Pensee
>   Par Souvenir est en moy engenree
>   Quelle est elle? (1048–50)

Could Machaut, carefully supervising the production of these manuscripts, have failed to notice the omission of this important section?

Without lines 1816–19, Raison's reply to Amours is colorless and undeveloped:

>   —"Comment, Amours?"
>   Ce dit Raison, "Est ce donc de voz tours
>   Qu'il aimera, sanz avoir nul secours,
>   Celle qui a donné son cuer aillours? 1815
>   *Et qui vous serft,*
>   *Qu'il n'a mie le loyer qu'il desert?*
>   *Certes, folz est qui a servir s'ahert*
>   *Sifait maistre, quant son garredon pert.*"

Finally, the loss of lines 1861–84 destroys the rhyme pattern of the first quatrain and leaves the sentence begun by Youth in lines 1857–60 without a verb for nominative case "cilz amis" in the result clause begun by "Car":

>   Car cilz amis, pour mal ne pour assaut
>   Qu'Amours li face, 1860
>   [N'iert ja partis de la belle toupasse ...]

and also fails to provide an antecedent for the relative "Qui" in line 1885:

>   [Qu'Amour, ma dame] 1884
>   Qui son cuer art, taint et bruit et enflame ...

Moreover, this last omission can better be explained as a scribal jump *du même au même*, from "Qu'Amours" in line 1860 to "Qu'Amour" in 1884.

Thus, these omissions bring strongly into question hypotheses of continuing authorial supervision, as well as the existence of a dependable exemplar of *Jugement* which Machaut would have maintained for the purpose of having authoritative copies made.

Further demonstration of the superiority of the early text is found in a detailed comparison of individual readings that differ from early to late tradition. Our careful inspection of the contrasting readings in the two sets of manuscripts reveals ninety-one instances in which there are two competing and distinctly different readings, each being supported by at least three manuscripts of its group. In all cases both readings make some kind of sense, but they are not always equally good. An impartial evaluation made before we had settled definitely upon a base manuscript revealed that forty-three of the ninety-one instances show a distinct difference in quality between the early and late readings. Of these forty-three, fourteen of the late-tradition readings were judged preferable, as opposed to twenty-nine of the early, a dramatic difference.[12]

Another feature of these variants supplies additional striking evidence of a lack of continuing authorial oversight. Not only do the early-text manuscripts have the better reading more than twice as often as the late, but of those fourteen instances in which the late seem better, all but three are shared by one of the better early manuscripts, C, P, or Pc. Conversely, of the twenty-nine readings in which the early seem better, only three are represented in the two late manuscripts that Hoepffner favored, A and F–G. From this one can infer that almost none of the better readings originate in these later texts, while once the good readings were lost, they remained lost.

We might look at several of the examples in which the text of our edition of *Jugement* differs from that of Hoepffner because of the respective manuscript preferences, A and F–G in his case, C, P, and Pc in ours. In line 531–33 of our early texts, the lady declares that Love at the appropriate time will give "Good reward" ["Bon guerredon"] to the lover, while Hoepffner's manuscripts use the colorless possessive, "His reward" ["Son guerredon"]. Just a few lines later (541–42), the lady in Wimsatt-Kibler tells the lover, "Therefore [Pour ce], good sir, go to Love, and make your complaints to her," while Hoepffner's manuscripts use the awkward connective, "So that" ["Si que"]. Again, in lines 789–90 the late-manuscript lover, speaking of Amour, claims ungrammatically that "it is a great friendship who [qui] has been his mother in prosperity"; the early texts have the necessary "que" plus pronoun: "it is great friendship that she [qu'el] has been my mother." In 1143–45, the lover of Hoepffner's version says he can't repent loving, and that he would be a false lover "if I departed [departoie] from it," which is quite maladroit. The early version has the logical "if I repented [repentoie] it." A little farther on (1257–58) the knight in the late version reports that the lady "inquired and conversed [m'enquist et aparla] whence he came there." The bothersome "aparla," inappropriate for a question, replaces the logical "demanda" of our early manuscripts. Again, in describing the approach to the castle of Durbuy, the poet in Hoepffner's text states (1401–03) that the valley echoed with the "noise" ["bruit"] of birds, and the water also continually makes "noise" ["bruit"], "so that one could not be in any [ne puet en nul] greater joy," while the early text uses the precise sensory verb to go with the preceding words of sound: "could not hear [ne puet oïr] greater joy." For a final example, in 1568–70 in our manuscripts the knight declares that his lady had "given and consigned to me all her heart with her love. She called me her lover." In Hoepffner's base, by contrast, there is an awkward repetition of "heart"; the knight states that she had "given and consigned to me all her heart. She called me her heart, her love, her lover."

There are, as we have said, many fewer examples in which the readings of the late manuscripts manifest superiority, and in virtually no case in our critical edition of the early manuscripts have we been forced to use inferior readings, as Hoepffner was repeatedly led to do by his editorial choice. As mentioned before, in only three cases where the late readings are superior (330, 1067, 1301) have all three of our preferred manuscripts lacked the better version. In two of these instances (330, 1301), J and K, part of the early tradition, have provided our edition good readings. In the solitary case of line 1067, the particle meaning "there" ["i"] in 'm'i fait mouvoir" gives Hoepffner's late reading somewhat more specificity and perhaps some superiority to the early-text "me fait mouvoir," which we use. That this is the *only* instance in which the beautiful vaunted late collections (ABDF–GPmVg) make a positive contribution to a critical edition of all the manuscripts of the *Jugement du roy de Behaigne* is surely strong testimony to the deterioration, rather than authorial revision, of the text.

The evidence of the manuscript versions of *Jugement* thus paints a different picture of the development of the Machaut text from that which a broader, but less complete and detailed, study of the evidence has suggested. It is manifest at least with *Jugement* that Machaut did not carefully supervise the text of the later manuscripts, and that the version printed by Hoepffner does not represent the poet's later and maturer judgment or preferences. However, since there remains substantial evidence that Machaut was involved in some way with the production of certain collective manuscripts (probably A and Vg), we would suggest that he was more concerned at this later stage of his life with the arrangement of the various works within the manuscripts and quite possibly with the illustrative programs to accompany specific works that he considered more important at this time,[13] and to which he wanted to accord special prominence by their physical presentation. The actual texts of the poems, however, he entrusted to the care of the scribes—and they were not always particularly careful. The exemplar from which all of the late-tradition collective manuscripts descended, missing as it did four important passages in *Jugement* and presenting numerous inferior readings, was most assuredly not Machaut's original, nor could it have been a copy personally maintained and updated by the author.

Our study of the text of *Remede de Fortune*, which as we have noted is preserved in ten collections and one individual manuscript, also reveals a lack of continuing authorial supervision, though in a less striking manner. As also remarked, here again we find well-defined "early" and "late" traditions in roughly the same two groups of manuscripts. Yet neither evidence from missing lines nor from competing readings reveals a clear superiority for either tradition. In the first place, the omissions from the *Remede* texts are by no means so extensive as with *Jugement*, nor are they so confined to the late tradition. The early C, E, and Pe lack 2111–12 (though J and K have them); the late A and Pm lack 3724–25; and only C and E have 3225, necessary for the lyric form at that point. Secondly, there is much less variation in total between the details of the early and late textual traditions. There are proportionately fewer distinct, competing readings for *Remede*, only seventy-four as compared with ninety for *Jugement*, a poem only half as long as *Remede*. And where differences do occur, the late reading is just as often superior as it is inferior. Of the forty-two variants which show some qualitative difference, twenty-one of the early readings and twenty-one of the late are superior.[14] Once more, however, one or more of the five early texts show almost all of the preferred late-tradition readings; only two of the readings are completely missing. At the same time, only four of the twenty-one better early-tradition readings appear in the six late texts.[15]

With such statistical balance, for most of these variants discussion will be inconclusive and probably tedious, but we might speak of the two that embody the most substantive changes between early and late. The first is found in lines 507–10, the lover's lai. Our text, based on C, reads, "Car en moy / Joye en croy, / Pour ce mon cuer vray / remaint en soy" ("For joy grows within me, since my true heart lives in her"). The later text has it, "Car de moy / A l'ottroy / Et de mon cuer vray / Qui maint en soy" ["For she has the gift of me and my true heart, which lives in her"]. The early text seems a shade better because of the effective parallel and contrast between "en moy" and "en soy." At any rate, it does not seem possible to claim that the late tradition is better. With the second case, there seems a definite decline from early to late. In the lover's complaint, our version of lines 1169–71, describing Fortune and based on C, states, "Sa foy est qu'a nul foy ne porte,/ Sa force est qu'en chëant est forte,/ En riant meschëance aporte" ["Her faith is that she's faithful to no one,/ Her strength is that she's strong in falling,/ Laughing, she brings misfortune"]. Here smooth syntax and nice rhetorical parallelism are abetted by the internal rhyme of present participles. Much of this effect is lost in the late version where the parallel is diffused and broken up: "Sa force est qu'en chëant est forte,/ En desconforte se reconforte/ En riant meschëance aporte" ["Her strength is that she's strong in falling: / In discomforting, she comforts herself,/ Laughing, she brings misfortune"]. In context this version appears even weaker, for the parallels set up are badly overdone in the quatrain that follows.

We can only speculate as to why the text of *Jugement* deteriorated so markedly between the early and late versions, while that of *Remede* remained at least comparable in quality. *Jugement* was an early and very popular poem, something of a *succès de scandale* in its day, attributing as it did the lion's share of the suffering to the Lover rather than to the Lady. This decision evidently was criticized in court circles and elicited Machaut's palinode in the *Jugement du roy de Navarre*. Because of its early date and notable success, *Jugement* undoubtedly had more opportunities to be copied, providing more occasions for variation to be introduced into the text before the ABF–GMPmVg group began to be composed in the early 1360s. *Remede*, composed some five to ten years after *Jugement*, was copied into all the major collections, but into only a single surviving "independent" manuscript. In the case of both poems, little indicates that the transmission of the text was accompanied by the poet's correction, emendation, or revision. Though Machaut obviously was concerned with general aspects of the presentation of his *oeuvre*, as with other poets of the time he left textual details largely to the scribes, whose standards of accuracy were hardly modern.*

NOTES

1. *Œuvres de Guillaume de Machaut.* 3 vols. (Paris: Firmin-Didot, 1908–21), 1: L. Earlier he had stated, more definitively, in speaking of these same manuscripts, "ils semblent avoir été écrits l'un

et l'autre du vivant du poète, peut-être même sous sa surveillance" (p. XLVI).
2. "An Author's Role in Fourteenth Century Book Production: Guillaume de Machaut's Livre ou je met toutes mes choses." *Romania*, 90, 4 (1969), 433–54.
3. Ibid., p. 445.
4. Madeleine Pelner Cosman and Bruce Chandler, eds. *Machaut's World: Science and Art in the Fourteenth Century*, Annals of the New York Academy of Sciences, vol. 314. (New York: New York Academy of Sciences, 1978). The articles referred to are Sarah Jane Manley Williams, "Machaut's Self-Awareness as Author and Producer," pp. 189–97; Kevin Brownlee, "The Poetic Œuvre of Guillaume de Machaut: The Identity of Discourse and the Discourse of Identity," pp. 219–33; Karl D. Uitti, "From *Clerc* to *Poète*: The Relevance of the *Romance of the Rose* to Machaut's World," pp. 209–16; and William Calin, "The Poet at the Fountain: Machaut as Narrative Poet," pp. 177–87.
5. Brownlee, "Poetic Œuvre," p. 229.
6. *Guillaume de Machaut: Le Jugement dou roy de Behaigne and Remede de Fortune*, ed. James I. Wimsatt and William W. Kibler (Athens: Univ. of Georgia Press, 1988).
7. Hoepffner, 1: XLIV; Williams, "Author's Role," pp. 448–53. See also Leo Schrade, ed., *Polyphonic Music of the Fourteenth Century* (4 vols. + Commentary, Monaco: Editions de l'Oiseau lyre, 1956–58), Commentary to vols. 2 and 3, p. 27.
8. The most recent and authoritative datings of the illuminated Machaut manuscripts (A, B, C, D, E, F–G, Pm, Vg) are in François Avril, "Les Manuscrits enluminés de Guillaume de Machaut," in *Guillaume de Machaut. Colloque – Table Ronde organisé par l'Université de Reims* (Paris: Klincksieck, 1982), pp. 117–33. The best overall study of the Machaut manuscript tradition remains that in vol. 2 (1926) of Friedrich Ludwig, *Guillaume de Machaut. Musikalische Werke*. 4 vols. (Leipzig: Breitkopf und Härtel, 1926–54).
9. *DL* is in Berlin, Staatsbibliothek lat. 2· 49; *DH* is in Clermont-Ferrand, 249; and *CA* is in Paris, B.N. f. fr. 994 and Chantilly, 485, with a fragment in Berne, A 95.
10. He writes in *Œuvres*, 1: XLV, "L'examen complet des rapports qu'ont ces manuscrits entre eux ne pourra être fait en détail qu'après la publication de l'oeuvre entière de Machaut. Pour le moment, nous nous bornerons à exposer brièvement la filiation de ces manuscrits telle qu'elle résulte des textes publiés dans ce premier

volume, nous réservant de faire connaître plus tard, dans l'étude d'ensemble, les faits sur lesquels se base notre classification." The promised "étude d'ensemble" never materialized. His stemma, which we reproduce here, is found in 1: XLVIII.
11. See Avril, "Manuscrits enluminés," p. 129.
12. We find the early readings better for the following lines (Our edition and Hoepffner's have the same line numbering): 147, 193, 317, 341, 342, 367, 393, 532, 541, 547, 678, 701, 790, 809, 849, 888, 1145, 1257, 1350, 1403, 1497, 1570, 1577, 1581, 1704, 1831, 1846, 1986, and 1987; the late are better for 151, 246, 330, 493, 626, 715, 821, 1067, 1197, 1286, 1301, 1325, 1343, and 1514.
13. Avril, "Manuscrits enluminés," pp. 131–32.
14. We find the early readings better for the following lines (Our line numbers agree with Hoepffner's up to our lines 3724–25, which Hoepffner omits because A lacks them; after this point, then, our numbers are two ahead of his): 220, 537, 611, 733, 740, 1169, 1170, 1295, 2277, 2477, 2576, 3019, 3074, 3225, 3246, 3267, 3382, 3423, 3762, 4089, and 4111. The late seems better for lines 426, 448, 669, 1489, 1836, 2102, 2240, 2340, 2478, 2719, 2801, 2812, 2984, 2993, 3345, 3391, 3861, 3871, 3903, 4040, and 4200.
15. This situation is somewhat qualified by the mixed filiations of J and K, which definitely belong to the early tradition for the *Jugement*. However, for *Remede* after line 1100, J and K have more in common with the late tradition. Our edition includes them with the early manuscripts C, E, and Pe, as do the statistics cited. Disregarding them, the generalizations made here hold, but not as firmly.
*Since this article was first published in Spring 1987, an additional manuscript of Machaut's collected works has been identified: Aberystwyth, National Library of Wales, MS NLW5010C (Bourdillon 10). The manuscript's existence was known from earlier accounts, but it was originally thought to contain only a single motet. It is badly mutilated by both water and vandalism (the removal of all leaves containing miniatures and music) and has therefore only recently been recognized as a complete works manuscript. A full description can be found in Lawrence Earp's forthcoming *Guillaume de Machaut: A Guide to Research*. The contents of W suggest that it is an early manuscript, from the 1350s, shortly posterior to C, although its version of the *Jugement du roy de Behaigne*

links it to the late text tradition of ABDF-GPmVg. This suggests that the text of *Jugement* was corrupted early but does not, we believe, vitiate the arguments of the present article relative to Machaut's supervision of the manuscripts of his collected works.

Steven R. Guthrie

Machaut and the *Octosyllabe*

My purpose is to discuss the rhythmic structure of Machaut's eight-syllable line. Because there has never been a systematic study of the octosyllabe, it has seemed advisable to formulate a theory of the line and to come at Machaut's practice by degrees, through a discussion of metrical practice during the preceding two and a half centuries. My presentation will focus on three issues: the eight-syllable line itself, the relationship between its lyric and narrative forms, and the spoken performance of verse.[1]

Prosodic studies of Old French as a rule deal adequately with the earliest period (the time of *Saint Leger* and the *Passion*), when the line is extremely regular and there is even a fairly concrete midline boundary. Where they run aground is in making the transition from the early period to the twelfth century and beyond. At this point, the linguistic line becomes obviously more complex, and prosodists speak of the added complexity in general terms as a means of avoiding monotony.[2] The precise nature of the variation encountered is not discussed, and when there are general observations to be made about Old French meter, scholars normally retreat to the safe ground of the early period. To make matters worse, when linguists confront the problem, they tend to generalize from a study of, say, *Saint Alexis*, which is decasyllabic, to a theory of Old French meter as a whole, regardless of line. Among linguistic studies, that by Klausenberger is a good recent example of both the strengths and the limitations of work to date.[3] Among more traditional studies, Paul Verrier's somewhat older treatise is noteworthy, both because it makes one indispensable point and because, by ignoring everything else, it does its own argument a disservice.[4]

Verrier's study is in good part a defense of Old French poetry against the depredations of German linguists, who, he argues, often forget that the poetry in question was frequently sung, and that song and spoken verse, not to mention verse read silently in the dust of Prussian libraries, do not necessarily follow the same rules. Verrier's treatise is passionate, informed, closely argued in places, and in some ways almost persuasive. And his central point is an excellent one. He carries it farther, however. *Everything* in French versification, he says, old and new, stems from the single rhythmic principle of binary recurrence.[5] Rhyme is obviously worth studying because the poets themselves talked about it; stanzaic structure is similarly important. But rhythm? A matter of ear, no more and no less.[6] In the first place, the rule of binarity takes precedence over everything else, and in the second place, rhythmic structure is intuitive, not planned—a part of the gift, not a part of the craft. The poets themselves had nothing to say on the subject, and why should we?

On this point Verrier is mistaken. Poetic rhythm is indeed very largely "a matter of ear"—intuitive, not consciously planned. But that is precisely why it *is* worth studying, if we can only find the right machinery for the job. The rhythmic structure of a poet's works can give us a cardiogram of his poetic character, of his epoch, and of a stage in the growth of his language. As it happens, the period loosely called Old French is anything but static. The language itself is evolving in a direction different from that of any language it has contact with, and poetry in the language develops resources to deal with, and perhaps even encourage, that evolution. There is wide diversity among individual poets and between periods, and at the same time there is a consistent direction in the growth of prosody during the age as a whole.

My conclusions are based on a generative metrical analysis which in part makes use of a method developed by Paul Kiparsky.[7] The method is controversial, and while this is not the place to examine it in detail, it will be worthwhile to state briefly its distinguishing characteristics. The underlying premise of generative metrics is that the linguistic structure of verse is worth studying because at some abstract level poets intuit rhythm in linguistic terms. To define a line as iambic tetrameter, or octosyllabe, then, is not to end the discussion but only to begin it. In each age and to a degree in each poet, there is a characteristic perception, linguistically expressed, of what will and will not work rhythmically in the verse line. What is metrical for one poet in the octosyllabe may be unmetrical for another poet in the same line.

Most generative methods measure stress morphologically. Kiparsky's, devised for the purpose of discussing English iambic pentameter, is alone in consistently maintaining access to phrase syntax. For English poetry, the method is quite good at articulating precise relationships between phrase structure and metrical pattern, but in some cases it probably understates line density by 5% or so (e.g., by ignoring the word stress of a preposed monosyllabic adjective). For French verse, given the certainty of phrase stress, and the relative uncertainty of most other stress even during late Old French, the method would seem to be nearly ideal.[8]

Two further notes will help clarify my method. First, I use the term *stress*, for lack of a better, to mean abstract linguistic prominence, not necessarily co-incidental with phonological emphasis. Second, I follow Klausenberger in accepting word stress in words with reduced -*e*,[9] and the graphs in my appendix, drawn in the interest of simplicity, reflect such stresses. It should be noted, however, that curves drawn for phrase stress alone present the same contours at somewhat lower levels.

I will offer a theory of the octosyllabe in which the metrical unit is the halfline whose ideal embodiment is a major linguistic phrase in an overall rising rhythm: "Au departir / / dou bel esté" (*Roy de Navarre*, 1). The abstract norm of the line, then, has phrase prominences at positions 4 and 8, with considerable variation permitted but with certain logically possible rhythmic patterns systematically avoided. The focus of these constraints is the boundary between metrical positions 4 and 5. In other words, in effect there is a caesura in the octosyllabe. This claim disputes the consensual view of prosodists that the octosyllabe is a *vers court* to which the concept of caesura is irrelevant.[10] It is true, after the earliest period, that there is no obligatory phrase boundary or even word boundary at position 4 in the line, but there is still an intuited metrical barrier which the linguistic line may cross freely only in certain ways. I would describe the midline boundary of the octosyllabe, then, as similar to the foot boundary of English iambic verse and to the caesural boundary of the French decasyllabe. Against the possible objection that the first halfline in *Navarre* 1, above, is not necessarily a full breath group, I would answer that prosodists have never hesitated to take similar phrases as caesural in the decasyllabe.

My analysis is based on sixteen narrative poems, including the *Dit dou Vergier* and *Jugement dou Roy de Navarre* of Machaut, and nine collections of lyric song, including separate studies of the ballades in Machaut's *Louange des Dames* and of his *Ballades Notées*. (A full list of texts is given in an appendix.) The metrical systems of these poets are compared in two ways: first, in terms of overall stress patterns; and second, in terms of specific syntactic constraints. Discussion of individual stress curves will refer to the graphs presented in the appendix.

The earliest narrative poem in the study is *Gormont et Isembart*, probably from the first third of the twelfth century. In this poem (see graph), the abstract norm of the line is strictly enforced: there are two primary peaks in the stress curve, at positions 4 and 8, and two secondary peaks at positions 2 and 6. Only 8% of all stresses occur at Weak (odd-numbered) metrical positions. The line is nonetheless an octosyllabe, not a tetrameter, as a comparison with the stress curve for Chaucer's *Book of the Duchess* will demonstrate. In the *Duchess*, as in *Gormont*, only 8% of stresses occur at Weak metrical positions, but the two graphs are much different in appearance. Stress at position 4 is much less frequent in the English poem, stress at positions 2 and 6 is much more frequent, and the overall weight of the line is somewhat higher, 3.1 stresses per line in the *Duchess* against 2.8 in *Gormont*. The line of *Gormont* is a legitimate *octosyllabe*, and despite great changes, Machaut's line is its direct descendant.

There is more to be learned about *Gormont* from a study of syntactically based rhythmic patterns. I have divided the relevant patterns into four groups, to which I will refer throughout the discussion. For the sake of convenience, all sample lines are drawn from Machaut's *Jugement dou Roy de Navarre*.

Group I is made up of lines with clear phrase boundaries at position 4:

Au departir / / dou bel esté	1
Que le soleil / / li amenistre	7
Tenu de sons / / et de hoqués	9
Pour li servir / / e honnourer	11
Pour le temps qui / / de sa nature	13
Se ma dame est / / preus et haitie	649

These are the norm, and in *Gormont* similar patterns occur in 79% of all lines.

Group II includes lines in which there is a virtual caesura at position 4:

A.	Et mettent a / / destruction	65
	Sans pitié ne / / compassion	66
B.	Si que de leur / / mervilleus plour	171
C.	Et me mis en / / estat de grace	439
	A quel fin ce / / porroit venir	447
D.	Arrousez de / / douce rousée	5
	Tout partout ou / / elles voloient	418
E.	Par nature, ou / / dou vent qui vente	23
	A souffrir, et / / qui plus me grieve	100
	Enchantant de / / la lopinelle	245
	Pour itant que / / leur baterie	255
F.	Des le premier / / commandement	1420

In each of these lines, the word in position 4 belongs to the major phrase in the second half of the line, but is in looser constituency with the elements there than they are with one another. In *Gormont*, Group II includes only 2% of all lines, bringing the total of lines with actual or virtual caesura to 81%.

Cadences in Group III represent variations of relatively little complexity on the basic model of the line:

G.	Par plains, par *aunois*, par bosques	10
	Pour ce me *tenoie* a couvert	31
	Si que grans *meschiés*, ce me samble	67
	Eins les cou*venoit* la morir	392
	Lors fui hors *d'esmay* et d'effroy	487
H.	Tous seuls en *ma chambre* et pensoie	38
	Li mondes *par tout* se gouverne	40
	Qu'on le scet *et voit* clerement	51
	Qui destruit *le monde* et tempeste	90
	Dou temps que *je vi* en m'enfance	96
I.	Mais cils qui *haut siet* et loing voit	299
	Pour rece*voir mort* en la place	440
J.	Et que la *fueille* chiet dou cherme	22
	Par la froi*dure* de s'espee	36
	Car les ba*tailles* et les guerres	189

In these lines, there is fifth position caesura, masculine in Types G, H, and I, and feminine in Type J. Types H and I differ in that in H, the word in position 4 is a proclitic, while in Type I, the boundary is between two major-class words. The relevance of the distinction to the metrical study is not entirely certain. Phrases like *haut siet* are much rarer than phrases like *et voit* at positions 4 and 5, but then they are rarer anywhere in the line. In *Gormont*, Types G through I are entirely proscribed. The reason for the constraint cannot be the refusal to permit Weak-position stress, because phrases like *par aunois* are allowed to end at metrical position 3. The primary issue is not binarity but reinforcement of the midline barrier. Type J cadences, with word boundary missing at position 4, but with stress at 4 and word and phrase boundaries at the adjacent position, appear in 15% of all lines. These are the only way of avoiding a fourth position word boundary which the poet intuits as acceptable.

Cadences in Group IV represent more complex variations:

K.	De celle *mervilleuse* mort	384
L.	Et si *generaument* savoir	233
	De cent n'en *demouroit* que nuef	406
	Si comme un *esprevier* qu'on mue	460
M.	Estoit, que *montagnes* et plains	29
	De penre *crueuse* vengence	351
	Car riens n'en *voioie* savoir	455
N.	Que tout ce *couvient* demourer	12
	Gisans mors *parmi* les eglises	372
O.	Gisoient *toutes* esperdues	416
	Venoit a *belle* compaignie	547
P.	Dont encor *les traces* en durent	200
	Et partout *le munde* couroit	363
	Et blez et *es vignes* paissoient	417
Q.	Les nues, *la mer* esmouvoir	290
R.	Dont villes *et citez* fondirent	174
	Dont on vit *par deffaut* de gent	407
	Car tuit li *plus hardi* trambloient	435
S.	Que li blez *en la terre* germe	21
T.	Tant que li *rois Artus* me ceingne	Cligés, 117
	Forment du *cuer pensif* par m'ame	Panthère, 49

These cadences occur in 4% of all lines in *Gormont*. (Type T lines do not occur in *Navarre*.) In the 661 lines of the poem, there is one instance of Type K, one of O, and one of P. Type O resembles Type J in Group III, except that in Type J there is a phrase boundary at position 5. Type J occurs in 15% of all lines, and Type O occurs in a fraction of 1%. The only other instances of complex lines in *Gormont* are of Type R, which occur at a 2.5% rate.

The line of *Gormont et Isembart*, then, is octosyllabe rather than tetrameter, but a very strict octosyllabe. The poem was apparently sung,[11] and it will be useful to compare its rhythmic structure with that of the work of a contemporary songwriter, Guillaume of Poitiers and Aquitaine. There are, of course, phonological differences between Guillaume's Provençal and the *Gormont* poet's Old French, but in the earlier period at least, relative stress appears to work similarly in the two languages, and the comparison seems to be a fair one.

In Guillaume, as in *Gormont*, there are primary prominences at positions 4 and 8 and secondary ones at positions 2 and 6, but there are also important differences between the two stress curves. The overall weight of the line is higher in Guillaume, 3.1 stresses against 2.8. The two curves are similar at positions 2 and 6, but in Guillaume the primary prominence at position 4 is considerably lower, and the rate of stress at positions 3 and 5 is considerably lower. In Guillaume, 20% of all stresses occur at Weak metrical positions, against 8% in *Gormont*.

There are related differences in the respective ranges of permitted syntactic variation. In Guillaume, fourth-position caesura occurs in 63% of lines, against 81% in *Gormont*. Fifth-position caesura occurs in 26% of lines against 16% in *Gormont*. Type G cadences, proscribed in *Gormont*, occur in 14% of the lines in Guillaume. Type H cadences, proscribed in *Gormont*, occur in 4% of lines. Group IV cadences, the most complex variations, occur in 11% of lines in Guillaume, against 4% in *Gormont*. In general, syntactic constraints which are rigid in narrative verse are only relative in contemporary lyric song.

The difference here is not simply one between spoken verse and song. Nor is it that the songwriter allows himself to be a sloppier versifier because he has the sentiment of his message or the skill of his performers or the glitter of the occasion to cover his mistakes. The linguistic rhythm of Guillaume's verse is comprehensible without music, and it may be that abstract linguistic rhythm is played off against concretely realized musical rhythm for the purpose of adding complexity to the whole composition. For the poet of *Gormont*, the same kind of complexity was not a goal.

These are the primitive forms of the line for the period under consideration. There are changes during the twelfth century, at the time of Chrétien, and they have often been noted but never systematically examined. As it happens, Chrétien himself is the extreme case, and I will suggest that his work represents one of two co-existing and later merging metrical approaches to the narrative octosyllabe.

During the twelfth century, the overall rate of Weak position stress increases, both in narrative verse (now spoken) and in lyric song. The increase has been difficult to explain, and attempts to account for it have produced some interesting logical contortions. Verrier notes the change, and suggests that in Chrétien's case the poet was more interested in telling a story than in minding his meter, and without music to guide him he strayed from his rhythmical way. Verrier acknowledges, in his next paragraph, that this hypothesis fails to account for the parallel loosening of rhythmic constraints in song, but he suggests that the songwriters neglected their meter because they were more interested in their melodies.[12]

Clearly the two explanations fail to wash one another or anything else. It seems to me that there are two reasons for the change. First, the language itself was changing. Word stress was undergoing a gradual levelling process in polysyllabic words without final -e, and as a result, the tendency toward overall rising rhythm in the phrase became stronger. The older kind of metrical tension, between linguistic rhythm and binary pattern, became relatively less important, and of relatively greater importance became a newer kind: rhythmic suspense created by a grading of stress upward in the breath group, resolved by phrase stress, simplified or complicated according to the patterning of the linguistic phrase with respect to the midline metrical boundary. The second, and related, reason is that from the twelfth century on, poets were engaged in building a metrical tradition in which rhythmic complexity counted for more than concrete binary recurrence, and in which even spoken narrative aimed at something like the intricacy of lyric song.

The two narrative approaches I have proposed are represented on the one hand by Chrétien de Troyes and on the other by Marie de France. (The dialect difference is suggestive in this case, but in general, dialect does not seem to be an adequate predictor of metrical complexity.) In Chrétien, in the overall stress curve there is no longer a secondary prominence at position 2, though a peak remains at position 6. The overall rate of stress is 2.6 per line (at about which level the line stabilizes for the rest of the period under consideration), and 20% of all stresses occur at Weak metrical positions.

In terms of syntactic constraints, the following figures are noteworthy. There is fourth position caesura in 68% of lines, and fifth position caesura in 16% of lines, and in these respects, Chrétien's line falls midway between those of the *Gormont* poet and Guillaume de Poitiers. Cadences of types G and H are permitted but restricted, accounting for 7% of all lines. Position 5 caesura remains the desired alternative to position 4 caesura: the ratio of Type G cadences (caesural) to type N cadences (non-caesural) is 8:1; Type H cadences (caesural) appear 5 times in the sample and Type Q cadences (non-caesural) do not appear at all. It is just as easy to construct a line of Type N as it is to construct one of type G, and the obvious explanation for the ratio is pressure toward a clear midline break, either at position 4 or, failing that, at position 5.

The signal characteristic of Chrétien's line is its permission of a relatively high rate of complex cadences of the types in Group IV. In some of these, there is also a masculine third position phrase boundary (rarely fully caesural):

Et le mors de l'espaule fist	Cligés, 4
Dex l'avoit as altres prestée	Cligés, 38

It is not the case, however, that the higher rate of Group IV cadences in Chrétien merely reflects a shift of normal emphasis away from the midline. Third position masculine phrase boundaries are in fact permitted everywhere in the octosyllabe, and the rate in Chrétien is about average. Typically, though, in Chrétien as in other poets, such cadences are followed either by cadences from Group II (which produce virtual fourth position caesura and thus mute the rhythmic effect of the phrase boundary at position 3) or by stronger (or simply additional) phrase boundaries at position 5, as in the lines in Group III. The majority of Chrétien's lines in which there are complex Group IV cadences do not involve clear third, fourth, or fifth position caesuras, and the goal in them appears to be sustained metrical tension: "Nus ne m'an porroit retourner" (Cligés, 146). Chrétien is an experimental poet, and the complex cadences he uses are rhythmic experiments comparable to, for example, his invention of rhyme-breaking.

In Marie de France, the rate of Weak position stress is 17%, or somewhat lower than in Chrétien. The two stress curves are similar, but in Marie the peak at position 4 is higher and the rates of stress at positions 2 and 3 are lower. Both curves have in common the loss of the valley at position 3 and the retention of the one at position 5, and in this they are characteristic of twelfth- and thirteenth-century narrative poetry overall. In Marie, the tendency toward fourth position caesura is stronger, 72% in *Lanval* against 68% in *Yvain* and 65% in *Cligés*. Rates of fifth position caesura are similar overall, 19% in Marie against 16% and 20% in Chrétien. The real difference comes in the incidence of complex variations, which occur at a 9.5% rate in Marie against 16% in Chrétien. Marie's line, then, is older, stricter, and less similar to the octosyllabe of lyric song than is Chrétien's.

If the line of at least some twelfth-century narrative poets has grown in complexity, the line of the songwriters has kept pace, in Old French proper at least. In Provençal, the rhythmic structure of the lyric octosyllabe is more complex in the works of Bernart de Ventadorn and Jaufré Rudel than it was in Guillaume of Poitiers, but in the stress curves of these poets there are still peaks at positions 2, 4, and 6, and valleys at 3, 5, and 7. Group IV complex variations account for 16% of lines in Bernart and 12% in Jaufré, compared to 11% in Guillaume. In the work of the trouvères, however, new rhythmic wrinkles have been added. Among the twelfth-century trouvères, Jean Bodel is included in this study, but Jean's metrical system is highly eccentric, and included here with his work is that of Thibaut de Champagne, who lived somewhat later but whose metrical system may be more representative than Jean's of the period from about 1150 to about 1250.

Jean Bodel is of course a competent versifier; he simply is more interested in experimentation than other poets are, and he is valuable to a study like this one in the same way that an eccentric like Donne is valuable to a study of English Renaissance pentameter: his work helps us to define the outer reaches of the metrical line. Fourth position caesura occurs in only 45% of Jean's lines, and that includes 12% from Group II with virtual rather than actual caesura. The rate of fourth position caesura in song is generally lower than the rate in contemporary narrative verse throughout Old and Middle French, but the rate in Jean is extravagantly low. Fifth position caesura, on the other hand, occurs at a 30% rate, the highest of any poet in the study. The rate of complex variations is 25% of all lines, the highest incidence but one in any poet analyzed. The highest rate of all—and this is another reason for discussing an obvious maverick like Jean—occurs much later in the *Ballades Notées* of Machaut.

A more representative lyricist of the period is probably Thibaut de Champagne. In the stress curve of his octosyllabic songs, the alternate peaks and valleys of earlier writers vanish completely, and the curve rises and falls symmetrically between positions 1 and 7. The overall rate of stress remains 2.7 per line, as in the narrative line, but the incidence of Weak-position stress rises to 27% of all stresses, from the 20% figure in Chrétien and Guillaume de Poitiers. Position 5 caesura occurs in 25%

of lines, against 15-20% in Chrétien and Marie. Position 4 caesura occurs in 61% of lines, against 65%-70% in Chrétien and Marie. Group IV cadences occur at a 15% rate, roughly the same as in Chrétien and considerably higher than in Marie.

The same general relationship between lyric meter and narrative meter appears to hold throughout the rest of the Old French period and into the fourteenth century. In lyric, and in the more experimental narrative line, the meter becomes gradually more abstract: the rate of fourth position caesura declines, and the rate of complex Group IV cadences increases. But the lyric is in general fifty to one hundred years ahead of the narrative line. The relatively weak syntactic constraints characteristic of Chrétien are reduced even further in Jean Renart, whose romance now called the *Guillaume de Dole* has a 19% rate of complex variations and only a 55% rate of fourth position caesura. The impulse toward complication appears to reach its limit here, however, and most other thirteenth- and fourteenth-century works are noticeably stricter, holding fairly well to levels of variation roughly halfway between those found in Chrétien and Marie. The lyric octosyllabe during the same period continues its experimentation, and the lyric line in Machaut, in some respects, approaches the statistical complexity of Jean Bodel's line. This does not mean that the two lines are close relatives in terms of overall style. The present account suggests points of interest to a more thorough stylistic analysis, but it is not meant to be mistaken for one.

It should be emphasized once more that the thirteen and fourteenth century line is a direct if now somewhat distant descendant of the earlier line. In narrative poetry, fourth position caesura still occurs between 60% and 70% of the time, and fifth position caesura is still the preferred variation. Poets intuitively prefer cadences in Groups II and III to cadences in Group IV. The ratio of Type G (simple) to Type N (complex) variations is at least 4:1; the ratio of Type H (simple) to Type Q (complex) is at least 3:1; and the ratio of Type J to Type O is at least 5:1. Narrative poets prefer the cadences in Group II to those with similar word boundaries in Group IV (that is, Types A-F to Types P-T) by at least a 5:1 ratio. The midline boundary is much more abstract than it was in *Gormont*, but it is still intuitively perceived as a ruled domain. As earlier, and more clearly now, the violation of binary recurrence is not the sole or even chief measure of metrical variation. (Of the eight syntactic patterns referred to here as complex variations, only three necessarily place a stress at a Weak metrical position.) Complexity is a function of the relationship between phrase structure and the midline metrical boundary.

In the fourteenth century, the stress curve of the narrative line catches up with the early thirteenth century lyric stress curve. In Nicole de Margival, the valley at position 5 is eliminated, and positions 5 and 6 are nearly level. In Machaut's narrative *dits*, the curve becomes symmetrical, as it had 100 years before in the songs of Thibaut de Champagne. The overall rate of stress remains at 2.6 to 2.7 per line, but the rate of Weak position stress rises from 17% in Marie and 20% in Chrétien to 25% in Guillaume de Lorris, 22% in Messire Thibaut, 20% in Jean de Meun, 26% in Nicole de Margival, and 27% in Machaut.

The metrical system of Machaut's first major narrative effort, the *Dit dou Vergier*, in some ways resembles that of the *Guillaume de Dole*. The rate of position 4 caesura is low (57% in *Vergier*, 55% in the *de Dole*, compared to an average of about 65% in narrative poetry overall), and the rate of complex variations is high (17% in *Vergier*, 19% in the *de Dole*). My guess is that the *Vergier* was strongly influenced by the lyric in general and by Machaut's own practice as a young lyric composer. In any case, the meter of *Navarre* is both stricter and more consistent with the overall direction of thirteenth and early fourteenth century practice. (The change is probably visible even within the *Vergier*: the rate of complex variations decreases from 17% in the first 500 lines to 14% near the end of the poem.)

In *Navarre*, as I have mentioned, the stress curve is symmetrical, and this is true of the *Vergier* as well. In *Navarre*, however, the impulse toward concrete reinforcement of the fourth position phrase boundary is somewhat stronger (61%), and the incidence of Group IV cadences is lower (13%). There is a third position phrase boundary in 20% of lines in *Navarre*. In about ⅗ of them, the remainder of the line is a Group II cadence, with virtual fourth position caesura, and in another ⅕ of them there is a strong fifth-position caesura. In other words, there is a strong tendency to seek a midline pause and to mute the effects of phrase breaks earlier in the line. If the pause is delayed until position 5, the effect is a temporary increase in rhythmic suspense, quickly resolved and therefore permissible at relatively high frequencies. It seems certain that at the very least, the kinds of phrases accepted as caesural in the decasyllabe are also caesural in the octosyllabe:

> Pour moy seront / / bonnes et belles   648
> Se ma dame est / / preus et haitie   649

In fact, although it has been thought necessary to defend such phrases as caesural even in the decasyllabe, there should be no doubt in the case of either line. Auxiliaries and forms of *estre* do not behave entirely like proclitics in Old and Middle French, just as they do not in Middle English, and it is entirely reasonable to suppose that they retain some notional value. In addition, there is a tendency to reinforce the separation in such lines in two ways: first, by ensuring the clarity of the rightward constituency (as in the pairing of elements in both lines above); and second, by beginning the rightward phrase with a paroxyton (as in line 648).

Machaut's narrative line, then, is much more abstract than that of the *Gormont* poet, both in terms of binary recurrence and in terms of the concrete enforcement of the caesura, but the two belong to the same essential metrical line, and Machaut's practice is an extension of the *Gormont* poet's practice. There is still an interest in binary recurrence, and a good index of it is the behavior of polysyllabic adverbs in *-ement* (*humblement, cointement*). In such words, if the poet allows the reduced *-e* to appear at a Strong metrical position, he must be willing to place both adjacent strong syllables at Weak metrical positions and thus to disrupt considerably a binary metrical expectation. In *Navarre*, the placement of such words against the grain of the binary pattern is permitted; but it only occurs in 14% of instances. The constraint is far from absolute, but it is strong enough to be felt. Overall, however, by the time of Machaut, for linguistic and prosodic reasons both, binary recurrence is a lower metrical priority than midline boundary, and the poetic phrase begins more and more to take on—or to anticipate—the characteristics of the Modern French breath group or cursus. Polysyllabic words appear at the ends of phrases (77% in *Navarre*), and vowel-reduced syllables at the beginning (and, in paroxytonic phrases, at the very ends). Rows of clitic syllables appear, so that the only possible stress in a phrase is phrase stress:

> Son proisme; *car je ne voy pere*   53
> A souffrir, *et qui plus me grieve*   100

This kind of line, of course, appears long before Machaut, but it becomes more important as the linguistic phrase becomes more central metrically. The cadences of the above lines are not imposed by the evolving natural language; they are prosodic contrivances, which imitate and perhaps even advance that evolution.

This is as much as the statistical study can say about Machaut's octosyllabe. The real craft of the meter appears in the ways Machaut manipulates rhythmic structure over a passage of several lines, and evidence of this manipulation is in fact crucial to the interpretation of the statistical results. The gradual levelling of overall stress curves during the period under consideration suggests the possibility that what is really at work is nothing more than the progressive levelling of word stress. In other words, stresses begin appearing more often at Weak metrical positions because they are no longer perceived as stresses in quite the same way they were earlier. The relative metrical simplicity of Provençal song at the end of the twelfth century would then indicate the relatively greater levelling of word stress in Old French.

On the face of it, this seems a reasonable explanation, and it seems certain that the evolution of word stress had something to do with changes in metrical structure, but the true explanation is probably more complex. Constraints on the placement of adverbs in *-ement* show the continued importance of at least one kind of word stress in the metrical line, and there are similar though somewhat weaker constraints on the placement of disyllabic words like *amor*. In addition, it is necessary to remember that, in the narrative line of the twelfth to fourteenth centuries, the trend toward greater and greater complexity proceeds only to a certain point, after which metrical constraints are considerably tightened once again. It would appear that poets in the octosyllabe experimented until they found or crossed the limits of the line and then retrenched.

If only the changing phonology of the language were involved in the evolution of metrical style, then by the time of Machaut variation would look more or less random to a syntactic analysis. This is not the case, however; rhythmic variation is patterned. The midline boundary is defined at position 4, "moved" temporarily to position 5 for several lines, moved back to position 4 or even 3 for a few lines, and so on. That this is conscious or intuitive manipulation, in either case intentional, there can be no doubt. That it is "merely a matter of syntax" or "merely a matter of ear"—both statements are equally true and actually somewhat redundant—is also beyond doubt. With the line types given above in mind, any passage of fifty lines or so in the *Roy de Navarre* (a good place to start is at the beginning of the poem, or, for example, at line 37) will illustrate the point.

This brings me to a consideration of Machaut's lyric meter. During the thirteenth century, following Thibaut de Champagne, the range of syntactic variation in French song appears to increase somewhat, with the rate of fourth position caesura falling below 60% (58% in Adam de la Halle), but with no radical change in the incidence of complex variations. The change comes with Machaut. I will discuss separately first the ballades in the *Louange*, without music, and second the *Ballades Notées*.

The stress curve for the ballades in the *Louange* is symmetrical, with one peak, relatively low, at position 4, and the obligatory one at position 8; 26% of all stresses occur at Weak positions. These figures are consistent with those for Machaut's narrative line. The incidence of caesura at position 4 is 55% in the *Louange*, compared to 61% in *Navarre*, 56% in the *Vergier*. The rate of complex variations is higher in the *Louange*, 20% of lines against 13% in *Navarre* and 17% in the *Vergier*. The meters of the *Dit dou Vergier*, the earliest *dit*, and the *Louange*, are rather similar, and the meter of *Navarre* is more conservative.

In the *Ballades Notées*, a curious thing happens to the stress curve. The rate of Weak-position stress (28%) is consistent with the narrative line and the *Louange*, but the curve is considerably flattened; the peak at position four is actually lower than the one at position 6; and a valley has reappeared at position 5. The rate of fourth position caesura is down to 50%, within five points of the rate in Jean Bodel, and the rate of Group IV cadences is 26% of lines, even higher than the rate in Jean Bodel. (The figures for the *Ballades Notées* are the same for songs in duple and triple meters.)

The meter of the *Ballades Notées* is more complex than that of the ballades without music, and the meter of the ballades in the *Louange*, while it resembles that of the early *Dit dou Vergier*, is more complex than the meter of *Navarre*. Machaut's mature intuition apparently tells him that he can get away with greater variation in a song than in a spoken lyric, and in a spoken lyric than in a narrative poem. In his earliest *dit* Machaut writes a more nearly lyric octosyllabe, which he modifies to a more nearly narrative form of the line by the time of *Navarre*.

There is no consistent minute relationship between linguistic rhythm and musical notation in Machaut. Music and poetry must obviously be compatible at the level of line length and stanza form, but beyond that the relationship is less direct, both in Machaut and throughout the period under consideration. In the songs of troubadours and trouvères, Beck derived musical rhythm from linguistic stress with apparent success, but the process is not reversible, and as Beck acknowledged, there are numerous exceptions to his correspondence theory.[13] Historically, or pre-historically, the recurrence of musical beat must have given birth to verse rhythm, but by the time of the troubadours and trouvères, musical rhythm and poetic rhythm are mutually complicating aspects of lyric song, and by the time of Chrétien, metrical expectation and poetic rhythm are mutually complicating aspects of spoken verse. It seems clear, however, that there is a general relationship between music and verse rhythm, evidenced by the fact that the range of permissible complication in the linguistic material is higher overall in song than in contemporary spoken verse. It seems likely, in view of the results given here, that the two primary influences on the evolution of narrative meter in Old French were the French language itself and lyric song. And it seems likely that, in the crucial area of the midline metrical boundary, the musical aspect of lyric song, with its often concrete caesura,[14] influenced both kinds of poetic meter.

The results of this study seem to me to justify speculation about fourteenth-century spoken performance of narrative poetry, for example the *Navarre*. Consensus among prosodists has it that there was a strong binary pulse in recitation, overpowering linguistic stress. The assumption for Old and Middle French combined (it is difficult to pin the commentators down to a period as narrow as the fourteenth century) is that word stress remains linguistically relevant at least in words with final or medial *-e*, but that the same word stress, or even phrase stress, is irrelevant to poetic performance. (This conclusion is based, e.g., on an observed 75% co-incidence between word stress and metrical ictus in a very early poem like *Saint Alexis*.)[15] The assumption of compelling binary recurrence, however, seems to me to be inconsistent with the evidence of purposeful rhythmic variation in the narrative line beginning with Chrétien. It seems more reasonable to suppose that phrase prominences were realized in recitation, wherever they occurred in the verse line, and that relevant word prominences were also realized. It seems possible that the midline boundary, at some abstract level, had an effect on the apprehension of the verse line, as it clearly did on its composition. It is difficult to say at this distance what the effect on performance might have been, and it is entirely possible that the boundary continued to influence both composition and apprehension without ever concretely affecting performance at all.

This necessarily sketchy treatment has also been speculative in some areas. I do not regard it as firmly established that the narrative rhythmic impulse represented by Chrétien played itself out by the time of Jean Renart or early Machaut, or that the mainstream of thirteen and fourteenth century practice in the octosyllabe amounted to a compromise between a strictly narrative version of the line and a more adventurous lyric version. These claims will easily be tested by the study of additional texts. I do regard the following as established: first, that the octosyllabe overall becomes more abstract during Old and Middle French, at least to the middle of the fourteenth century; second, that contemporary lyric and narrative lines are different from one another, and that the lyric line influences the narrative; and third, that Machaut's practice is a comprehensible extension of Old French practice, relatively strict in the narrative line and highly experimental in the lyric. It seems worth repeating that this study is meant to demonstrate the need for a really thorough stylistic analysis and not to take the place of one. Rhythmic structure, like the other elements of prosody, is indeed a matter of ear, but the poet's ear is a crafty thing, accessible to systematic analysis and rewarding of the effort.

LIST OF TEXTS

Stress curves and figures for metrical variation are based on samples of 500 lines each in the narrative works listed below. Lyric samples are necessarily much smaller, averaging 200 lines. Samples drawn from heterometric lyrics include only the octosyllabic lines. In many cases, discussion of metrical variation in a particular poet reflects study of an entire narrative text. Rutebeuf's "La Complainte d'outremer" is classed as narrative for the purposes of this study because, while lyric in some ways, it is clearly not song.

A metrical study based on published texts is to some extent at the mercy of editors, for whom the urge to restore and the urge to improve have not always been entirely separable. I am reasonably sure, however, on the basis of collations provided, that on the whole my statistical results are fair to the manuscript evidence. Whether or not that evidence is fair to the poems themselves is another problem, whose dimensions are well known and which cannot possibly be solved by this paper.

Texts

Gormont et Isembart, ed. Alphonse Bayot (Paris: Champion, 1931).
Enéas, ed. J. Salverda de Grave (Paris: Champion, 1964), vol. 1.
La Vie de Saint Laurent, ed. D. W. Russell (London: Anglo-Norman Text Society, 1976).
Benoît de Sainte-Maure, *Le Roman de Troie*, ed. Leopold Constans (Paris: Firmin Didot, 1904), vol. 1.
Chrétien de Troyes, *Cligés*, ed. Alexandre Micha (Paris: Champion, 1965); *Yvain*, ed. Wendelin Foerster, introd. T. B. Reid (Manchester Univ. Press, 1948).
Le Roman de Renart: Première Branche, ed. Mario Roques (Paris: Champion, 1957).
Marie de France, *Le Lai de Lanval*, ed. Jean Rychner, introd. Paul Aebischer (Paris: Minard, 1958).
Jean Renart, *Le Roman de la Rose ou de Guillaume de Dole*, ed. Felix Lecoy (Paris: Champion, 1962).
Guillaume de Lorris et Jean de Meun, *Le Roman de la Rose*, ed. Ernest Langlois (Paris: Firmin-Didot, 1920), vol. 2 (samples from each poet).
Messire Thibaut, *Li Romanz de la Poire*, ed. Friedrich Stehlich (Halle: Niemeyer, 1881).
Rutebeuf, "La Complainte d'outremer," in his *Œuvres Completes*, eds. Edmond Faral and Julia Bastin (Paris: Picard, 1959), vol. 1.
Nicole de Margival, *Le Dit de la Panthère d'Amours*, ed. Henry A. Todd (Paris: Firmin Didot, 1888).
Guillaume de Machaut, *Le Dit dou Vergier* and *Le Jugement dou Roy de Navarre*, in his *Œuvres*, ed. Ernest Hoepffner (Paris: Firmin Didot, 1908), vol. 1.

Lyric Texts:

Guillaume IX, *Les Chansons*, ed. Alfred Jeanroy (Paris: Champion, 1964).
Jaufre Rudel, *Les Chansons*, ed. Alfred Jeanroy (Paris: Champion, 1924).

Bernart de Ventadour, "Joie d'aimer," "Declaration amoureuse," "Melancolie," in Joseph Anglade, ed., *Anthologie des Troubadours* (Paris: Boccard, n.d.).

Jean Bodel, *Les Congés, Romania*, 9 (1880), 216–47.

Thibaut de Champagne, *Les Chansons*, ed. A. Wallenskold (Paris: Champion, 1925).

Colin Muset, *Les Chansons*, ed. Joseph Bédier (Paris: Champion, 1938).

Adam de la Halle, *Œuvres Complaintes*, ed. E. de Coussemaker (Paris: 1872; rpt. Genève: Slatkine Reprints, 1970).

Guillaume de Machaut, *La Louange des Dames*, ed. Nigel Wilkins (New York: Barnes and Noble, 1972); *Musikalische Werke: Erster Band: Balladen, Rondeaux, und Virelais*, ed. Friedrich Ludwig (Wiesbaden: Breitkopf & Hartel, 1977).

APPENDIX
STRESS CURVES (IN ROUGH CHRONOLOGICAL ORDER)

Vertical axis represents rate of stress per 100 lines.
Horizontal axis represents metrical positions in line.
S/W = % of stresses occurring at weak metrical positions.
CAES = Rate of fourth position caesura
GRP IV = Rate of complex variations from group IV

NARRATIVE

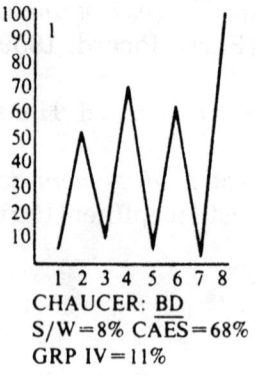

1
CHAUCER: BD
S/W=8% CAES=68%
GRP IV=11%

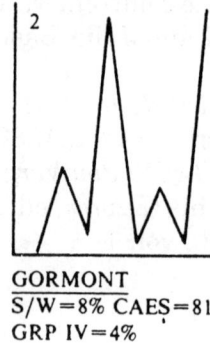

2
GORMONT
S/W=8% CAES=81%
GRP IV=4%

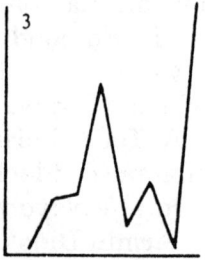

3
ENÉAS
S/W=16% CAES=70%
GRP IV=9%

STRESS CURVES (continued)
NARRATIVE

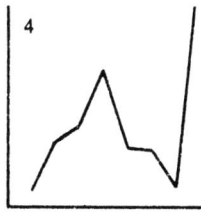

ST. LAURENT
S/W = 26% CAES = 70%
GRP IV = 17%

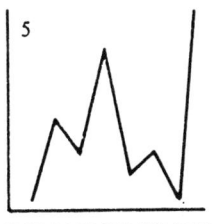

ROMAN DE TROIE
S/W = 16% CAES = 69%
GRP IV = 11%

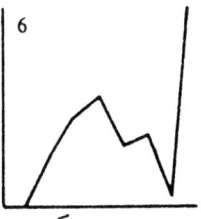

CLIGÉS
S/W = 25% CAES = 66%
GRP IV = 16%

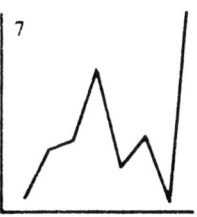

YVAIN
S/W = 20% CAES = 68%
GRP IV = 17%

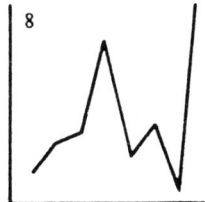

RENART, I
S/W = 17% CAES = 65%
GRP IV = 13%

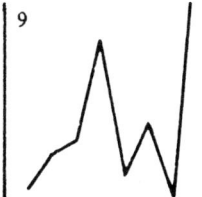

LANVAL
S/W = 17% CAES = 72%
GRP IV = 10%

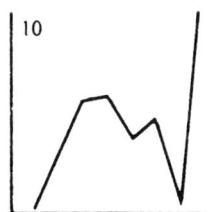

GME. DE DOLE
S/W = 28% CAES = 55%
GRP IV = 19%

ROSE (GME.)
S/W = 25% CAES = 63%
GRP IV = 11%

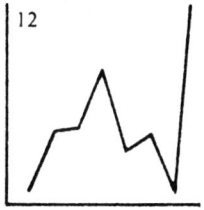

POIRE
S/W = 22% CAES = 70%
GRP IV = 11%

RUTEBEUF
S/W=24% CAES=68%
GRP IV=13%

ROSE (JEAN)
S/W=20% CAES=63%
GRP IV=13%

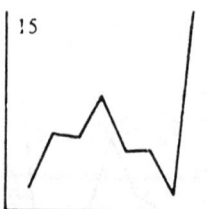

PANTHERE
S/W=26% CAES=62%
GRP IV=12%

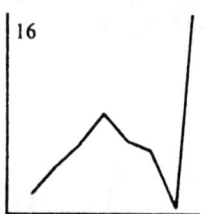

VERGIER
S/W=28% CAES=57%
GRP IV=17%

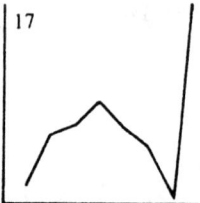

NAVARRE
S/W=27% CAES=61%
GRP IV=13%

LYRIC

GME. DE POITIERS
S/W=20% CAES=63%
GRP IV=11%

JAUFRÉ RUDEL
S/W=15% CAES=70%
GRP IV=12%

BERNART
S/W=20% CAES=63%
GRP IV=16%

STRESS CURVES (continued)
LYRIC

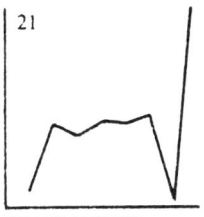

JEAN BODEL
S/W=26% CAES 45%
GRP IV=25%

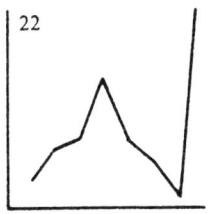

THIBAUT
S/W=27% CAES=61%
GRP IV=15%

COLIN MUSET
S/W=24% CAES=63%
GRP IV=17%

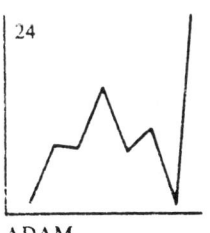

ADAM
S/W=22% CAES=58%
GRP IV=15%

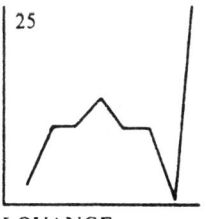

LOUANGE
S/W=26% CAES=55%
GRP IV=20%

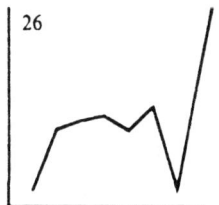

BAL. NOTÉES
S/W=28% CAES=50%
GRP IV=26%

NOTES

1. This paper presents part of the material covered in an address titled "Meter and Performance in Machaut and Chaucer," given at the University of Texas Symposium, Music and Poetry in the Middle Ages, April 3, 1987.
2. W. Theodor Elwert, *Traité de Versification Française des Origines à nos Jours* (Paris: Klincksieck, 1965), p. 123.
3. Jürgen Klausenberger, *French Prosodics and Phonotactics* (Tübingen: Niemeyer, 1970).
4. Paul Verrier, *Le Vers Français*, vol. 2, *Les Mètres* (Paris: Didier, 1932).
5. Ibid., pp. 5, 18, 20, etc.
6. Ibid., p. 22.
7. Paul Kiparsky, "The Rhythmic Structure of English Verse," *Linguistic Inquiry*, 8 (1977), 189-247.
8. Kiparsky's method is used on Middle English in my "Prosody and the Study of Chaucer: A Generative Reply to Halle-Keyser," *The Chaucer Review*, 23 (1988), 30–49. The method, and responses to it, are discussed in detail in my 1985 Brown University dissertation, "Chaucer's French Pentameter."
9. Klausenberger, p. 20.
10. See, e.g., Verrier, p. 54; Elwert, p. 123; Maurice Grammont, *Petit Traité de versification Française*, 5th ed., rev. (Paris: Colin, 1924).
11. Implicit in Verrier's discussion, p. 34.
12. Ibid., p. 58.
13. Jean Beck, *La Musique des Troubadours* (Paris: Librairie Renouard, 1910; rpt. New York: AMS Press, 1973), p. 60.
14. Robert L. Gieber, "Poetic Elements of Rhythm in the Ballades, Rondeaux and Virelais of Guillaume de Machaut," *Romanic Review*, 73 (1982), p. 5, notes the strength of the musical caesura in Machaut's octosyllabic *Ballades Notées*.
15. Klausenberger, p. 25.

Margaret J. Ehrhart

Only Connect: Machaut's Book of Morpheus and the Powers of the Weak

Though not often thought of as a political poem, the *Dit de la fonteinne amoureuse* is Machaut's response to the political turmoil that characterized fourteenth-century France.[1] Composed between 1357 and 1364, it dates from the reign of John the Good (1350–64), a period characterized by royal extravagance and bad advisors. When John was captured at Poitiers in 1356, political disorder, the result of his ill-conceived policies, followed.[2] Drawing on the tradition of the *speculum principis*, or mirror for princes, Machaut sketches a portrait of a realm whose leadership has failed it. In keeping with the *speculum principis* tradition as well, he links the fate of the ruled with the character of those who rule, and he foresees an inevitable end to France's days of glory.

But as a poet-clerk, Machaut is dependent on the goodwill of his noble patrons. Reluctant to speak openly about the abuses of power around him, he hides behind the mask of the inept and tentative Guillaume. Abdicating responsibility for the significance of his material, he thrusts the burden of interpretation on his audience. Moreover, Machaut exploits the dream's traditional association with the veiled or oblique message, drawing on classical myth, particularly the Trojan legend, for themes that resonate with the political situation in contemporary France.

And, finally, if Machaut understands the dynamics of hierarchy created by royal power, he understands too the sexual politics defined by power and male prerogative. As a clerk, he knows that his allies are those constituencies likewise excluded from the power structure. In a brilliant insight, he recognizes that the truth he offers in his poem is most likely to be understood only by the weak and disenfranchised.

The "plot" of the poem is simple. Restless and unable to sleep in an unfamiliar room, Machaut's clerkly narrator, Guillaume, overhears and transcribes a *complainte*. In the *complainte*, an unrequited lover laments the voyage he must soon make; it will separate him from the lady whom he loves but who currently ignores him. The next morning, Guillaume meets the *complainte*'s author and learns that he is the prince whose acquaintance Guillaume has sought. Welcomed on the strength of his reputation and requested to give voice to the prince's love longing, Guillaume presents the young man with a transcription of his own *complainte*. Then the two enter the prince's pleasure garden, dominated by a fountain whose water induces love in those who drink it. They share a dream during which Venus presents the prince with his beloved, and they awake to discover that the prince now wears his lady's ruby ring on his finger in place of his own diamond. A few days later, Guillaume accompanies the prince to the coast for his voyage and watches his ships depart.

This simple plot is richly embellished with classical allusion. The prince's *complainte* includes the story of Ceyx and Alcyone. The fountain in his private garden is decorated with scenes from the Trojan saga. When Venus appears in the shared dream, she describes the Wedding of Peleus and Thetis (inserting the story of Midas and his asses' ears) and the Judgment of Paris, and she recounts how Vergil loved the emperor's daughter. Within Venus's narrative, Mercury tells of the founding of Troy and the dream of Hecuba. When he and the prince awake from their dream, Guillaume describes the dream of the one hundred Roman senators.

At first glance, then, the *Fonteinne amoureuse* seems an amorous adventure decked out with erudite references. Yet Machaut alludes as well to a darker world, a world in which noblesse oblige fails and the ideals of courtly culture give way to the realities of dishonesty, cowardice, vice, and greed. When we consider the political context within which the poem was composed, it seems clear that he is referring specifically to conditions around him.

Early in the poem, Guillaume observes,

> cils fait *honnourable* chasse
> Qui grace par honneur pourchasse
> *Sans* flaterie, *sans* lober,
> *Sans* pillerie et *sans* rober. (177–80; my emphasis)[3]

I speak generally, he adds, as if to excuse the implication that some in his milieu *do* flatter, cheat, pillage, and rob. And there are many, he continues, whom one must serve though one recognizes their deceitful intentions (181–89).

In a subsequent passage, Guillaume describes the handsome prince whose court he is visiting, then notes that one can be handsome but disloyal, that one can be strong but unwilling to fight, and that some who pride themselves on wisdom know scarcely a page of good. "Je le di pour les riches hommes," he cautions—if they do not fulfill the duties of their station. And in fact they do not; in an explicit reference to themes from the *speculum principis* tradition, which specified in text after text that the good ruler maintains justice, protects the church, and looks after widows and orphans,[4] he complains that justice has fled, the church is destroyed, and widows and orphans go unprovided for (1161–88).

An underlying theme in the *Fonteinne amoureuse*, then, is that the powerful abuse power; the result is social and political disorder. A second theme is that, just as courtly culture has its darker dimension, so too does human sexuality. The prince's garden, locus of the dream that he and Guillaume share, is linked with sexual pleasure. The prince tells Guillaume that the garden was once the trysting place of Jupiter and Venus (1380–86), the spot where they enjoyed

>   le deduit ou nature
> Mist plus son entente et sa cure,
> Pour avoir plaisence et solas.... (1387–89)

But, Machaut adds, this delight can bring unhappiness; sometimes it is more harmful than a long rain after good weather (1390–92). The garden's focal point is the amorous fountain that induces love in those who drink its water. Since the fountain's circulating water flows into its basin through a golden twelve-headed serpent (1343–48) with obvious phallic associations, the flowing stream resembles rather more than slightly the discharge of seminal fluid in the sex act. The fountain likewise mingles sorrow with the pleasure of love; its stream is "De joie *et* de tristece pleinne" (1560; my emphasis).

Sexuality's darker dimension is also recalled in the dew that blankets the garden. This dew results from the tears of Aurora, who weeps every day at dawn for her son, Memnon, killed in the Trojan War (1653–60). The Trojan War figures significantly in the *Fonteinne amoureuse*, as we shall see. We know that the war was fought because the Trojan prince Paris could not resist his passion for the Greek queen Helen. Because he stole her from her husband, Memnon lost his life and Paris's own country was destroyed. Thus Aurora's tears, the garden's dew, are a sorrowful reminder that the human sexual impulse can be destructive—particularly in those with access to power.

It is clear, then, that despite its courtly surface, the *Fonteinne amoureuse* raises serious issues. Machaut alludes to contemporary social and political problems, he notes character flaws in the powerful, and he recalls that the romantic indulgence often considered a prerogative of the nobility can lead to political disaster. As a member of the clerkly estate, Machaut was certainly in a position to comment on issues such as these. Clerks were the traditional advisors of the nobility, and a good advisor was a faithful mirror. With access to the wisdom of the past, he could instruct and exhort, drawing on classical precedent to elucidate the causes and effects of human failing.

Indeed, the persona that Machaut creates for himself in the *Fonteinne amoureuse* is that of poet-clerk. Realizing, early in the poem, that the frightening sounds he hears are poetry, he prepares, clerk-like, to transcribe what he hears:

>   je pris mon escriptoire,
> Qui est entaillie d'ivoire,
> Et tous mes outils pour escrire
> La complainte.... (229–32)

Finishing the transcription, he takes professional interest in this product of a so-far unknown poet, rereading it to see whether any rhymes have been repeated (1046–48). When he is subsequently singled out by the prince at whose court he is a guest, it is his clerkly persona that gives him his identity and validity. He is able to make his way in the rarified milieu of his patrons thanks to his métier, the literary culture that he has mastered. Acknowledging the narrator's clerkly role, the prince requests that Guillaume produce a poem (1501–4).

But Machaut is skeptical about his audience's willingness to be advised, its ability to recognize the truth and choose the good. This skepticism is revealed in a passage that he interpolates into Venus's narrative of the Wedding of Peleus and Thetis: the story of how King Midas chose Pan's music over that of Phoebus. Phoebus Apollo, the god of light, played the lyre; Pan, the goat-footed god of sexuality and chthonic forces, identified in the *Fonteinne amoureuse* as the god of beasts (1692), played the pipes. Midas, a king who was unable to recognize the good, preferred the pipes of Pan to the lyre of Phoebus. Phoebus took vengeance by giving him asses' ears—which, though he hid them under a hat, were revealed by his barber (1689–1702). A rich symbol of the inability to hear and discriminate,[5] these ears make explicit his stupidity.

Machaut may well imagine that in his courtly audience there are those who would likewise choose the pipes of Pan to the lyre of Phoebus, and on whose deaf ears his own words, as clerk and advisor, would fall. As an intimate and confidant of nobles, he may see himself as not unlike a royal barber. No man is a hero to his valet, nor perhaps to his clerk. If it is true that Machaut notes abuse of power and its results in his milieu, yet fears to speak openly to the powerful about their failings, it is tempting to see in the Midas episode a classical parallel to his own situation. The powerful within his own milieu, may, he feels, be unable to discriminate good and truth from the empty piping of Pan.

Thus the guise under which he presents himself in the poem—Guillaume, the poet-clerk—is humble and comical, as if to downplay the status and value of the profession that he represents. Machaut emphasizes his awareness of the poet's role vis-à-vis that of the prince, sketching a portrait of Guillaume as a fixture of a princely retinue yet knowing well his role's parameters.[6] Overhearing the prince's *complainte*, he is at first comically fearful; were he armed on a battlefield, he would be equally fearful, he says, and he would flee if given a chance. Neither a cowardly knight nor a clerk who wants to be brave is worth a fistful of straw, he says (69–135). And he *is* a clerk: "rudes, nices et malapers" (140).

If we examine the passage with which the *Fonteinne amoureuse* opens, we can see that Machaut establishes Guillaume's ineptitude early in the poem. This passage functions as a prologue, setting forth the circumstances of the poem's composition, instructing the audience on its role in the poem's reception, and offering in anagram form the author's name and the name of the person for whom the poem was composed. Yet the prologue's chief effect is to demonstrate Guillaume's ineffectiveness and to deflect his responsibility for the significance of his material.

As the prologue opens, our first perception of Guillaume is that he is an unrequited lover. We are already familiar with this aspect of Machaut's self-presentation. In his earlier narratives, the lover stance took precedence over the clerkly stance, and the lover persona that Machaut created for his *dits amoureux* no doubt derives ultimately from the *Roman de la Rose*. Yet as Machaut's clerkly persona comes to the fore in the later *dits*, he remains an unrequited lover as well. By the time we reach the *Fonteinne amoureuse*, with its pessimistic view of the clerk's ability to influence those in power, the stance of unrequited lover has become a metaphor for powerlessness. In awe of his lady, the unrequited lover is unable to break through to her. Deferring to the prince's position, the clerk can speak only obliquely when he addresses his patron on moral or political topics. He thus *must* portray himself as inept and ineffectual.

Guillaume's lady is unreachable and un-named. "To delight and comfort myself, and to bind my thought in loyal love that binds me in its bonds," the *Fonteinne amoureuse* begins, "I want to begin with happy demeanor in the honor of my pretty lady a thing that will be happily seen and prettily done with pretty sentiment and true heart dedicated to her."

> Pour moy deduire et soulacier
> Et pour ma pensee lacier
> En loial amour qui me lace
> En ses las. . . .
> . . . .
> Vueil commencier a chiere lie,
> En l'onneur ma dame jolie,
> Chose qui sera liement
> Vëuë, et joliement
> Faite de sentement joli
> Et de vray cuer, qui est a li. (1–12)

His love is a circular process. Even the rhymes in the first few lines imply circularity and enclosure: sou*lacier* / *lacier; lace*, with an internal rhyme on *las*. The work will be done *for* his lady, but the only verb that implies transmission to an audience is in the passive voice. The work *will be seen* ("sera . . . -vëuë")—but by whom? He has been inspired to write a poem to bind himself more firmly in the love that has inspired his poem.

In the central section of the prologue, Guillaume explicitly renounces authority over the significance of the *Fonteinne amoureuse*, entrusting his audience with the responsibility of interpretation. And he implies that only a certain segment of his audience will truly understand his poem: those who are capable of discriminating between the "good" and the "bad." If they find any good, they should choose it, and they should leave aside the bad:

> Or pri a ceuls qui le liront,
> Qui le bien dou mal esliront,
> S'il y est, qu'il vueillent au lire
> Laissier le mal, le bien eslire. (13–16)

Punning on *eslire*, *eslite*, and *esleüs*, he goes on to suggest that the reader of such a perfect work, perfect because susceptible to discriminating reading, is numbered among the elect or chosen. And he envisions a scene in which an "elect" or chosen reader reads to an audience of ladies whose delight is the greater for their superior discrimination:

> quant la chose est bien eslite,
> Par raison homs plus s'i delite,
> Et dames et cils qui le lit
> Penre y doivent plus grant delit,
> Et cils dont il sera leüs
> Soit ou nombre des esleüs. (18–22)

On what basis, however, is this audience to choose the good from the bad?

Perhaps a clue resides in the passage that follows: Guillaume declares that he does not wish to include anything *laide*—"ugly"—or *villeinne* in his poem; even bad weather is sweet compared to *Mesdit* (23–29)—scandal, slander, or backbiting. In other words, he wants to exclude negative or critical material. Choosing the "good" might then mean overlooking any negative or critical passages, such as those we examined earlier: indictments of the nobility for failing to carry out their duties or reminders that sex can be destructive.

Yet such an interpretation is contradicted elsewhere in the poem. Immediately after the long passage I discussed above, in which Guillaume criticizes the abuses he sees around him

(1161–88), he announces suddenly, "Now I want to leave this matter . . . because sometimes one makes things worse by speaking of good and truth" ("Car aucune fois on empire/ De bien et de verité dire" (1203–4). *Bien*, the "good' parts of the poem, would thus be those parts in which the poet-clerk takes seriously his mission to see the truth and tell it, to be a mirror for princes.

In the third section of the prologue, Guillaume presents the anagram that encodes his name and the name of "the one" for whom the book was made—a woman's name, if we are to go by his opening statement that the *Fonteinne amoureuse* is being written in honor of his lady.[7] The anagram occupies vv. 40–41; the passage that surrounds it focuses on Guillaume's feelings for his beloved. Love commands him to present his name and the name of the person for whom the poem was made, and *deduis* demands that he attend to this command,

> Et toutevoie ne vuet mie
> Deduis nulle grant muserie.
> Avec mon cuer y ha bon gage,
> Car mes corps en est en ostage,
> Qui jamais jour ne cessera
> Jusques atant que fais sera. (39–44)

His body is in hostage until he accomplishes this chore of naming. And yet the onus is on his audience. They must decode the anagram in order to free him.[8] Again there is a sense of circularity and enclosure—even futility. If the other name in the anagram is the name of a woman, then the tradition of keeping one's beloved a secret would dictate that her name be hidden—would dictate, in fact, that the anagram be insoluble. Thus the prologue to the *Fonteinne amoureuse* establishes right at the outset Machaut's stance vis-à-vis his audience. Portrayed as Guillaume, he is weak, tentative, and ineffectual; he cannot reach his lady, nor is he certain that he can reach his audience. If his audience takes any serious message from the poem, it is their doing, not his.

Once we have recognized that Machaut's strategy in the *Fonteinne amoureuse* is to retreat from claiming the prerogatives bestowed by his mastery of literary culture, two subsequent passages take on new significance. In Venus's long narrative of the Judgment of Paris, she describes how Mercury leads the goddesses to the Trojan prince for his decision concerning their beauty. Before entrusting him with judgment, the god reveals to the young man the truth about his ancestry. Paris is a prince of Troy, not the shepherd he seems. In the midst of enumerating Paris's royal siblings, however, Mercury suddenly qualifies his spate of information with the phrase "se l'istoire ne ment": if the history does not lie (1958).

Mercury, as god of eloquence, was associated with learning and scholarship; he was often identified as a cleric in allegorizing treatments of the pagan gods.[9] Machaut must have viewed this scene in which Mercury lectures the Trojan prince on his own ancestry and the history of his nation as an image of the poet-prince relationship. Yet, tellingly, Machaut makes Mercury drop out of character—or perhaps more accurately, usurps the character of Mercury—in order to offer a self-deprecating comment that devalues the role of the clerk as anything other than a transcriber.

Slightly later, when Mercury is describing how Hecuba circumvented Priam's order that the infant Paris be put to death, the god observes,

> —Mais loange ne vueil ne gloire
> De ceste geste ou ceste hystoire,
> Qu'on scet bien que pas nez n'estoie
> Eins la fondation de Troie,
> Mais ci l'ay mot a mot escript,
> Si com veü l'ay en escript.—(1989–94)

Handed over to a servant, Paris grew up among shepherds. He now learns for the first time the truth of his noble origins. Yet Machaut backs off from the responsibility of knowing so much, on such an emotion-laden topic, about a member of the nobility. It is as if the scene imitated too closely a poet-prince encounter in which authority had been usurped by the traditional subordinate, the poet or clerk.

Because Machaut is reluctant to speak openly to his patrons about issues of personal character and political duty, the *Fonteinne amoureuse*, as we have seen, downplays the potential power over the powerful that literacy bestows on the poet-clerk. Conversely the poem exalts a mode of communication associated with covert revelation: the dream—significantly linked with political commentary and prophecy as well.[10] The Middle Ages traced to Macrobius the tradition that dreams offered glimpses of otherwise hidden truths. The *somnium* veiled the truth in enigma, requiring interpretation to pierce its mystery. The *oraculum* featured the visit of an authority figure who revealed the truth. The *visio* was a prophetic dream whose truth was borne out in reality.[11]

The prince places his trust in dreams, discounting messengers, writing, ink, and parchment as means of reaching his lady. The narrative of Ceyx and Alcyone in his *complainte* exalts the superiority of dreams over written messages. When Ceyx drowned at sea, Alcyone prayed to Juno to learn what had become of her beloved husband. Juno requested the god of sleep to communicate the dead king's fate to his wife, and the god's son Morpheus took Ceyx's form and revealed his fate to Alcyone as she slept. The prince is confident that if Morpheus will take *his* form and tell his lady of his misery, she will pity him. Macrobian tradition would characterize Alcyone's dream as an *oraculum* or *visio* since Morpheus revealed to the queen the truth about her husband's fate.

Two other dreams that figure in the *Fonteinne amoureuse* likewise prove true. These latter two are examples of *somnia* since they operate by means of images that require interpretation. Mercury relates Hecuba's dream to Paris as an explanation of why the young prince has been raised as a shepherd. When his mother was pregnant, she dreamed she bore a flaming torch that destroyed all of Troy. She recounted the dream to her husband Priam, he sent for sages, and on their advice commanded that when Paris was born he should be killed. Moved by his great beauty, his mother spared him (1967–86). But her dream proved an accurate prediction, and it would have been better for Troy had Priam's command been heeded. When Paris stole the Spartan queen Helen from her husband, the Greeks laid siege to Troy, finally burning the city.

The second example of a *somnium*, or enigmatic prophetic dream, is the dream shared by the Roman senators; it is the dream cited by Guillaume when he and the prince discover that they have shared the dream of Venus's visit. One hundred Roman senators dreamed that they saw nine various-colored suns. Puzzled, they summoned the sibyl, who led them up to "Mont Apennin" and rendered her interpretation. Guillaume withholds the interpretation, but refers his audience to "Istoire des Rommains" for the dream's meaning (2695–96). It would be too long to include here, he adds, placing the burden of interpretation on his audience.

But this dream likewise proved true, as we can determine by consulting what was probably Machaut's immediate source, the *Ovide moralisé*. The story of the senators and their dream appears in Book 14 as part of an elaboration of Aeneas's meeting with the Sibyl of Cumae, who escorts him to the underworld.[12] The interpretation is an apocalyptic message based on an ages-of-the-world scheme, as can be seen from the passage in the *Ovide moralisé* that leads into the sibyl's interpretation:

Par ceste fiere avision
Velt manifester nostre Sires
La diversitez des empires
Du monde et les mutacions
De toutes generacions. (14.119–94)

In the interpretation itself, we learn that the first two suns, both clear, signify ages in which people lived in simplicity and sanctity. The third, which was red, signifies a fierce, warlike, people and, says the sibyl, "En Rome avra mainte bataille" (14.1209). The fourth, also red, denotes a disloyal people that will turn from right and truth, but during this era, Christ will be born. The fifth, dark, then clear, signifies "La quinte gent.../ Plaine de toute felonie" (14.1309–10). During this era, however, the message of Christ will be preached throughout the world. The sixth sun, dark with a scorpion tail in its center, signifies "l'occision et le martire" that will come upon the Romans:

Trois ans et sis mois tout le mains

Durera la bataille à Rome.
Et des mors y avra grant some. (14.1322-24)

The seventh, red with a black dagger in its middle, shows again a fierce people, full of rage, who will persecute the Jews. The eighth, red, signifies the era when Rome will be destroyed and deserted. Finally, the ninth, dark with a single gleaming ray, covers the whole era from the fall of Rome to the second coming.

These three dreams that figure in the *Fonteinne amoureuse* all prove, then, to be true. Alcyone learned in a dream that her husband Ceyx had perished at sea; Hecuba dreamed she bore a flaming torch that destroyed Troy, and her son Paris subsequently brought war and destruction on the city; the dream shared by the Roman senators revealed Rome's rise and fall in the inevitable succession of empires.

But the central episode of the *Fonteinne amoureuse* is a dream as well. A prince and a poet-clerk dream that Venus comes before them, explains the story behind the golden apple she carries, and presents the prince with the lady he loves. The lady pledges herself to her lover and they exchange rings. When the two dreamers awake, they discover that the prince wears his lady's ring. At the conclusion of the *Fonteinne amoureuse*, moreover, Guillaume asks, "Tell me, was this well dreamed?" ("Dites moy, fu ce bien songié?" [2848]), forcing us suddenly to look at not only the dream within the poem but perhaps the entire poem as a dream.

I have suggested elsewhere that in his focus on love to the exclusion of his royal duties, the prince resembles Paris, whose story is recounted in his dream, and that Machaut emphasizes this resemblance.[13] Paris judged in favor of Venus, awarded her the golden apple that was the prize of beauty, and won Helen as his reward. He thus brought war and ruin to Troy. The prince compares his love for his lady with Paris's love for Helen: "plus vous aimme et pris/ Qu'onques ne fist belle Heleinne Paris" (344-45). Like the Trojan Paris and the Greek Helen, too, the prince and his lady are separated by sea (493-98). Similar phrases are used in describing the two men. As Mercury approaches Paris leading the three goddesses, we are told "tant estoit de bel arroy/ Qu'estre sambloit bien fils a roy" (1885–86). When Guillaume observes the prince entering his court, he comments "tant estoit de bel arroy/ Qu'il sambloit estre fils a roy" (1157–58). The shepherd Paris carries with him a bow that Hecuba gave him (1891–95). About to enter his garden, the prince is offered a bow (1293–95). Paris, we know, was raised as a shepherd; when the prince welcomes Guillaume to his court, his domain is referred to as a "pascoy," or pasturage (1234). Paris caused the ruin of his kingdom, and passages in the *Fonteinne amoureuse* allude to the political disorder prevalent in Machaut's France. It is thus hard to escape the notion that Machaut intends the dream of the Judgment of Paris as a kind of index to the character of the un-named prince, and sees the whole poem as a comment on how the character of the nobility is reflected in the condition of the realm.

Let us return, however, to the three dreams that we know proved true. Like the content of the dream we have just considered, the contents of these three dreams parallel the situation of the prince and his realm. And if the entire *Fonteinne amoureuse* is a dream—"Dites moy, fu ce bien songié?"—the complex web of Machaut's allusions invites us to search for patterns in the poem itself with which these enigmatic, prophetic, and oracular dreams might resonate.

King Ceyx perished at sea, and Morpheus took his form to reveal his fate to his beloved queen. The lovelorn prince claims that he is half-dead of love, and that, could his lady see his state, she would pity him. Yet there is a much stronger parallel between the prince and Ceyx—one that he himself does not see. Like Ceyx, he departs at the end of the poem on a sea voyage. The allusion to Ceyx, then, creates a sense of foreboding. Perhaps Ceyx's dark fate awaits the prince as well.

Hecuba's dream that she bore a flaming torch predicted Paris's destruction of his own city. In fact, he did destroy it, and he himself lost his life through his judgment in favor of Venus and his choice of the life of love. The flaming torch is an allusion not only to Troy's eventual burning, but also to the fact that lust caused Paris's undoing. This connection is not lost on Machaut, who emphasizes the parallel in a scene from the Trojan saga depicted on the fountain in the prince's garden. This scene, the first he describes, shows Venus, Paris, and Helen, and how she was carried off to Troy on Paris's ship. Paris wooed her—"li disoit sa karelle"—and Venus was the "maquerelle," or procuress,

> Et dou brandon qu'art sans fumee
> Dame Helainne a si alumee
> Qu'elle n'i savoit quel tour prendre
> Dont elle se peüst deffendre. (1321–24)

Helen is rendered helpless, inflamed with lust against her will, by the torch with which Venus assists Paris in the conquest of the woman that she has promised him.

Not only does Machaut see Paris's theft of Helen as the cause of his city's ruin, but he also looks back in time to situate Paris and his actions in a context of dynastic succession. As Mercury enlightens Paris concerning his royal origins, he delineates not only Paris's own genealogy but the founding of Troy, tracing the dynasty back to Jupiter. Enamored of Atlas's daughter Electra, Jupiter engendered Dardanon, whose nephew Tros founded Troy. Ultimately the line gave rise to the Trojan kings Laomedon and Priam, who ruled after Laomedon's death. Priam was the father of Paris (1919–49).

Machaut's treatment of the Trojan saga, then, spans the rise and fall of this great, ancient empire. He includes its origin with the eponymous Tros, Paris's judgment of the goddesses and rape of Helen, the war itself—alluded to in the depiction of the battle between Achilles and Hector on the "fonteinne amoureuse" (1330–34), and the city's ultimate destruction. Troy's fall is evoked in the recollection that Peleus and Thetis were the parents of Achilles

> Par qui Troie fu mise a fin
> Et Prians et tuit si affin,
> Fors aucuns qui en eschaperent,
> Qui par mer nagent s'en alerent
> En essil. . . . (1637–41)

It is also evoked in the description of Hecuba's grief when she saw "le fort chastel d'Ylion" put to destruction (1651–52). In its imagery of the burning torch that issues from her body, the dream of Hecuba thus telescopes Paris's birth, his rape of Helen, his personal fate, and the fate of his realm.

Rome succeeded Troy, founded, as Vergil has it in the *Aeneid*, by the fleeing Trojan Aeneas. But we know, not only from hindsight but from the dream of the Roman senators, which predicted it, that Rome eventually fell. When Venus includes in her paean to the irresistible power of love the episode of Vergil and the emperor's daughter, we recognize a second allusion to the power of lust in a dynastic context. As the poet of the *Aeneid*, Vergil represents the transfer of empire from Troy to Rome. Yet Venus can make the wise foolish and humble the highest ("le plus riche"). As one example she cites Vergil "qui s'assote/De la fille l'empereour" (1820–21). The tradition that Vergil was a magician accounts for this tale of how the epic poet became embroiled in the affair of the emperor's daughter.[14] Pretending to welcome his romantic attentions, the young woman marooned him in a box halfway between her window and the ground, to the great amusement of the Romans. In retaliation, Vergil arranged it so that the only source of fire in Rome was her pudendum—Machaut uses the euphemism "dos" (1823–33)—and Romans came to her one by one with unlit torches, departing with the fire they had sought. Immediately after this anecdote, Venus reminds her hearers that when she inflames one with her torch all is forgotten but the love of one's lady (1839–42).

No empire, no matter how powerful, lasts forever. Human nature sees to that. Taken together, the classical allusions in the *Fonteinne amoureuse* remind us that before France there was Rome, and before Rome there was Troy.[15] Not only is there a direct relationship between the fall of Troy and the founding of Rome, but there is also a direct relationship between Troy and France. Imitating Vergil's *Aeneid*, France too traced its founding to fleeing Trojans in a tradition that dates back to the Merovingian Fredegarius.[16] *Translatio imperii*: empires rise and they fall, succeeding one another. But as Karl Heisig points out, the tradition that saw the origin of the Franks in fleeing Trojans sought in it a justification for *translatio imperii* from Romans to

Franks. The Franks would become the valid successors of the Romans in part because they too were descended from Troy.[17]

Paris was his country's torch; his lust was Troy's downfall. The sibyl's interpretation of the senators' dream in the *Ovide moralisé* sees in suns number three through eight a panorama of Roman history in which human vice alternates with social and political unrest. Suns number three and four, both red, signify eras characterized by many battles and by disloyalty. Suns number five and six, both dark, signify eras of felony and suffering. In the eras signified by the seventh and eighth suns, both red, Rome persecutes the Jews, including Jesus, and is then destroyed. The ninth sun, dark with a single gleaming ray, signifies the long period from the fall of Rome to the second coming of Christ, but in her interpretation the sibyl focuses most of her attention on political events in France. Some kings are good, some are bad, but there is much unrest. For example:

> Empres vendra uns rois de France.
> Lors sera si grant habondance
> De barat et de tricherie,
> De traïson et de boisdie,
> Que dès que li monde fu fais
> N'avront esté tant de malz fais. (14.1521–26)

Following Fredegarian tradition, the sibyl's interpretation sees France as the successor to Rome—and sees in France simply a continuation of the vice and unrest that had marked Rome's years of ascendancy.[18] The story of Vergil and the emperor's daughter reminds us that the Romans were no strangers to the power of lust to move the powerful.

Machaut knows that his France is free from neither political turmoil nor the influence of Venus. When the prince awakes from his dream to discover a ruby on his finger in place of his own diamond, it is even possible to see an allusion to the senators portentous dream of nine suns—particularly since the dream is described between the time that the prince first notes the ruby on his finger (2523–26) and then reflects on it again (2711–12). The most striking feature of the nine suns is that the first two are clear and bright—like diamonds—and they signify peaceful and good people, but the decline in empire is reflected in the change to red for three and four. Seven and eight again are red and Rome's destruction occurs during the era signified by eight. Vivid images empower enigmatic dreams to capture the sleeping imagination, and they demand to be glossed upon awaking. So too the image of the ruby that replaces the diamond on the prince's finger: it demands glossing, even as it alludes to the portentous dream of the senators in which alternation from clear suns to red signalled decline of empire.

When the prince journeys to the coast and departs by sea, "par mer nagent" (2841) this action too resonates with dream material from earlier in the poem. Describing the fall of Troy, Venus recalls that most noble Trojans were killed,

> Fors aucuns qui en eschaperent,
> Qui *par mer nagent* s'en alerent
> En essil. . . . (1639–41; my italics)

Some Trojans escaped—among them, we know, those who founded new empires in the tradition of *translatio imperii*. To found a great empire is a noble deed, yet the scheme of history on which Machaut draws so insistently in the *Fonteinne amoureuse* emphasizes that new empires rise only when old ones fall. The departure of the prince "par mer nagent" at the conclusion of the poem suggests that he is leaving behind a realm whose days of glory are at an end. In fact, the little town from which he sets out is described as "De barat pleinne et de riote" (2810) evoking a last sense of a disordered France. Perhaps it is only coincidence that the sibyl's prophecy in the *Ovide moralisé* includes a French king's reign characterized by

>   grant habondance
> De barat et de tricherie,
> De traïson et de boisdie. . . . (14.1522–24)

Perhaps it is not.

Machaut's interest in the theme of dynastic rise and fall is suggested early in the shared dream when he introduces the figure of the sibyl into the Wedding of Peleus and Thetis. When

Discord enters the wedding feast, jealous that she has been excluded, she casts before Venus, Juno, and Pallas the golden apple that gives rise to the quarrel subsequently resolved by Paris. But the description of the table at which the goddesses sit differs from the description in the *Ovide moralisé*, the source that Machaut otherwise followed quite closely. Machaut looked ahead in his source and took from Book 14 the reference to the ten sibyls that precedes the senators' dream (14.1067–74):

> Nous trois seiens a une table
> Qui n'estoit pas de bois d'erable,
> Eins estoit d'or fin esmaillie,
> Car les ymages et la vie
> Y estoient des dis Sebilles
> Qui sages furent et abilles
> Et qui tant fort estudierent
> Que toutes dis prophetiserent
> De l'avenement Jhesucrit,
> Si com veü l'ay en escript. (1715–24)

Why would Machaut include the sibyls at this point in the *Fonteinne amoureuse*—when he incorporates most of the *Ovide moralisé*'s treatment of the senators' dream into a much later segment of the poem? Because, I would argue, the *Fonteinne amoureuse* resonates with themes of portent and prophecy, cause and effect, dynastic rise and fall. And the figure of the sibyl rises above the limited view of most of the characters in the poem—and most of its audience too—because she alone can grasp the implications of such veiled truths as the dream of the senators. At the very moment that Discord casts her apple—the action that led ultimately to the fall of Troy—the sibyl is introduced.

The *Fonteinne amoureuse*, then, situates late fourteenth-century France in a context of dynastic rise and fall. Machaut knows that power inevitably corrupts, that noblesse oblige fails. But patronage dictates content. Only on royal sufferance may the poet speak the truth, though he may see it clearly. Thus the voice we hear in the *Fonteinne amoureuse* is comical and self-deprecating; Guillaume disavows responsibility for speaking of "bien et ... verité" and presents his poem as an enigma.

Machaut's stance vis-à-vis his audience acknowledges the disparity between noble and clerk in the courtly hierarchy. Guillaume's reticence and self-abnegation imply that ultimate power lies in the hands of the prince. But his survey of dynastic rise and fall has shown that failure of empire is ultimately due to human failing: abuse of power and failure to govern oneself. If power corrupts, if royal prerogative lays claim to all that power can claim, then corruption begins in that most basic arena where power is exercised: the sexual arena. The parallel love relationships of Paris and the prince are defined by power and male prerogative.

When the Trojan Paris won Helen, whom Venus had promised him in exchange for the golden apple, he stole her from Greece against her will. Machaut does not gloss over the fact that winning Helen was an act of aggression. First to be described among the scenes depicted on the fountain in the prince's garden is the scene that shows how Helen was ravished—"ravie"—"Et menee a Troie a navie" (1317–18). Venus had so inflamed the Spartan queen with her torch that Helen was reduced to tears, unable to defend herself (1320–24).

The prince, master of the garden and its fountain, likes this scene very much:

> Et comment qu'Heleinne esplouree
> Fust, si bien estoit figuree
> Qu'il sambloit que bien li seïst,
> Quelque samblant qu'elle feïst,
> Et bien li plaisoit il sans faille. (1325–29)

His admiration for the sight of Paris stealing the tearful Helen from her homeland seems an index of his own character in love.

If we look at the episode in which Venus brings his lady to him in his dream, we can see that his view of love is a fantasy in which a compliant woman is made available to fulfill male sexual needs—thanks to the magical power of Venus to arouse women. In his dream, Venus stresses her power: "Il ne scet rien de ma puissance" (2149). As "maquerelle," the same role she performed for Paris, she offers him the silent and passive woman that he desires, displaying her like a product:

> vesci sa dame et sa drue
> Qui est aveques moy venue
> Pour li soulacier et deduire. (2165-67)
> . . . .
> Est elle belle et douce et gente? (2172).

I *give* her to him, Venus says, and command her to comfort him:

> Sans retollir li doing et baille,
> Et avec ce je li commande
> Que a li conforter entende. . . . (2174-76)

I do not want her to be ashamed of anything, but she ought to be humble and pitying to do his good and his will (2181-83).

As Venus continues, she coaches the lady in her speech to the prince. The speech takes the form of a poem in which the lady assures him that she is his—but a small contretemps midway through is revealing. The lady appears to be *qualifying* the commitment she offers the prince, specifying that she pledges herself emotionally but not sexually. And she appears, in a passage whose grammatical convolution mirrors her modesty and embarrassment, to believe that Venus upholds the claim that sexual favors are not to be part of her commitment.[19]

But Venus intrudes. Though she appears to support what the lady has just said—

> Lors prist a rire
> Venus et dist: "Je diray: Voir!
> Dieus et deesses ont pooir
> Tel qu'il faut faire leur voloir
> Sans contredire." (2346-50)

—consider the force of her laughter. And consider that her words can be taken as a restatement of her earlier boasting about the power of love, not to mention an allusion to her role in the ravishing of Helen. The statement thus becomes a confirmation of her power to arouse women sexually, with the implication that the prince can expect sexual gratification from his lady.

The story of Paris and Helen, with its striking parallel in the relationship between the lovelorn prince and his lady, offers an example of power used abusively. The prince, like Paris, seeks sexual compliance. The pleasure he takes in the depiction of a tearful woman inflamed by passion against her will and then ravished suggests that he revels in images of royal and male power. In the symbolic landscape of his pleasure garden, the amorous fountain celebrates the connection between political power and sexual conquest.

Machaut apparently considered "Morpheus" an appropriate alternative name for his poem.[20] In fact he is a kind of Morpheus, a god of sleep who presents the dream to which attention must be paid. If he withdraws into the humorous Guillaume, that is only a disarming persona. The poet-clerk looks up to the prince, but as Morpheus he can encode a message for those of his audience who do not share the asses' ears of Midas. Only connect, then, and take the good from Machaut's richly allusive text. "Dites moy, fu ce bien songié?" (2848), he asks at the conclusion.

But who are the members of that ideal audience on whom he calls to understand that the truth resides in the poem's darker passages? Machaut exalts the sibyls as prophetesses, powerful women from whom the secrets of dreams are not hidden. They see the truth, and so too perhaps do the ladies in the audience he envisions in the poem's prologue. Outside the power structure, ladies and clerks can see in the depiction of the helpless Helen, tearful at her inability to defend herself from Paris, an allusion to the abuse of power, the unthinking domination of the princely class.[21]

NOTES

1. For previous readings of the *Fonteinne amoureuse* see William Calin, *A Poet at the Fountain: Essays on the Narrative Verse of Guillaume de Machaut* (Lexington: Univ. Press of Kentucky, 1974) Chapter 8; Kevin Brownlee, *Poetic Identity in Guillaume de Machaut* (Madison: Univ. of Wisconsin Press, 1984) 188–207; R. Barton Palmer, "Vision and Experience in Machaut's *Fonteinne amoureuse*," *Journal of the Rocky Mountain Medieval and Renaissance Association* 2 (1981): 79–86.

2. Generally on this period: Raymond Cazelles, *Société, politique, noblesse et couronne sous Jean le Bon et Charles V* (Geneva: Droz, 1982). According to Cazelles, Machaut ranged himself among the reformers of 1357 (30). Cazelles also notes, "De plus on rencontre dans l'opposition des familiers de la maison de Luxembourg, notamment des anciens officiers du roi Jean l'Aveugle, père de Bonne. Guillaume de Machaut, secrétaire de ce roi, n'a quitté son service, puis celui de sa fille, que pour se donner au roi de Navarre, alors qu'on se serait plutôt attendu à le voir s'attacher à Jean le Bon, protecteur des poètes" (88). On Machaut's political stance, see also Claude Gauvard, "Portrait du prince d'après l'oeuvre de Guillaume de Machaut: Etude sur les idées politiques du poète," *Guillaume de Machaut: Poète et compositeur*, ed. Daniel Poirion, Actes et Colloques No. 23 (Paris: Klincksieck, 1982) 23–39. Gauvard sees Machaut's sentiments as lying with the reformers as well (27–28, 37).
3. Citations are to the edition of the *Fonteinne amoureuse* in *Oeuvres de Guillaume de Machaut*, ed. Ernest Hoepffner, 3 (Paris: E. Champion, 1921).
4. See my article, "Machaut's *Dit de la fonteinne amoureuse*, the Choice of Paris, and the Duties of Rulers," *Philological Quarterly* 59 (1980): 119–39, on this tradition and Machaut's use of it. On the *speculum principis* tradition, see also J. H. Burns, ed., *The Cambridge History of Medieval Political Thought* (Cambridge, Eng.: Cambridge Univ. Press, 1988) esp. 326–28, 483–85; Wilhelm Berges, *Die Fürstenspiegel des hohen und späten Mittelalters* (Leipzig: Hiersemann, 1938). Machaut's view of the ideal ruler emerges clearly in the *Jugement dou roy de Navarre*, written in 1349. The *Navarre*, originally edited by Ernest Hoepffner in *Oeuvres de Guillaume de Machaut*, 1 (Paris: Firmin-Didot, 1908), has recently been reedited and translated by R. Barton Palmer (New York: Garland, 1988). See also Gauvard 32–37.
5. " 'Ovide moralisé': Poème du commencement du quatorzième siècle," ed. Cornelis de Boer, *Verhandelingen der Koninklijke Akademie van Wetenschappen te Amsterdam, Afdeeling Letterkunde*, NS 15, 21, 30, 37, 43 (Amsterdam, 1915–38). The Midas story (11.670–770) is in the same book that contains the Wedding of Peleus and Thetis and the Judgment of Paris, but it precedes that episode. The pipes of Pan are interpreted as the praise offered those who want earthly honor and glory (11.835–45).
6. Daniel Poirion's book, *Le Poète et le prince: L'évolution du lyrisme*

courtois de Guillaume de Machaut à Charles d'Orléans (Paris: Presses Universitaires de France, 1965), is structured around the complementary roles of poet and prince; see 192–205 for his discussion of Machaut as a court poet. See also, for an explicitly structuralist analysis of the relationship, Jacqueline Cerquiglini, *"Un engin si soutil": Guillaume de Machaut et l'écriture au XIVe siècle* (Paris: H. Champion, 1985) 107–37. Alexandre Leupin offers a brief analysis of the power relationships implied by hierarchy: "The Powerlessness of Writing: Guillaume de Machaut, the Gorgon, and *Ordenance*," *Yale French Studies* 70 (1986): 127. See also Palmer, "Vision and Experience," 84–85; "*The Book of the Duchess* and *Fonteinne amoureuse*: Chaucer and Machaut Reconsidered," *Canadian Review of Comparative Literature* Fall 1980:389–91.

7. See my "Machaut's *Dit de la fonteinne amoureuse*, the Choice of Paris, and the Duties of Rulers," 122. The lines that contain the anagram, 40 and 41, read "Deduis nulle grant muserie./ Avec mon cuer y ha bon gage." Ernest Hoepffner believed that the anagram could be solved to reveal the name of the Duc de Berry. In arriving at his solution, however, he did not follow Machaut's instructions precisely, he used a reading of lines 40 and 41 that appears in only one manuscript, and he added an *h*. See Ernest Hoepffner, "Anagramme und Rätselgedichte bei Guillaume de Machaut," *Zeitschrift für romanische Philologie* 30 (1906): 401–13, and *Oeuvres* 3, xxvi, n 2. Machaut's instructions for solving the anagram read as follows:

> Jusqu'a quarante compteras
> Ces vers ci, et quarante et un,
> Si qu'après vin et a geün
> Nos noms entiers y trouveras,
> Mais trois lettres en osteras
> Droit en la fin dou ver quarante. (46–51)

8. Alexandre Leupin sees the use of the anagram as displacing "control of the work toward the adventure of reading" (133). Laurence de Looze too sees Machaut's anagrams as important chiefly because of the relationship they encourage between the reader and the text, not because they are genuine puzzles: "Mon nom trouveras": A New Look at the Anagrams of Guillaume de Machaut—The Enigmas, Responses, and Solutions," *Romanic Review* 79 (1988): 537–57.

9. E.g., Petrus Berchorius, *Reductorium Morale, Liber XV: Ovidius Moralizatus, cap. 1, De Formis Figurisque Deorum*, ed. J. Engels

(Utrecht: Instituut voor Laat Latijn der Rijksuniversiteit, 1966) 25–26. See also Jean Seznec, *The Survival of the Pagan Gods: The Mythological Tradition and Its Place in Renaissance Humanism and Art*, trans. Barbara F. Sessions (1953; rpt. Princeton: Princeton Univ. Press, 1972): as bishop with a book, 156; scholarly, 158; as a scribe 159–60, and my *The Judgment of the Trojan Prince Paris in Medieval Literature* (Philadelphia: Univ. of Pennsylvania Press, 1987) 106.

10. On the tradition of vision literature and its application to political purposes somewhat later in the fourteenth century, see Jeannine Quillet, "Songes et songeries dans l'art de la politique," *Les Études Philosophiques* 30 (1975): 327–49.

11. F. X. Newman, "*Somnium*: Medieval Theories of Dreaming and the Form of Vision Poetry," diss. Princeton 1962. Macrobius and John of Salisbury are two dream theorists whose work was particularly important for the Middle Ages. Macrobius categorizes dreams into five types in his *Commentary on the Dream of Scipio* (trans. William Harris Stahl [New York: Columbia Univ. Press, 1952]), and John follows this division in the *Policraticus* (trans. Joseph B. Pike as *Frivolities of Courtiers and Footprints of Philosophers* [Minneapolis: Univ. of Minnesota Press, 1938]). The terms in my text are Macrobian. For *somnium*, see Macrobius 90; also John 76–77: for *oraculum* and *visio*, Macrobius 90; John 78–79.

12. Machaut's reliance on the *Ovide moralisé* for his mythological material is well documented. See Cornelis de Boer, "Guillaume de Machaut et l'*Ovide moralisé*," *Romania* 43 (1914): 335–52. Machaut follows the description of the dream in the *Ovide moralisé* quite closely, abridging a bit but sometimes taking whole lines word for word. The story actually dates from a fourth-century Greek original, was rehandled in Latin, and with over 130 known mss. was, as Bernard McGinn puts it, "a medieval best-seller." See his "*Teste David cum Sibylla*: The Significance of the Sibylline Tradition in the Middle Ages," *Women of the Medieval World*, ed. Julius Kirshner and Suzanne F. Wemple (Oxford: Blackwell, 1985) 24. Whether Machaut also knew the story from a version of the *Histoire ancienne*—thus "Istoire des Rommains"—its interpretation was standard.

13. "Machaut's *Dit de la fonteinne amoureuse*, the Choice of Paris, and the Duties of Rulers," 130; *The Judgment of the Trojan Prince Paris in Medieval Literature*, 130–41.

14. Domenico Comparetti, *Vergil in the Middle Ages*, trans. E. F. M. Benecke (New York: Stechert, 1929) 326–36.

15. On the medieval theme of world rule passed from Troy to Rome, see Karl Heisig, "Zur fränkischen Trojanersage," *Zeitschrift für romanische Philologie* 90 (1974): 443–44.
16. *Chronicarum quae Dicuntur Fredegarii Scholastici Libri IV cum Continuationibus*, ed. Bruno Krusch, *Monumenta Germaniae Historica, Scriptores Rerum Merovingicarum*, 2 (Hannover: Hahn, 1888); on the theme see also Maria Klippel, *Die Darstellung der Fränkischen Trojanersage in Geschichtsschreibung und Dichtung vom Mittelalter bis zur Renaissance in Frankreich* (Marburg: Beyer und Hausknecht, 1936); Ernst Robert Curtius, *European Literature and the Latin Middle Ages*, trans. Willard R. Trask (1953; rpt. Princeton: Princeton Univ. Press, 1973) 27–30.
17. Heisig 445.
18. The sibylline prophecies were for the most part "history cast as prophecy" (McGinn 25). Because the sibyl talked authoritatively about things that had actually happened, as if she was foreseeing them, her glimpses of the future tended to be believed as well—useful especially for the political purposes to which these texts were often put. Though Machaut drew on the *Ovide moralisé* for this section of the *Fonteinne amoureuse*, the sibyl's interpretation of the senators' dream could not, of course, genuinely cover Machaut's own contemporary France since the *Ovide moralisé* was completed before 1328.
19. Mais qui autre mercy desire
    Et qui dit qu'il pleure et soupire,
    Dont il le couvient a martyre
    Vivre et manoir,
    Il a tort et assés s'empire.
    Venus scet bien ceste matyre.
    Pour ç'ose bien devant li dire
    Qu'on doit savoir
    Qu'il ne fait mie son devoir,
    Eins vuet sa dame decevoir
    Qui autre mercy vuet avoir. (2335–45)
20. The words "alias morpheus" are added to the *explicit* in ms. M. This is a later manuscript, Hoepffner acknowledges, but he points out that Machaut also refers to the *Fonteinne amoureuse* as "Morpheus" in the *Voir Dit*. See *Oeuvres* 3, xx–xxii.
21. I would like to thank John Block Friedman for reading this essay and making valuable suggestions.

Constance B. Hieatt

Falconry and Fantasy in Guillaume de Machaut's *Dit de l'Alerion*

Guillaume de Machaut's *Dit de l'Alerion* was not the first work in the *ars amandi* tradition based on an analogy drawn from natural (or unnatural) history. A prominent earlier example is Richard de Fournival's *Bestiaire d'amour*. Bossuat remarked that this work revived the *Physiologus* tradition by substituting for the usual Christian allegorization a more subtle and ingenious intepretation: "C'est, tout compte fait, un traité d'amour courtois adressé par l'auteur à sa dame pour tenter une dernière fois de vaincre sa résistance. L'attitude et les sentiments de l'un et de l'autre se retrouvent dans le comportement de divers animaux."[1] These animals do not include falcons; but in another, more "learned," bestiary, the widely disseminated Latin *Aviarium*, Machaut may have found remarks about hawks which suggested that birds of prey could provide an appropriate analogy to correct human behaviour. This treatise includes, unusually for such a work, several chapters on the use and training of hawks "described as a means of depicting the righteous life which a man should lead."[2] In the *Alerion*, Machaut proclaimed that he was going to explain how to lead a righteous life (lines 1–8), and proceeded to discuss "experience" with four different falcons,[3] to which experiences he compared, in turn, various presumably hypothetical amatory situations. In doing so, he went considerably beyond the bounds of either sort of bestiary and produced what seems to have been the first poem making an extensive comparison between the arts of falconry and love.

It was by no means the last. While I am not the only critic who has suspected that the influence of the *Alerion* lies behind two sequences portraying falcons as lovers in Chaucer (in the "Squire's Tale" and "The Parliament of Fowls"),[4] Machaut does not in fact depict falcons as lovers of *each other* in the *Alerion*: he describes the falconer's desire for, and delight in, the falcon, and the falcon's attachment to the falconer, as "love"—as the work of the god "Amours," a figure familiar to readers of *The Romance of the Rose*. The falcons are treated as non-anthropomorphic hunting birds, with human lovers represented by hypothetical cases whose fortunes and misfortunes are compared to various incidents which the narrator claims as his experience in falconry. The metamorphosis of falcon characters into lovers with human problems would appear to be Chaucer's invention.

A clearer indication of the influence of Machaut's falcon poem on his English admirer may well be Chaucer's use of the terminology of falconry as metaphor for human relationships. For example, Criseyde, greeting her lover from a window as he returns from riding out on a hawking expedition, is described as "As fressh as faukoun comen out of muwe"[5]: Chaucer's description of a lady as a hawk and her lover as a falconer is the earliest use of this metaphorical nexus I have found in English literature, and it is particularly apt. That is, the falcons used for hawking were always assumed to be female (the males being much smaller and thus of less use); appropriately, then, Criseyde, not Troilus, is compared to a bird of prey.

And at this point in *Troilus and Criseyde*, the lady, who had previously been "mewed" in the seclusion of her home in her widowhood, as a falcon is confined to the mews when it is moulting, has been gradually coaxed into willing cooperation with the falconer Troilus—who proclaims, in the consummation scene, that she has been "kaught" (3.1207)—by steps bearing some resemblance to those by which a captured falcon's resistance to the will of her captor is gradually broken down. We can say, then, that at this point in Book 3 of the *Troilus* Criseyde has completely changed her coat and has been "reclaimed" by her new lover as, we are told by some of the falconry manuals, a sparrowhawk must be reclaimed (i.e., tamed, persuaded to obey the falconer) when it completes its molt.[6]

While Chaucer was not the first English writer to compare a lady to a falcon,[7] he was almost surely the first to make repeated use of the analogy of the lover (or husband) as falconer. Other examples in his work include the *Legend of Good Women*'s apostrophe to Jason (1369–72):

> Thow sly devourere and confusioun
> Of gentil wemen, tendre creatures,
> Thow madest thy recleymyng and thy lures
> To ladyes of thy statly aparaunce

(Note that the juxtaposition of the hawking terms "reclaiming" and "lure" confirm the poet's intention of invoking the falconry sense of the words here); and the Wife of Bath's characterization of herself as a falcon in the context of her explanation of how she would not submit to her elderly husbands until she had been suitably bribed (*WB Prol* 413–15):

> And therfore every man this tale I telle,
> Wynne whoso may, for al is for to selle;
> With empty hand men may none haukes lure.

(One lures a falcon with an apparatus called a "lure," which must be baited with meat.) And among Chaucer's metaphorical falconers there is one who has several birds to command: the summoner of the *Friar's Tale* (1339–40)

Hadde alwey bawdes redy to his hond,
As any hauk to lure in Englelond,

to bring him back their prey in the form of information which the summoner could use as a basis for blackmail.

Metaphorical use of the lover or husband as falconer and the woman to be won or controlled as a falcon became a widespread commonplace in the work of English writers of the next few centuries after Chaucer, most remarkably in the pervasive and fundamental use of the comparison in Shakespeare's *The Taming of the Shrew*.[8] But this was no commonplace in Chaucer's time, and the best (and possibly only) precedent he could have found for it would have been, of course, Machaut's *Dit de l'Alerion*. Chaucer, anticipating Spenser, Shakespeare, and dozens of other writers after him, would—unlike many readers of Machaut in our own time[9]—have found the analogy very suitable, for falconers seem to make the reverse analogy constantly, and speak of their "love" for their falcons and the "courteous" reciprocal relationship between the falcon and the falconer.[10]

However, it must be admitted that Machaut's choice of parallels between falconry and various aspects of courtship does not always fall on points where the comparison seems a natural one. Some of these parallels are certainly reasonable enough, such as the suggestion that a lover must be just as careful in considering how to attract the lady he desires as the falcon-fancier must be in arranging a trap to catch a wild falcon; here Machaut compares the tame bird the falconer uses as a decoy to the lover's bait of "dous amoureus regart" (sweet, amorous glance, 803)[11] and "bel et courtoisement parler" (lovely courteous speech, 808). But what in the world does he mean by attributing to a falcon called an "alerion" feathers called "pelles" (2554, 2830–31) which are as sharp as knives, and which he proceeds to allegorize as corresponding to, on the one side, "judgement, honesty, and courtesy," and on the other to their reverse (in love)?

The ground of the presumed comparison is elusive. Machaut suggests that the would-be lover who lacks the good qualities he associates with the right-hand knifelike feathers will be punished by being cut by those on the left; this would appear to ignore the fact that the feathers on the right and on the left have been said to be equally sharp and cutting. How, then, can it be that the lover who approaches from the correct right-hand side avoids being wounded? Could Machaut have been thinking about right and wrong ways of approaching the blade of a knife, assuming that it is sharp along only one edge? Perhaps, but that is certainly not quite what emerges from the passage itself, although it does indeed compare correct and faulty approaches to love with table manners. False lovers, we hear, are rude gluttons who bolt the food which is offered to them at love's table in such a way that they can derive no nourishment from it,[12] while the true ones are appreciative guests who derive sustaining nourishment from whatever tidbits are offered them.[13]

But, in the course of almost a hundred lines on this subject (lines 2838–2924), we do not hear very much about the presumed ground of the analogy, knife blades, except that the nourishment offered to the false lovers is properly cut into suitable serving pieces, "trés honnestement taillie" (2870); and, in the end those gluttons may be wounded and torn by their experience, as if cut with a knife (if that is what Machaut means when he says they are "tiré" and "mal atiré") and therefore assailed by pain they do not know how to endure (lines 2891–96). Finally, we are told that the basis of the comparison is that each man has an appropriate serving cut for him, according to what he deserves (2908–24): but it is not at all clear what the connection of all this is to the claim that the right-hand feather means one thing and the left-hand its opposite.

If Machaut's analogy seems somewhat far-fetched and not perfectly logical in its working out here, that is not the only problem this passage presents. Another is the puzzle of where he got the idea of those sharp feathers in the first place. The only way he could have derived this information from any of the falconry manuals would have been to misinterpret grossly a description of a falcon's wing feathers. The falconry section of the contemporary *Ménagier de Paris* tells us that some of the falcon's feathers consist of "bons cousteaulx," and the most influential medieval falconry text of all, Emperor Frederick II's *De arte venandi cum avibus*, tells us that the most exterior of a bird's ten primary wing feathers is called the *saxellus*, and that these feathers, and those just preceding them, are shaped like knifes; we are told, "It is for this, in our opinion, that they are called 'the knives' [*curtelli*]."[14] But note that this does not mean that these feathers (to be found on any bird: not just falcons, or a particular kind of falcon) are sharp; all it means is that each of them is shaped like a knife and its handle.

These statements, and others like them elsewhere in descriptions of falcons (and/or birds in general), might have misled Machaut, but if so, why would he have associated knifelike feathers with one particular bird, which he called the "alerion"? The answer is not to be found in descriptions of this bird in the falconry manuals: alerions are conspicuously absent from most of the treatises on falconry written, and circulating, in medieval Europe. *Les livres du roy Modus et de la royne Ratio*, known as *Modus*, is typical enough in its treatment of birds suitable for falconry; it states flatly that there are only eight kinds of birds of prey suitable for falconry, and that these are the (peregrine) falcon, the lanner, the saker, the hobby, the goshawk, the gerfalcon, the sparrowhawk, and the merlin.[15] No other is considered even worthy of mention. Of the approved eight, "Modus" says that the (peregrine) falcon and the sparrowhawk are best (line 228).

In fact, the only work on falconry which even mentions a bird called an alerion appears to be Gace de la Buigne's *Roman des deduis*,[16] from which we can learn only that alerions are not common in the West (lines 10481–2). This agrees with Machaut's claim that they are rare (1578–1608, e.g., line 1583, "Car ce n'est pas chose commune") and that they capture pheasants, partridge, and other small birds (lines 10489–90), which implies that they are a small species—as Machaut says (line 2531: "Ce n'est pas uns oiseaus moult grans"). Yet Blomqvist, the editor of the *Roman*, defines the alerion in his glossary as a "grande espèce d'aigle"!

In this conclusion he agrees with the majority of dictionaries, especially French dictionaries, with the exception of Tobler-Lommatzch, which does not try to define "alerion" at all: it simply refers us to the description to be found in the Jubenal edition of Rutebeuf. The word does not appear in English dictionaries in any helpful sense. The *OED* defines "alerion" as a heraldic term, meaning "an eagle without beak or feet," obviously a bird which could *only* exist in heraldry. The *OED*'s derivation of the original (presumably pre-heraldic) word is:

> Fr. *alerion* (12th c.), med.L. *aleriōn-em* some large bird of prey of the eagle kind. Of unkn. origin. Borel makes it an augmentative of OFr *eillier*, which Diez considered might be Germ. *adler* or *adelar*, an eagle.

While most French dictionaries seem to assume a similar derivation (Greimas, for example, derives the word from Latin *aquilarionem*, and defines it as "Oiseau de proie, grand aigle"), there have long been some doubters. La Curne de Sainte-Palaye's *Dictionnaire Historique de l'Ancien Langue Français*[17] expresses dubiety about ths derivation as well as about an alternative suggestion that the word is derived from *ala, aile*, and remarks that there is nothing in any source of information mentioning an alerion which indicates that it is a kind of eagle. In fact, the word "alerion" may well derive from Pliny, an authority frequently invoked by bestiaries, who speaks of a small type of eagle called *Valeria*.[18]

Many medieval references to the "alerion" agree that it is particularly powerful, as well as swift, including the account Hoepffner points to as a possible source of Machaut in the *Speculum naturale* of Vincent of Beauvais. This work has, within a very few pages of Book 16 (*De avibus*), first, in Chapter 19, the story of how a hawk captures a small bird as a footwarmer;[19] second, in Chapter 23, a description of the high-flying "aerophilon" ("vulgaritur aelion appellata est"), which Hoepffner assumed to be the alerion; and third, in Chapter 32, various details about the eagle, including information about how a gerfalcon committed culpable lèse majesté in attacking an eagle.

This sequence contains several striking elements of the *Alerion*, and in the same order; but, as Hoepffner rather tentatively suggests (n. 2, p. lxviii), Machaut may have gone directly to Thomas of Cantimpré, Vincent's source for most of this information. Hoepffner is wrong, however, in stating that Thomas is the more likely source "car c'est là qu'il a encore pu trouver certains détails sur l'élevage des oiseaux que Vincent n'a pas reproduits"; in fact, while Vincent rearranged some sentences and moved one to an entirely different place in the chapter, he includes everything in Thomas's account except for one sentence on the sighting of the birds which does not parallel anything Machaut says.[20] It may be more significant that Thomas tells the "captive bird" story in his chapter on the sparrow hawk, while Vincent omits it in his (taken from Thomas) account of the sparrowhawk (Ch. 92): no doubt because he has already introduced the same story (basing his account on another source, stated to be "Philosophus"—i.e., Aristotle?) in his earlier chapter on hawks (Ch. 19) without specifying what kind of a hawk the "accipiter" of this story is.

Thomas is Vincent's source of information about the "aelion" and the eagle—including the story of the gerfalcon's attack on an eagle (Ch. 2, p. 179); but this means only that he is as likely as Vincent to be Machaut's source, not necessarily *more* likely, since the only detail he includes which Vincent omits is the identity of the sparrowhawk as the bird with cold feet, and that Machaut could have learned from Gace de la Buigne, who tells the story in l. 6367–77 of the *Roman de deduis*.

A glance at, or recollection of, the relevant chapters of either Thomas or Vincent could have suggested to Machaut all four of the birds he chose to describe in his poem. The shocking behavior of the gerfalcon, which Thomas and Vincent say is the *only* bird known to have attacked an eagle, could have led Machaut to use a gerfalcon as his one example of a misbehaving bird. This is likely to be why he gave no generic identity to the bird he describes as attacking an eagle (identified only as an especially good hunting "oiseau"; line 3422), if he had decided to save the gerfalcon for separate treatment. Other details in the description Vincent derives from Thomas of the "aelion" suggest that it was indeed likely to have been a source for Machaut; for example, that it flies so high a man cannot see it (cf. 2534–35, "Et prent de voler si haut estre/ Qu'on en puet perdre la veüe"). And, perhaps the most important point, Thomas and Vincent say that the alerion is the most noble of all birds, "avis avium noblissima": Machaut begins the alerion sequence with an account of a conversation with a group of falcon fanciers assessing birds according to their degree of nobility ("selonc leur noblece," line 1564), leading to a general agreement on the superiority of the alerion (1565–68).

Note, however, that Thomas and Vincent claim that this bird is somewhat larger than an eagle ("Aquila parum maior est," ch. 16, p. 185; in Vincent, "paulo maior aquila"). Whatever Machaut thought an alerion might be, he evidently did not think it was a "grand aigle," a species he deals with quite separately. While he may have learned that alerions were relatively small from Gace de la Buigne, he is equally likely to have taken the point from the same source which led him to think that the alerion had knife-like feathers—a source which was neither the *roman des deduis* nor *De natura rerum*.

Information on this point comes only from the world of the bestiary, not that of "natural history," much less that of the falconry manual. One of these is the early thirteenth-century *Bestiaire* of Pierre de Beauvais, which tells us,

> Phisiologes dist que li alerions a moult grant segnorie sor tous les oiseaus del monde, et sa colors est semblant a fu. Et ses èles sont alsi tranchants comme un rasoirs; et il est petis I pou, et il est plus grant d'un aigle.[21]

If Pierre is an important source of traditional information about the alerion, as appears to be the case,[22] perhaps this contradictory statement explains the confusion about the alerion's size, but the editors (Cahier and Martin) understandably suggest that the last clause may be a copyist's error. If Machaut's source was Pierre, he may have seen a copy which made better sense. Another passage of the *Bestiare* which could have influenced Machaut is the "moral," which informs us that "Les trencans èles del alerion, ce sont li fait de mal hom", as against the good, who will be saved by "mesure et raison";[23] while this is not exactly what Machaut says about those wings, the passage could certainly have suggested that the sharp feathers had a connection with dividing good from bad behavior, and its emphasis on "mesure" could have suggested the treatment of false lovers as gluttons in this connection.

But if Machaut knew Pierre's account, he chose to ignore the rest of it: the further characteristics attributed there to the alerion clearly derive from the phoenix legend. The alerion is not to be found in most other bestiaries, nor in the usual "learned" sources from which bestiaries drew[24]; it is not to be found in (for example) the *Aviarium*, which has been mentioned above as a possible source for Machaut. However, Pierre de Beauvais was not *necessarily* a direct (or even indirect) source of Machaut's information: the most widely disseminated "bestiary" account of the alerion is that found in the Old French prose version of the famous medieval forgery known as the "Letter of Prester John." It is this document which Tobler-Lommatzsch is referring to when it tells us to see Jubinal's edition of Rutebeuf for a description of this bird—although *T-L* neither quotes the description nor makes it clear that the actual source is that notorious letter.[25] This version of "The Letter of Prester John" just may have been the source of the information passed on by Pierre de Beauvais: no other source has been found for his account of the alerion, and the "Letter" predates him; but since we do not know just when the alerion passage found its way into the letter, the influence could have gone the other way around.

The original Latin "letter" (which began to circulate in the twelfth century) does not mention the alerion; the phoenix, however, does appear in a list of the exotic inhabitants of Prester John's kingdom—briefly: "avis, quae vocatur fenix."[26] This reference is considerably elaborated in some of the German versions of the next century or so,[27] and was apparently replaced by the description of the alerion in continental French versions, all of which credit the alerion with phoenix-like qualities.[28] One of these French translations, which does not say anything about the size of such birds, calls them "yllerions" and says "leurs helles sont tranchantes comme rasoirs."[29] Note the spelling of the word for wings: *helles*. Here we may have the origin of Machaut's razor-sharp "pelles," by which he evidently meant "feathers" rather than "wings," since he rhymed it with "elles." A confusion of *p* and *h* is not a particularly common error in medieval manuscript hands, but it is far from impossible.[30]

Machaut's sources were probably multiple and various, but the "fact" about the alerion he gives most attention to, those feathers, seems to be literary (and fantastic) in origin, owing little (if anything) to falconry treatises, let alone experience with the sport. The same is true of Machaut's use of the eagle as one of his four birds. While the eagle is mentioned in various works on falconry, it is only mentioned in passing: eagles were not recommended for use in falconry and were apparently never used for this purpose in western Europe. The Emperor Frederick says: "There are raptors not generally regarded as hunting birds, such, for example, as the higher order of eagles, that, on account of their weight, cannot be held on the fist."[31] The *Roman des deduis* mentions eagles a number of times, but never as birds used in hunting. The sole reference in the *Ménagier* to an eagle says that it can be used to hunt deer, hares, and bustards, but the practical writer of that work recommends that hounds, instead, be used for hunting such large game.[32] In the Near and Far East, where eagles *were* sometimes used to hunt larger game, they had to be carried about on specially constructed frames.[33] Machaut gives no indication that he knew any of this.

Machaut scholars are likely to suspect that the poet's information about falconry owed more to books than to experience, although this is not necessarily the case—he certainly *says* he has hunted in other works in which he is not an unnamed "narrator" (e.g., the *Jugement dou Roy de Navarre*), and he could easily have learned a great deal about falcons from casual acquaintance with falconers. In a period when people thought it perfectly proper to take their falcons to church with them,[34] he would have had plenty of opportunities to become acquainted with falcons and their owners. Brownlee remarks that the "falconry register" "makes extensive use of the vocabulary and constructs of twelfth- and thirteenth-century manuals of falconry considered as a genre" (p. 66), and so it does, especially in relation to the sparrowhawk—but the technical vocabulary of falconry is almost entirely limited to the sparrowhawk sequence, and is remarkably selective even there.

If we examine the technical matters here and compare them with what is found in even the briefest of falconry manuals, we can easily see that Machaut's omissions are as notable as what he includes. Having captured a sparrowhawk by means approved and described in some manuals (means which, as noted above, actually do lend themselves to comparison with the lover's tactics in wooing a lady), the narrator equips her (recall that a falcon is always "she," regardless of French grammatical gender) with leather "longes et prolongues" (1035); these were the shorter and longer leashes known to English falconers of the period as "lunes" and "creance," both of which were basic equipment for training and handling the bird. Machaut does not attempt to equate these with lovers' gifts or in any way integrate them with the "amatory register," which may show commendable restraint on his part. While many ladies might not mind the idea that they can be "lured," they would be unlikely to appreciate the notion of being controlled by a lover's leashes.

But he omits any mention of the tame falcon's other necessary equipment, such as bells and jesses, or the vital necessity of temporarily depriving the newly-taken falcon of sight, either by the use of a hood or by the older expedient of "seeling" the falcon's eyes by sewing down the eyelids.[35] Any falconry manual sufficiently thorough as to explain how to capture a "ramage" hawk[36] also spells out the need for temporary blinding during the training period. It may well be suspected that however "separate" the falconry and amatory "registers" appear to be in this early part of the poem, they are still so closely related that Machaut may well have wanted to avoid the suggestion that a lover should blind his lady's eyes.

The narrator next discusses his care in the proper feeding of his hawk (1042–48), saying he measured her food precisely, gave it at the proper times, and always from his own hand: just as prescribed by the falconry manuals. But he does *not* say that he withheld food to keep the hawk "sharp," as the manuals recommend, and while he makes an allusion to the practice of keeping a newly-caught hawk continually awake for two or three nights to get her to submit to his will, a procedure which was considered essential at that time,[37] he turns this into the need for *him* to suffer sleepless nights, not mentioning the fact that she, too, would be forced to go without sleep. Again, it may well appear that this had to be passed over because it might have suggested tactics unacceptable for a lover courting a noble lady, however well similar tactics served Shakespeare's Petruchio in taming his shrew.

Machaut makes use of some rather more important special vocabulary when he tells us that his hawk was easily "reclaimed" (*fu reclamez*, 1123), the technically correct term for the falcon's return to the falconer in response to his signal (or lure); and he refers to the falconer's call (for which the proper term was *atrais*) when he says that the hawk came "tost ou attrait" (1148).[38] These latter points are of course of first importance to the comparison between falcons and ladies that he is in the process of setting up: the good falcons (and ladies) are those which attend the falconer/lover's signals and can be "reclaimed," unlike the fickle bird/dame whose heart changes, like that of his sparrowhawk after it molted, or, worse, the capricious, unreliable falcon/lady who behaves like Machaut's gerfalcon and thus forfeits all claim to her good reputation.

On the other hand, the technical details about how the falconer persuades the falcon to hunt exactly as he wishes her to hunt, while given at some length in the manuals, are passed over in almost complete silence; they would not have been very helpful to the amatory comparison. For example, any use of an already prepared lady (as a "makefalcon") or a cooperative companion to help the lover "train" his prospective lady certainly sounds like matter more appropriate to a fabliau than to a courtly *dit*.

Machaut, then, selected from the falconry manuals almost nothing beyond those points which he could make use of in drawing his comparisons. He also made highly selective use of bestiary materials and the like for the anecdotes on which his more fantastic "falconry" sections depend.[39] Note that he was drawing from two distinctly different types of literature for these materials, one group of which contained reliable information about the art of falconry as against another which most certainly did not. Thomas of Cantimpré, Vincent of Beauvais and the *Aviarium*, representing "learned" sources, contained a little of both, but neither was likely to have been Machaut's primary source of information about the actual practices of falconers. The striking differences in the nature of Machaut's sources need to be taken into account by all readers because they suggest at least one important reason for the relative brevity of the falconry sequences involving the alerion and the eagle.

That is, while Machaut could easily have learned all he needed to know about how to catch, tame, and care for a sparrowhawk from any of the falconry manuals circulating in the fourteenth century, he could not have learned any special points about hunting with an alerion or an eagle from such sources of information. Brownlee has remarked that the falconry component of the narrative is sharply reduced after the first section, saying that "an important development . . . takes place as the dit progresses: an increasing reduction of the size and importance of the falconry narrative [is] linked to an increasing emphasis placed on the process of comparing, on metaphoric discourse" (p. 77). I suspect that this was precisely why Machaut found it useful to switch from a (reasonably) realistically treated falcon to birds more at home in the pages of a bestiary.

He must indeed have intended to make "the narrator figure" take "on an increasingly artificial cast" (Brownlee, p. 73) at this point; he was thereby enabled to turn attention to the elaborate metaphorical discussion of *fin' amours* which was his true subject (as usual), despite his reiterated claims, as he turns back to the subject of falconry, that he must now get back to this, his "true subject" (e.g., 3657–59: "Si vueil ceste division/ Amener a conclusion,/ Pour au droit procès revenir"). In scanting a narrative tied to realistic descriptions of the falconer's experiences in favor of one loosely related by a number of generally apocryphal stories about birds of prey which he could exploit for their metaphorical relationship to love situations, Machaut was released from the need to keep his metaphorical discourse inconveniently closely tied to the "real life" situation he had chosen to exploit.

Note that there is only one episode in the entire sparrowhawk sequence which could be said to be from bestiary, as against falconry-manual, sources—and that is a very late one, coming *after* the narrator's explanation of how he lost the sparrowhawk. This is the tale of how the sparrowhawk captures a small bird to keep her feet warm at night, but then lets it go free and guards it against other possible predators on the following day, which Machaut gives as an example of the hawk's courtesy, and, inevitably, the courtesy of a lady who does not harm the lover's heart which has in some sense warmed *her* through a (metaphorical) cold night. The story is a widely circulated one, although in England it was told of the merlin, not the sparrowhawk.[40] Everything else Machaut has told us specifically about the sparrowhawk, up to the point where he tells us how she was lost after her molting (ll. 1211–61), can be seen as perfectly plausible "realism," in complete conformity with the falconry manuals.

The only point on which we might question his knowledgeability about falcons this far would be why, if he knew that much about sparrowhawks, he did not anticipate inevitable difficulties, and the need for re-training, when his hawk finished her molt. But hereafter, for a good deal more than 2,000 lines of the poem, and thus for about half its total length, he has nothing at all substantive to tell about the two "falcons" who form the basis of the "narrative" (as against the metaphorical comparison to love situations) except similar tales about such birds in general, mostly drawn from the kind of material we associate with the bestiaries. Brownlee is absolutely right when he notes that what the narrator tells us about the alerion describes "the alerion in general (rather than the particular one who figures in the narrative episodes" (p. 75) and that most of what is said about eagles similarly "concerns eagles in general, rather than the particular eagle" of the falconry narrative (p. 80).

But, as I have remarked above, Machaut could not have found out anything about the character traits of eagles as observed by falconers since there was no such material; nor could he have found much about alerions. The sparrowhawk was enough to set up the frame of reference; in turning next to two other birds of prey with a literary reputation for excellence and nobility, Machaut was able to take advantage of the tales told of them as parallels to excellent traits in noble ladies: and note that he used these tales as selectively as he did technical details of falconry, choosing only those which might usefully form the basis of amatory comparison.

No wonder, then, that the "falconry" content in the alerion and eagle episodes is almost entirely limited to the basic point that they were good falcons in that they cooperated with, and promptly returned to, their handler, but that eventually they were lost to him. And no wonder he does not tell us exactly *how* those two birds were lost to him. If he had done so, he would have had to suggest that they were less than faultless: the sparrowhawk is seriously undermined as an ideal in that her change of coat became a change of heart when she turned away from the "lover" (*bons amis*, 1247) with whom she had previously cooperated enthusiastically. No doubt this is why the bird which returns in the final sequence could not be the sparrowhawk; nor could it be the gerfalcon, since the reasons for that bird's loss are even more discreditable.

Brownlee describes the gerfalcon episode as "the most abbreviated version in the *dit* of the basic model established in the esprivier segment" (p. 85); he thinks it has a "somewhat comic air that functions to undercut still further the lyrico-narrative 'experience' ostensibly recounted in the falconry register" (p. 88). But what this sequence is in greatest danger of undermining is the amatory parallel: it concerns the bad falcon/worthless lady, and if it had not been kept shorter than the other sections it might have given an overly misogynistic emphasis. The function of the gerfalcon section is, however, basic to the plan Machaut indicates at the beginning of the poem when he sets forth his subject as, first, four points necessary for happiness in this world. As I have suggested elsewhere, the four birds correspond to the four "points," with the gerfalcon illustrating the negative effects of behaving in a manner contrary to what is dictated by the first three.[41] That she did not "eschuer tout le contraire" (line 14) is emphasized by the reiteration of the word *contraire* four times in the section leading up to a description of her misbehaviour (4028, 4039, 4047, and 4060). Since this narrative sequence (3872–4248) is, then, entirely negative, there is further reason why it should be the shortest of the four.

It is not one of a "program of variations on the model plot pattern"[42] but a necessary reversal of it, which was part of the plan from the beginning, providing an anticipated contrast. It is true that the "falconry" sections dealing with the sparrowhawk, the alerion, and the eagle constitute a threefold repetition of the "good" pattern which may seem more repetitious than readers of 500 or so years later find desirable, and our problem may, in part, be blamed on the poet in that he did not succeed in differentiating clearly between behavior representing "bien penser" and "bien dire" as against "bien faire" (line 13). Nevertheless, there are some real differences between those three sections, as Machaut moved increasingly from the initial analogy between the falconer's relationship with the falcon and turned to more fantastic narratives drawn from traditional sources.

If Machaut had worked out the falconry parallel with more attention to the possibilities of "realism" in the model throughout, he might have been more successful with later critics, paradoxical as this may sound when so many critics have expressed doubt about the appropriateness of the falconry nexus as a parallel to the discussion of *fin' amours*. But the problem may well be that he has distracted the critics' attention from even considering the possibilities of falconry by constantly increasing the dose of learned fantasy, so that by the time he gets back to falconry the basis of his analogy has been forgotten, and his poem seems to have joined the more familiar (to medievalists, anyway) world of bestiary allegory.

Note that while the alerion is presented as a more exotic creature altogether than a sparrowhawk, she is treated in a vaguely realistic way; no doubt vagueness was unavoidable because available descriptions of the presumed species gave Machaut very little to work with (even if he wanted to, which is another question). The only notably non-realistic departure is that concerning the significance of the alerion's peculiar feathers, which, like the tale of the sparrowhawk's captive, is the only more-or-less "learned" anecdote concerning the species. But when Machaut gets to the eagle, his entire purpose would seem to have been to capitalize on the eagle's traditional and literary reputation, which had nothing whatsoever to do with the practices of falconry.

Thus when Machaut returns to the problems of the falconer as the basis of his narrative in the gerfalcon sequence, the reader—especially a modern reader who has come to the poem without much knowledge of falconry—may well have lost the thread and not even realize that what we see here *is* a return to the basic analogy. Medieval readers would at least have been likely to know that when a falcon turns away from the "proper" quarry at which the falconer has directed her and flies toward another prey of a kind undesirable to her master (an action known to modern falconers as "checking"), this is unmitigated disaster, demonstrating the worst fault a falconer can find in an otherwise properly trained bird. Whether or not Machaut was actually a falconer, he must certainly have heard of, or read about, such problems.[43]

Just as reasonably realistic descriptions of the falcon's cooperation with the falconer in the case of the sparrowhawk, and, to a lesser extent, the alerion, served as parallels to the behavior of praiseworthy loved ladies, so this example of a misbehaving falcon provides an appropriate parallel to a lady who betrays her lover in a similar manner. Shakespeare uses the same metaphor when he has Othello accuse Desdemona of being just such an unsatisfactory falcon (III.3.260–263); but, of course, Shakespeare was writing a tragedy, not a *dit amoureux*. In the case of the *Alerion*'s gerfalcon, the usual *fin' amours* code is clearly being subverted. Machaut is giving an example to justify the point he also made in the *Jugement dou roy de Behaigne*, that a bad woman should be, as Othello put it, "whistled off" like a bad falcon,[44] just as, on the other hand, a good one is worth any amount of trouble to keep by one's side—one of the principal points of the *Alerion*'s epilogue, which ends with the narrator's vow to love his alerion for life.

The falconry parallel gave Machaut a strikingly appropriate vehicle for the message "But she wol love hym, lat hym love another,"[45] a doctrine Machaut has attributed to "Amours" throughout the poem—at least, in regard to falcons. But this amendment to the code of *fin' amours* was certainly not all that he had in mind in writing this poem; he needed the more fantastic component too, for reasons suggested above, among other considerations. I do not intend to make understanding Machaut seem simple. That would be, to say the least, misleading.

NOTES

1. Robert Bossuat, *Le Moyen age* (Paris: Presses de l'imprimerie moderne, 1955), p. 191.
2. Summarized by Florence McCulloch, *Medieval Latin and French Bestiaries* (Chapel Hill: Univ. of North Carolina Press, rev. ed., 1962), pp.123–24. The *Aviarium*, now credited to Hugo of Folieto (see McCulloch, p. 211), is printed in Migne, *PL* CLXXVII, as the first book of the *De bestiis* formerly attributed to Hugo of St. Victor; the chapters on hawks are 12–19. A critical edition and English translation of this work by Willene B. Clark has recently appeared see *The Medieval Books of Birds: Hugh of Fouilloy's 'Aviarium'* (Binghamton: MRTS 80, 1992). That Machaut may indeed have drawn on this work is suggested by several correspondences; the question is discussed in the introduction to the translation of the poem by C. B. Hieatt and Minnette Gaudet *The Tale of the Alerion* (Toronto: Univ. of Toronto Press, 1994).
3. Note that falcon and hawk are generally interchangeable terms: medieval terminology was confused and variable, but today the term falcon is used for a "long-winged hawk." Eagles are hawks which do not fall into either the long-winged or the short-winged categories.
4. Especially in the case of the "faithless" falcon of *SqT*.
5. 3. 1779, 1784; all quotations from Chaucer are from *The Riverside Chaucer*, ed. Larry D. Benson, et al. (Boston: Houghton Mifflin, 1987).
6. See, e.g., the falconry manual in the 14th-century *Ménagier de Paris*, ed. Jérôme Pichon (Paris: Société des Bibliophiles françois, 1846; repr. Geneva: Slatkine, n.d.; the falconry text is in vol. 2) and Georgine E. Brereton and Janet M. Ferrier (Oxford: Oxford Univ. Press, 1981); unless otherwise noted, page references herein are to this latter edition: p. 163.
7. *Guy of Warwick*'s Felice is said to be "as demure . . . /As girfauk, or fawkon to lure,/That oute of muwe were drawe"; ed. Julius Zupitza (London: E.E.T.S. o.s. 42, 1883) p. 7.

8. For a discussion of the uses of falconry in this play, see C. B. Hieatt, "Stooping at a Simile: Some Literary Uses of Falconry," *PLL* 19 (1983), pp. 357–79. To summarize the most important points as briefly as possible, Petruchio's method of taming Kate is, as he states himself, the classic method for taming a falcon: he deprives her of both food and sleep, doing without both himself at the same time in such a way that she does not realize what he is up to, and always treating her with what appears to be "kindness": a hawk cannot be openly forced into obedience and must perceive its compliance with the will of the falconer as voluntary, as Katherine perceives her capitulation to Petruchio. Both Kate and her sister Bianca are referred to in hawking metaphors throughout the play, and in the final scene Petruchio wins a wager against his fellow bridegrooms by dispatching Kate, who, unlike the other young women has come at once when summoned, to round up the lesser "birds" and bring them to the husband she refers to as her "keeper."

9. Such as William Calin, who remarks (justly enough), "A modern reader finds it difficult to enjoy a love story narrated in terms of falconry; he simply does not have enough knowledge of, or interest in, or emotional attachment to 'l'art de chasse aux oiseaux' to react to the tale as poetry"; *A Poet at the Fountain* (Lexington: Univ. of Kentucky Press, 1974), pp. 100–101. However, in the last decade the tide may have turned: see, for example, Alexandre Leupin, "The Powerlessness of Writing: Guillaume de Machaut, the Gorgon, and *Ordenance*," trans. Peggy McCracken, *Yale French Studies* 70 (1986), 127–49. Leupin devotes several pages to the *Alerion*, exploring its use of birds as symbols of words (among other things).

10. The *Ménagier de Paris* warns that the trainer must not upset the hawk in any way, "car se vous le courroucez une seule foiz ja puis ne vous aimera" (p. 149). The *Traité de fauconnerie* of Adam des Aigles warns, right at the beginning, "Fauconnerie vielt que luy soyez doulx et courtoys et debonnaire": ed. Åke Blomqvist (Karlshamn, 1966), p. 22. Medieval, renaissance, and even modern falconry accounts are full of such statements; for example, T. H. White's account of training a goshawk, which points out that one must never try to punish a hawk, includes many references to the love and courtesy between the keeper and the hawk: see *The Goshawk* (London: Jonathan Cape, 1951).

11. Quotations from the *Alerion* are from the *Oeuvres*, ed. E. Hoepffner (Paris: Société des anciens textes français, 1908–11), vol. 2.

12. "Il ne la fait que devourer,/Car il ne la scet savourer," 2871–2.
13. These "N'ont chose qui bien ne leur plaise" (2899); if they do not gain *merci*, "il prennent substance" from Love and Hope (2900–01).
14. See *The Art of Falconry*, ed. and trans. Casey A. Wood and Marjorie Fyfe (Stanford: Stanford Univ. Press, 1943; repr. Boston: Charles T. Branford Co., and London: Oxford Univ. Press, 1955), 1.50; references to the translated text, as against editorial material, are given by Book and Chapter numbers). In the Old French translation ed. Gustaf Holmer, *Traductions en vieux français du "De arte venandi cum avibus" de l'empereur Frédéric II de Hohenstaufen* (Lund: Bloms, 1960), the word is given as "coutiaus" (p. 84); this edition contains only Book 2 and is thus of limited usefulness. (Note also that the chapter numbers are not always the same.)
15. Ed. Gunnar Tilander (Paris: Société des anciens textes français, 1932), 1, pp. 173–74 and 228.
16. Ed. Åke Blomqvist (Karlshamn, 1951); on the author's expertise in falconry, see p. 9.
17. 1 (Paris: Vieweg, 1881), p. 218.
18. The relevant passage is the beginning of the book X, Ch. 3, of the *Natural History* (not X.6, as stated in W. L. Bevan and H. W. Phillott, *An Essay in Illustration of the Hereford Mappa Mundi* (London, 1873), pp. 30–31). The phrase printed as "eadem in Valeria" in editions of the 19th century, and earlier, appears as "leporaria" ("hare-eagle") in recent editions, but the "valeria" reading was obviously unquestioned for many centuries before ours.
19. Hoepffner (p. lxviii) reports that this is in Ch. 21; he was using a different edition of the *Spec. nat.* (Venice, 1591), but I suspect 'xix' has been miscopied as 'xxi' since the other chapter numbers he cites correspond with those in the editions I have used: Strassburg, 1481 (?), and Douai, 1624.
20. "Serenitate tamen aeris aliquando videtur, et hoc ab illis, qui visum habent acutum," 'However, in good weather it is sometimes seen by those who have acute vision'; *Liber de Natura Rerum*, ed. H. Boese (Berlin and New York: Walter de Gruyter, 1973), I, Book 5, Ch. 16, p. 185.
21. ("Physiologus says that the alerion has great lordship over all the other birds of the world, and its color resembles fire. And its wings are as cutting as a razor; and it is little and small, and it is larger than an eagle."), ed. Charles Cahier and Arthur M. Martin (who

refer to the author as "Pierre le Picard"), *Mélanges d'Archéologie, d'histoire et de littérature sur le moyen âge* (Paris, 1868), vol. ii, p. 162; Guy Mermier is currently preparing a new edition: see Mermier's "The Phoenix," *Beasts and Birds of the Middle Ages*, ed. Clark and McMunn, n. 88, pp. 84–85. On this bestiary, see also Bevan and Phillott (cited in note 18), pp. 30–31.

22. It is the primary source of the *Bestiaire d'amour* of Richard de Fournival: see McCulloch, pp. 62–69 and 197–98. This *Bestiaire*'s reference to an alerion has been frequently cited, e.g., by Hoepffner (p. lxviii) and Tobler-Lommatzch; but in fact Richard skipped the account of the alerion. His reference to an alerion is only a phrase or two in his account of the "serre," a sort of flying fish which follows boats, which he says is as swift as an alerion chasing a crane ("se lance parmi la mer plus tost ke alerions ne vole a grue, ki a le pene tranchante comme raisoirs"; ed. Cesare Segre (Milan and Naples: Riccardo Ricciardi, 1957), p. 78. The phrase "ki a le pene tranchante comme rasoirs," 'which has feathers as sharp as razors,' is obviously confusing, since the antecedent could be cranes, and is reported to be missing from three of the manuscripts. In any case, it is obviously unlikely that this particular bestiary was a prime source for Machaut's information about alerions, since this is only a passing reference.

23. The "moral" is a long one, most of which is not really relevant to Machaut's use of those cutting wings; see Cahier and Martin, p. 163. The razor-sharp feathers of Machaut's alerion are also *wing* feathers, despite the occasional confusions of Machaut scholars on this point: Kevin Brownlee, for example, translates *pelles* as "tail feathers": *Poetic Identity in Guillaume de Machaut* (Madison: Univ. of Wisconsin Press, 1984), p. 78. Machaut specifically says that the "pelles" are "parmis ses eles" (2553).

24. Unless we see the "aelion" described by Thomas and Vincent as an example: and note that they did not say that this bird had razor-sharp wings, etc.

25. II. 456. Hoepffner notes this and the account in the *Bestiaire d'amour* as the only sources he had seen for the alerion's sharp feathers (note 3, p. lxviii).

26. See Friedrich Zarnke, *Der Priester Johannes* (Leipzig, 1875 and 1876, repr. Hildesheim: Georg Olms, 1980), p. 911. 27. See Zarnke, pp. 950, 960, and 997.

28. The only medieval reference to alerions found in an English (or Anglo-Norman) source appears to be that on the Hereford map

(cf. n. 18, above). For further information on the French "Prester John" version, see Vsevolod Slessarev, *Prester John: The Letter and the Legend* (Minneapolis: Univ. of Minnesota Press, 1959), which includes a facsimile of a fifteenth-century printed edition between pp. 66 and 67. This version's description of the alerion is identical to that printed by Denis (see below), except that the spelling for 'wings' is a more conventional "elles."

29. Ferdinand Denis, ed., in *Le monde enchanté: cosmographie et histoire naturelle fantastique du moyen âge* (Paris, 1845; repr. New York: Burt Franklin, n.d.), p. 188.
30. None of the dictionaries of Old French mention Machaut's use of the word "pelle." They all give, under this spelling, only referrals to other words: Tobler-Lommatzsch refers us to 'päele' (pot) and 'perle' (pearl), for both of which 'pelle' is an alternate spelling; Godefroy refers us to 'pelleterie' (fur) and 'pesle' (bolt), and Greimas to 'pesle' and 'perle.' Actually, Machaut's "pelles" must be Modern French 'pelle,' shovel or scoop, in the sense of what English speakers call a "pie-slice" or "cake server," which is one of the senses of 'pelle' in Modern French.
31. 2.2; the Old French translation does not limit the comment to "the higher orders": it says, "Des oisiaus de proie li home n'usent point, ainsi com toutes meniers d'aigles, qui pour lor pois ne sont pas abiles ne ligiers a porteir" (2.3, p. 65).
32. Pichon adds a note pointing out that it is dubious that such game as deer was ever hunted with any variety of hunting bird in France; he remarks that "L'aigle n'a donc jamais été employé habituellement dans la fauconnerie" (p. 321).
33. See Wood and Fyfe, pp. xl and 525.
34. See the *Ménagier de Paris*, and Pichon's note (which cites the *Roman de deduis* and other evidence), p. 296.
35. Many manuals explain how to do this; the *Traité de fauconnerie* of Adam des Aigles simply takes it for granted: without having told us how to seel the ramage hawk's eyes, he warns strongly against unseeling too soon: "Se voustre oyseau est ramage, aprenez le bien et ne le dessillez point jusques atant qu'il mengeue bien sur le poing et saiche bien aler sur la main par luy" (ed. Åke Blomqvist, Karlshamn, 1966, p. 22).
36. One which had left the nest to hunt for herself but which was still in her first year and had not yet molted; there are good reasons behind Machaut's "narrator" voice for preferring such a hawk (ll. 305–18), which would have begun to learn how to hunt, but not

be so well accustomed to caring for herself as to be completely unamenable to human assistance/interference.
37. See, e.g., *Modus* 1.180.
38. Note his application of the same vocabulary to a lover and his lady throughout: e.g., lines 207, 844, 2568.
39. For example, he prefers the distinctly eccentric report that the eagle does not hesitate to take away the prey of lesser birds to the information in the *Roman des deduis* (credited to Pliny) that the eagle courteously shares his prey with lesser birds (lines 5969–89).
40. Cf. Hieatt, "Stooping at a Simile," p. 348.
41. See " 'Une autre fourme': Guilliaume de Machaut and the Dream Vision Form," *Chaucer Review* 14 (1980), 97–115 (especially p. 112). Observations on the possibility of a numerical structure related to fours (and possibly threes) appear in our translation of the poem; these are too complex to touch upon here. We suspect that Machaut was up to something characteristically tricky—as he was in his obviously numerical signature.
42. Brownlee, p. 85.
43. Emperor Frederick II discusses this problem in considerable detail; e.g., 5.17; p. 339 in Wood/Fyfe translation.
44. "Reason," seconded by the royal judge, gives advice to this effect in the *Jugement de roy de Behaigne*, lines 1744–1988; pp. 122–32 in *Oeuvres*, ed. Hoepffner, vol. 1.
45. *PF* 567; some Chaucerians will, of course, think that this means Chaucer thought it a "goosish" idea.

Murray L. Brown

Poets, Peace, the Passion, and the Prince: Eustache Deschamps's "Ballade to Chaucer"

Eustache Deschamps (b. 1346) is best known to readers of English poetry for his ballade addressed to, and in praise of Geoffrey Chaucer:

> O Socrates plains de philosophie,
> Seneque en meurs et Anglux en practique,
> Ovides grans en ta poeterie,
> Bries en parler, saiges en rethorique,
> Aigles treshaulz, qui par ta theorique
> Enlumines le regne d'Eneas,
> L'Isle aux Geans, ceuls de Bruth, et qui as
> Semé les fleurs et planté le rosier,
> Aux ignorans de la langue pandras,
> Grant translateur, noble Geffroy Chaucier.

Tu es d'amours mondains Dieux en Albie:
Et de la Rose, en la terre Angelique,
Qui d'Angela saxonne, est puis flourie
Angleterre, d'elle ce nom s'applique
Le derrenier en l'ethimologique;
En bon anglès le livre translatas;
Et un vergier ou du plant demandas
De ceuls qui font pour eulx auctorisier,
A ja longtemps que tu edifas
Grand translateur, noble Geffroy Chaucier.

A toy pour ce de la fountaine Helye
Requier avoir un buvraige authentique,
Dont la doys est du tout en ta baillie,
Pour rafrener d'elle ma soif ethique,
Qui en Gaule seray paralitique
Jusques a ce que tu m'abuveras.
Eustaces sui, qui de mon plant aras:
Mais pran en gré les euvres d'escolier
Que par Clifford de moy avoir pourras,
Grand translateur, noble Gieffroy Chaucier.

L'ENVOY

Poete hault, loenge destruye,
En ton jardin ne seroye qu'ortie:
Considere ce que j'ay dit premier,
Ton noble plant, ta douce mélodie.
Mais pour sçavoir, de rescripre te prie,
Grant translateur, noble Geffroy Chaucier.[1]

Although the influence of Deschamps's writing on Chaucer's has been explored, most notably by John Lowes, no one has explained why Deschamps wrote this poem or when it was written. Although Lowes suggests that it comes from the period 1384–90, he favors placing the poem's composition in the mid 1380s.[2] The poem probably dates, however, from Sir Lewis Clifford's diplomatic mission to the French court in 1391; and the demonstration of this date is relevant to the understanding of Deschamps's rhetoric, of the praise he heaps on Chaucer, and of the poem's probable reception at the English court. Given the war and the relationship of the English and French monarchies, it is remarkable that this poem ever came to exist. The fact that it does exist raises questions concerning the foundation of a new relationship between the two kingdoms; more importantly, it addresses the relationship between the two poets and their several patrons-princes-pupils.

Elsewhere in this volume Douglas Kelly considers the patron as donor, as poet, as master, lady/love, and finally as pupil. This final category is what must ultimately concern us here because although Deschamps is working on the king's behalf and interest, his object is to instruct both monarchs. He waits their pleasure in these matters—until the prince is disposed to counseled instruction. Deschamps's "Ballade to Chaucer" is unusual because patronage appears to be either very distant or entirely absent. On the surface, Deschamps writes as a poet to a master poet on the subjects and business of poetry. Given that for his patron's benefit Deschamps had often composed martial verse, it is intriguing to here find him lauding England's most prominent court poet, praising the greatness of his genius, but more largely, applauding the society which fosters and appreciates it. A survey of Deschamps's writings reveals that the wishes and policies of his patron usually inform the poet's subjects. Deschamps would not make an ovation, such as we have here, without the support of the highest patronage. To date the poem is to seek explanation for its rhetoric, and it is therefore necessary to discover when the position of Deschamps's patronage softened toward the English, why it changed, and why it hardened again. My thesis is that, though Chaucer and Deschamps may have known one another as early as 1360, this poem was occasioned by their association (in the late 1380s, early '90s) with the Order of the Passion of Jesus Christ.[3] This is the crusading order which finally provided the French and English nobility with both the foundation and the agenda to end The Hundred Years War.

On the public, or rather, on the courtly level, this is an occasional poem, and these poets are acting as high-level, cultural diplomats; Deschamps praises Chaucer for having translated and transplanted the *Roman de la Rose* in Albie. He therefore applauds Chaucer for having taken a step toward reconciliation (the underlying assertion being that if there is an increased harmony of artistic and cultural interest between the courts then genuine peace is sure to follow).

On the personal and private level, an exploration of the poets' possible acquaintance is in order. Although Deschamps and Clifford may have crossed paths on several occasions during 1390–91,[4] no one has taken seriously Oliver Emerson's suggestion that Deschamps and Chaucer met in Reims during Chaucer's captivity.[5] Chaucer, at the approximate age of twenty, saw his first military service in France and was captured with Richard Stury by the French near Reims in early 1360.[6] He was ransomed for the sum of £16 on March 1, 1360.[7] After his release he returned to England (probably in May, 1360), but visited France again the following year as a courier to Calais. Significantly, Deschamps was in Reims assisting in the defense of that city, and in the company of his famous mentor, Guillaume de Machaut, during the same time that Chaucer and Stury were captive there.[8] Since the Exchequer issued payment for Chaucer's release on the first of March, a transaction which required some considerable time for conveying messages, Chaucer had probably been held for several weeks, perhaps longer. Because Deschamps was present in Reims and witnessed the siege,[9] he was probably aware of Chaucer's presence, especially in view of the relatively small size of the city and its embattled state.[10] Stury was a well known courtier and probably familiar with Machaut's compositions, and Chaucer, who knew Machaut's work by this time, may well have been the kind of company Machaut and Deschamps would have sought. Though Deschamps and Chaucer were serving concurrently as soldiers, it is equally certain that both these young men were seeking poetic and courtly repute. By 1369–70 Chaucer was already writing English poetry (most notably, *The Book of the Duchess*), and his French poems probably date from at least a decade earlier. Since, in the course of their careers, neither Chaucer nor Deschamps exhibited any social diffidence whatsoever, it is difficult to believe that Chaucer would not have taken advantage of this opportunity to meet with the Europe's foremost poet and composer. Thus, when Deschamps gave his ballade to Sir Lewis Clifford, who delivered it to Chaucer, probably for a reading before the court, it is also probable that Deschamps was not only corresponding with a great poet, thinker, and his recognized counterpart, but with an acquaintance of thirty years.[11]

The two youths may also have met in England during the fulfilment of obligations imposed by the Treaty of Brétigny (1360–62). Deschamps's whereabouts are unknown in the year 1361. In 1360, he accompanied Isabella of France (daughter of Jean II) to Italy where she met with her future husband, Galeas Visconti; Deschamps did not remain with Isabella for her entire Italian sojourn and quickly returned to France. While Deschamps's whereabouts from this point through 1362 are unknown, they probably relate to the exchange of Jean II for several peers of France. The English and the French agreed that King Jean, captured by the English at Poitiers in 1356, would be released if the dukes of Anjou, Berry, Burgundy, and Orléans and a number of other influential men would take his place.[12] The 1360 exchange provided that the hostages would be changed on a rotating basis until Jean's ransom had been paid, but unfortunately for Philippe d'Orléans and the others, no one else was willing to replace them, and they remained in England for two years, at considerable expense to themselves and to the French people in general.[13] The dukes negotiated their own release for the sum of 200,000 gold florins in November of 1362 and were then allowed to move to Calais until other terms were met.[14]

Philippe d'Orléans was certainly not mistreated during his stay in England and probably took part in court society much after the fashion of his king, and at his own expense.[15] He took sixteen personal servants and a retinue of sixty with him to England,[16] and the young Deschamps was probably in Orléans's train—he was a squire in the Duke's household.[17] The nature of his hurried visit to Italy—the outright sale of Isabelle to the highest bidder, the Visconti of Milan, the princess's illness,[18] and the surrender of his patron, Philippe d'Orléans—made his return to France all the more urgent. If he accompanied the duke, or followed the household, he may have had the opportunity to make the acquaintance of Geoffrey Chaucer, a young poet of his own age, at the English court.[19] Jean had been lodged in

Lancaster's own Savoy, a house with which Chaucer was certainly familiar. It is also obvious that Deschamps must have developed a sophisticated command of English at some point before he composed his "Ballade de Chaucer," and the possibility he stayed in England with his patron offers an explanation.[20]

The conjectural foundation of this relationship is supported by remarkable circumstantial parallels in the poets' lives, careers, and positions: Deschamps and Chaucer were of precisely the same generation; both were witnesses to the ongoing war since childhood; both were attached to the households of dukes who urgently sought to establish their own dynasties; both had access to the political debates of the day; both may have been students of law; both were involved in the siege of Reims; both participated in the peace negotiations; both had been involved in marriage negotiations with Visconti Italy for the houses to which they were attached; and, both travelled to Italy in royal service. Both men were powerful satirists, called upon at a crucial moment to influence the course their nations chose to pursue. The Order of the Passion facilitated this dialogue largely because it recognized a threat from the east. While these early encounters remain uncertain, by the time his "Ballade to Chaucer" was composed, Deschamps was probably attracted to Chaucer's work more by virtue of Lancastrian association with The Order of the Passion of Jesus Christ and its agenda than he was by Chaucer's poetic genius. To my knowledge, there exists no hard evidence that links our two poets in the 1360s. This ballade was written not only to renew, or to re-establish a former acquaintance, it was written to facilitate peace and the defense of Europe.

The Order's membership included the most powerful dukes of both England and France, Richard II, and Charles VI.[21] It also included supporters and members from Spain, Savoy, Aragon, Gascony, Navarre, Germany, Scotland, and Lombardy. Simply stated, the Order was dedicated to the restoration of peace in Christendom, ending the schism, and mounting a unified crusade against the Ottoman Turks who now genuinely threatened all of eastern Europe and valuable commercial trade centers such as Cyprus. It was the Order of the Passion which apparently led to the renewed acquaintance that both poets and both courts enjoyed in the 1390s.

The Order's main proponent and chief organizer, Philippe de Mézières, was formerly a soldier under Lucchino Visconti, Lord of Milan.[22] He was Chancellor under Peter of Lusignan, King of Cyprus, and accompanied that monarch on a tour of several European courts (1362–65) with the aim of raising a crusade to halt further Turkish encroachment. In 1364, he witnessed Charles V's coronation at Reims and by that time had surely made a great impression upon both Machaut and Deschamps. Machaut later based his epic poem, *La Prise d'Alexandrie* (c. 1370), on Peter Lusignan's campaign of 1365 and he was obviously an ardent supporter of Peter's crusading mission, transmitting that enthusiasm to Deschamps all through the mid-sixties.[23] Having served Charles V, Philippe acted as tutor to Charles VI and continued to advise the young king.[24] During the 1380–90's Mézières, continued to be a prolific and persuasive writer on behalf of the Order.

Mézières's emissary in England, Robert the Hermit, was an able representative and a career diplomat.[25] His efforts in England were enhanced, no doubt, by Oton de Granson, "Chevalier d'onneur du roy d'Engleterre et du Duke de Lencastre," who, along with John de Blaisy and Louis de Giac, had sworn support for the Order at the conclusion of the peace negotiations of 1385.[26] These four are aptly referred to by Mézières as his "four evangelists."[27] Granson certainly had to be a central figure in any relationship between Chaucer and Deschamps simply because his large circle included both poets. Chaucer, who imitated his Valentine poetry,[28] refers to him in "The Complaint of Venus" as the "flour of hem that make in France," and he must also be counted among Deschamps's favored contacts.[29]

Granson greatly admired Machaut, as did Chaucer; in addition, Granson had many opportunities to meet and speak with Deschamps. It is likely that Deschamps met Granson through his mentor, Machaut, and it is certain that Granson and Deschamps were already well acquainted by 1384[30] when they travelled together to Calais (during the first peace of Leulinghem) where Deschamps was to inspect a fortress.[31] During this visit, and while in Granson's company, Deschamps was detained by English soldiers because, unlike his companion, he possessed no safe-conduct pass. Granson evidently saved him from incarceration. Deschamps's rondeau, addressed to Granson, recounts the tale (*Oeuvres* IV, 55), and dates from immediately before Granson's enrollment in the Order of the Passion and before the break-up of the negotiations the following year.[32]

An associate of Granson's in the Order was Sir Lewis Clifford, a close associate of Chaucer's and a Chamber knight who served on diplomatic missions during the critical period of the organization of the Leulinghem conferences of the early 1390s.[33] Clifford is known to have travelled with Thomas Percy to the French court in 1391 (undoubtedly on the Order's business) and Richard issued a letter of credence for their safe passage in February. He was a friend of Granson's and many other of Chaucer's friends, such as Boucicaut, Philip de la Vache, and Guichard d'Angle.[34] Clifford was a trusted envoy for the two courts, as well as a naturally adept diplomat.

If the date for Deschamps's "Ballade to Chaucer" is 1391, it was probably part of a cultural exchange which accompanied, and to some degree facilitated, both the coming peace negotiations and the royal marriage. The opportunity for such a dialogue was provided by the Order of the Passion, which encouraged much gift-giving between the courts during this period (e.g., exchanging of tapestries); and this is probably when the Wilton Diptych was executed, a painting clearly illustrating the Order's agenda.[35] It is likely that the Ballade and numerous other works were part of a cultural exchange, an informal dialogue between the two courts; and, as the conferences approached and hopes for peace became greater, so did the gifts attending them. The exchanging of gifts probably explains not only when, but why Deschamps received what he did of Chaucer's poetry and why he offers his own plants for the poet's garden of verses. The later date (1390–91) not only allows Clifford ample opportunity to come into contact with Deschamps, it allows Deschamps sufficient time to alter his responses and to speak respectfully of the English.

Deschamps's patron, Louis d'Orléans, did not embrace the Order until late 1389 (see pp. 201–02).[36] A decade earlier Deschamps temporarily used his poetic talents for Enguerran de Coucy and his *Ordre de la Couronne* which was dedicated to winning the Imperial crown for its founder.[37] Deschamps was surely cognizant of similar ambitions on the part of the leading members of The Order of the Passion, and perhaps questioned its usefulness. It appears he did not address the Order's full agenda until after his patron initially promised his support to it and the support of Royal and ducal support on both sides of the Channel appeared established and assured. Indeed, unless Deschamps already knew Chaucer and counted him as a friend, there would be little reason for him to write a ballade to Chaucer in the mid 1380s, and little political reason before the very late 1380s, when constructive dialogue between the courts resumed.

Deschamps begins the "Ballade" by calling Chaucer a "Socrates full of wisdom, a Seneca in uprightness of life, an Aulus Gellius in practical affairs, an Ovid great in thy poetic lore" (see n. 1), a man "wise in the arts of the versifier," and "a lofty eagle (genius)." Chaucer would not have deserved praise as a serious, "philosophical" poet before the production of *The Parlement of Foules* (probably from the early 1380s).[38] From his considerable distance, he demonstrates a knowledge of Chaucer and his work beyond what we might expect. His allusion to the eagle appears to indicate he had seen Chaucer's *Parlement of Foules*, but as I shall show, Deschamps wrote disparagingly of English well into the 1380s. However, if the date is 1391 (or any time after 1385–86), the poem, in mentioning the matter of Troy, probably refers to *Troilus* as well as the *Roman de la Rose. Troilus*, like Gower's *Vox Clamantis*, is based on the notion that England is a "New Troy," descended through Aeneas and Brutus from the old Trojans. Deschamps calls Chaucer a "mundane god of Love," or Cupid, probably drawing this image from Chaucer's reference to himself: "For I, that God of Loves servantz serve" (*Troilus*, 1.15), a servant of the servants of love. In any case, Deschamps clearly indicates that he has been aware of Chaucer's poetry for some considerable, but undetermined length of time: "A ja long temps que tu edifias" (1.19).

Deschamps's praise of Chaucer's translation of *The Romaunt of the Rose* is also significant in view of the debate surrounding the authorship of the extant Middle English translation. While it seems unlikely that Chaucer would have sent an unfinished manuscript to Deschamps, it is possible that the poem was produced, or possibly finished, by a number of English poets and that Deschamps here praises specific sections that Chaucer wrote. Chaucer may have only translated, or interpreted, the *Rose*'s first portion, condensing it and making far more effective headway in only seventeen hundred lines when compared to the author of Fragment B, who adds nearly four thousand more. Chaucer is retransmitting the poem. This explains, perhaps, why Deschamps praises Chaucer as being brief in expression and wise in rhetoric. A joint effort and presentation of the complete poem, however, would be in the spirit of reconciliation and in keeping with the established practice of exchanging gifts between the two courts.

Alternately, the French poet may not be referring to a literal translation of the *Rose* at all, but to the *Troilus* as a transformation of its ideas and philosophic assumptions.[39] The fact that Deschamps is evidently reciprocating Chaucer's gift and sends plants of his own for the poet's garden of verses is a clear indication that this poem is not an isolated encounter; rather it implies an ongoing poetic correspondence before a courtly audience: shared tastes and friendships soothe differences and decrease political distance.

David Lampe has provided a persuasive explication of Deschamps's "Ballade to Chaucer"; he stresses the poem's public nature, its fine show of courtly erudition, and playfulness (see n. 11). In contrast, Jenkins finds the poem to be stiff and forced. I feel that it speaks both on a personal level—albeit an intellectual one—and on a courtly or ceremonial level. Deschamps sets this personal tone with his use of "tu," the familiar address, and much could be made of this point alone. Jenkins questions Deschamps's usage and calls it "high brow." While he does not point to this *faux pas* as justification for his rather cynical reading, it does indeed darken his interpretation of the poem. Perhaps Jenkins's reading would be justifiable were there no evidence of previous relationship between the two poets, but, even if the two were not acquainted from their youth, there is textual evidence that Deschamps was long familiar with Chaucer's work (line 19, above), and Deschamps most probably uses the familiar pronoun simply because he feels at ease when he writes to his English counterpart.[40]

To balance this personal touch, and bowing to the poem's public function, Deschamps flatters Clifford, a well-known figure at both courts, and alludes to his amorous reputation. Admittedly, he first refers to England as "L'Isle aux Geans, ceuls de Bruth" (line 7);[41] but we soon find Chaucer presented as the earthly god of love in "Albie" (l. 11; see p. 193) who plants the rose (his translation) "en la terre Angelique" (l. 12). In pointing to their current refinement and achievement, the overall effect is to elevate the position of the English people in view of their supposed base beginnings. This "Ovid grans en [sa] poetrie" illustrates the worthiness and sophistication of the society which produced him. Rhetorically speaking, the offspring of the Trojan Brutus, well interpreted by Jenkins as the "rough Greek" (p. 273), move out of ignorance to become the inhabitants of the angelic land. This type of language play would not be lost on the poem's courtly audience;[42] it is intended to first raise an eyebrow and feign a hostile tone, but just as quickly it soothes and charms.

The poem's first ten lines attempt to define Chaucer's public stature as teacher, poet, rhetorician, theoretician and philosopher. Perhaps Deschamps perversely chooses Socrates, Seneca, and Ovid with an eye to their relationships with states and with monarchs. A courtly audience must then interpret Deschamps's choices as chiding counsel to an inferior culture, one that cannot recognize genius but has somehow produced it. Chaucer is to Seneca as Richard is to Nero. This is the most hostile reading one could give these lines; and to sustain such an interpretation would also be to force the unuttered and the cryptic beyond their proper measure.

Deschamps turns from this cataloging of ancients, moves into the "Angelic land," and enters into the garden; here the Rose has been translated and the profile spring of Hippocrene flows. The stanza begins with "Tu" and first establishes a personal tone. Chaucer is addressed as England's god of love and his request for plants from Deschamps's garden of verses is honored. Chaucer is maintaining a flourishing garden, which, of course, in its larger context is England; he provides the environment and the enabling genius to sustain a living translation of the *Roman de la Rose*.

The third stanza admits the fecundity of Chaucer's garden when fed with the waters of the Hippocrene. This garden, therefore provides common cultural and political ground and represents the hope for an end to hostility. The poem's function is twofold: it intimately addresses and praises a mutual friend while it delights its larger courtly audience. It praises the court's good taste and its acquaintance with the poet. Deschamps lets Chaucer provide the link between himself, representing French interest, and what is held dear in both courts. This is surely the language of reconciliation, not of hauteur.[43]

Deschamps's repetition of the word *translateur* is interesting in view of his reference to the *Rose*, to *Troilus and Criseyde* ("la langue Pandras," line 9) and his rhetorical elevation of the English people. Translate and translation (L. *transfero, translatio*) carried more elevated and various meanings than the modern English equivalents. In English, the verb form still means: to carry or convey to heaven without death (s.v. *translate* OED I.1.b.); to interpret (II.3.); and to transport with the strength of some feeling, to enrapture (III.6.). These meanings are and have been likewise attached to the French noun "translation." Deschamps evidently wanted to convey to his English auditors the transport he felt in recognizing true genius—these meanings are intended to build upon one another and ennoble their subject in much the same fashion that Deschamps elevated the sons of Brutus and made them angels. I am suggesting that by way of his puns Deschamps hints he has seen the *Troilus* (l. 9), and he offers his praise, recognizing how the *Rose* figures there; that is, he saw how well Chaucer translated its ideas and revitalized them in verse; this, in addition to his translation of the *Rose* itself: "Tu es d'amours mondains Dieux en Albie: et de la Rose" (lines 11, 12).[44]

Deschamps could not have written such a poem prior to the late eighties or early nineties. The *Troilus* was not completed until the mid-eighties and Clifford's earlier missions occurred when there would have been very little occasion for *cultural*, as opposed to diplomatic, exchanges. It is difficult to argue that Deschamps would have addressed any English poet prior to 1386, and though it has been argued that the poem is not intended to be flattering, better arguments suggest it is.[45] Deschamps was a combatant as late as 1380, a date which also marks the beginning of Deschamps's career at the court of Charles VI—the same year he refers to the English king as *l'Ane Pesant* (the ponderous ass). In 1383 Deschamps urged Charles to reaffirm his love of arms and show his enemies no mercy.[46] Indeed, up until 1386 he expresses a vehement hatred for the English; yet, war and its sorrows had taken a heavy personal toll. He writes in 1380 of having his home and lands at Vertus burned by English soldiers (*Oeuvres* V, 5–6), referring to "leur guerre," and to himself as "Brulé des Champs," or "Scorched of the Fields." But, even in the face of disaster and great personal loss, he seems to have kept a sense of humor and doesn't fail to estimate his monetary losses.[47]

Even five years later (during, or even after the period when Lowes dates the "Ballade to Chaucer"), and apparently still very embittered against the English, Deschamps urges his countrymen to victory on the eve of the ill-fated invasion effort of 1386. In 1385, he writes a ballade on the occasion of Jean de Vienne's departure for Scotland where the French and the Scots were to sweep down on the English from the north in support of the main invasion:

> Du sang des mors de chascune partie
> Fleuves courront, et veritablement
> Les fils de Bruth mourront la a tourment,
> Et, des ce jour, n'ont espoir de merci:
> Destruiz seront, c'est leur definement,
> Tant qu'om dira: Angleterre fut cy.

(*Oeuvres* I, 107:25–30)

> The blood of death will run from every limb and truly the sons of Brutus will die in torment and from that day they will have no hope of mercy; their fate is to be destroyed and one will say: this was England.

Here the poet hopes for a complete and bloody vanquishing of the English, literally demanding their total destruction. He uses the "sons of Brutus" in a most unflattering context—there is no rhetorical ennobling—and the English remain the sons of the "rough Greek" (see p. 195). The "Ballade to Chaucer" could not have come from this period—why would Deschamps praise the transplanting of the French Rose in the garden of the new Troy, if he intended that land to be destroyed?

A change came over Deschamps and many other court leaders; although Deschamps earlier had vowed always that "gens d'armes ameray" (*Oeuvres* IV, 25), [I will love the warrior], and despite the fact he had given this same advice to Charles in 1383, in 1386 he wrote:

> Las! que j'ay veu de tribulacion
> De tempestes et de mortalitez,
> De haines, de peuples mocion,
> De grans orgueilz et de grans vanitez,
> De traisons et de crudelitez,
> Puis .L. ans, et vengence soudaine,
> Conflis de roys en France et en Espaigne
> Pour nos pechiez, et universel guerre
> Pour le debat de France et d'Angleterre,
> Pais ardoir, tout detruire a la ronde
> Pour convoitier et seignourie acquerre!
> C'est tout neant des choses de ce monde.
>   (*Oeuvres* VI, 40:1–12)

> Alas! I have seen tribulations: storms and death, hatred, a whole people shaken, pride, vanity, treason and cruelty; then fifty years and sudden vengeance, conflicts of kings in France and Spain for our sins, and universal war of France and England; burning the country, destroying everything out of desire to acquire lands and titles. All in this world is for nought.

During nearly the same period that he praises the Scottish campaign, he completely reverses his position in "Guerre Sans Fin" and laments that peace would never be achieved, probably suggesting that the breakdown of peace negotiations in 1385 and the failure of the 1386 invasion effort contributed to the poem's despairing tone. The poet has heard the Requiem sung too often—it seems as though no other Mass will ever be sung: "De *Requiem* chantera desormais: / Sanz paix avoir, nous aurons guerre, guerre" (*Oeuvres* I, 136:9–10). [The Requiem will be sung from this day forward; without peace we will have but war, war.]

Thereafter, Deschamps moves away from the notion that the English are the sole source of the ongoing conflict and finds the French people themselves deficient in faith and piety, suggesting that they have ceased to be a Christian nation. The war is both the consequence and the punishment of their break with God. The first ten lines of his ballade "Pourquoi Nous Ne Pouvons Jamais Avoir de Paix" advise the auditor to read Leviticus and heed what was told the shepherds. Peace is destined to those who keep goodwill and God's commandments; all earthly happiness, including children, riches, honor, power and knowledge, will attend the blessed. The poet concludes, however, that "Le contraire faisons, si qu'en ce temps / Nous ne devons ne bien ne paix avoir" (*Oeuvres* II, 142–43:9, 10). [We are doing just the contrary and in these times—we will never have peace.] In Leviticus 26 God warns he will lay waste to the land of Israel, put the people to the sword, subject them to foreign domination, afflict them with plague and famine, and make them suffer a host of other ills; here Deschamps makes France as Israel in the desert, failing to keep faith and breaking with God's laws (26:1–34). Because the church has also failed in its role and has been divided, the people lack faith, engage in idolatry, and will receive punishment for their sins. The world will not be restored to order until they reform.

What makes Deschamps's use of the third book of Moses in an anti-war ballade of particular interest is that Philippe de Mézières's *Songe du Vieil Pèlerin* and *Epistre au Roi Richart II* also cast Charles VI in the role of Moses. Mosaic analogies were rarely used to interpret national events or the nature of kingship

(David and Solomon furnished appropriate models of biblical kingship in most cases), but Deschamps uses Moses as a model of the good ruler quite often; the figure appears in some thirteen different locations (*Oeuvres* X, 214) in Deschamps's writings: "Pour signe nul que Moyses eust fait: / Par leur orgueil en Rouge Mer perirent, / Car Dieux pugnist chascun de son meffait" (*Oeuvres* VII, 7:8–10). [They did not repent despite all that Moses did, they perished in the Red Sea by their own pride as God punishes everyone who is sinful.]

While there are many textual and rhetorical similarities connecting Deschamps with Philippe de Mézières and the Order, Mézières personally recommends Deschamps to Charles VI in the third book of the *Songe du Vieil Pelerin* (1389):

> Tu puez bien lire aussi et ouyr les dictez vertueulx de ton serviteur et officier Eustache Morel [Deschamps], et toutes autres escriptures vrayes, honnestes et catholiques, tendans a bonne edification . . .
>
> (II, 223)
>
> You would also do well to read and hear the virtuous writings of your servant and officer, Eustache Morel, these and any other true, honest, and catholic writings which aid in your good instruction.

The context of this passage is germane and all of Mézières's recommended reading, in the passages which precede and follow, revolve around the resurrection of the crusading spirit and Christian conquest. Because of its influence on Charlemagne, perhaps the greatest crusader in the history of Christendom, Mézières recommends Augustine's *City of God* and suggests that Charles also read the life history of Godefroy de Bouillon and of his "noble compaigne et sainte chevalerie" (Deschamps refers to this crusader approximately twenty times in his writings). Because we know that by 1389, the date of the *Songe* and of Louis's enrollment in the Order, we may conclude that Mézières' recommends Deschamps to the king because he is sufficiently familiar with Deschamps's writings and trusts that their author will continue to support the Order's program.

Mézières strongly influenced Deschamps's work during the period immediately following the production of the *Songe du*

Vieil Pèlerin, and although Deschamps's changeability on matters political has been noticed frequently, he eventually, and most ardently, embraced the ideals of the Order.[48] Jarry reports (pp. 52–53) that shortly after "le roi repara les desordres de l'administration du duc de Berry," and while the king was with Orléans at Toulouse [Nov. 29–Jan. 7, 1389–90]:

> une ambassade genoise vint trouver le roi de France, pour implorer son secours contre les Musulmans, dont les progres effrayants sur les côtes de la Mediterranée inquietaient Genes et troublaient son commerece. Les Genois demandaient pour chef le frère du roi; mais le commandement fut confié au duc de Bourbon.
>
> C'est probablement à cette époque que le duc de Touraine [Louis, future Duke of Orléans, Deschamps' patron] promit son concours à l'ordre fondé par Philippe de Mézières, sous le nom de *Chevalerie de la Passion*.

In 1389–90 Louis had sought to solidify his position by marrying Valentina, the daughter of Giangaleazzo Visconti, infamous first Duke of Milan.[49] Through this marriage Louis hoped to take advantage of the schism: by supporting the Clementist cause, he could establish himself in Italy and overcome the Urbanites (perhaps Louis had his eye on the Imperial throne as did Richard and Charles). Louis supported the Order only while it was politically advantageous to do so; peace between France and England meant there would be more resources to achieve his goals in Italy. Furthermore, by promising aid to the Genoese, he could ally himself with Visconti of Milan, who sought to extend their influence in the West. Although Orléans nominally supported the Order, and initially made great promises, as Charles's brother he was also a contender for the throne. With Charles's illness in 1392, this became more apparent.[50] This is also true of Burgundy. Apparently, the tension between Louis and Philip drew Louis away from fully supporting the Order as early as 1392,[51] and Louis's position relative to the throne and to the Order was altered twice that year: on June 4 he was given the duchy of Orléans in apanage,[52] and the King's first attack of madness occurred in August.[53] Raynaud reports (p. 66) that immediately upon Louis's taking up his new residence, he made Deschamps "un des ses conseillers et maîtres d'hôtel"; these were, evidently, the posts Deschamps held when the king took ill. It was feared Charles would not survive his illness and perhaps Louis was anticipating his brother's death—obviously there was a great deal at stake. Crusades, it seems, are usually more attractive to the dispossessed and Louis was clearly no longer in that category. From his acquisition of the duchy of Orléans he pursued a campaign of personal aggrandizement which accelerated during the crucial Leulinghem conferences with the death in February of Blanche de France, widow of Philippe d'Orléans.[54] With his mother's death Louis came into large holdings in Valois and Beaumont-sur-Oise.

Louis's new wealth must have cooled his crusading spirit because he did not attend the second round of the conferences reconvening that same month, but stayed close to the king,[55] where his best interests were served.[56] In addition, rumors (c. 1395) later accused the Duke of Milan, his daughter (the Duchess of Orléans), and so Louis himself, of having poisoned Charles and causing his insanity.[57] According to the Chronicler of Saint-Denys these rumors were unfounded, but they were certainly aimed both at discrediting any alliance with Visconti Italy and damaging Louis's close relationship with the king. Because Visconti Italy and its interests ran counter to the Order's agenda, the Visconti were increasingly perceived by Burgundian and Lancastrian factions both as hindering the English-French peace, and the united crusade which depended upon peace in Christendom.

By 1391, the probable year for Deschamps's "Ballade to Chaucer," France and England were closer to peace than they had been in almost a decade. Urban VI was dead, and with the election of Boniface IX, Charles attempted an invasion of Italy in the hope of replacing the newly elected pope with Clement, winning the imperial throne for himself and installing his brother in the Romagna.[58] Both Charles and Louis sought the aid of the Visconti to help accomplish their goals, but neither received the aid needed to succeed. The English were not pleased with French intervention in Italy and threatened to renew the war, and Charles, evidently preferring to continue the truce with England over renewing the conflict, quickly withdrew his army and returned to France. By abandoning the Italian invasion and admitting English pressure, however, he also abandoned Louis's plans in Italy. Louis returned to France with nothing more than the second installment of his bride's dowry. At this point, peace between France and England meant peace in Italy: Louis could not profit from an Anglo/French peace, and he eventually abandoned the program offered by the Order and advocated renewed hostility with England.

Peace held its attractions for Burgundy because of his tenuous hold over Flanders and most of the Low Countries. His support for the Order, that is, his alliance with Lancaster, allowed him to use his resources elsewhere. Between the years 1391 and 1393 differences between Louis and Philip intensified as France and England moved closer to a strengthened truce and perhaps toward a complete and permanent peace.

My hypothesis is that Deschamps's disillusion with the war led him, at least informally, and temporarily, to switch patrons. He was in the company of Philip of Burgundy at the Leulinghem negotiations in 1393. The dukes of Lancaster, Burgundy, Gloucester, and Berry were all present at this important meeting. Orléans, apparently, was not. This body endorsed Mézières's program. The Chronicler of Saint-Denys reports that Leulinghem was chosen as a site for the conferences not only because of its central location, but because its chapel was nearly in ruins and the town was itself reduced to rubble.[59] The private sessions were held in the chapel where the Duke of Berry had hung tapestries to hide the shabby appearance of its walls. Lancaster objected, not to their hanging, but to their subjects; apparently, all of them glorified wars and the warlike. These were removed and replaced with tapestries representing "les principaux traits de la Passion de Notre Seigneur Jesus-Christ."[60]

The need for an alliance in the west was evident. In 1391 a large Anglo/French contingent went to crusade in Prussia, this while urgent requests for assistance had been coming regularly for years from Hungary. The Turks posed a formidable threat not only to Christendom, but to Eastern trade in general; and for this reason Louis finally pledged his support for the Order to merchant supplicants and not to noblemen or churchmen. Both Richard and Charles had been bombarded by Mézières's pleas for a number of years, and now that many of the personal ambitions that had kept the war going had been satisfied (except in Louis's case), Burgundy and Berry knew they must rid the countryside of marauding, unemployed mercenaries, reunite the church, and deal with the Turks. As the powerful dukes spoke, both kings made ready to step in and endorse the treaty. The Order of the Passion provided the common ground for this important meeting and helped break down the apparent differences that had kept the many factions from uniting in the past. Had it not been that Charles was suddenly taken with one of his frequent fits, the issues might have been resolved at the 1393 meeting. To underscore the important role the Order played in this and other meetings that followed, J. J. N. Palmer (p. 189) states that "when Philip de Mézières described the Hermit [Robert] as 'the special messenger of God and Saint James to the kings of England and France to conclude peace, end the Schism, and arrange a crusade, he was stating no more than the bare truth."

At Leulinghem in April of 1393, Burgundy asked Deschamps to translate his Latin treatise, *Complaint de l'Eglise* into French and to read it for all present (*Oeuvres* VII, pp. 293–311).[61] Here Deschamps truly steps into the role of revered teacher; he is, in fact, instructing and pacifying the most powerful men in Europe. While the treatise sums up Burgundian hopes, it also illustrates Mézières's influence. Deschamps chides these noblemen for their failure to fear God and for following the prince of the world. To paraphrase the *Complaint*: In his pride, he [Satan] also rises up to oppose the Lord; he drives away divine thought, and seduces them with covetousness, pride, and sins of the flesh. For his glorification, he places wars, hatred, and treason among Christian people, leads them to spill human blood, rape virgins, massacre innocents, destroy God's temples, and ravage sacred objects with sacrilegious hands. Deschamps warns that by reducing to nothing the patrimony of their Father, they will lose the legacy of his knighthood. Deschamps's own version of the Beatitudes follows (*Oeuvres* VII, 306, 08), tailored to fit the situation and addressed to the warriors of France and England. He argues that if faith is kept, the warriors could bring about a good union and the Christian religion could be reformed. To effect this they must inflict the vengeance of the Father and his law upon his enemies. They must take the Sepulcher from the Saracens who hold it in disrespect and return the Holy Land to the hands of the Father. By so doing, and repenting of their iniquities, they can conquer and obtain Paradise.

Deschamps's ideas (as well as the way he displays them) closely resemble those Mézières expresses in his *Epistres au Roi Richart* (1395). His audience is the noblemen of France and England and, like Deschamps, he catalogues their faults and the consequences of their break with God: the church is poisoned, cities and castles destroyed; virgins and nuns are raped and delivered to despair while homeless children die of hunger. But worst of all, the Catholic faith is forgotten and perishes by pride, covetousness, and a desire for transitory wealth: a king commands only a few years of worldly pleasure, and then loses paradise in the bargain.[62]

A comparison of Mézières's language with that of Deschamps's "Complainte de l'Eglise" reveals both writers soundly chiding the leaders of the day. Both specifically point out the same principle faults as the primary reasons for continued hostilities: "[Satan] . . . qui par couvoitize, orgeuil, et pechie de char vous a seduit . . ." (*Oeuvres* VII, 295). [Satan has seduced you by covetousness, pride and sins of the flesh.] Deschamps points out where he thinks the lords have gone astray, admonishes them for their sins, supports his assertions with scripture, assigns a fitting penance, and finally points to the reward; Mézières does the same in the passage described above and in many other places in his writings. Both monarchs are repeatedly warned that the church has been divided and weakened by their continued hostilities, and though Mézières does not propose a crusade in the paraphrased passage above, both writers view this as the way to set things right.[63]

Neither Deschamps's rhetoric nor his point of view could have been genuinely shared by his patron. Louis had too much to gain from continued hostilities with England and with England's allies in Italy. Yet, even though Louis probably was not in favor of a lasting peace with England, he may have felt that the Order of the Passion and the crusade that sprang from it might be used to serve his interests by keeping the king of France and Burgundy occupied. If this were the case, we might expect Deschamps to praise the crusading effort while remaining somewhat cool toward a lasting settlement with England—especially if peace were cemented by a royal marriage between Richard and Isabelle, the daughter of Charles VI. This, however, was not the case. In 1395 Deschamps endorses the marriage (*Oeuvres* VI, 133–34). He considers Eve's temptation, the resulting strife and death, and concludes his treatment by underscoring the redemptive qualities offered by the royal marriage: "Toute paix vint par un saint mariiage." Since the 1396 marriage was arranged by Robert the Hermit and Lancastrian deputies, Deschamps's poem clearly supports the Order's program of reconciliation.[64]

A survey of the correspondence offered by the Chronicler of Saint-Denys between the two courts relative to the marriage negotiations indicates, however, that the crusading component was not seriously considered until the marriage itself was firmly settled.[65] An alliance had to precede the crusade, and Deschamps buys the whole package. The English are the first to address this issue in their correspondence of March 13, 1395, so Louis's lack of preparation does not clearly speak against his supporting the Order in 1394.[66] Both sides regarded this marriage and the resultant treaty as prerequisites to their support for mounting a crusade. The Chronicler also illustrates how deeply Charles believed in the spiritual power of the Order; he called upon it to heal not only the many social, religious, financial, and political ills plaguing his realm and all of Christendom, but also his personal maladies. The king's pilgrimage procession to Paris in January, 1396 was staged according to terms provided by the Order.[67] All those in the king's train wore silk capes which bore the insignia of the Passion. Even well after the defeat at Nicopolis, as late as 1399, Charles was firmly convinced that the

Order would provide a cure for his malady.[68] The Chronicler also reveals that Charles was under the watchful care of Burgundy and Berry, who frequently sheltered him from influences and opinion which might lead the king seriously to consider alternative proposals.[69]

By supporting the Order's program during the years 1386–1397 and associating himself fully with the interests of the Lancastrian, Burgundian policies and only partially with the interests of the Orléanist factions, Deschamps placed himself with a distinguished group of poets and literary figures: Chaucer, Mézières, Boucicaut (Marshal of France), Granson, and Clifford, to name only a few. All were involved, in varying degrees, in the political and religious debates of the tumultuous 1390s, and all were associated with the Order of the Passion. This is the context in which Deschamps's "Ballade to Chaucer" should be read: the poem is most valuable because it provides the essential evidence that, at the very least, Deschamps was encouraging a poetic dialogue with Geoffrey Chaucer—who was apparently doing the same when he offered his translation (probably through Clifford) of *Le Roman de la Rose* and possibly his *Troilus* to Deschamps. The war-weariness of the *Troilus* should have appealed to Deschamps in this period. His ballade was probably written well after the ill-fated invasion effort of 1386 when French victory seemed assured, and closer to 1391, a period when dialogue between the two courts was re-established and Clifford frequented the French court. In the late 1380s Deschamps turned away from his pro-war stance, away from what must have been a considerable share of personal bitterness, and embraced Mézières's Order in the hope that it could bring peace between France and England—the first step toward a final cure for many social, political, and religious ills. The *Ballade* likely dates from that critical period in early 1390 when for the first time Charles, Orléans, and Bourbon were operating in concert with Lancastrian England. Deschamps's poetic tribute to Geoffrey Chaucer is crucial evidence of this turning.

NOTES

Some of the material in this essay appears in "The Order of the Passion of Jesus Christ: A Reconsideration of Eustache Deschamps's "Ballade to Chaucer," *Mediaevalia* 11 (1985, for 1989), 219–44. I extend my thanks to *Mediaevalia*'s editor, Professor Bernard Levy, for giving his permission to use material from that article.

1. This ballade appears in *Oeuvres Completes de Eustache Deschamps*, gen. ed. Le Marquis de Saint-Hillaire (Paris: Société des Anciens Textes Français, 1880), 11 vols. (1878–1903), 2, 138–39. All subsequent references to this work will be noted simply as *Oeuvres*. The following translation of Deschamps's "Ballade to Chaucer" is by Atkinson T. Jenkins, "Deschamps' Ballade to Chaucer," *Modern Language Notes* 33 (1918): 268–78:

> O Socrates full of wisdom, a Seneca in uprightness of life, an Aulus Gellius in practical affairs, an Ovid great in thy poetic lore, brief in expression, wise in the art of the versifier: —lofty eagle (genius), who by thy science dost illuminate the kingdom of Aeneas, the Isle of the Giants—they of Brutus—and who hast sown there the flowers (of verse) and planted the Rose-tree for (the benefit of) those ignorant of the Grecian tongue, O great translator noble Geoffrey Chaucer;—
>
> Thou art a mundane god of love in Albia: and (thou translatedst the *Book*) *of the Rose* in the Angelic land, which from the Saxon lady Angela has since developed (into) Angle-land, (for it is) from her this name now is applied, being the last in the series of names: —thou translated the *Book* (*of the Rose*) into good English; and now for a long time thou hast been constructing a fruit-garden, for which thou didst ask some plants from those who poetize to win themselves solid reputation, O great translator, noble Geoffrey Chaucer;—
>
> Wherefore I ask that I may have from thee a genuine draught from the spring of Hippocrene, whose rill is altogether in thy possession, so that I may check my feverish thirst for it: here in Gaul I shall be as a paralytic until thou shalt make me drink. A Eustache am I, thou shalt have some of my plants; but look with favor upon the schoolboy productions which thou mayst receive from me through Clifford, O great translator, noble Geoffrey Chaucer.
>
> High poet, (the) glory of squirehood, in thy garden I should be only a nettle: bethink thee of what I have described above,

thy noble plants, thy sweet music! Nevertheless, that I may not be left in doubt, I beg thee to return me an official opinion, O great translator, noble Geoffrey Chaucer.
2. John Livingston Lowes, "The Prologue to the *Legend of Good Women* Considered in its Chronological Relations," *PMLA* 20 (1905): 749–864.
3. See: Paul A. Olson, *The Canterbury Tales and the Good Society* (Princeton Univ. Press, 1986), pp. 49–84; J. N. N. Palmer, *England, France and Christendom* (Chapel Hill: Univ. of North Carolina Press, 1972).
4. Lowes (1905), p. 769.
5. See: Oliver F. Emerson, "Chaucer's First Military Service—A Study of Edward Third's Invasion of France in 1359–60," *The Romanic Review* 3.4 (1912): 353–54, n. 114.
6. See: D. W. Brewer *Chaucer and His World*, (New York: Dodd, Mead, 1978), p. 28.
7. Martin M. Crow and Clair C. Olson, eds., *Chaucer Life Records*, (Oxford: Oxford Univ. Press, 1966), p. 24.
8. See: Gaston Raynaud, "Vie de Deschamps," *Oeuvres* vol. 11, p. 12.
9. Raynaud indicates (*Oeuvres* vol. 11, p. 12) that Deschamps was present in Reims from December 4, 1359 through January 11, 1360.
10. For information on Reims prior to and during this period see: Pierre Desportes, *Reims et les Remois aux XIIIe et XIVe Siècles* (Paris: Picard, 1979), pp. 549–62, 697. Crow and Olson consider the chances of Chaucer meeting Deschamps during his captivity at Reims, but conclude a meeting was unlikely (*Chaucer Life Records*, n. 27).
11. For a discussion of the courtly nature of Deschamps' "Ballade to Chaucer," see: David Lampe, "The Courtly Rhetoric of Chaucer's Advisory Poetry," *Reading Medieval Studies* 9 (1983): 70–83.
12. See: Pierre Chaplais, ed., *Some Documents Regarding the Fulfilment and Interpretations of the Treaty of Bretigny, 1361–1369*, Camden Miscellany 19 (London: Offices of the Royal Historical Societe, 1952), p. 5.
13. See: Jean Devoise, *Jean le Bon* (Paris: Fayard, 1985), pp. 378–416; and Edouard Perroy, *The Hundred Years War* (Bloomington: Indiana Univ. Press, 1960), pp. 132ff.
14. See: Perroy [1960], p. 142; and Barbara Tuchman, *A Distant Mirror: The Calamitous 14th Century* (New York: Ballantine, 1978), p. 200.

15. See: Perroy [1960], p. 137–39; and H. d'Orléans, *Notes et Documents Relatifs à Jean, Roi de France, et sa Captivité en Angleterre* (London: C. Whittingham, 1855 [?]), pp. 26–35.
16. Tuchman, p. 194, n. 2.
17. Raynaud, p. 12.
18. See: Tuchman, p. 191.
19. For information on Deschamps's age see: Raynaud, pp. 9–10; For a discussion of Chaucer's date of birth, see: John Gardner, *The Life and Times of Geoffrey Chaucer* (New York: Knopf, 1980), p. 21, n. 1.
20. For information concerning Jean's English residence see: Devoise, p. 409; and d'Orléans, p. 27.

    It is interesting to speculate that the few English words Deschamps used in his verse (*Oeuvres*, V, 79), written during his visit to Calais with Oton de Granson in 1384, playfully demonstrate not only Deschamps's knowledge of English, but that he learned what he knew in England (see: Lowes [1905], pp. 758–60). French, of course, was the language of both courts and Deschamps probably had little opportunity to use English in France. His comic renditions: "commidre" (come hither); "dogue" (dog); and "goday" (good day), poke fun at the English soldiers' accents and their apparent practice of running words together. In his "Ballade to Chaucer" Deschamps overtly praises Chaucer's translation of the *Roman*, calling it "good English," and any qualitative judgment of Chaucer's poetry would be difficult to make if Deschamps did not possess a sophisticated command of English. Given the war, it seems unlikely that he learned English while a student at Orléans in the mid-sixties (Raynaud, p. 13). His use of English in 1384 is witty, but rather thin, and probably not sufficiently sophisticated to make the well-informed judgments that appear in his "Ballade to Chaucer." Nor does it seem possible that he learned English from the soldiers he parodies. Unless Deschamps had a firm grasp of the language since the early 1360s (above), in view of the Calais poem, one must conclude that Deschamps's understanding, as demonstrated in his "Ballade to Chaucer," is too developed to have been written in 1384 and probably dates from almost a decade later when Deschamps had better reason and opportunity to use English.
21. See: Aziz Suryal Atiya, *The Crusade of Nicopolis* (London: Methuen, 1934; rpt. AMS, 1978), p. 133–35.
22. See: Philippe de Mézières, *Songe du Vieil Pèlerin*, 2 vols., G. W. Coopland, ed. (Cambridge Univ. Press, 1969), vol. I, p. 4.

23. See: David Lanoue, "*La Prise d'Alexandrie*: Guillaume de Machaut's Epic," *Nottingham Medieval Studies* 24 (1985): 99–108.
24. See: Olson (1986), p. 57; and Françoise Autrand, *Charles VI* (Paris: Fayard, 1986), p. 29.
25. Palmer, pp. 188ff.
26. Atiya cites these men as being among the Order's original members (p. 133).
27. Palmer, p. 188.
28. See: James I. Wimsatt, *Chaucer and the Poems of 'CH' in University of Pennsylvania MS French 15*. Chaucer Studies IX (Totowa, NJ: Rowman and Littlefield, 1982): 50–1; and Haldeen Braddy, "Chaucer and Graunson: the Valentine Tradition," *PMLA* 54:2 (1939): 359–68.
29. See: Haldeen Braddy, "Messire Oton de Granson, Chaucer's Savoyard Friend," *Studies in Philology* 35:4 (Oct. 1938): 515–31. It is interesting that Crow and Olson report (p. 24) that "Sir William de Gransaun (Grauntson), knt. of Burgundy," a supporter of the English, was ransomed for the sum of £20 on December 13 and his name appears in William de Farley's account along with both Stury's and Chaucer's. This "Graunsaun" may have been Oton's brother, or at least a close relative (see: M. L. de Charrière, *Les Dynastes de Grandson* [Lausanne: Georges Bridel, 1866, table IV B]; Arthur Piaget, *Oton de Grandson sa Vie et ses Poesies,* Société d'Histoire de la Suisse Romande, 3rd Series, vol. 1 (Lausanne: Payot, 1941) p. 9, n. 1. he was evidently held with this same group of prisoners. Chaucer and Deschamps may well have encountered Oton himself in Reims, or heard of him there as early as 1360.
30. See: William Calin, "Machaut's Legacy: The Chaucerian Inheritance Reconsidered," in this volume.
31. See: Lowes (1905), pp. 758–60; and Raynaud, p. 42.
32. By the 1380s Granson was a knight of legendary stature and his early support of the Order must have contributed greatly to its success. He was certainly in the service of John of Gaunt in 1374 (see: Haldeen Braddy, *Chaucer and the French Poet Graunson* [Baton Rouge: Louisiana State Univ. Press, 1947], pp. 40–41) and was later a favorite in the company of the Earl of Derby (the future Henry IV of England), accompanying the Earl on his second Prussian campaign in July of 1392. He was an eyewitness to the trouble in Cyprus when he visited there in February of that same year (see: Lucy Toulmin Smith, ed., *Expeditions to Prussia and the Holy Land Made by the Earl of Derby [. . .] in the years 1390–1*

and *1392–3*, The Camden Society, 52. [London: Camden Society, Second Series, 1894], rpt [New York: Johnson, 1965], p. 309); his association with the Order (Piaget, 6–8), and his presence in England during the crucial years immediately before the recommencement of peace negotiations (Smith, 45 ff) indicates that he was probably playing a major role in bringing an end to Anglo-French hostilities.

33. See: Paul A. Olson, "Chaucer's Epic Statement and the Political Milieu of the Late Fourteenth Century," *Mediaevalia* 5 (1979): 83, n. 21.
34. For information concerning Clifford's business in France, see: Edouard Perroy, ed., *The Diplomatic Correspondence of Richard II*, Camden Third Series, 48 (London: Offices of the Royal Historical Society, 1933), p. 85, item 26, 223. See: Braddy [1947], p. 36 for information about Granson's circle.
35. See: Olson [1986], pp. 112, 113, n. 14; Maude Violet Clarke, *Fourteenth Century Studies*, L. S. Sunderland and M. McKisack, eds., (Oxford Univ. Press, 1937), pp. 272–92; Palmer, pp. 242–44.
36. See: Lowes [1905], p. 769; Lampe, pp. 70–83; Eugene Jarry, *La Vie Politique de Louis de France, Duc de Orléans, 1372–1407* (Paris: 1889), rpt. (Geneve: Slatkine-Megariots Reprints, 1976), p. 53.
37. See: Raynaud, pp. 27–28.
38. See: Paul A. Olson, "*The Parlement of Foules*: Aristotle's *Politics* and the Foundations of Human Society," *Studies in the Age of Chaucer* 2 (1980): 53–69. D. W. Robertson, in his *Preface to Chaucer* (pp. 280, 81), places the date of the *Troilus*' composition in the year 1385 (see also: "The Probable Date and Purpose of Chaucer's *Troilus*," *Medievalia et Humanistica*, New Series, 13 (1985): 143–71; and John Tatlock, *The Development and Chronology of Chaucer's Works,1*, (Gloucester, Mass: Peter Smith, 1963), x, pp. 41–44.
39. See: John Fleming, *Classical Imitation and Interpretation in Chaucer's Troilus* (Lincoln: Univ. of Nebraska Press, 1990), ch. 3.
40. See: Jenkins, p. 274.
41. Deschamps alludes to the parricide, Brutus, who after slaying his father, Sylvius, fled to Greece and later went to Britain, becoming its first king. He captured the giants Gog and Magog (generally interpreted as the enemies of God), and made them serve him (see: Gertrude Jobes, *Dictionary of Mythology, Folklore and Symbols* [New York: Scarecrow Press, 1962], vol. 1, pp. 669, 670).

42. See: Lampe, p. 72; Richard Firth Green, *Poets and Princepleasers* (Toronto: Univ. of Toronto Press, 1980), p. 71.
43. See: Jenkins, p. 268.
44. See: Fleming, ch. 3; R. A. Shoaf, "Notes Towards Chaucer's Poetics of Translation," *Studies in the Age of Chaucer*, vol. 1 (1979): 55–66.
45. Compare Jenkins, pp. 268ff., with Lampe, pp. 70ff.
46. Raynaud, pp. 30, 31. 38.
47. Three years later Deschamps successfully brought suit against a certain Huguenin de Charmes, a *pillard*, in the employ of Jean de Vergy, Senechal de Bourbourg, for having raided the village of Vertus and taken goods from his *hostel* (Raynaud, pp. 40, 41).
48. See: Lowes [1905], 757ff.; Olson [1978], 83, n. 20.
49. See: Richard Vaughan, *Philip the Bold* (London: Longmans, Green & Co., 1962), p. 44.
50. See: Jarry, p. 53; Atiya, p. 36.
51. Palmer, pp. 192, 222–23.
52. See: Jarry, pp. 89–90; Vaughan, p. 44; M. L. Bellaguet, trans., *Chronique du Religieux de Saint-Denys*, 2 vols. (Paris: De Crapelet, 1839–40), vol. 2, pp. 61–3.
53. Vaughan, p. 42.
54. Vaughan, p. 44.
55. Raynaud, p. 68.
56. Jarry, pp. 90ff.
57. Bellaguet, vol. 2, p. 407.
58. Palmer, pp. 192–93.
59. Bellaguet, vol. 2, pp. 75–76.
60. Bellaguet, vol. 2, p. 79.
61. Raynaud, pp. 67–68.
62. Philippe de Mézières, *Letter to King Richard II*, G. W. Coopland, ed. (Liverpool: Liverpool Univ. Press, 1975), p. 79. All future references to this work will appear simply as Letter.
63. See: *Oeuvres*, vol. 7, p. 308; Letter, pp. 30ff; Philippe de Mézières, "Philippe de Mézières' *Order of the Passion*, Muriel Brown, ed. (Diss., Univ. of Nebraska, 1971), pp. 1–258.
64. See: Palmer, p. 189; Bellaguet, vol. 2, pp. 357–87.
65. See: Bellaguet, vol. 2, p. 365.
66. Palmer, p. 201.
67. Bellaguet, vol. 2, pp. 409ff.
68. Autrand, pp. 327–28.
69. Bellaguet, vol. 2, pp. 131ff.

Barbara K. Altmann

"Trop peu en sçay": the Reluctant Narrator in Christine de Pizan's Works on Love

We are drawn to Christine de Pizan not only because of the quality and nature of her works, but perhaps first and foremost because of those aspects of her career that make her unique among late-medieval French authors: a woman writing; a woman writing politically-engaged literature; a woman writing to rehabilitate the reputation of women, in the face of the misogynistic lessons of the male canon. These facets of her *oeuvre* have captured our attention as particularly germane to late-20th century critical preoccupations. But what of the more conventional love poetry she wrote? Easily dismissed as derivative of Machaut and his successors, Christine's lyric poetry and the longer narrative works that speak about love may lull the reader by virtue of their familiar subject matter and form. We can assume that it has all been heard before, while losing sight of another startling fact, an almost paradoxical combination of authorial voice and topic. Although deriving from a poetic tradition almost exclusively the domain of the male voice, Christine's works about love contain a female narrator and focalizer who bears a striking resemblance to the historical personage Christine herself.

It is the narrator/poet figure in Christine's love poetry that will be the focus of this study. This construct, a woman-writer figure identified as "Christine," is portrayed with remarkable consistency from the earliest to the latest writings in Christine's literary production. It is the woman writer we know from one of the often-reproduced miniatures in Christine's manuscripts, wearing a high head-dress and simple gown as she sits at her desk with a writing instrument in hand.[1] We find this personage in the bold allegorical and political works such as the *Livre de la Cité des Dames*, for example, or in Christine's last work, the *Ditié de Jehanne d'Arc*. But somewhat to the reader's surprise, the same figure is already present in her earlier compositions, those which presumably established her reputation as a writer and which conform more closely in subject matter to popular courtly models.

The seven works to be considered in the present paper fall into the latter category; each of them, written in verse, has to do with love and traces the evolution of one or more affairs of the heart. The group consists of the two *ballade* cycles (*Cent Ballades*; *Cent Ballades d'Amant et de Dame*), the three "debate" poems (*Le Livre du dit de Poissy; Le Debat de deux amans; Le Livre des trois jugemens*), the *Dit de la Pastoure*, and the *Livre du Duc des vrais amans*.[2] In every one of these works, the narrator plays a small but important role, whether her presence is confined to a prologue or whether her character is integrated into the narrative. In every instance, through the use of certain rhetorical figures and/or staging within the fiction, this narrator establishes a distance between herself and the material she is presenting. In other words, in every instance, she disassociates herself from the topic of love. This distance constitutes a significant break with the tradition that inspires and informs these works, and as such, makes the "conventional" portion of Christine's corpus rather less conventional than it might at first seem.

The model which serves as a point of departure for Christine's works dealing with love is the notion of *fin'amors* as adapted by Machaut, Froissart, Deschamps and others. As inherited from her predecessors, the "je" of courtly love poetry was necessarily an advocate of and participant in the game he wrote about. However problematic the sincerity of the first-person voice in the love lyric, that voice sang what purported to be personal experience. In the narrative genres, the narrator did not necessarily tell his own tale; he could also serve as the witness and recorder of someone else's affairs of the heart. The works of Guillaume de Machaut are the most useful basis of comparison for Christine's work, because she drew on them for both subject matter and poetic form.[3]

The narrator in Machaut's "dits amoureux" embodies, as Kevin Brownlee writes, a figure in whom are conflated the voices of the professional writer, the clerk, and the lover.[4] Machaut's great innovation was the elaboration of the notion of himself as "poète," and this conception of himself unifies the various genres in his corpus as the work of one artist. Machaut's poet-narrator can play a variety of roles, can be either protagonist or witness. But the fundamental element in his relationship to the text he produces is that Love furnishes the inspiration for his poetry and the poet-narrator is always that god's vassal. In Brownlee's words:

> Perhaps the single most important result of Machaut's concept of poetic identity involves a widening of the range of contexts in which the poet could portray himself qua poet, an increase in the range and number of poetic stances open to him—*all under the general rubric of serving love through poetry*. (p. 20; emphasis added)

Machaut's *Prologue*, the statement of his poetic program, tells us, after all, that Nature gives him three of her children (Scens, Retorique and Musique), in order that he write about love.[5] The introductory paragraph preceding the first *ballade* of the *Prologue* tells us:

> Comment Nature, volant orendroit plus que onques mais reveler et faire essaucier les biens et honneurs qui sont en Amours, vient a Guillaume de Machaut et li ordonne et encharge a faire sur ce nouviaus dis amoureus ... (p. 1)

Amours, in turn, makes Machaut the gift of Dous Penser, Plaisance and Esperance, to provide him with "matere et exemplaire" (III, v. 28). The poet complies willingly with his orders from Nature and Amours, and undertakes to devote himself to the task entirely.[6]

In following Machaut's example by presenting a poet-narrator figure in her work, Christine demonstrates that she shares his preoccupations concerning the process of literary creation and her status as a professional author.[7] Her narrator corresponds to the scholarly writer that her autobiographical texts tell us she aspired to be.[8] But there are two major differences between her narrator and Machaut's; these constitute a radical break with tradition. The first, obviously, is that Christine's narrator is a woman. The second is that even when this narrator is telling stories about love, she is not in Love's service.

The latter is to a large degree the result of the former. In the theory and practice of *fin'amors* as we find it represented in literature, the lady was the passive party. It was certainly not her role to sing or write about it. She was rarely allowed any voice at all, let alone the license of equating love service with the making of poetry. Christine, of course, could have chosen a narrator like Machaut's, a lover (or perhaps even a lady beloved) moved to compose love poetry by hope, sweet thoughts, and the pleasure of loving; but by choosing a figure that reflects and emphasizes the singularity of her own historical situation, she breaks so thoroughly with her model that it is not then too great a step to defy the commonplace of proclaiming oneself to be Love's acolyte. Indeed, she categorically and repeatedly places herself outside the system, using a variety of strategies that will be examined below with reference to the individual texts.

Other critics have recently recognized Christine's anomalous position *vis à vis* her love poetry, and have explained it in various ways. Nicole Zeeman, for example, in an article on love as 'matere' in medieval French love poetry, takes the position that Christine, as opposed to Machaut, simply denied the need for personal experience as inspiration and guarantee behind love lyrics.[9] The innovative nature of Christine's narrator's voice and her position outside the traditional roles is discussed by Kevin Brownlee in "Discourses of the Self: Christine de Pizan and the *Rose*."[10] With regard to the *Dit de la Rose*, Brownlee describes Christine's woman author's voice as one which speaks "neither as beloved nor as lover" (p. 209). Christine expands the courtly system "to include a new kind of female voice, outside the economy of desire but empowered to comment authoritatively upon that economy by means of courtly discourse" (p. 212). In works such as the *Cité des dames* or the *Dit de la rose*, works which are explicitly didactic, Christine establishes the authority of her text, despite or by means of its unexpected female poet figure, by evoking and reworking powerful models.[11] In the more conventional poetry, it is convention itself that makes the works acceptable. Christine's deft handling of familiar subject matter and format reassures the reader, countering any resistance to the unfamiliar voice telling the tale. These works are more subtly surprising than many of the others, because the fresh perspective from which the material is presented is well disguised in the midst of tried-and-true elements.

II

I have stated repeatedly that Christine disassociates herself from the game of courtly love; now it is time to turn to the texts to see first how and then why she does so. The most explicit denials that she has or wishes to have anything to do with the kind of love she is writing about occur in some of her earliest poetry, the *Cent ballades*. Just as the *Cent ballades* introduces many of the themes to be found in much of Christine's other work,[12] it also fixes many aspects of the narrator's persona. The explicit statements made here about Christine the narrator's position *vis à vis* her subject matter establish the paradigm we find reproduced in the other, later love poetry.

The *Cent ballades* was Christine's first extended work, and seems to have been written over a period of five years or so, probably between 1394 and 1399.[13] Like other collections of *ballades* of the time, it contains poems written on a variety of topics. Poems 2, 3, and 4 deal with themes taken from antiquity; numbers 5 to 20 are primarily about sorrow, the loss of a loved one, and the fickle nature of Fortune. Then comes a sequence of poems, numbers 21 to 49, which can be considered a self-contained story in that they trace the development of the relationship between a young lover and his lady.[14] This and the later *ballade* cycle can be treated for our purposes as narrative works. While each individual poem is the lyric expression of the emotional state of the lover speaking at one particular moment, they establish a linear development when taken together, tracing the changes in the relations between the lovers over time.[15] A second cycle runs from poem number 65 to number 88 and is both preceded and followed by other incidental poems about love.

A quick inventory of the collection demonstrates that although it is predominantly about love, there is also a significant portion (particularly numbers 2 through 20), that deals with entirely different subjects, some of them almost antithetical to love. Any kind of global reading leaves the reader wondering how to read the multiplicity of voices in the collection, and how the very different emotional tenor of the first poems—sorrowful *ballades* describing widowhood, desolation and despair—can be reconciled with the story about the relationship between two lovers that follows.

We are not left stranded. There are signposts, in the form of poems number one, 50 and 100, to help dispel any confusion as to who is saying what (or, in the case of Ballade 50, to anticipate a little, who is *not* saying what). In these three *ballades*, an author's voice gives us what is in essence a reader's guide to the poems included in the collection. Ballade 1 allows this poet to establish three points with regard to the composition of the poetry that follows. First, she is writing at the request of others: "Aucunes gens me prient que je face / Aucuns beaulz diz, et que je leur envoye" (vv. 1–2). Second, while these patrons say that she is gifted in the art of poetry (v. 3), she is inexperienced at it: "Puis que prié m'en ont de leur bonté, / Peine y mettray, combien qu'ignorant soie" (vv. 6–7). This theme is repeated in the *envoi*, where she states: "Princes, prenez en gré se je failloie; / Car le ditter je n'ay mie henté" (vv. 25–26). Third, she is incapable of writing happy poetry because a personal sorrow has extinguished all her joy (vv. 9–12). Instead, she will willingly write about her unhappiness: "du grant dueil qui me tient morne et coye / Puis bien parler assez et a plenté; / Si en diray" (vv. 13–15). The third stanza explains the source of her pain, which was the death of "Cellui de qui trestout mon bien avoye" (v. 20). The reference to a male beloved first indicates the gender of the speaking subject and therefore justifies the use of the feminine pronoun for the poet.

After the interruption of the three poems dealing with classical themes, there follows upon this statement of identity and intent the seventeen poems about grief and widowhood, including the well-known "Seulete suy" (number 11), which sums up the desolation of them all. At number 21, without a transition, the first love story begins, and from then on we read about love.

Number 50, however, occurring at the exact middle of the collection and immediately after the cycle of love *ballades*, reminds us of the presence of the poet figure behind the tale we have just read. This poem is often quoted as an explicit statement of the poetic mandate Christine sets for herself. In the absence of a metafictional, comprehensive *ars poetica* like Machaut's *Prologue*, critics interested in Christine's conception of her art must look to the words her narrator speaks within the works themselves. Here, the first stanza immediately warns the reader:

> Aucunes gens porroient mesjugier
> Pour ce sur moy que je fais ditz d'amours;
> Et diroient que l'amoureux dongier,
> Je sçay trop bien compter et tous les tours,
>   Et que ja si vivement
> N'en parlasse, sanz l'essay proprement,
> Mais, sauve soit la grace des diseurs,

Je m'en raport a tous sages ditteurs. (1–8)

In other words, the vivid and skilful rendering of the love story just told must not mislead us into thinking that the "je" of this fiftieth poem is drawing on personal history. This first stanza reinforces the fictional nature of the love story, by references to her skill as a poet (she knows "trop bien compter" the ways and dangers of love and speaks of it "si vivement"), and by the appeal to the expertise and good sense of "tous sage ditteurs," a group among whom she, by implication, should be numbered.

The second stanza, well known by now, contains an assessment of love as subject matter:

> Car qui se veult de faire ditz chargier
> Biaulz et plaisans, soient ou longs ou cours,
> Le sentement qui est le plus legier,
> Et qui mieulx plaist a tous de commun cours,
>   C'est d'amours, ne autrement
> Ne seront fait ne bien ne doulcement,
> Ou, se ce n'est, d'aucunes belles meurs,
> Je m'en raport a tous sages ditteurs. (9–16)

The effect of this expert, dispassionate assessment is to do away completely with the notion of love as the inspiration for poetry and reduce it to the status of an expedient choice for writers who hope to please a patron or other audience. The moral elitism of *fin'amors*, the assumption that it is an appropriate occupation only for the worthy, is denied to some extent by declaring that love generally appeals to everyone. Its ennobling qualities are no longer at issue—this poet, unlike Machaut, is not a happier, better person for thinking and speaking of love. In place of the Machaut-type narrator, whose poetry is both inspired by and offered to Amours and his powers, one finds a poet figure who considers love a convenient and pleasing subject matter for poetry, one topic among others, however privileged it may be.

An explicit denial that the poet writing the *Cent ballades* belongs to the world of lovers finally appears in the third stanza of Ballade 50. Referring back to the mistaken assumptions about her personal experience mentioned in the first stanza, she says;

> Qui pensé l'a, s'en vueille deschargier,
> Qu'en verité ailleurs sont mes labours.
> Pour m'excuser ne le dis ne purgier;
> Car amé ont assez de moy meillours,
>   Mais d'amours je n'ay tourment[,]
> Joye ne dueil; mais pour esbatement
> En parlent maint qui ont ailleurs leurs cuers,
> Je m'en raport a tous sages ditteurs. (17–24)

Using as an antecedent (in "Qui pense l'a") the misapprehensions raised at the beginning, which she hopes to quell, she insists that her own preoccupations are truly with other matters. While conceding that many others more worthy than she have loved, she states that love brings her neither torment nor happiness. Rather, like others whose thoughts are elsewhere, she speaks of love simply for enjoyment or entertainment ("pour esbatement"), the artist's pleasure derived from dealing with pleasing material.

"Esbatement" is repeated in Ballade 100, the final poem in the collection. The first lines pronounce the completion of the collection and the fulfillment of her obligation to the patron for whom it was composed:

> Cent balades ay cy escriptes,
> Trestoutes de mon sentement.
> Si en sont mes promesses quites
> A qui m'en pria chierement. (1–4)

Then she requests that all those who read or hear these one hundred *ballades* understand that they are meant to entertain, without reading anything else into them ("Qu'on le tiengne a esbatement, / Sanz y gloser mauvaisement," vv. 12–13).

The main purpose of this last poem, however, is to give a name to the creative voice that we hear in numbers 1, 50, and 100, commenting on her material. The first stanza reveals that in this poem:

> Nommée m'i suis proprement;
> Qui le vouldra savoir ou non,
> En la centiesme entierement

En escrit y ay mis mon nom. (5–8)

On the simplest level of the puzzle, the words "en escrit" render "Crestine" (or "Cristene"), and thus give us a name for the poet we have been listening to. The temptation, of course, has been to identify this "je" as Christine-the-author all along, on the basis of our knowledge of Christine's biography. Knowing that at a young age she lost her much-beloved husband and that she never remarried, we are predisposed to read the widowhood poems as "sincere" and the love story as fiction, and to assume that the voice encouraging us at the beginning and middle to do just that is Christine. But, in fact, the only textual evidence that buttresses our instinct is the anagram provided in number 100. Once we unscramble the anagram and equate the speaker of this *ballade* with Christine the author, we read back and attribute the words of the first and the fiftieth poems to her as well.[16]

The nature of the words from which one deciphers the name is of obvious significance, too. Their importance is marked by repetition; the capsule anagram—"En escrit y ay mis mon nom"—forms the refrain of this *ballade*, and is thus repeated three times. This line is an obvious play on words, as well. One can read it either as, "I have concealed my name there in 'en escrit,'" or as, "I have put my name there in writing." The double emphasis inherent in the ambiguity, the importance of inscribing her name, of "writing" as equivalent as "Christine," sums up in the last line of the collection the self-conscious literariness of this particular *ballade* and recalls the self-reflexive quality of Ballades 1 and 50. The author is equated with her poetry and vice versa, and this, Christine's first work of considerable length, sets the tone for both the poetry and prose that follow.[17]

To review, then, the information provided for the reader by the poet figure in the *Cent ballades*: the first poem tells us that she writes at the behest of a patron; at that point, the beginning of the collection, her preferred subject matter is the sorrow that overwhelms her. Half way through, interrupting the love poetry to which the sad poems have given way, she reminds us of her presence, says that she herself has no stake in the game of love, and insists that we not read the "ditz d'amours" as representative of her own experience or desires. At the end, she signs off with a flourish (or, at the least, with an anagram), emphasizing again the creative process that drives the work.

III

None of the other works that tell love stories states quite as baldly as Ballade 50 that Christine-the-poet herself wants nothing to do with love. But each of them clearly establishes her position outside the system by reproducing some, if not all, of the other elements introduced by the metafictional framework of the *Cent ballades*.

In the six other works that contain love stories, the framework itself follows one of two recognizable patterns, with the visibility of the narrator and the extent of her role varying accordingly. The first is the model just seen in the *Cent ballades*, where the poet figure appears in poems number one, 50 and 100. Because these poems are counted in the numbering of the collection, they function on two levels; they constitute a commentary on the collection as a whole, but are also simply three of the one hundred *ballades*, adding to the plurality of voices heard.

In contrast, there are three works—The *Cent ballades d'amant et de dame*, the *Dit de la pastoure* and the *Livre du duc des vrais amans*—in which the poet figure's presence is even more limited. In these, she appears only in a prologue, and, in one, in an epilogue, rather than being integrated more thoroughly into the structure of the poem. The *Cent ballades d'amant et de dame* confines the poet figure's voice to an introductory *ballade* which sets up the following sequence: In contrast to the first poem of the earlier collection, this first *ballade* does not count as one of the hundred. The "Amant" is given the floor immediately in poem number one, and each subsequent poem is labeled with the name of the character speaking (or writing) it. In the *Dit de la pastoure* a short introduction (vv. 1–34) is set off from the narrative by the notation "La Pastoure," who then tells her own story. The extra-diegetic narrator does not speak again. The *Duc des vrais amans* follows the same pattern: a similarly short prologue (vv. 1–40) precedes the duke's tale; then his name is given, and the break indicates where the poet figure falls silent and the protagonist begins to speak. In the *Duc*, however, there is a short epilogue as well. Between the "Explicit" and the fixed-form lyric poems that follow,[18] the poet's voice is heard again in a short passage (3557–80), commenting on the complexity of the rhyme she has managed to maintain throughout the book.

In all three of the works in this second group, the formal break between the poet figure's words and the story highlights the narrator's absence from the narrative proper. In *Cent ballades d'amant et de dame*, in *Dit de la Pastoure* and in *Duc des vrais amans*, Christine-the-narrator is textually removed from the love stories she is presenting, actually outside the boundaries of those fictions. This device establishes her position quite literally outside the discourse of courtly love.

The three debate poems, *Le Livre du dit de Poissy*, *Le Debat de deux amans* and *Le Livre des trois jugemens*, adopt a pattern closer to that of the *Cent Ballades*. In these works, the narrator functions on both the extra- and the intradiegetic levels, that is, comments on the production of the story while also playing a part as one of several characters. With due allowance for the difference in the formal properties of the two works (interlocking, rhyming octosyllabic quatrains, as opposed to a sequence of *ballades*), the *Livre du dit de Poissy* has a structure very similar to that of the *Cent ballades*. In *Poissy*, just as in the *Cent ballades*, the narrator introduces the work, reappears in the middle to address the reader (represented, in *Poissy*, by a patron), and closes the poem by referring to the process of its creation. She also, however, in her intradiegetic role, plans, and participates in, the excursion that the *Dit* recounts and witnesses the debate it contains after launching it by encouraging one of the characters involved to tell her unhappy story. In the *Livre des trois jugemens*, a text that assumes the tripartite structure suggested in its title, the narrator comments on her material four times: at the beginning, and after each of the three debates. She also interacts with the debaters, in that it is she to whom they turn in search of a judge to resolve their arguments. In the *Debat de deux amans*, as in *Poissy*, she is on stage for the duration of the work as a limited participant, with comments directed to her patron at the beginning and the end.

Even in these debate poems where the narrator is present throughout the text, her position on the fringe of the action underscores her removal from the sphere of activity that the lovers portrayed participate in. Each of the three has its own strategy for isolating her from the material. In the *Dit de Poissy*, the narrator converses about love with the friends who accompany her on an excursion to Poissy, but her reason for undertaking the trip is to visit her daughter at a Dominican priory, through which she and the others are led on a tour before the debate portion of the poem begins. Christine launches the debate on the return to Paris by gently questioning a young lady whom she sees to be suffering. Throughout the unhappy stories that the lady and the knight tell, however, and during their disagreement over which of them has greater grounds to be pitied, the narrator remains silent, speaking up only at the end, when they ask her to find a suitable judge for their dispute. While a sympathetic companion to her love-lorn friends, she is distanced from them by two attributes that preclude an empathetic response: her strong association with the religious community that stands for a very different life from that led by the young nobles and by her status as a devoted mother. The love she represents is maternal.

The *Debat de deux amans* graphically places Christine on the periphery of the world of lovers by showing her on the sidelines of the party which sets the scene for the debate. At a splendid Paris townhouse, there is assembled a company of attractive young ladies and knights, all of whom were "deligent / De joye faire" (vv. 99–100). Sixty lines (vv. 82–144) are given to a description of the happy, joyful ambiance of the gathering: the dancing, the laughter, the amorous glances. It is a most lighthearted affair: "[t]oute tristece en estoit hors banie" (v. 109). There is one sad figure, however. The narrator herself is preoccupied with the sorrow that never leaves her, resulting from the death of "cil que je porte en ma memoire / Sanz nul oubly" (vv. 151–52). So she stays "sus un banc en cellui lieu assise / Sanz mot sonner, regardant la devise / Des fins amans gentilz"

(157–59). The opposition is drawn in strong terms: against the background of the lively, dancing, flirtatious crowd, we see a solitary, seated figure, steeped in mourning that she has no wish to relieve.

The narrator's position gives her an excellent vantage point from which to observe the action. She picks out among the company one squire, the most handsome and gracious of all. She is able to discern from the way he gazes at one of the ladies present that this young man is clearly "surpris d'amours" (v. 207). In contrast, another pensive, unhappy figure appears, this one a knight (vv. 209 ff.). He is seated near the narrator, his head on his hand, sighing. Christine sizes up this character, too, with her keen eye: "Soingneusement son maintien regardoie / Pour ce que si pensif je le veoie" (vv. 226–27). It is clear to her that he is suffering for love. No one else notices his despondent behaviour, because everyone but the knight and Christine is dancing.

Several elements in this scenario instruct us about the narrator's situation. Her position on the sidelines is perfect for fulfilling her function as witness to the events as they unfold. The knight at first shares her status as outsider; like her, he is cut off from the group by his unhappiness. The similarities in their demeanor, however, only temporarily disguise the essential difference between their sorrow. The knight, while disenchanted and unhappy, is still a lover, and thus belongs to the assembly in a way that Christine does not. For a short time, he and she converse apart from the others, after he gallantly approaches to speak with her. But soon they are joined by the young squire who engages them in a discussion about love, and the knight then shifts from a marginal role to a major one, as he becomes one of the "deux amans" whose debate Christine is recounting. She, on the other hand, remains a witness and, ultimately, the reporter of the case. She does not take part in the debate and resurfaces at the end only to propose the Duc d'Orléans as the judge for their disagreement (vv. 1939–76). The debaters then praise her skills as a writer and ask that she compose a "dit" to explain their case to the duke.

In accordance with the narrator's position as witness, there is an emphasis in *Deux amans* on the act of hearing what the other characters say. The same emphasis is found even more strongly in *Trois jugemens*: the narrator will report on the debates "De mot a mot, si com j'en ay record" (v. 29); the first case, as she heard it ("ainsi com j'oÿ dire" [v. 33]), is about a very beautiful lady; this lady's lover soon proves fickle, however, as the narrator heard tell ("j'oÿ recorder" [v. 213]); and so on.[19] One particularly significant example occurs in a passage describing the mutability of all things, including love:

> ... n'il n'est chose tant dure
> Qui ne s'use, soit chaleur ou froidure,
>   Et qui ne tire
> A quelque fin, et ainsi tire a tire
> S'usent amours souvent, s'ay je *ouy dire*.
>   (1298–1303, my emphasis)

Once again, she speaks from hearsay, rather than personal experience.

Her involvement is further limited by her refusal to act as a judge in the cases she reports on, despite the fact that all three couples seek her out with that request. In declining, she asserts that she is too little versed in the matters of love to serve as arbiter. This can in part be dismissed as a mark of deference to the Sénéschal de Hainaut, on whom she prevails to judge the debates in her stead. Nevertheless, the repeated statements about her ignorance in the domain of love exceed the necessary modesty and give the impression that she is going to some lengths to convince the protagonists and the reader that she is a disinterested party. In her address to the patron before the first debate begins, she says that she presents the cases to him because she herself knows too little about the subject to decide fairly ("trop peu sçay pour en bien jugier," [v. 26]). She replies much the same thing to the first couple who comes to her for help. Her first reason for demurring is that she wouldn't want to favour one side and anger the other, but she adds: "Et autressi ne sçay tout ou partie / De tel debat jugier, pou apertie / Y suis sans faille" (vv. 670–72). To the second and third couples, she answers simply that they could certainly find a much better judge than she (vv. 1243–61; 1504–11). As reflected in the opinion of the characters, she is wise enough to be considered among the possible judges, and she does not protest the implication that in this regard she is equal to her patron—she simply bows to his greater expertise in this particular area. After all, a wounded man's cure depends on his doctor:

> ... a bon mire
> Doit le naivré
> Soy adrecier, s'estre veult delivré
> De son grief mal" (1511–14).

She is evidently not the specialist these lovers need, and in each case she agrees, therefore, to act only as an intermediary.

IV

In all six works, those in which the narrator witnesses all phases of the development as well as those where her presence is more limited, the prologues make use of the first rhetorical device found in the *Cent ballades*: that is, they begin with an appeal to the patron for whom the work was composed. The three debate poems, two of which name this person (the *Debat de deux amans* is addressed to the Duc d'Orléans and the *Livre des trois jugemens* to the Sénéschal de Hainaut)—praise the patron extravagantly, extolling his courtly attributes and particularly, as befits the context, his ability to judge fairly on matters of the heart. The equivalent passage from the *Dit de la pastoure* is shorter, but contains the essentials and is representative of the type:

> Ay fait ce dittié en rimes,
> A mon pouoir leonimes,
> A requeste de personne
> Dont par le mond le nom sonne,
> Qui bien me puet commander
> Et son bon vouloir mander. (15–20)

Invariably, the patron is of high rank, someone who must be obeyed. In four cases including the *Dit de la Pastoure* (the others are *Duc des vrais amans, Cent ballades d'amant et de dame* and *Dit de Poissy*), this person has specifically commissioned a "dittié" of some kind. Indeed, in the case of the *Duc*, the "seigneur" making the request (who may or may not represent a true, historical patron of Christine's) asks that Christine-the-poet record his own story. As the prologue states:

> Si lui plaist que je raconte,
> Tout ainsi comme il me conte,
> Les griefs anuis et les joyes,
> Les fais, les estranges voyes
> Par ou est depuis passez,
> Pluseurs ans a ja passez. (25–30)

Christine accedes to the request and says that she will tell his tale "en sa personne" (v. 39), that is, in his own words.

Here, obviously, whether the request is real or imagined, it provides the material for the story and therefore takes the choice of topic out of Christine's hands. In the *Cent Ballades d'amant et de dame*, as well, she has been ordered to write "Cent balades d'amoureux sentement" about "un amoureux et sa dame" (vv. 6, 8), in punishment for having counselled ladies to avoid love. In *Poissy*, the *Trois jugemens* and *Deux amans*, it is not the patron who dictates the contents; rather, it is the lovers involved in the debates who have asked her to find them a judge, and she obliges both debaters and judge by presenting the arguments to an arbiter who will enjoy the case.

The imposition of subject matter is one of the ways in which Christine can maintain her distance from love as a topic. The source of the order is unimportant. It makes no difference whether the patron requests a love story or whether such a work, supposedly written at the behest of the protagonists, is considered suitable for presentation to a courtly patron. In either case, Christine can present her material as something she writes about dutifully, to fulfill a promise. As she takes care to point out on several occasions, her own preferences lie elsewhere.

Her statement of these preferences occurs in conjunction with her deference to a patron and reinforces the notion that she goes against her personal inclination in writing about love.

The prologues of *Cent ballades d'amant et de dame* and *Duc des vrais amans* both declare that the obligation to produce love poetry takes her away from the pursuit of other, and, by implication, more worthwhile projects.

In *Duc des vrais amans*, the opening lines of the prologue establish her reluctance:

> Combien que occupacion
> Je n'eusse ne entencion
> A present de dittiez faire
> D'amours, car en aultre affaire
> Ou trop plus me delittoye
> Toute m'entente mettoye . . . (1–6)

She will begin this "nouvel dit," however, because she has been asked to by someone whose request must be honoured.

The *Cent ballades d'amant et de dame* adopts a more judgmental tone about the relative merits of composing love poetry as opposed to other kinds of work. Like the equivalent passage in *Duc*, the opening *ballade* begins in a neutral voice with the statement that she had had no intention of writing about love because her thoughts were elsewhere: "Quoy que n'eusse corage ne pensée, / Quant a present, de dits amoureus faire / Car autre part adés suis apensée..." (vv. 1–3). In contrast, the third stanza betrays a certain irritation: "Or pry je a Dieu que n'en soye lassée / Car mieulx me pleust entendre a autre afaire / De trop greigneur estude" (vv. 17–19). The show of reluctance is certainly deliberate. Because the composition of this sequence of poems is purportedly undertaken as punishment for having displeased an important person with one of her earlier works, Christine must maintain the pose of an author being censured. She cannot, therefore, appear to be very pleased to comply with the order.

Nevertheless, a professional writer such as Christine depended for her livelihood on her patrons and their interest in her work. The kind of request that generates the debates, the *ballade* sequences and stories such as the *Duc* and *Pastoure* would, therefore, hardly have constituted an unwelcome demand. Daniel Poirion remarks on this aspect of the professional writer's career in discussing the order behind the *Cent Ballades d'amant et de dame*:

> cette contrainte extérieure, cette détermination par le public n'impliquent pas une servitude étroite, une censure, ou une direction qui s'exercerait sur toute la création littéraire. Après tout, le poète de cette époque est un artisan pour qui la commande d'un ouvrage représente une impulsion positive, et non une contrainte négative.[20]

In this context, the prologues in which she stresses her sorrow and her reluctance to write yet another love story can be read, to some extent, as a pose, a variation of the modesty topos she also employs. Her protestations help define the image the reader forms of both the poet and the patron as represented in the text. The patron's prestige is augmented by the notion that his request is important enough to cause the writer to leave more serious work and write about love despite her reluctance and her sorrow. In turn, the emphasis on Christine's other preoccupations and literary endeavors enhances her reputation as an author: she is a learned woman, generally occupied with studies more serious than love stories; she is professional enough, however, to write on demand rather than from personal inspiration alone.

The effect of stressing that the choice of subject matter reflects public tastes or a specific request is to focus the readers' attention on the skill with which the old themes are treated. A comment by Suzanne Bagoly regarding the creation of Christine's lyric poetry applies equally well to the narrative works about love: "Mieux qu'un devoir, la réponse à une commande appelle la perfection, l'achèvement de l'offrande; quand le thème en est donné, tout gît dans la façon que lui modèlera l'auteur."[21] In acknowledgement of this concern with style and technique, each of the works discussed above refers again and again to the process of its own composition.

Some of these references comment on the difficult task the poet has set herself. The passage following the completion of the lover's tale in *Duc des vrais amans*, for example, appeals to others "ditteurs" to recognize the technical accomplishment demonstrated in the rhyme scheme:

> A tous ditteurs, qui savoir
> Ont en eulx, celle savoir
> Fait, qui ce dittié ditta,
> Qu'en trestous les vers dit a
> Rime leonime ou livre,
> Et tel tout au long le livre. (3557–62)

There follows a description of what a "rime leonime" entails, and then an explanation for undertaking such a challenge: the poet "Ainsi l'a voulu parfaire / Pour monstrer son essience" (vv. 3570–71). It takes skill and hard work to maintain such a rhyme scheme while treating diverse subjects, she says, and she invites anyone who is skeptical about her success to check for themselves. The *Dit de la pastoure* likewise points out that it is written "en rimes, / A mon pouoir leonimes" (vv. 15–16) and then adds, in eight lines, the enigmatic advice that a pretty tale can hide a deeper meaning (vv. 24–32).

Statements such as these, dealing with the theoretical concerns behind Christine's writing, are rare, particularly in the works on love, and so the most obvious evidence of her preoccupation with the process of composition lies in the play between various levels of the text. In the debate poems one finds, as noted earlier, repeated asides from the poet to the patron. The works label themselves variously as a "dit," a "dittié," a "rommans," or an "oeuvre."[22] There are also frequent references to something that occurs either earlier or later in a particular text. Examples from *Deux amans* can be used to demonstrate the device: "vers nous vint cellui tout a esture, / Dont j'ay parlé / Ycy dessus" (vv. 347–49); "[l'escuier] Parla ainsi com m'orrez affermer" (v. 1003); "ainsi leur devisay / Com vous pourrez / Yci ouïr" (vv. 1939–41).

These features are not exclusive to Christine's stories about love, nor indeed to Christine's corpus. Like Machaut before her, all of Christine's writing is self-conscious, as one might expect in the corpus of an author for whom her status as a writer was of such a fundamental importance.[23] The manner in which she draws attention to the mechanics of making poetry and prose in fact becomes part of her self-portrait as an author, and results in texts that frequently refer to themselves. Nevertheless, the high degree of self-reflexivity in the love stories coupled with the deliberate undermining of love as a subject matter gives the impression that these works, even more than Christine's others, are about the art of writing.

Various comments are sprinkled through her work to the effect that the writing of love poetry can constitute an entertainment for the writer just as the final product entertains the reader. These statements are found in conjunction with a description of the personal misfortunes (often expressed as the harsh treatment of Fortune) that have caused the author so much unhappiness. Virelay XV, for example, a poem from another early collection, speaks of composing poetry as a diversion that can bring a bit of relief from the sorrow that overwhelms her.[24] She speaks first of how hard she must work because of her grief to write happier verse for others (vv. 1–13). But then she adds that despite the difficulty of the task, accomplishing it can be a pleasure for her, as well.[25] The *Dit de la pastoure* repeats the same theme, opening with the statement that, however little she knows about it, she has often entertained herself by writing poetry:

> Moy de sagece pou duitte
> Ja par mainte fois deduitte
> Me suis de faire dittiez
> De plusieurs cas apointiez,
> Combien que pou entremettre
> M'en sache, pour desmettre
> Aucunement la pesance
> Dont je suis en mesaisance,
> Que jamais ne me fauldra
> Jusques vie me fauldra (1–10).

These lines echo what one finds in *Lavision-Christine*, where Christine reflects on her career. In the early stages, she says, she composed poems about her unhappiness; but also, "pour passer temps et pour aucune gayete attraire a mon cuer doloureux [des musetes des pouetes . . . me faisoient] faire ditz amoureux et fais dautrui sentement" (p. 161). There can be no doubt that it is not love itself, but writing about love that brings her pleasure.

From this perspective, that is, viewing the works on love as a self-conscious entertainment or distraction, one should not be surprised to find one final element of writerly awareness. Four of the texts extend and elaborate the ludic dimension by ending in an anagram giving Christine's name. One of the four is the *Cent ballades*, as mentioned above. The others are the *Deux amans*, the *Trois jugemens* and the *Dit de Poissy*. Together they constitute half of all the works that end this way. The other four are all also early works, written during the same stage of Christine's career as those under discussion here.[26] Furthermore, two of the others, the *Epistre au dieu d'amours* and *Dit de la rose*, are the two other books in Christine's corpus which are primarily concerned with some aspect of *fin'amors*. In other words, the use of anagrams is a feature employed in only a small segment of Christine's work, a group limited by period of composition and to a somewhat lesser extent, by subject matter.

The significance of the words in which the author's name is hidden has been touched on in the discussion of the last poem in the *Cent ballades*, where Christine's name (or more exactly a variant of it) is scrambled to form "en escrit." The adjective "creintis," found in *Poissy* and in the *Epistre au dieu d'amour*, can be seen as characterizing the bewilderment, difficulty and despair by which she was overwhelmed for so long after the death of her husband. The nouns "cristienté" and "crist," found in *Deux amans* and *Trois jugements*, reflect her strong personal religious belief, a theme which is given greater prominence in her later books. Jacqueline Cerquiglini, commenting briefly on the anagrams, feels that Christine read in her name, "un programme, une définition et peut-être un destin,"[27] choosing to conceal her name in words that emblematize her life and livelihood. Certainly to the extent that these metaphors reflect her preoccupations and purpose, they could not place her further from the courtly values espoused by the characters on stage before the author closes the work.

V

The question that remains is, what effect does the distancing of the narrator in the books about love have on the reader's perception of those works? One immediate answer is that the narrator's distance from the material creates and justifies critical distance. Because she makes it clear that she does not espouse the values of the game of love as portrayed, we are forced to consider carefully the implications of the stories told. Such analysis leads to the argument that Charity Cannon Willard and other critics have recently expounded, namely that Christine emphasizes the destructive potential of illicit love, particularly for the woman involved.[28] One of Willard's conclusions is, in fact, that close examination of the early works in verse proves that there is greater coherence in Christine's corpus than is first apparent.[29] The unhappy stories found in the works about love do seem to bear out the lessons stated explicitly for the first time in the *Duc des vrais amans*. This warning takes the form of a letter from the Dame de la Tour to the lady in love, in which she warns of the "perilz et dongiers qui sont en tel amour" (*Duc* p. 168), particularly for a woman of high birth.[30] The "Lay de Dame" which concludes the *Cent ballades d'amant et de dame*, addressed to "Amours dure et sauvage," speaks for itself as to the despair love can bring. I have argued elsewhere that the juxtaposition in the *Dit de Poissy* of a description of a religious community for women with a debate on questions of love reflects unfavourably on fashionable, worldly pursuits as opposed to a life dedicated to religion. Similarly, the failure of any of the debates to reach a resolution, the stalemate the lovers are left in, seems to point out the futility and frustration that dalliance with love entails.[31] All of these interpretations are supported by the determination of the narrator to hold herself above and apart from the tales she tells.

None of the works that tell love stories is primarily didactic. There are, however, two works from the same period that are. To quote again from Ballade 50 of the *Cent ballades*, Christine maintained, whatever her opinion of it, that love constituted, "le sentement le plus legier, qui mieulx plaist a tous." She used it to good effect in the *Epistre du dieu d'amours* and in the *Dit de la rose* to teach and reinforce good behaviour by emphasizing the honourable conduct expected of worthy lovers.[32] The *Epistre* takes the form of a royal letter from Cupid to all his "vrais loiaulx servans subgiez" (v. 6), addressing the complaints that have been brought before him by women in all stations of life about the many wrongs done to them by disloyal lovers. The punishment for those who indulge in such unworthy actions is excommunication and banishment from Cupid's court. The *Dit de la rose*, on a more optimistic note, recounts the founding of a new chivalric order, the Order of the Rose, to reward those who faithfully uphold the honor and reputation of women as they ought.

These two works share much with the seven that tell of individual lovers. At the same time, however, they manifest important differences in the treatment of the narrator's role. The *Epistre* and the *Dit de la rose* clearly adopt many of the principal elements of the world of *fin'amors*—Cupid as the sovereign to whom all lovers are subject; the moral code to which one must adhere in order to be worthy of love; the rose as an emblem of love—but use them as a sugar-coating to encourage responsible social interaction. The author capitalizes on the admirable facets of the code in an effort to correct injustice. There is nothing in the love/Love described which could offend the moral standards of the poet figure who presents these works. Consequently, there is no need for her to detach herself from the subject matter, or incorporate in the poem the devices that deflect any attempt to identify her as an advocate of the system.

Accordingly, as in the long allegorical works, there is within the text no appeal to a patron, nor any hint of outside influence as to choice of topic. Such dedications and references to a patron prove to be a feature unique to Christine's lyric poetry and the stories about love. Nor is there any mention of other preoccupations, more serious tasks or sorrow, from which the work at hand distracts her. In the *Epistre*, Christine the narrator is, in fact, completely absent.[33] It has been suggested that Christine can be seen as the royal secretary who would have read Cupid's letter aloud to his subjects.[34] Knowledgeable readers would undoubtedly have been amused by the royal "we" issuing from the hand of a woman writer who generally condemned the male version of the courtly game. They might also have quickly recognized behind the letter format the skills Christine had learned from her father and her husband (who before his death had held the position of royal secretary at the court of Charles V). But there is in fact no textual evidence to support this interpretation. In comparison with the works in which she goes to some lengths to establish her distance from Cupid and his machinations, her absence here seems to indicate tacit approval of the mission he is undertaking.

The opening of the *Dit de la rose*, as well, imitates the style of a royal letter. While the formal, somewhat ponderous nature of the address in verses 1–14 would have us believe that the speaker is a personage who commands some respect, there is no indication as to the identity or mandate of this "je" until well into the poem. The narrative and intercalated poems (several *ballades* and one "rondelet") of the first part describe the gathering that was taking place in a Paris townhouse when Dame Loyauté, an emissary from Amours, appears to a highly select group of nobles to found the new Order of the Rose. Christine finally presents herself (at v. 264 of 649), and only then do we learn that she has been present at the "manoir" throughout the entire event. From that point on, she herself appears as one of the cast of characters just as she does in the debate poems but again seems to be more of a witness of, rather than a participant in, the events that transpire. The detached nature of her presence and the initial impression that she speaks with authority are vindicated when we discover that she is Loyauté's handmaiden, a role that becomes clear to her in a dream as she spends the night in the townhouse. Christine has been chosen, Loyauté tells her, to select in her turn the "procuresses" who will spread the word about the Order to all countries and bestow a rose on all those who pledge to fulfil the Order's purpose.

Again the narrator is an intermediary, but in this instance, unlike her resistance to any involvement in the debates, she is far from reluctant:

> Lye fuz de la vision
> Et d'avoir tel commission;
> Car combien que je ne le vaille
> Ay je desir que nul ne faille,
> Et pour ce moy, qui suis commise
> A ce, ne doy estre remise
> De faire si bien mon devoir

Que je n'en doye blasme avoir. (594–601)

Because she is participating in a cause she espouses—ensuring that the honour of all ladies be upheld—she gives herself to the task wholeheartedly. Such is the inspiration behind this particular "dictié," in contrast to those which claim an obligation to a patron and/or those who have approached her for advice. Christine's role as amanuensis to the allegorical deities (as well as the framing dream sequence) in *Dit de la rose* anticipates her role in *Le Livre de la cité des dames* and *Le Livre des trois vertus*, to be written a few years later. In the *Dit de la rose* she is not simply the witness/recorder of others' adventures, the respected writer aloof from the lovers whose stories she tells; instead, while maintaining her distance from the acolytes of Love, she joins the ranks of those who legislate their behaviour.

The treatment of the narrator in the stories about love as contrasted to the same in Christine's other works points out on the level of the entire corpus the tension expressed by the narrator's anomalous status within the textual boundaries of each of those love stories themselves: the tension between courtly, relatively conventional themes and more purely didactic and political material. The tendency is to rate the alternatives, to place more value on the latter than on the former. Christine herself, in the autobiographical portion of *Lavision-Christine*, mentions the *Cent ballades* as a work of her youth (p. 160), and describes how she later moved from the composition of "choses iolies a mon commencement plus legieres" to a "plus grant soubtillete et plus haulte matiere" (p. 164) as her learning and skills increased. Nevertheless, with the exception of the *Cent ballades*, all the works dealing with love must be included in the total of ".xv. volumes principaulx" that she says she produced between 1399 and 1405 (p. 164), works of which the author obviously speaks with some pride.

The devaluation in the status of love that occurs from Machaut to Christine, from inspiration to convenient subject matter, explains certain unexpected features in some of her texts. If love is only one of many topics, there is no incongruity in incorporating almost anti-courtly themes—such as widowhood and sorrow, or praise of marriage—into a collection of what are mostly love poems. Viewed from this perspective, the transitions in the *Cent ballades* are less jarring than one might at first think, and the collection does not suffer from a lack of cohesion. The well-developed narrator's persona acts as a structuring device that binds together a variety of subjects. In more purely narrative works, one sees this structure in the *Dit de Poissy*, which combines a description of a religious community with a love debate; in the *Trois jugemens* which contains three independent segments; and even in the *Dit de la rose*, in which the third-person recounting of a courtly gathering is linked to a first-person dream vision by virtue of the narrator-poet.[35] Undoubtedly, the god Amours, prime source of poetic inspiration for the love poets of the fourteenth century, is replaced by Raison, Droiture, Justice and their sisters in Christine's pantheon. Because Christine's narrator, unlike Machaut's narrator, does not aspire to belong to the world she represents in the love stories, these poems avoid the conflict inevitable in Machaut's, namely the impossibility that a clerk, no matter how worthy his character and strong his desire, could ever fully participate in the game of love exclusive to the rarified social circles he was writing for. Machaut's *Voir dit* is the culmination of his literary quest to reconcile the unreconcilable.[36] In Christine, the social tension is replaced by a personal and professional one: must she play court poet and write the love stories that are so well-received or can she devote herself to the more studious pursuits suitable to a woman of high intelligence and thorough education? Christine's own ambivalence in no way undermines the pleasure that the modern reader, like the fifteenth-century reader, can take in the poems about love. One must look for the subtle ways in which Christine alters the compendium of topics she had inherited. And meanwhile, the narrator also guides us through the art of reading and writing the type of tale in hand.[37]

NOTES

1. It is significant that this image, often used as a portrait of Christine, actually appears at the beginning of the *Cent ballades*, one

of the works to be discussed here. Two slightly different versions of the picture can be found in British Library ms. Harley 4431 [folio 4r] and Bibliothèque Nationale f.fr. 835 [folio 1r]. For a reproduction of the Harley miniature, see the frontispiece in: Enid McLeod, *The Order of the Rose: the Life and Ideas of Christine de Pizan* (Totowa, N.J.: Rowman and Littlefield, 1976); the B.N. portrait is reproduced as the frontispiece in Josette Wisman, ed. and trans., *"The Epistle of the Prison of Human Life" with "An Epistle to the Queen of France" and "Lament on the Evils of the Civil War"* (N.Y.: Garland, 1984).

2. My references to the *Cent ballades d'amant et de dame* are taken from the edition by Jacqueline Cerquiglini (Paris: Union Générale d'Editions, 1982). All the others are from Maurice Roy, ed., *Oeuvres poétiques de Christine de Pisan*, 3 vols. (Paris: Firmin Didot [SATF], 1886-96); *Cent ballades*, t.I: 1-100; *Le Dit de la rose*, t.II: 29-48; *Le Debat de deux amans*, t.II: 49-109; *Le Livre des trois jugemens*, t.II: 111-57; *Le Livre du dit de Poissy*, t.II: 159-222; *Le Dit de la pastoure*, t.II: 223-94; *Le Livre du duc des vrais amans*, t.III: 59-208.

3. For a discussion on Christine's indebtedness to Machaut, see: Annie Reese Pugh, "Le jugement du roy de Behaigne et le Dit de Poissy de Christine de Pisan" in *Romania* XXIII (1894): 581-86; Johanna Catharina Schilperoort, *Guillaume de Machaut et Christine de Pisan, étude comparative* (The Hague: Mouton, 1936); Barbara K. Altmann, "Reopening the Case: Machaut's Jugement Poems as a Source in Christine de Pizan," in *Reinterpreting Christine de Pizan*, Earl Jeffrey Richards, ed., (Athens: Univ. of Georgia Press, pp. 137-56).

4. See Brownlee, *Poetic Identity in Guillaume de Machaut* (Madison, Wis.: University of Wisconsin Press, 1984). My discussion of Machaut's narrator figure is indebted to Brownlee's work.

5. For the text of the *Prologue*, see Ernest Hoepffner, ed., *Oeuvres de Guillaume de Machaut*, 3 vols., (Paris: Firmin Didot [SATF], 1918-21) vol. I, pp. 1-12.

6. See in particular Part IV, vv. 13-17, and V, vv. 21-23.

7. What differs in her conception of her profession is, of course, that she does not aspire to compose musical accompaniments for her texts.

8. See particularly Part III of *Lavision-Christine*, Mary Louise Towner, ed. (New York: AMS Press, 1969 [reprint of a dissertation, Catholic University of America, 1932]). Biographical notes are also

to be found in the *Livre de la mutacion de fortune*, Suzanne Solente, ed., 4 vols., (Paris: Picard [SATF], 1959–66); and in *Le Livre du chemin de long estude*, Robert Püschel, ed. (Geneva: Slatkine, 1974 [originally Berlin: Damköhler, 1887]).

9. Zeeman, "The Lover-Poet and Love as the Most Pleasing 'Matere' in Medieval French Love Poetry" in *Modern Language Review* 83 (1988): 820–42. See particularly p. 840: "what is important and innovatory in [Christine's] claim is that such personal experience of love is *not necessary* for composition" [original emphasis].

10. *Romanic Review* 79 (1988): 199–221. Brownlee's argument converges closely with mine particularly in his analysis of the *Dit de la rose*.

11. This approach has been taken by the following: Brownlee, "Discourse of the Self"; Lori Walters, "The Woman Writer and Literary History: Christine de Pizan's Redefinition of the Poetic Translation in the *Epistre au dieu d'amour*" in *French Literary Studies* 16 (1989); Maureen Quilligan, "Allegory and the Textual Body: Female Authority in Christine de Pizan's *Livre de la cité des dames*," *Romanic Review* 79 (Jan. 1988): 222–42 plus plates; Patricia A. Phillippy, "Establishing Authority: Boccaccio's *De claris mulieribus* and Christine de Pizan's *Le Livre de la cité des dames*," *Romanic Review* 77.3 (May 1986): 167–93.

12. On this point, see Charity Cannon Willard, *Christine de Pizan: Her Life and Works* (N.Y.: Persea, 1984), pp. 59–60.

13. This dating is based on internal evidence to be found in two poems, numbers IX and XX, which state, respectively, that the "je" writing has been widowed for five and ten years. See Roy's introduction to the *Cent ballades*, t.I: xxvi–xxvii. Needless to say, the dating depends on the assumption that the lyric voice in question can be identified with the historic Christine, whose husband Etienne died in 1389.

14. In her article "Lovers' Dialogues in Christine de Pizan's Lyric Poetry from the *Cent ballades* to the *Cent ballades d'amant et de dame*," Charity Cannon Willard treats poems 21–49 as a unit. In a more recent article, however, she calls poem 43 the end of the sequence: "Punishment and Reward in Christine de Pizan's Lyric Poetry," *Rewards and Punishments in the Arthurian Romances and Lyric Poetry of Medieval France: Essays for Kenneth Varty* [Woodbridge, Suffolk: D. S. Brewer, 1987], p. 168.

15. On the narrative properties inherent in poem cycles, see Jacqueline Cerquiglini, "Le lyrisme en mouvement," *Perspectives médiévales* 6 (juin 1980): 75–86.

16. The "logic" of anagrams and the way they function in Machaut's work is the topic of an article by Laurence de Looze, "Mon nom trouveras": A New Look at the Anagrams of Guillaume de Machaut—the Enigmas, Responses, and Solutions" in *Romanic Review* 79.4 (November 1988): 537–57. Particularly relevant to the discussion of Christine's anagram in Ballade 100 are the following points: an author must already be well known in order to use this device successfully; the solution is known to the reader even before the instructions for solving the puzzle are given; and the name to be found in the scrambled letters is not always "correct," that is, does not match the name as we find it elsewhere.
17. Another of Christine's collections of poetry, the *Jeux à vendre* (Roy t.I: 187–205), ends with a similar anagram. Number 70 apparently conceals both Christine's name and that of her late husband, Etienne, in the word "escrinet." This variation obviously carries the same connotations as "en escrit"—the importance of the author's literary production is stressed, as well as the equivalence of Christine and her work.
18. These poems—nine *ballades*, three *Virelais*, four *Rondeaulx* and one *Complainte*—are announced before the "Explicit" by the duke, who says that he will append the poems that he and his lady exchanged when they were far from each other (3515–19).
19. Other similar usages can be found, for example, at vv. 220; 329; 365; 1245; 1273; and 1518.
20. Poirion *Le Poète et le prince* (Paris: PUF, 1965), p. 247.
21. "Christine de Pizan et l'art de 'dictier' ballades," *Le Moyen Age* 92:1 (1986), p. 67.
22. "Dit" is used frequently: see *Deux amans* vv. 10, 1990; *Poissy* v. 2066. "Dittié" can be found in *Deux amans* v. 2009; "rommans" in *Deux amans* v. 53; "oeuvre" in *Trois jugemens* v. 1519. The *Cent ballades d'amant et de dame* refers to the "livret" in which the *ballades* are being written (v. 14). This list of references is meant simply to provide examples of such usage; it is by no means exhaustive.
23. On the self-consciousness of Machaut's work, see Brownlee, *Poetic Identity*, particularly the Introduction: "Machaut and the Concept of *Poète*," pp. 3–23.
24. Roy t.I: 116–17.
25. Et se le cuer dolent é
    Il ne m'est mie legier
    Joyeux ditz faire a plenté,

> Mais pour un pou alegier
> La doulour qui m'est prochaine
> Je les fais communement
> Joyeux . . . (14–20).

26. I am relying for the number of works containing anagrams on my own count and on the list provided by Cerquiglini in the introduction to her edition of the *Cent ballades d'amant et de dame* (see pp. 23–23). The other four are: *Mutacion de fortune, Jeux à vendre* number 70 (the last poem in that collection), *Epistre au dieu d'amours* and *Dit de la rose*.
27. Introduction to *Cent ballades d'amant et de dame*, p. 22.
28. Willard has written several articles on the subject, including: "Lovers' Dialogues in Christine de Pizan's Lyric Poetry from the 'Cent Ballades' to the 'Cent Ballades d'Amant et de Dame," *Fifteenth Century Studies* 4 (1981): 167–80; "Christine de Pizan: Cent ballades d'amant et de dame: Criticism of Courtly Love," in Glynn Burgess et al., eds., *Court and Poet: Selected Proceedings of the Third Congress of the International Courtly Literature Society* (Liverpool: Cairns, 1981): 357–64; "Concepts of Love According to Guillaume de Machaut, Christine de Pizan, and Pietro Bembo," Glynn Burgess and Robert Taylor eds., *The Spirit of the Court: Selected Proceedings of the Fourth Congress of the International Courtly Literature Society* (Dover, N.H.: Brewer, 1985): 386–92. See also Liliane Dulac, "Christine de Pisan et le malheur des 'vrais amans,' " in *Mélanges de langue et de littérature médiévales offerts à Pierre Le Gentil* (Paris: S.E.D.E.S., 1973): 223–33; and "Dissymétrie et échec de la communication dans les *Cent Ballades d'Amant et de Dame* de Christine de Pizan," *Lengas* 22 (1987): 133–46.
29. See Willard's introduction to "Christine de Pizan's *Cent Ballades d'amant et de dame*: Criticism of Courtly Love."
30. The same letter is repeated verbatim in the *Livre des trois vertus*. See the modern edition by Charity Cannon Willard, *Le livre des trois vertus* (Paris: Champion, 1989); pp. 109–20. There also exists an English translation by Willard, *A Medieval Woman's Mirror of Honor: The Treasury of the City of Ladies* (N.Y.: Bard Hall Press/Persea Books, 1989).
31. See B. Altmann, "Coherence and Diversity in Christine de Pizan's *Livre du dit de Poissy*," *French Forum* 12.3 (Sept. 1987), 261–71 and "Reopening the Case: Machaut's Jugement Poems as a Source in Christine de Pizan."
32. The *Epistre au Dieu d'amours*, written in 1399, and the *Dit de la rose*, dated Valentine's day 1401, are available in a new critical

edition and English translation by Thelma Fenster. See Fenster and Mary C. Erler, eds., *Poems of Cupid, God of Love: Christine de Pizan's "Epistre au dieu d'amour" and "Dit de la Rose"; Thomas Hoccleve's "The Letter of Cupid"; with George Sewell's "Proclamation of Cupid"* (Leiden: Brill, 1990).

33. She is absent with the exception that one single manuscript of the text, B.N. f.fr. 835, contains the anagram "Creintis" before the "Explicit" with no indication of how the word is to be unscrambled or what it signifies.

34. See Willard, *Christine de Pizan: Her Life and Works*, pp. 47, 62. Kevin Brownlee is of Willard's opinion, insofar as the construct of a letter written by Cupid "allows Christine to present herself indirectly as Cupid's secretary who writes down and then, presumably, reads out her royal master's missive." He acknowledges, however, that there is "no explicit self-figuration [of Christine] at the diegetic level." See Brownlee, "Discourses of the Self," p. 201.

35. Christine uses even at the level of the individual text the unifying presence of the poet figure that binds the various different works in Machaut's whole corpus. On this aspect of Machaut, see Brownlee, *Poetic Identity*, p. 14 and elsewhere.

36. An introduction to these issues can be found in Poirion, *Le Poète et le prince*, p. 205. For a much more detailed analysis, see Jacqueline Cerquiglini: "Tension sociale et tension d'écriture au XIVème siècle: les dits de Guillaume de Machaut" in *Littérature et société au moyen âge* (Paris: Champion, 1978), pp. 111–29; and the chapter "Le clerc-écrivain" in *"Un engin si soutil": Guillaume de Machaut et l'écriture au XIVe siècle* (Paris: Champion, 1985), pp. 107–38.

37. This article was finished in 1990, and therefore does not take into consideration the abundance of new research published since then on Christine, some of which bears more or less directly on the issues I have raised. Works to be considered include: Liliane Dulac, "La Figure de l'Ecrivain dans quelques traités en prose de Christine de Pizan," in *Figures de l'Ecrivain au Moyen âge. Actes du Colloque / Université Picardie, 1988*, Danielle Buschinger, ed. (Göppingen: Kümmerle, 1991); Dulac (trans. Christine Reno), "The Representations and Functions of Feminine Speech in Christine de Pizan's *Livre des Trois Vertus*," in E. J. Richards et al. eds., *Reinterpreting Christine de Pizan* (Athens, Georgia: University of Georgia Press, 1992); Maureen Quilligan, "The Name of the Author: Self-Representation in Christine de Pizan's *Livre de la Cité*

des Dames," Exemplaria 4.1 (Spring 1992), 201–228, and Chpt. 1, "The Name of the Author," in Quilligan's book, *The Allegory of Female Authority: Christine de Pizan's Cité des Dames* (Ithaca, N.Y.: Cornell University Press, 1991).

Claire Nouvet

The "Marguerite": a Distinctive Signature

Two new figures appear on the literary scene of the fourteenth century: the figure of the professional poet and the corollary figure of the patron of letters. With the emergence of these two figures, literature engages in a distinctive practice of self-reflexivity; representing himself in his text, the professional poet stages his role as well as his patron's role in its creation. A commissioned and remunerative narrative, the text inscribes the social constraints presiding over its composition; it becomes the story of its own production.

Two works exemplify in a privileged manner this explicit thematization of the poet/patron relationship: Guillaume de Machaut's *Voir-Dit*, and Jean Froissart's *Prison amoureuse*. Although it borrows from Machaut the idea of representing in the text both poet and patron, Froissart's text departs from its model. While Machaut's text conjoins the professional relation between poet and patron and the lyric relation between lover and lady by making the lady play the role of the patron, Froissart's text disjoins these relations. The *Prison amoureuse* stages an "I" who is both Narrator and Protagonist, this last figure assuming the role of the lyric lover-poet. This love-adventure is, however, soon brought to an end. A disappointed lover at the outset of the narrative, the Progatonist withdraws into a retreat where he receives a letter signed "Rose." Despite the apparent femininity of this name, "Rose" is not a lady but a lover who requires the protagonist's advice. At first an advisor in matters of love, the Progatonist of the *Prison amoureuse* soon becomes an advisor on the subject of courtly writing, before finally assuming the role of professional poet when Rose asks him to collect their correspondence into a "volume."[1]

The *Prison amoureuse* thus converts the lyric Protagonist into a professional poet writing to and for Rose. By doing so, it seems to expose the predicament that the historical "Jean Froissart" faced when writing at his patron's command. This mirror-effect, however, reveals a major difference; in sharp contrast to Guillaume de Machaut's text, where the professional poet represented in the text bears the author's first name, "Guillaume," the *Prison amoureuse* refuses to name the professional poet that it represents "Jean Froissart." At his patron's request, the professional poet adopts a "devise," a pseudonym, as well as a "signet," a specific figure, a seal, which functions as his signature. Although invoked in the name of lyric secrecy, the pseudonym and the signet, fulfill, I believe, another function. Refusing to identify himself by his proper name, the poet "Jean Froissart" resorts to another mode of identification, a mode which radically redefines the very notion of poetic identity.

The patron initiates this alternative mode of identification when he chooses the pseudonym "Rose." With this pseudonym, the patron redefines his identity. Renouncing the sociality of his proper name, he exchanges his social identity for a lyric identity since "Rose" is the pseudonym that he has given to the lady he loves. Read in this perspective, the name "Rose" would mean "I am the one who loves Rose." With this name, the patron not only presents himself as a lyric lover, he also identifies himself as a poet or, rather, he demonstrates that these two identities are inextricably entangled. The choice of the name "Rose" proceeds from the following comparison:

> Car tout ensi com la rose est souverainne sur toutes flours, elle est tant qu'a moi souverainne sur toutes; et pour s'amour je porte une rose pour ma devise, coment que je n'ai mie bien matere dou faire.[2]

Naming himself "Rose," the patron presents himself as the one who, out of love, *likens* his lady to a rose. The lover is thus from the very beginning a poet, a poet who, moreover, identifies himself by (and with) the performance of a rhetorical move: the metaphorical process which turns a lady into a flower. In other words, it is the metaphorical process which produces the lady's name that identifies the poet *as poet*; poetic identity ceases to refer to the historical person in order to refer to a rhetorical performance. No wonder then if the poet is better named by the lady's name than by his own proper name. This feminine name exposes the poetic gesture which his own proper name can never hope to designate; it functions as the poet's true proper name. For this name to become a signature, a supplementary twist must be added to this already complex sequence. Rose does not sign his letters with the name "Rose," but appends to them the "signet," the figure, of a rose. This "signet" redefines the very notion of signature. A poetic signature can no longer be equated with the mere writing down of one's proper name, it becomes the *figuration* of this name.

According to Rose, then, the poet identifies himself in his text by performing a rather complicated sequence of rhetorical moves: he must first liken his lady to a flower (a rose), then turn this noun into a proper name (Rose) which is itself turned into a figure (the graphic representation of a rose), and it is this last move which constitutes his true signature, a signature more "proper" than the mere inscription of his "proper" name. As Rose's name already suggests, this mode of poetic identification cites a specific text: the *Romance of the Rose*. This text seems to accomplish the intricate performance that Rose requires; implicitly likening the lady to a rose, it gives her the pseudonym of "Rose" before turning this proper name into the figure of a rose. Citing the *Romance of the Rose*, Rose is then asking the poet to identify himself by repeating the rhetorical performance which, according to him, constitutes the distinctive signature of this text.

Confronted with Rose's request, the poet of the *Prison amoureuse* decides, after some hesitation, to choose the pseudonym "Flos" and to adopt the daisy as a "signet." As he himself stresses, "Flos" is the Latin translation of the French "Flower: "Flos en latin, fleur en français" (v. 890). Using the Latin to translate a noun into a proper name, the professional poet thus distinguishes himself from his patron by opposing the generic "Flower" to the patron's particular flower. This generic designation, which implicitly defines him as a general figure capable of comprehending all particularities, is susceptible to several interpretations. First, as Douglas Kelly points out, it can refer to the poet's general knowledge of love by opposition to the patron's particular knowledge of it: "The poet retains his general referentiality—Flos is a generic name—so as to speak for all flowers to Rose.... As Flos he comprehends all specific loves (Letter II. 29–32) as the genus flower does all species of flower."[3] And, indeed, having taken in the correspondence the pedagogic stance of the advisor in courtly writing and courtly love, the poet seems to be endowed with a general understanding that comprehends all particular loves.

But the generic name "Flos" can also point to another kind of generality and comprehension. A professional writer, Flos is expected to collect both the letters and the lyric poems that he and Rose have exchanged in a single "volume," a text. The *Prison amoureuse* implicitly compares the constitution of this "volume" to the creation of a "comprehensive" container. Implicitly thematizing its own constitution, it describes the various boxes in which Flos encloses Rose's letters and poems; it even represents Flos making the box in which the correspondence is to be collected. This emphasis on the material container metaphorizes the double function of the new-born author. First, this author must constitute a text as a comprehensive whole capable of containing elements as heterogeneous as the ones which compose the *Prison amoureuse* itself: narrative, letters, and lyric poems. Second, he must collect these fragmented texts into one complete work, an *"oeuvre,"* which the name of "Jean Froissart" will circumscribe. In other words, the author who creates textual containers promotes his own name to the status of an all-comprehending container.[4] A generic name, the name "Flos" would then designate the general function of the author's name. It would in effect "properly" name the function of the author's proper name: that of comprehending, circumscribing, not only one text but a whole body of work.

We should take into account a third and last interpretation. The generic name "Flower" can also indicate the general rhetorical understanding which characterizes the professional poet by opposition to the particular rhetorical move which characterizes the patron. While the patron can only liken a lady to a particular flower, the poet is gifted with a general comprehension of the rhetorical process in which the patron engages in particular terms. The poet distinguishes himself by his general rhetorical understanding of the "flowers" of rhetoric.

Having thus designated in his *"devise"* the multi-faceted generality inherent to the poetic function, Flos encounters a significant difficulty when the time comes to face the question of the *"signet."* While Rose has no problem figuring his own name, the generic name that "Flos" has chosen clearly resists such a figuration; the generality of the flower cannot be figured. By promoting himself to the status of a general figure, the poet has thus placed himself beyond representation: he can no more be represented than can the generic flower. Although beyond representation, he must nevertheless comply with his patron's demand and represent himself in a figure. While apparently limited to the correspondence of the *Prison amoureuse*, this representative constraint can be said to define Froissart's entire poetic production, which is thus characterized by an unresolvable contradiction. On the one hand, the poet elevates himself to a general and therefore unrepresentable status from which he derives his author-ity. On the other hand, he must submit to the patron's pressure and represent himself in his text. But how can he represent this general poetic self?

Confronted with this dilemma, Flos resolves it by adopting as a *"signet"* the *"margherite."* The choice of this particular figure, in the context of Froissart's *"oeuvre,"* is far from indifferent. Running through his entire corpus, the *"margherite"* functions as the privileged signifier which no single text can pretend to contain. Froissart devotes an entire Dit to it, the *Dit de la margherite*, and keeps referring to it in the *Espinette amoureuse*, in a *pastourelle*, and in his last *dittier*, the *Joli Buisson de Jonece*. This textual recurrence has led some to believe that "Margherite" was the name of the lady that Froissart loved, an hypothesis which the *Espinette amoureuse* apparently confirms.[5] At the end of the *Espinette amoureuse*, the narrator signals the specific lines in which his name as well as his lady's name are anagrammatized:

> Là estoit, ses mains sus son pis
> Et son chief sus les orilliers.
> N'i ot roses ni violiers,
> Mès j'appelloie ce par m'ame,
> Le Vregier de ma Droite Dame
> *je hantoie* là tempre et tart,
> Dont *frois*, dont chaux, navrés d'un *dart*
> D'amours; et lors de flours petites,
> Violetes et *margherites*
> Semoie dessus le tapis
> Qui dedens la chambre estoit mis.[6]
>   (emphasis added)

Choosing the daisy as *"signet,"* Froissart would then have recourse, as Rose did, to a lyric identity; he would be "the one who loves Margherite." The recourse to this lyric identity apparently gives a referential basis to his courtly authority. Having loved a real lady named "Margherite," the poet presumably gained from this particular experience the general understanding of love that the patron now seeks. Moreover, it is his ability to move from the particular to the general which distinguishes him from the patron and grants him his pedagogical authority over him.

If this strictly referential understanding of the name "Margherite" can account for the poet's pedagogical authority, it cannot, however, account for his poetic and, more precisely, rhetorical authority. Whether or not the poet Jean Froissart loved a real lady named "Margherite," what matters is the rhetorical use that he made of this referential or pseudo-referential love. In other words, the daisy can function as the poet's signature because it is exemplary of a poetic practice. Thanks to this particular flower, the poet Jean Froissart illustrates his general rhetorical understanding of the metaphorical process which turns ladies into flowers, a metaphorical process which he, moreover, understands as exemplary of a whole textual tradition.

This textual tradition discreetly appears in the very passage which seems to ground a strictly referential understanding of "Margherite." The passage of the *Espinette amoureuse* which reveals the lady's name makes an implicit reference to the *Romance of the Rose* when it represents the lover and his lady in a room which the lover calls the "Vregier de ma Droite Dame." This metaphorical *Vregier* recalls the literal *"vergier"* of the *Romance of the Rose*, an intertextual allusion which the seemingly unwarranted addition of a negative indication confirms. In contradistinction to the *Romance of the Rose*'s *"vergier"*, which contains a rose, Froissart's metaphorical *vregier* is characterized by the absence of roses: *"N'i ot roses ni violers"* (v. 3377). Having thus defined his *vregier* (i.e., his textual space) as the negative image of the *Romance of the Rose*'s textual space, the poet inscribes on it his proper name: *"Je han*toie la tempre et tart" (v. 3380; emphasis added). Thanks to this anagram, the poet *Jehan* Froissart represents himself as "haunting" the textual space of the *Romance of the Rose*, a space which he nevertheless modifies by strewing it with *"margherites"* instead of roses. Haunting the *Romance of the Rose*, Jean Froissart is thus engaged in a specific activity: the "strewing" of *margherites* on a carpet. The performance of this curious gesture constitutes in fact an implicit reading of the *Romance of the Rose*. The unnatural strewing of daisies on a carpet metaphorically represents the poetic gesture that the *Romance of the Rose* performed; while apparently describing natural flowers, it was in effect strewing flowers of rhetoric on its textual canvas. The substitution of a daisy for a rose thus enables the poet to re-read the pseudo-natural space of the *Romance of the Rose* as a rhetorical space where a flower like the rose is to be read as a flower of rhetoric. This understanding of the rose (and, by extension, of the daisy) as a rhetorical flower singularly problematizes its referential status, a problematization that the poet of the *Prison amoureuse* increases when he uses a daisy to sign his letters to Rose. By so doing, he stresses the privileged status of this flower of rhetoric. Functioning as a poetic signature, the daisy signals, in the text, the rhetorical performance which alone identifies the poet as a poet. Although apparently meant to name the referential lady that the poet loves, the daisy, as well as the rose, illustrate in fact the poetic process which creates "her" as a distinctive flower of rhetoric, a flower endowed with the privilege of signaling in the text the rhetorical performance which presided over its composition. Rendering explicit that which remained implicit in the *Espinette amoureuse*, the *Prison amoureuse* undoes the referential pretext of the courtly narrative. Although this narrative must posit the polarity I/She and endow this "she" with a degree of referentiality in order to provide a love story, this "she" is in fact a signature which reflects in the text the poet's distinctive figurative ability. Submitting himself to the representative constraints that his patron has imposed on him, the poet represents himself in his text. This representation, however, has nothing to do with a mimetic representation of his historical and social figure. The poet represents himself by signaling, whether in the figure of a rose or of a daisy, that which constitutes his only identity: his figurative capacity, his rhetorical ability to create a figure.

A specific signature which signals a distinctive figurative process, the *"marguerite,"* runs through Froissart's entire corpus. But why substitute a daisy for a rose? Why use this specific signature? As we shall see, Froissart substitutes a daisy for the rose because this flower allows him to encompass the entire poetic tradition of which he is the inheritor, a poetic tradition which includes Guillaume de Machaut as well as the *Romance of the Rose*. Machaut indeed devoted two Dits to the daisy, the *Dit de la fleur de lis et de la marguerite* and the *Dit de la margherite*, which Froissart explicitly recites in his *Dit de la margherite*, in a *pastourelle* and in his last dittier, the *Joli Buisson de*

The "Marguerite": a Distinctive Signature 259

Jonece. The question then becomes: how does Froissart reread the rose of the *Romance of the Rose* through his rereading and rewriting of Machaut's daisy poetry? How does he, thanks to a distinctive practice of rewriting and rereading, sign his work?

In his *Dit de la marguerite*, Machaut presents the daisy as the sun flower which follows the sun from dawn to dusk: [7]

> J'aim une fleur, qui s'uevre et qui s'encline
> Vers le soleil de jours quant il chemine,
> Et, quant il est couchiez sous sa courtine
>   Par nuit obscure,
> Elle se clot, ensois que li jours fine;
> Ses feuilles ont dessus coulour sanguine,
> Blanche dessous plus que gente n'ermine
>   De blancheur pure.   (vv. 1–8)

Machaut's text interprets the "inclination" of the daisy toward the sun as the metaphorical representation of the lady's humility and *"courtois accueil."* Like the daisy open to the sun, the lady is "open" to the lover's declarations. This open quality implicitly explains the puzzling resurrecting power granted to the daisy:

> Sa grant douceur garist les mauls d'amer,
> Sa grainne puet les mors ressusciter
> Car elle m'a geri d'outre la mer
>   De ma dolours   (vv. 25–28)

Metaphorically "dead," the lover is "resurrected," that is, cured of his sorrow, when the lady at last welcomes his love. That this cure should occur while the lover is separated from the lady (he is *"outre le mer"*) suggests, however, that it is less the daisy itself than its representation that resurrects the dead lover. The text confirms this suggestion when it describes the daisy as the image which is "represented" and "figured" in the lover's heart.[8] A reader of the *Romance of the Rose*, Machaut obviously expands on the God of Love's remedies. The figure of a daisy resurrects the dying lover as the figure of the rose remedied the Lover's metaphorical death in the *Romance of the Rose*.

In the *Dit de la fleur de lis et de la marguerite*, Machaut explicitly posits the comparison between the daisy and the lady which his first Dit only implicitly posited. Surprisingly, however, he creates a comparison to the second degree when he compares the comparison itself to an adornment, a clothing. As he *himself* states, he "clothed" his lady with the daisy: "De la marguerite ensement/ Li ay je fait un vestement" (vv. 385–86).[9] Moreover, it seems that it is this ability to "adorn" the lady with a metaphor which defines his poetic talent. The poet thus implicitly identifies himself with the metaphorical process which "dresses" ladies as flowers, an implicit mode of identification which Froissart's signature in the *Prison amoureuse* brings to explicitness. As for the description of the daisy, it apparently repeats with some modifications the basic description provided by the *Dit de la marguerite*. Like the *Dit de la marguerite* did, Machaut's *Dit de la fleur de lis et de la marguerite* insists on its resurrecting power:

> Un grant acteur de medecine
> Parle de li e determine
> Si com veü l'ay en son livre,
> Que les mors puet faire revivre,
> tant en fait on bons ongnemens.
>   (vv. 275–79)

The rest of the text explains this resurrecting power with an explicit analogy. As the daisy "Froide est et seche et restreintive" (v. 291), "Ensi ma dame debonnaire/Refroide, seche et fait garir/ Tous maus amoureus et tarir" (vv. 320–22—emphasis added). And if we wonder how the daisy/lady "cools down" and thus cures the lover, another curative flower, the lily, provides the indirect answer to our question. Machaut's Dit indeed compares the lady to both a lily and a daisy. According to Machaut, the lily produces a medicinal water "plus froide que n'est glace" (v. 98) which cures men of "*chalour*" (fever). Likewise, the lady cures the lover of his love "fever" when her tears

> Arrouse les yex et la face
> De son chier et loial amy,
> Et qu'elle die: Amis, aymi!
> Pour quoy ne vous confortez vous?

Certes mes cuers est vostres tous:
Tenez, amis, je le vous baille
        (vv. 118–23)

The curative value granted to the daisy/lady therefore resides in her ability to cry "cold" tears which both alleviate the lover's fever and "dry" his tears. A sign of love, these tears coincide with the "welcoming" discourse in which she grants her love to her long-suffering lover. Compared to a daisy, the lady is thus turned into the ideal courtly lady capable of "crying," that is, of responding, of "welcoming" the lover's sorrow.

Froissart's *Dit de la margherite* extensively quotes Machaut's Dit. As Anthime Fourrier points out in his introduction, it repeats nearly verbatim the description found in Machaut's *Dit de la margherite*:

Car tout ensi que li solaus cemine
De son lever jusqu'a tant qu'il decline,
La margherite encontre lui s'encline
        Comme celi
Qui monstrer voelt son bien et sa doctrine,
Car li solaus, qui en biauté l'afine,
Naturelment li est cambre et courdine
Et le deffent contre toute bruïne
Et ses coulours de blanc et de sanguine
Li par acroist. (vv. 53–62)

Froissart, however, introduces a modification in Machaut's first Dit when he declares that:

La margherite encontre lui s'encline
        Comme celi
Qui monstrer voelt son bien et sa doctrine

This modification seems to proceed from a reading of Machaut's second Dit in which the solar inclination of the daisy signifies its knowledge of the sun's power: "Et samble qu'elle ait cognoissance/Dou soleil et de sa puissance." Reread in the light of Machaut's second Dit, the "*doctrine*" of Froissart's daisy implicitly refers to its acknowledgement of the sun's creative power. A reading of Machaut's second Dit can also account for the further modification that Froissart's text introduces in its recitation of Machaut's first Dit. While Machaut represented the sun *"couchiez sous sa courtine."* Froissart transforms the sun into a *"cambre et courdine"* which protects the daisy against *"toute bruïne"* and thus *"ses coulours de blanc et de sanguine / Li par acroist."* *Le Joli mois de mai* describes the lady in nearly identical terms:

> Car elle est la flour souverainne
> De bonté et de biauté plainne,
> *Qui nulle bruïne n'estaint,*
> En tous temps elle est clere et certainne
> Et Nature forment se painne
> De li donner couleur et taint
> (vv. 287–94—emphasis added)[10]

The absence of any *"bruïne"* ensures the "clarity" of the daisy/lady. Although the description of the daisy as "dry" and therefore "clear" seems at first to innovate on Machaut's text, this innovation in fact refers to a detail of Machaut's text which Froissart apparently elided. Machaut's *Dit de la fleur de lis et de la marguerite* indeed endows the daisy with a clarity which is explicitly likened to a mirror effect:

> Sa couleur qu'est blanche et vermeille,
> Qui n'a seconde ne pareille,
> *Est si tresclere qu'on s'i mire*
> Clerement, qui bien la remire.
> La voit on bien s'il y a tache
> Qui le cuer de l'amoureus tache.
> (vv. 343–48—emphasis added)

The "dryness" and the "clarity" of Froissart's daisy/lady must therefore be read as a discreet echo of its mirror effect. By drying any fog or dew that might dampen its colors, the sun produces the daisy/lady as the *speculum* which reflects a clear image of the lover/poet.

While explicitly reciting Machaut's daisy poetry, Froissart's text inscribes this recitation within an implicit reference to the *Romance of the Rose*. If the *Romance of the Rose* "enclosed" a rose, Froissart's lover wishes to "enclose" the daisy in a tower which recalls the central tower of the *Romance of the Rose*. As if to strengthen the intertextual echo, Froissart even mentions the *"destor"* in which the *Romance of the Rose* repeatedly localizes the rose:

[. . . .] Pleuïst au dieu d'Amour
Que je veïsse enclos en une tour
O le closier la gratieuse flour,
Et si n'euïst homme ne femme au tour
     Qui sourvenir
Peuïst illuec, et fust en un destour
A mon cuesir, n'ai cure en quel contour!
     (vv. 148–54)

By placing the daisy in the tower where the *Romance of the Rose* imprisons Bel Accueil (the allegorical figuration of the lady/rose "welcoming"), Froissart's text discreetly assimilates the daisy to Bel Acueil; the daisy substitutes for the rose as the *"flour des flours"* because, like Bel Accueil substituting for the rose's muteness, its welcoming quality substitutes for the lady's unresponsiveness. Although the daisy now seems to be an unequivocally curative flower, Froissart endows it with a contradictory effect. The daisy that the lover wishes to pluck is implicitly likened to the lady because of the wound that it inflicted on him:

Car en cascun floron, je vous creant,
Porte la flour un droit dart a taillant
Dont navrés sui si, en soi regardant,
Que membre n'ai ou li cops ne s'espant.
     (vv. 187–90)

Adding to the description of the daisy the wounding effect that Machaut's description presupposed but omitted to mention, Froissart's text presents the daisy as both the wounding and the healing agent; the flower which induced the lover's "fever" can also "cool" it. This innovation with regard to Machaut's poetry enables it to cite the *Romance of the Rose*; while Love's arrows in the *Romance of the Rose* implicitly represent the wounding qualities of the rose, this implicit representation becomes explicit in the Froissardian comparison of the daisy's *"floron"* to a *"dart."* We find the duality imparted to the daisy curiously represented in the anagram of Froissart's own name. Anagrammatizing his last name in the *Espinette amoureuse*, he chooses two signifiers (*"frois"* and *"dard"*) which we can now identify as exemplary of the daisy dual quality:

> Je hantoie là tempre et tart,
> Dont *frois*, dont chaux, navrés d'un *dart*
>
> (emphasis added)

Literally, the poet identifies himself with the ambivalent figure of the daisy; "Froissart" is the daisy which both cools and wounds. "She" functions as his true mirror-image, as his true signature.

Thanks to the daisy, then, Jean Froissart signals his poetic rewriting of en entire tradition, a poetic rewriting which culminates in a distinctive poetic practice: the creation of a pseudomyth. Froissart's *Dit de la margherite* distinguishes itself from Machaut's poetry by the addition of a myth regarding the origin of the flower. This myth constitutes a truly original creation, a creation which announces all the pseudomyths that we later encounter in Froissart's major Dittiers.[11] Praising the *"flour des flours"* which is "written in his heart," the lover of the *Dit de la margherite* recounts the story of its origin. A flower generated "sans semence et sans semeur ossi" (v. 67), the "margherite" proceeds from Hero's tears:

> Une pucelle ama tant son ami,
> Ce fu Heros, qui tamaint mal souffri
> Pour bien amer loyaument Cepheï,
> Que des larmes que la belle espandi
>   Sus la vredure
> Ou son ami on ot enseveli,
> Tant y ploura, dolousa et gemi
> Que la terre les larmes requelli.
> Pitié en ot, encontre elle s'ouvri
> Et Jupiter qui ceste amour senti
> Par le pouoir de Phebus les nourri;
> En belles flours toutes les converti (vv. 68–69)

Disguised as a "true" Ovidian myth, the story is in fact Froissart's own mythical invention. It is repeated in the *pastourelle* XVII:

> Plus vant, Cephey li biaus
> Nes de Thesalle la contree,
> Pour qui Heros reut par ruissiaus
> Plours et larmes en Galatee:
> La fu premierement trouvee
> La margherite sans falir;
> La le fist hors de terre issir
> Jupiter, li diex des planetes,
> Qui l'aoura de ses saiettes;
> Zephirus li donna oudours. (vv. 57–66)

As for the *Joli Buisson de Jonece*, it at last provides the beginning of this disseminated story. Out of *"merancolie,"* Cepheus climbs onto a laurel to wait for Hero whom he meets everyday in a garden. When evening comes and she does not appear, Cepheus believes himself to be abandoned, falls from the laurel and kills himself.

Expanding on the solar myth already implicit in Machaut's text, Froissart explains the solar inclination of the daisy by its solar origin. The daisy follows the sun, that is, recognizes its power, because it is itself a testimony of its creative power; a sun flower, it was generated by the sun. The earth opened itself to hero's tears, the light of the sun "nourished" them and converted them into a flower: the "margherite." Since the lady is likened to the daisy, we must conclude that the story which accounts for the origin of the daisy accounts as well for the origin of the lady. In other words, thanks to the daisy, Froissart exposes the highly unnatural strewing in which the poet of the *Espinette amoureuse* indulges when he "strews" daisies on a carpet. He in effect exposes this strewing as a figurative process: as the sun produces the daisy, so does the poet produce his "Margherite," that is, create the figure of a lady. Moreover, as the daisy testifies to the sun's creative power, so does "Margherite" signal in the text the poet's creative power.

This poetic power is explicitly defined as a work of "conversion." The poet/sun turns tears into a flower/lady. This myth about poetic conversion is itself the product of a poetic conversion. It proceeds from a rereading and rewriting of both Machaut and the *Romance of the Rose* which testifies to Froissart's own inventive power. A figure for the lady's responsiveness, the daisy is implicitly likened in Machaut's text to the sign of this responsiveness: the tears that the lady sheds. Froissart expands on this implicit and discreet link between the daisy and the lady's tears. In his myth, the daisy can figure the responsive lady who "cries" over her lover's fate because it itself has been generated from the compassionate tears of a lady: Hero. This inventive rewriting of Machaut's poetry is itself part of a distinctive rereading of the *Romance of the Rose*. Inspired by Machaut's text, the conversion of tears into a flower enables Froissart to cite the conversion of the dew into a rose which the *Romance of the Rose* performed.

Note first that the daisy does not have the exclusive privilege of being generated out of water. This watery origin is a recurrent motif in Froissart's poetry. Thus, in the *Plaidoirie de la rose et de la violette*, the advocate of the violette insists on the flower's watery origin: [12]

> Et quant dou chiel furent venues
> Avoecques la vapeur des nues,
> La terre la semence en but
> Dont les violettes conchut;
> Si les tieng en tres grant chierté.
> (vv. 207–11)

Again, a flower is generated out of a mixture of water and earth. The advocate uses this watery origin in order to contest the superiority of the rose. The daughter of the *"firmament,"* the violette, supersedes the rose as the daisy did and for the same reason: its creation testifies to a conversion process. The similarity between the violette and the daisy does not stop here. Like the daisy, the violette is also a very dry flower. Against the advocate who praises the rose as the perfect figure of the sun, its advocate denies the suitability of this figuration because *"Rose est muiste et li solaus chaus*" (v. 185). Another variation on the daisy myth, the story of the violette explains that which remained enigmatic in this myth: the apparently contradictory combination of water and dryness. Although the sun created the flower out of water, it dries it in order to turn it into the perfect mirror which reflects its creative power. Likewise the poet/sun creates the lady out of water but then erases any trace of this watery origin in order to turn her into the resplendent figure which reflects in the text his poetic power.

The watery origin of a flower (be it the daisy or the violette) is thus used to justify its substitution for the rose as the supreme flower. Ironically enough, however, this watery origin in fact brings to explicitness the watery origin of the rose itself. In other words, Froissart's daisy can claim to supersede the rose because it exposes the poetic conversion which generates in the *Romance of the Rose* the figure of the rose. The story of its origin narrates the poetic conversion that the *Romance of the Rose* performed but refused to narrate. In order to read the conversion at work in the *Romance of the Rose* we must pay close attention to the way in which this text plays with the signifier "rose" before the rose is finally allowed to appear in Narcissus's pool. The description of Leesce first introduces the rose as a term of comparison:

El resembloit rose novele
de la color sus la char tendre,
que l'en li peust tote fendre
a une petitete ronce.   (vv. 838-41)[13]

The color "rose" evokes the flower "rose": Leesce is "like a rose" because of her rosy color. As for this rosy complexion, it is produced by the tenderness of her flesh, a carnal tenderness which is mentioned in another description, the description of Beauty:

el ne fu oscure ne brune,
mes reluisant come la lune
envers qui les autres estoilles
resemblent petites chandailles.
Tendre ot la char come rosee   (vv. 995-99)

The "rosée," "dew," is too close to "rose" not to have caught the attention of a translator like André Lanly:

> On peut se demander si dans cette expression devenue traditionnelle (doux, tendre comme la rosée) le mot n'évoque pas la rose elle-même. On peut même se demander si, d'une façon générale l'étymon *rosata (le mot simple est ros, roris en latin) ne résulte pas d'un croisement avec rosa.[14]

We do not need, however, to invoke an etymological link to take note of the fact that the *Romance of the Rose* culminates its play with the signifier "rose" as both color and flower by likening the "rose" to a "rosée." As we can now reconstruct the sequence, the color "rose" evokes the flower "rose" because it is the sign of a tender flesh which is itself like a "rosée," like dew. In other words, the flesh, the body, is no more than the condensation of water into dew drops. The "tender" beauty of the rose is thus implicitly defined as the beauty of a colorless and shapeless water condensing itself into a shape and a color, into the figure of a rose. In this perspective, an apparently insignificant detail retroactively takes on a new significance. Describing the earth which in May creates its "dress of flowers," the narrator implicitly designates the "rosée," the dew, as the agent responsible for this "proud" ornamentation:

> la terre meïsmes s'orgueille
> por la rosee qui la mueille,
> . . .
> lors devient la terre si gobe
> qu'el velt avoir novele robe (vv. 55–60)

Thus it is the "rosée" which generates the flowers of the *Romance of the Rose*. Far from being the result of a natural process, these flowers are flowers of rhetoric, mere figures. They are the colorful condensation of a colorless and shapeless water into the figure of a flower. And no flower better exemplifies this proud process of figuration, by which water "converts" itself into the colorful figure of a flower, than the rose.

In *Le temple d'honneur*, Froissart remembers this association flesh/*rosée*. Describing the beauty of the newly wed, the Narrator likens it to dew:

N'i avoit ceste ne cesti
De l'espeus et de l'espousee
Qui ne fut tendre com rousee. (vv. 235-37)

In the following Dit, however, the description of the lady's beauty erases any reference to the dew of the *Romance of the Rose*. The lady is now the *"flour souverainne"* "Qui nulle bruïne n'estaint" (v. 289). From the *Temple d'honneur* to the *Joli mois de mai* (two Dits which precede the *Dit de la margherite*), Froissart has thus erased the play of signifiers between *"rosée"* and *"rose"* in order to endow the daisy with the watery origin of the rose. Having thus both displaced and explicated the watery origin of the rose, he can now turn the daisy into the poetic flower *par excellence*, the one which signals in the text the poetic power of conversion from which it proceeds.

To read Jean Froissart's signature is thus to read a distinctive figurative process. Signed "Margherite," the text refers to the power of the solar light to convert a pool of tears into a figure, the daisy/lady, which becomes the testimony to the sun/poet's creative power. Citing the figurative process at work in the *Romance of the Rose*, Froissart's daisy myth gives a central importance to the sun which becomes a figure for the poet himself. The *Prison amoureuse* stresses this identification of poet and sun by turning the myth of Pygmalion into another variation on the daisy myth. Reworking the Ovidian myth, the poet of the *Prison amoureuse* tells the story of Pynoteus, who created a statue of his lady, not, like Pygmalion did, out of ivory, but *"d'aige et de terre muiste et mole"* (v. 1718). The statue is the product of a *"coumellure,"* of the mixing of water and earth. This *"coumellure"* can only recall the pool of tears collected in the earth which allowed the sun/Phebus to produce the daisy. And, indeed, it is Phebus, the sun, who is given the power to turn the statue into a living body. While Pygmalion addresses his prayer to Venus, Pynoteus instead prays Phebus who *"escrips lettres et signaux"* in the earth.

The solar generation of flowers (and of ladies) is thus assimilated to writing and, more specifically, to the inscription of letters. Illuminating the earth, penetrating it in order to "work in it," the sun is writing letters which function as "signaux," that is, as signs, signatures. In this perspective, the daisy is to be considered as the privileged solar letter which "signals" the sun as the principle of a literal inscription which is in fact a figuration. In Froissart's solar myth, the inscription of letters is indeed a necessarily figurative process: the shapeless light of the sun (which constitutes an appropriate metaphor for the generality which deprives the poet of any particular shape of figure) imprints on the earth the specific shapes of letters which signal its figurative power. Written by the sun, the letter is light signaling itself in the production of a shaped figure: literality itself becomes the sign of a figural process.

Froissart's last *dittier*, the *Joli Buisson de Jonece*, brings to a new and final degree of explicitness this figural conception of the literal inscription. The entire text presents itself as a parenthesis in a movement away from courtly love. At the beginning of the narration, the Protagonist desires only one thing: to say his daily prayer to "Sainte Margherite." Venus intervenes to delay the untimely prayer:

> Un aultre heure rara son lieu!
> Tout dis s'aquite on bien a Dieu. (vv. 1116–17)[15]

Deferred, the prayer is not forgotten. As soon as the narrative ends, the Protagonist pays his debt to God. However, in place of the expected prayer to Marguerite, we find a *Lay de Nostre Dame*. Mary replaces Marguerite. This replacement allows the text to cite the story of the incarnation as the last version of the solar myth of the "Margherite." In the *Lay de Nostre Dame*, Christ takes Phebus's place and becomes the "*vrais feus habondans, / Caritables et redondans*" (vv. 5188–89), "*li feus plaisans, / Non ardanz, / Mais enluminans*" (vv. 5408–10). This fire which shines without burning incarnates itself in Mary, the "*flour d'onnour tres souveraine.*" A receptacle of light, this flower converts dew into flesh:

> Car en lui vint la rousee
> 　Des chieux nee,
> 　　Inspiree,

> En char fourmee,
> Quant li angles dist: Ave. (vv. 5397–401)

Like the pseudo-Ovidian myth of the daisy, the Christian incarnation is made to depend on the conversion of water. Christ, who is pure light, can incarnate himself because Mary drank the divine *"rousee,"* a "dew" which recalls the "dew" of the *Romance of the Rose*. Furthermore, his incarnation is explicitly described as a figuration:

> Moult nous cheri
>   et ossi
> Bien nous servi
>   Quant ensi
> *Il se vesti*
>   Et offri
> A nostre humanite legiere.
>   (vv. 5281–87—emphasis added)

The incarnation thus becomes the story of an immaterial light or dew taking on a body which is in fact a clothing, a veiling figure. A last recitation of the daisy solar myth, the incarnation illustrates the writing process: a pure and shapeless light inscribes itself in the "bodies" of letters, a body which is in fact a figural veil.

Writing himself in a text, the poet does not therefore transcribe an already constituted self. As shapeless as light or dew, the poetic "I" writes its self in the letter of a text which gives form and figure to that which precisely has no form or figure. The letter of the text functions, in other words, as the figurative veil through which the "I" constitutes its self as a mere figure, an imago. Disseminated throughout Froissart's *"oeuvre,"* "Margherite" summarizes this solar figuration. Named "Margherite," "she" functions as the privileged letter which signals in the text the process of figuration from which the text proceeds. "She" mirrors the textual body in which she is inserted; like her body, this textual body is but the figurative veil thanks to which the "I" incarnates its self, that is, takes on the figure of a self.

Although the Froissardian text repeatedly stresses the simulacrum quality of the self, the narrative is designed to avoid any recognition of this status. It does so by anchoring the figurative process which generates the daisy in a lyric pretext which itself mirrors the lyric pretext that we find at the beginning of all Froissart's narratives. Instead of merely narrating the conversion of water into a flower, Froissart's myth prefaces this conversion with a lyric story: the daisy is generated because Hero cried over Cepheus's death. In other words, the happy love affair between Hero and Cepheus must be brought to a premature and tragic end for the figural process to take place. By presenting the figural process as the consequence of the lyric failure, Froissart's myth stages the tension which characterizes his major narratives, a tension that it inherits from the *Romance of the Rose*. On the one hand, the daisy myth points to the purely figural status of the lady: "she" is no more than the product of a poetic conversion of water into the figure of a flower/lady. On the other hand, it complies with a textual tradition which requires a lyric and pseudo-referential pre-text. The conversion of water into the figure of a lady is therefore introduced by the story of a love affair with a "real" lady who provides the moisture, the "semence," necessary for the figural creation of "Margherite." Since "Margherite," the figural lady, is endowed with the welcoming quality that characterizes Hero, the supposedly real lady, the figural lady is not only generated out of the real lady's tears but is also substituted for her. "Margherite" is in fact the replica of "Hero," who somehow disappears after having performed her function of referential model.

Forced by the literary tradition in which he writes to give a referential origin to his figural process. Froissart, however, undoes this referential basis thanks to a complex work of intertextual echoes. The story of Cepheus and Hero's reciprocal but doomed love is inspired by an Ovidian myth, the myth of Pyramus and Thisbe. From this Ovidian story (which he again uses in the *Prison amoureuse* at the beginning of the story of Pynoteus and Neptisphele), Froissart retains three main elements: the reciprocal love, the meeting, and the lover's error. Like Pyramus and Thisbe, Cepheus and Hero love each other; unlike Pyramus and Thisbe, however, they repeatedly meet each other. Like Pyramus, Cepheus dies because of a mistaken assumption: as

Pyramus assumed Thisbe to be dead, so he assumes that Hero abandoned him. Finally, like Thisbe, Hero discovers the dead body of her lover; although, unlike Thisbe, she does not kill herself, but rather mourns him. While rewriting the Ovidian story of Pyramus and Thisbe, Froissart inscribes within this story another Ovidian story: the story of Daphne who was turned into a laurel for having refused Phebus's love. By perching Cepheus on a laurel, Froissart refers to the Ovidian myth which describes that which his own myth pretends to perform without fully acknowledging it: the "conversion" of a real lady into a flower which can then be used to glorify the poetic power. Conjoining elements of both Daphne and Thisbe, "Hero" is like Daphne, metamorphosized into a poetic figure: the daisy. Unlike Daphne's metamorphosis, however, this metamorphosis is not provoked by her lack of love but by the love which she shares with Thisbe. While positing Hero as a real lady, the daisy myth implicitly defines this referential lady as being in fact an intertextual product, a composite of two Ovidian figures: Thisbe and Daphne. A textual composite, this intertextual figure is endowed with a dual quality. While explicitly presenting Hero as the ideal of the responsive lady, Froissart's myth inscribes within this responsive figure an allusion to a most unresponsive figure, Daphne. Hero, it seems, functions as a palimpsest. Behind the name of "Hero" we first discover the name of "Thisbe" and then the name of "Daphne." The juxtaposition of these two antithetical names emblematizes the highly ambivalent attitude which characterizes the feminine figure in Froissart's narratives. A composite of "Thisbe" and "Daphne," "Margherite" tends to oscillate between Daphne's unresponsiveness and Thisbe's welcoming. We can now begin to understand why this oscillation is deprived of any convincing psychological motivation. The lady's ambivalence proceeds not from a psychological but a textual ambivalence, a textual ambivalence which implicitly denounces the lady's "welcoming" as but a mask put on an irreducible unresponsiveness.

Although she seems at first to function as the referential model for the figural lady, Hero ends up by denouncing this referential model as being nothing more than an intertextual "*coumellure.*" Complying with the referential requirements of the poetic tradition which he inherited, Froissart creates out of textual material a "real" lady, engages her in a love-affair with his Protagonist, and brings this love-affair to a premature end in order explicitly to engage in a process in which he has in effect been engaged all along without, however, acknowledging it: that of producing the figure of a lady. In this perspective, the production of the daisy out of a "*coumellure*" of water and earth merely repeats the creation of the pseudo-referential lady out of an intertextual "*coumellure.*" An intertextual product, the lady can then appropriately mirror the text in which she figures; like the lady, the Froissardian text is characterized by its intricate and inventive weaving of other texts such as Ovid, Machaut, and the *Romance of the Rose*. Like the lady, this intertextual "*coumellure*" functions as a simulacrum; both lady and text figure the poetic self. As for this simulacrum of the self, it is supposed to glorify the poetic power of incarnation which generated it. This function of glorification implicitly likens the daisy to the laurel which Phebus uses to glorify his own poetic power. And, indeed, Froissart's texts repeatedly link the daisy to the laurel; first, by conferring upon it an evergreen quality,[16] and second, by explicitly inscribing the laurel in the daisy myth. Cepheus is perched on a laurel before falling to his death. Presented as the privileged evidence of Froissart's figurative power, the daisy/text would constitute his poetic "laurel."

As the *Dit de la margherite* reminds us, however, in order to fulfill this function of glorification, the daisy/text must be turned into a very dry flower. No trace of water must obscure the resplendent mirror that it is supposed to be. In other words, the daisy/text must forget its origin: the watery tears from which it proceeds. Presented exclusively as a remedy against sorrow in Machaut's Dits, the "margherite" becomes in Froissart's text the trace of sorrow itself. A resurrecting flower which cures the lover's sorrow, it is engendered by the tears shed over a lover's death: Cepheüs. To name "her" "Margherite" is then to turn her into the figure generated by the mourning over the death of the lyric "I." Moreover, since the figure of the daisy figures the poetic self, it is this poetic self which in fact emerges out of the lyric death. This emergence both points to and covers the death inherent in the constitution of the self as a mere figure. Although Froissart's myth describes as two distinct temporal moments the death of the lyric "I" and the emergence of the poetic self in the figure of the daisy, these two moments are in fact simultaneous. In the very process of constituting itself in and as a simulacrum (be it the simulacrum of the daisy or of the text as a whole), the self "dies," that is, "falls" (like Cepheus falling from the laurel tree) into the simulacrum, the image that it is. Apparently used to mirror the poetic "glory," the daisy/text in fact signals that which the poetic self cannot recognize: its constitution as an original simulacrum. Although unrecognized, this simulacrum nonetheless "wounds" the author's name as the anagram of Froissart's own name suggests. Composed with the two signifiers associated with the daisy *"frois"* and *"dart,"* this anagram inscribes the simulacrum that "she" is in the very heart of the author's name. "Froissart" "is" the daisy, that is, the simulacrum which gives a figure to an original "fall": the fall occasioned here by the notion of a substantial self. The authorial figure that appears in fourteenth-century literature might then have to be reassessed less as a radical departure from the lyric identity than as an extreme extension of the problematic surrounding this figure. If the lyric "I" exemplifies the "dying" inherent in the very constitution of the self in and as an image, the emergence of the professional writer "echoes" this original disappearance. Generated out of the death of the lyric "I," the professional poet appears as the funereal flower which embalms, preserves in a figure the original death, the original "fall," of the lyric "I." Undertaking to write the self, fourteenth-century literature may implicitly define this writing as an inherently funereal writing, an interminable and therefore highly productive work of mourning.

NOTES

1. See William Kibler's article: "Poet and Patron: Froissart's *Prison amoureuse*" in *L'Esprit créateur* 18 no. 1 (Spring 1978): 32–46.

2. I am using Anthime Fourrier's edition (Paris: Klinksieck, 1963), p. 58, lines 35–38.
3. "The Genius of the Patron: the Prince, the Poet and Fourteenth-Century Invention" in this volume, pp. 1–27.
4. See on the function of the author's name Michel Foucault's study "What is an author?" in *Textual Strategies: Perspectives in Post-Structural Criticism*, edited by Josué Harrari (Ithaca, NY: Cornell Univ. Press, 1975).
5. This hypothesis is presented by both Anthime Fourrier in his Introduction to the *Dit de la margherite* in Froissart's *Dits et Débats*, (ed. A. Fourrier, Genève: Droz, 1979) and John Whiting in "Froissart as Poet," *Mediaeval Studies* 8 (1946).
6. Ed. Anthime Fourrier, Paris: Klincksieck, 1972.
7. I am using Anthime Fourrier's edition of the *Dits et Débats*.
8. Let us note that Froissart's *Espinette amoureuse* seemed to rework, among other texts, Machaut's daisy poetry. After having compared himself to Phebus and his lady to Daphne, the lover of the *Espinette amoureuse* concludes that the lady who refuses his love deserves to be turned into a laurel, that is, into a lifeless figure, be it a statue or a portrait. Shortly after he makes this wish, he goes abroad ("oultre la mer" like Machaut's lover in his *Dit de la marguerite*) and in his sleep sees his lady "figured" in a mirror. Deserving her name of "Margherite," she now "welcomes" the love that she previously has rejected. Froissart's *Espinette* thus makes explicit that which was implicit in Machaut's Dit: the potentially imaginary and therefore deceptive quality of the lady's welcoming.
9. In Anthime Fourrier's edition of Froissart's *Dits et Débats*.
10. Ibid.
11. See on this aspect of Froissart's work Douglas Kelly's article, "Les Inventions ovidiennes de Froissart: Reflexions intertextuelles comme imagination," *Littérature* 41 (1981): 82–92.
12. In Froissart's *Dits et Débats*.
13. I am using Félix Lecoy's edition of *Le Roman de la Rose* (Paris: Champion, 1970).
14. *Le Roman de la Rose* translated by André Lanly (Paris: Champion, 1973) p. 120.
15. Ed. Anthime Fourrier (Genève: Droz, 1975).
16. Car en jenvier.
   Que toutes flours sont mortes pour l'ivier,
   Celle perchut blancir et vermillier
   Et sa coulour viveté tesmongnier.
   —*Dit de la Margherite*, vv. 96–99

Peter F. Dembowski

Tradition, Dream Literature, and Poetic Craft in *Le Paradis d'amour* of Jean Froissart

Until quite recently, the reputation of Jean Froissart, the poet, suffered from a serious handicap. Critics, particularly in the French-speaking countries, tended to denigrate his poetry, simply because it was not as important as his *Chronicles*. Consciously or not, his poetry was treated as his "second" achievement, as his avocation.[1] The poet Froissart did not fare much better in the Anglo-Saxon world. He was studied, of course, as one of the influences on Chaucer, but his poetry *per se* was little appreciated. This critical attitude can be best illustrated by the exasperated outburst against his poetry emitted by Bartlett J. Whiting some fifty years ago.[2] The neglect of Froissart's poetry has been reflected, for a long time, in the editorial situation. His poetry, that is to say, his lyrico-narrative *dits* as well as his lyric poems, was edited some one hundred and twenty years ago by Auguste Scheler.[3] This edition was prepared rather hastily in Paris under difficult conditions caused by the Franco-Prussian war. In the last twenty years, however, the poetry of Froissart has been published in a series of modern critical editions.[4] The last of these new editions containing *Le Paradis d'Amour* was prepared by myself.[5]

The traditional negative attitude towards the poetry of Froissart is no longer prevalent. There is no doubt that the availability of new editions, coupled, of course, with a general shift in literary criticism, has resulted in a number of studies of Froissart's narrative *dits*. But whereas *L'Espinette amoureuse, La Prison amoureuse, Le Joli Buisson de Jonece, L'Orloge amoureus*, as well as certain shorter *dits* have been analyzed in recently published studies,[6] the first of Froissart's lyrico-narrative *dits*, that is, *Le Paradis*, has not, as far as I know, been an object of a modern critical analysis, except as a source for or imitation of other works.[7]

There is no doubt that *Le Paradis* is indeed the first of Froissart's longer *dits* that has come to us. The chronology of his poetical works need not occupy us here. It suffices to say that it has been well established[8] (thanks chiefly to the efforts of modern editors), and that we are quite certain Froissart composed this *dit* either in 1361 or 1362,[9] probably just before entering the service of Philippa de Hainaut, Queen of England. He was, at that time, about twenty-four years old.

The young poet wrote his *Paradis* no doubt consciously following tradition. The fact that he exploited the then most current literary topos should not startle anyone acquainted with the literary history of the period. The very aspect of dream vision upon which *Le Paradis* is based represents, of course, a "continuation" of Guillaume de Machaut's utilization of the *songe* motif, which Guillaume de Lorris made so popular in French literature. But despite our young poet's obviously voluntary embracing of this tradition, despite the absence of any trace of "originality anxiety" in his writing, this poem discloses, as I shall try to demonstrate, certain concrete aspects of Froissart's poetic self.

The subject of *Le Paradis* is traditionally simple. In 1723 lines,[10] Froissart presents a story of a dream, told in the first person singular. The poetic "I" (whom we will know later as belonging to the poet-lover-narrator) begins by telling us about his insomnia[11] induced by melancholy amorous thoughts about *la belle*, whom he does not want to forget. He prays to Morpheus, to Juno, and to Æolus (whom his text calls *Oleüs*) to grant him the gift of sleep. Juno, having received a golden ring from the sad insomniac, takes pity on him and sends her messenger, Iris, to intervene before the "noble god of sleep." Morpheus grants the request of Juno, sending one of his sons, Enclinpostair[12] to the lover. As soon as Enclinpostair enters the chamber, by some mysterious opening (". . . entrés fu,/ Je ne sçai le pertuis par u" ll. 29–30), the poet falls asleep "in such thoughts as shall be reviewed for you here."

At the outset of the dream, the lover finds himself in the beautiful month of May in a lovely woodland, sometimes referred to as the "orchard." It is full of luscious grass, flowers, fruit trees, singing birds and all the other attributes of a traditional *locus amoenus*. But these beautiful surroundings only deepen the melancholy felt by the lover, for they bring back the sad memories of an unhappy love. Seized by despair, he recites to *Amour* and to himself *La Complainte de l'Amant*[13] in which he tells the story of his unfortunate love. The point of the *Complainte* is not so much a narration of his misfortunes, but rather a formal renunciation of his fealty to Love. The lyric poem begins with "Amours, je te fis ja hommage / Pour la plus belle et plus sage" (ll. 75–76) and ends with a real *cri du coeur* (the poet addresses himself to Lady *Plaisance*, whom we shall meet later—a sort of "administrative assistant" to the god of Love):

> Ja te soel
> Honnourer, löer et cherir,
> Mais je te maudis par aïr.
> Mors, preng moi tost, el ne desir
>   Ne el ne voel.   (ll. 198–202)

The *Complainte* is the only inserted lyric poem in our *dit* which is not commented by Froissart as to its quality or its form.

Sad and dejected, despite the joyful singing of birds, the protagonist is in this terrible state of unhappy lovers in which the tears are the least of their sufferings. Suddenly, he encounters two lovely and most elegantly dressed ladies. Later, we shall know their names, they are *Dame Plaisance* and her cousin, *Dame Esperance*. *Plaisance*, having apparently heard the lover's poem, is outraged by his renunciation of the fealty to the god of Love, and by his subsequent despair. She is also incensed by his attacks on the master of this place. The lover excuses his behavior immediately and expresses his desire to know who this master is. The ladies, softened by his good manners, inform him that he is no other than the god of Love. We are in the woods of the master, known to us now as the king or the god of Love, or simply Love.

Plaisance continues to chastise the lover for having reproached the master to whom he formerly paid homage. She preaches to him a good sermon on the duties of the vassals of Love. They must be, she says, faithful, obedient and forever patient. Without ever succumbing to excessive jealousy, they must always be capable and willing to endure gladly all the ordeals of love. A sight of a loyal lover fills her with joy, for she herself loves, serves and adores her master, the god of Love. He has given to her, as a heritage, all her powers. She cannot exist without him.

The poet asks *Plaisance* about her role at the court of the king of Love. She is his spokeswoman (*avantparliere* l. 467), that is to say, an advocate of all lovers before her master, and, at the same time his trusted adviser. *Plaisance* gives the poet another lecture, this time on the powers of the god of Love, illustrating it with the examples taken from Classical mythology in its more or less Ovidian version.[14] She describes, thus, the fatal effects of Cupid's arrows in the case of the great loves of Achilles and Plyxena, Neptune and *Eqeulenta* (Leucothea?), Leander and Hero. These examples are followed by a brief *ars amandi* in which lady *Plaisance* again explains the proper behavior of loyal lovers.

The poet-lover complains once more about his *dame* who "ne voelt avoir pité" (l. 573) on him. She whom he calls here "la flour sur toutes aultres flours" (l. 593)—foreshadowing thus the culminating love ballade inserted in his *dit*—is not even aware of his love.

Here *Plaisance* enlists the assistance of her cousin, *Esperance*. This splendid lady takes pity on the poet for his suffering and also lectures to him on the duties and obligations of the *amoureuse vie* (l. 649). She promises to be his advocate before his lady and before the god of Love, but she insists that he must resist excessive jealousy and practice steadfastly the virtue of hope. She also promises him help from her constant allies: *Atemprance* ('moderation'), *Advis* ('prudence'), *Maniere* ('propriety,' 'decency'), *Congnissance* ('knowledge,' 'tact,' 'ability'), *Francise* ('nobility,' 'generosity'), *Debonnaireté* ('mildness,' 'meekness'), *Sens* ('good sense,' 'prudence'), *Pité, Humilité* ('tender, generous and gracious condescension'[15]). All of them, says *Esperance*, will fight for my cause (*tout soustenront ma baniere*, l. 757). Many of the allegorical personifications in our *dit* are those traditional figures from *Le Roman de la Rose*, but Froissart creates some new ones.[16] Much of the "ideological" content of *Le Paradis* depends on the meaning of these personified abstractions, and other such figures that the lover will meet later in the *dit*. I am sure that the contemporaries of Froissart saw more semantic substance in them than we are able. Notice also that most of those allies of *Esperance* are fundamentally social virtues: they are necessary qualities of a gentleman or a gentlewoman.

Esperance continues her exhortations. She advises the lover to be discreet, courteous, and faithful to her *doctrines* (line 780). She concludes, with a kind of a "believe or perish" motto: "Se tu me crois, tu iés garis, / Se tu me faus ('fail'), tu iés peris" (ll. 799–800).

Greatly encouraged by *Esperance*, the lover inquires about the dwelling place of the king and master of this woodland. *Plaisance* and *Esperance* lead the now much comforted protagonist towards this dwelling which is, we shall know soon, a splendid tent pavillion. The atmosphere of the *dit* has changed. All three walk cheerfully and playfully repeatedly singing the two rondeaus which the lover has himself composed. The first (lines

851–58) proclaims, quite appropriately, the liberation from anxieties through the intervention of *Plaisance* and *Esperance*; the second (lines 888–96) celebrates the joyful submission to whatever Love commands. It is important to note that *Plaisance* becomes a literary critic of sorts. She comments on the first with a visible enthusiasm: ". . . par le corps Dé, / Moult bien me plaist en tous endrois. / Or le chantons encor . . ." (lines 861–63). After the first rondeau, *Plaisance* asks the poet to make her one more. He answers that it is necessary to have one since she so commands. He promises to compose up to three of them only to please the lady. And thus "A che que Plaisance me tente, / Si fis un rondelet joli" (lines 885–86). The second rondeau also elicits a favorable but nuanced comment from *Plaisance*: "Chils rondelés bien me suffist, / Je le prise bien autrement" (lines 899–900).

Between the two rondeaus the singers come upon a young gentleman with two fine greyhounds. It is *Douls Pensers* ('sweet thought'), *Plaisance*'s own brother. She inquires about her master, whether he is where he was yesterday. No, answers *Douls Pensers*, he is now near the Fountain of Narcissus. After a while our voyagers encounter a group of hunters: *Biaus Semblans* ('fair appearance') leading three greyhounds on a leash. Also with him is his brother *Bien Besongnans* ('he who acquits himself well from all his duties'), as well as *Plaisance*'s other brother *Douls Regars* ('tender gaze'), who blows a hunting horn. Further, *Plaisance* identifies *Franc Voloir* ('noble wish'), *Desir, Oïr* ('hearing'), and *Souvenir* ('memory'). All these gentlemen, members of the king's retinue, plus countless kings, dukes, counts, knights and other persons of noble love comportment, are all good "veneour / Au dieu d'Amours" (lines 931–32). The *locus amoenus* of *Le Paradis* is portrayed as a happy hunting ground.

Le Paradis becomes more and more populated. We see a great company of elegant ladies and gentlemen, all dressed in green, the color of hope, readying themselves for a dance. *Plaisance* continues her role as guide and explicator. She identifies to the poet and to us the great lovers of the ancient world, Troilus and Paris. She also points out to us those who belong to the world of French romances: Lancelot, Tristan, Drumart, Perceval, Lot,

Galahaut, Mordred, Meliaduc, Agravain, Brun, Yvain, Gauvain and an unidentifiable Erbaus.

Here, Froissart plays one of those authorial deceptions, which points to his rightful pride in this *métier*, and which has caused a great deal of discussion among contemporary scholars. He places in this "procession" of famous lovers three heroes from his own verse romance: Meliador, Tanghis, and Camel de Camois (lines 985–88). There is no doubt in my mind that this insertion of the knights of *Meliador*[17] (written some twenty years after *Le Paradis*) represents an interpolation in the two manuscripts of our *dit*, which are dated 1382 and 1383.[18] Among the numerous ladies present, eight are identified by *Plaisance*. Five of them are "ancient": Helen of Troy, Hero, Plyxena, Echo and Medea, and three modern (none of them from *Meliador*): Guenevere, the Châtelaine de Vergi, and Isolde. We are, says *Plaisance*, very close to the "entree / Dou paradis a mon signour" (lines 1002–03). In a beautiful tent, she presents the lover to the god of Love. *Plaisance* asks the lover to disclose to her master the state of his soul in the form of a lyric lay. The poet declares that the composition of a new lay would require a great deal of time, but he happens to have one already composed, which can certainly fit the present need. Sitting at the feet of the king of Love, the poet recites his long lay.[19] He will learn later from *Plaisance* that throughout the long recitation, the god of Love, enraptured by the poetry, listened with total attention. Neither his eyes nor his mouth moved "Tant li fu la matere douce" (l. 1076). Thus Froissart not only inserts his lay into the narrative text, but he also supplies his own "critical" comments in the form of a kind of advertisement.

The lay retells the story of an unrequited love, or more precisely recalls the emotions of this love. But like the lay inserted by Machaut in his *Remede de Fortune*,[20] it contributes to the plot development, for it ends with the poet striking a new, distinctly hopeful note, showing thus a simple psychological evolution in the protagonist. He asks *Pité* and *Droiture* ('justice') to intervene on his behalf and to tell the *dame* about his love sufferings.

The god of Love, moved by the beauty of the lay, once more receives the poet as his vassal and orders *Esperance* to continue to comfort the lover. The poet in company of his two ladies and mentors, takes leave of the king singing a virelay (lines 1423–44), the theme of which is gratitude. The poet is grateful to the god of Love for having removed all the lover's anxieties and placed them in his own domain. The poet confidently anticipates the joy of love. The happy end must be near.

Plaisance praises the virelay ("Par le corps Dé / . . . il est moult bien fais" ll. 1446–47), while they continue their cheerful journey, picking flowers and listening to the songs of birds. Suddenly (l. 1472), in the midst of a meadow they see *Biel Aquel* ('Good Welcome') who is weaving a wreath. The lover kneels before his lady love (line 1477), who appeared with *Biel Aquel*,[21] and begs her mercy. The lady asks rather coquetishly: "Compains, que volés vous avoir? / En demande gist grant savoir, / Or demandés courtoisement" (lines 1503–05). Nevertheless, she promises him the assuagement of his pains, provided that he does not transgress the rules of conduct (*ordenance*, l. 1508). The lover asks nothing except that the lady may speak to him, and that he may always be her loyal servant. A perfect understanding is reached between the *dame* and her lover. Lady *Plaisance* is also happy about this state of affairs. Her cousin *Esperance* has disappeared from the scene, for after all, the wishes of the poet-lover having been fulfilled, she is no longer needed.

The lady asks whether the poet has made a new composition: "Avés vous riens fait de nouvel" (line 1602). The proud and happy poet answers promptly and precisely: "Oïl, dame, de sentement / Et de coer amoureus et sade ('glad') / Ai ordonné une balade" (lines 1604–06).

Sitting down in the company of *Plaisance* and other allegorical figures, some of whom we have encountered before: *Biauté sans Envie, Francise, Honneur, Gaie Vie, Maniere, Sens, Atemprance, Cremeur* ('fear,' 'modesty'), *Advis, Pourveance* ('forethought,' 'prudence'), the poet recites his final ballade, the theme of which, contained in the last line of each stanza "Sur toutes flours j'aimme la margerite,"[22] was hinted at, as we have seen in line 593. This theme is the one which resumes the final atmosphere of the *dit*. In the final lines of the ballade, the poet contemplates the happiness of the "Deus coers navrés d'une playsans saiette" (line 1648) who are now enjoying the company of *Plaisance* and *Courtoisie* (line 1650), as well as of *Douls Regars* (line 1651), the three attributes of *bonne amour*. Just as the poet recites the last line "Above all flowers I love the daisy" (line 1653), the lady weaves the last daisy into the wreath.

After the recitation, not only *Plaisance*, but also the lady praise the poem, the former finding it "nouvelle" (line 1659), never having heard it before; the latter saying: ". . . La balade est moult bone, / S'est drois que le caplet ('wreath') donne / A celui qui la ordonné" (lines 1666–68). Beautiful is the wreath. The lady gives it to the poet to be kissed, and she kisses it herself. Then she places it on his head, and says ". . . Alons, alons, / Esbanoiier d'une autre part" (lines 1679–80).

Here Froissart demonstrates that he is capable of writing a *dit* more psychologically realistic, or, in the language soon to be used by Machaut, a *dit plus voir*. He describes the moment of waking in a way that gives us a sense of witnessing a real "lived" experience. So great is the pleasure that the poet takes in contemplating his lady's movements and her gaze, that he feels suddenly touched by *Plaisance*, and thus, he says, "Pour ceste cause tressalli, / Adont a mon songe failli" (lines 1684–85). The dream ends as a result of an excess of pleasure.

The story also ends, but, and this is very important, the poet comments upon his vision, now that he is fully awake. He is astonished by what has happened to him, that is to say, by what he saw in the dream. He begins to wonder what caused this vision. He recalls that he prayed to Morpheus to grant him sleep. That "pleasant" god of sleep, who is also a "reasonable" god of dreams (line 1701), granted him his prayer: ". . . il m'endormi en tel songe / Ou nulle riens n'a de mençonge" (lines 1710–11), he assures us in this rhyme so well tested by tradition. But Morpheus did more than that. The poet thanks him and also Orpheus for having shown him in this comforting dream the art and the usage of composing the ballade, the rondeau, the virelay, and the well made lay ("Et le lai qui bien a maniere" line 1716).

Having thus made what I consider to be the main ideological point, Froissart closes his *dit amoureux* by thanking Iris, the messenger of Morpheus, through whose gifts all true lovers are comforted in dreams and in visions. And rather abruptly, he concludes: "Ensi fui je ravis jadis / Dedens l'Amoureus Paradis" (lines 1722–23).

It is evident that the young Froissart composed a very traditional *dit*. It is also evident that he imitated his unacknowledged master, Guillaume de Machaut throughout this poem, just as he imitated him in his other lyrico-narrative poetry. *Le Paradis* is very traditional in its basic concept of the *Visio amorosa* that it exploits. The self of the protagonist-dreamer in such poetry cannot really be very individualized. He is an Everyman-Dreamer, who is both the receiver of the vision and its narrator. The main function of dream literature was not only to free the author from the accusation of telling "lies," but also to expand his poetic consciousness and his protagonist's experience. This protagonist-dreamer-narrator sees, talks to, rubs shoulders, so to speak, not only with all sorts of allegorical personifications, but also with the heroes and heroines of the Classical and of his own literary world. It is a traditional experience of a traditional literary hero.

But Froissart adds to it what I consider a truly individual touch. His strong professional personality, his poetic self is seen in the poem. It is seen first of all in the very role of his lyric inserts. They are not merely decorative. They not only express the main situation from which and around which the narration evolves, but they also bear the greater part of the ideological underpinnings, *sine qua non* of such a *dit*. The inserted lyrics in this *dit* are as important as the narrative verse. If this *dit* shows us the man behind the traditional protagonist of dream literature, it does so by presenting him to us as a lyric poet thoroughly conscious of his craft.

It is for this reason that the ending of *Le Paradis* is so important. The poet thanks the gods not only for the gift of an expanding and comforting experience, but also, and explicitly, for having received the gift of poetry writing. The dream has opened to him not only a paradise of love, a land of love's imagination, but also (and concretely) the domain of creativity.

Thanks to Morpheus and Orpheus, he has the ability to understand and to create the traditional art. This is, no doubt, what the phrase "l'art et l'us" (line 1713) means. We, the twentieth-century readers, see him as a "real" person chiefly when he speaks about his own craft. It is mostly then that we can catch a glimpse of the real self of this extraordinarily dedicated and proud maker of traditional poetry.

NOTES

1. I discussed both the old neglect, as well as the new, more positive attitude towards Froissart's poetry in: "La Position de Froissart-poète dans l'histoire littéraire: bilan provisoire," *Mélanges ... Jean Rychner: Travaux de Linguistique et de Littérature* (Strasbourg), 16, 1 (1978), 131–47.
2. "Froissart as Poet," *Mediaeval Studies* (Toronto) 8 (1946), 189–216.
3. *Œuvres de Froissart. Poésies* (Brussels: Devaux, 3 vols., 1869–1872).
4. The following *dits* were edited by Anthime Fourrier: *L'Espinette amoureuse* (Paris: Klincksieck, 1963; 2 éd. entièrement revue, (Paris: Klincksieck, 1972); *La Prison amoureuse* (Paris: Klincksieck, 1974); *Le Jolie Buisson de Jonece* (Geneva: Droz, 1975); *Dits et Débats avec en appendice quelques poèmes de Guillaume de Machaut* (Geneva: Droz, 1979). In addition, the lyric poetry of Froissart was edited by Rob Roy McGregor, Jr., *The Lyric Poems of Jehan Froissart: A Critical Edition* (Chapel Hill: University of North Carolina, 1975). This good edition, published in English in the United States, is therefore practically unknown in the French-speaking world. Thus, Rae S. Baudouin published Froissart's *Ballades et rondeaux* (Geneva: Droz, 1978) apparently unaware of McGregor's edition. Recently these poems received the attention of Kristen Mossler Figg, *The Short Lyric Poems of Jean Froissart. Fixed Forms and the Expression of the Courtly Idid,* New York & London, Garland, 1994.
5. *Le Paradis d'Amour et l'Orloge amoureus* (Geneva: Droz, 1986). The edition and the *dit* here analyzed will henceforth be referred to as *Le Paradis*.

6. William W. Kibler, "Self-Delusion in Froissart's *Espinette amoureuse*," *Romania*, 97 (1976): 77–98; Alice Planche, "Culture et contre-culture dans l'*Espinette amoureuse* de Jean Froissart: Les Ecoles et les jeux," *L'Enfant au moyen âge. Littérature et Civilisation* (Aix-en-Provence: Université de Provence, 1980), pp. 389–403; Nancy Bradley-Cromey, "Mythological Typology in Froissart's *Espinette amoureuse*," *Res Publica Litterarum*, 3 (1980): 207–21; William W. Kibler, "Poet and Patron: Froissart's *Prison amoureuse*," *L'Esprit Créateur*, 18 (1978): 32–46; Claude Thiery, "Allégorie et histoire dans la *Prison amoureuse* de Froissart," *Studi Francesi*:61–62 (1977), 15–29; Michelle A. Freeman, "Froissart's *Le Joli Buisson de Jonece*: A Farewell to Poetry?," *Machaut's World: Science and Art in the Fourteenth Century* (New York: New York Academy of Sciences, 1978), pp. 235–47; Jean-Louis Picherit, "Le Rôle des éléments mythologiques dans *Le Joli Buisson de Jonece* de Jean Froissart," *Neophilologus*, 63 (1979): 498–508; Alice Planche, "Du *Joli Buisson de jeunesse* au Buisson ardent: Le Lay de Notre-Dame dans le *dit* de Froissart," *La Prière au Moyen Age: Littérature et Civilisation* (Aix-en-Provence: Université de Provence, 1980), 395–413; Peter F. Dembowski, "*Li Orloge amoureus* de Froissart," *L'Ésprit Créateur*, 18 (1978): 19–31; Normand R. Cartier, "*Le Bleu Chevalier*," *Romania*, 87 (1966): 289–314. The following two items, which deal with an important aspect of the whole of Froissart's poetic output should also be mentioned: Audrey Graham, "Froissart's Use of Classical Allusion in his Poems," *Medium Ævum*, 32 (1963), 24–33, and Douglas Kelly, "Les Inventions ovidiennes de Froissart: Reflexions intertextuelles comme imagination," *Littérature*, 41 (1981): 82–92.
7. James Wimsatt studied *Le Paradis* as one of the sources for Chaucer's *Book of the Duchess* in his now classic *Chaucer and the French Love Poets. The Literary Background of the Book of the Duchess* (Chapel Hill: University of North Carolina Press, 1968, reprinted New York: Johnson Corporation, 1972). In his analysis of Machaut's *dits* William Calin, *A Poet at the Fountain. Essays on the Narrative Verse of Guillaume de Machaut* (Lexington, KY: The University of Kentucky Press, 1974) points out the indebtedness of Froissart to Machaut. The fact that Froissart imitated Machaut has always been well understood. The basic "factology" of this imitation has been exposed in the Jena dissertation of Jakob Geiselhardt, *Machaut und Froissart. Ihre literarische Beziehungen* (Weida i. Th.: Thomas und Hubert, 1914).

8. See my "La Position de Froissart" (above, n. 1), pp. 132–33.
9. *Le Paradis*, pp. 12–13. See also below, n. 18.
10. The narrative parts of the *dit* comprise 1252 traditional octosyllabic rhymed couplets. The rest is composed of six lyric inserts: a long *Complainte*, a very long lay, two rondeaus, one virelay and one ballade.
11. The opening lines of *Le Paradis* are echoed quite closely by Chaucer in his beginning of *The Book of the Duchess*. Froissart in turn was probably inspired by a passage in Machaut's *Le Dit de la Fonteinne amoureuse* (see Ernest Hoepffner, *Œuvres de Guillaume de Machaut* [Paris: S.A.T.F., III, 1921], lines 699 ff).
12. The name of this son of Morpheus, unknown in Classical mythology, figures also in *The Book of the Duchess* as "Eclymposteyre." See Normand R. Cartier, "Froissart, Chaucer and Enclimpostair," *Revue de Littérature Comparée*, 38 (1964): 18–34, for the long history of conjectures concerning this name which was, no doubt, invented by Froissart.
13. This *Complainte* doubtless imitates a similar *complainte* inserted by Machaut in his *Fonteinne amoureuse* (above, n. 11, lines 235–1034), except that Froissart's is much shorter. It has eight stanzas, whereas Machaut's has fifty. (Later, in *L'Espinette*, Froissart will also be able to write a fifty-stanza *Complainte*, lines 1556–2355.) Each stanza is composed of sixteen lines and is based on a two-rhyme pattern. (For the form, see *Le Paradis*, p. 26.) The main formal difficulty of such lyric form lies in the necessity of finding two different rhymes for each stanza. There is no doubt in my mind that this *Complainte*, like all other inserted lyrics, constitutes both an integral part of the narration as well as an independent poem. It is strange that the *Complaintes* from our *dit* and from *L'Espinette* were not included in McGregor's edition (see above, n. 4).
14. There cannot be any doubt that Froissart, like all the members of the educated class, knew Ovid chiefly through the extraordinarily popular *Ovide moralisé*.
15. See *Table des noms propres, Le Paradis*, p. 130.
16. The personifications marked with a (*) in *Tables des noms propres* are those which do not exist in *Le Roman de la Rose*. Froissart might have "borrowed" some of them from Machaut.
17. Auguste Longnon, éd., *Méliador, Roman comprenant les poésies lyriques de Wenceslas de Bohême, duc de Luxembourg et de Brabant* (Paris: S.A.T.F. 3 vols. 1895–1899).

18.   Et chils a che biel Solel d'Or,
       On l'appelle Melyador,
       Tanghis et Camel de Camois
       Sont la ensus dedens ce bois . . . (lines 895–88)

    These lines inserted here provoked a debate between George L. Kittredge and Auguste Longnon, editor of *Meliador*. In his "Chaucer and Froissart (with a Discussion of the Date of *Méliador*)," *Englische Studien*, 26 (1899): 321–36. Kittredge demonstrated quite convincingly that the two couplets quoted here are an interpolation, and as such cannot support the hypothesis of an early date (*circa* 1373) of the composition of *Meliador*. Longnon argued (in is "Réponse aux objections de M. Kittredge relativement à la date de *Méliador*" in an appendix to vol. III of his edition, pp. 383–69) precisely for such a date for an early version of Froissart's romance. I discussed the exchange between Kittredge and Longnon in my *Jean Froissart and his Meliador: Context, Craft, and Sense* (Lexington, Ky.: French Forum, 1983), pp. 57–59. I mention this matter here not only because it touches upon Froissart's literary consciousness, and because it bears upon the relationship between Froissart and Chaucer, but also because Longnon's hypothesis would postulate a much later date for the composition of *Le Paradis*.

19. This traditional lyric lay is indeed long: 312 lines. It has a complex strophic structure: the twelve stanzas are all different in their rhyme and meter pattern (except the first which is like the last, and the third which repeats the metric pattern of the eleventh). See *Le Paradis*, pp. 26–27, for an analysis of the structure of this lay. McGregor (above, n.2) prints the lay on pp. 136–44. All of Froissart's *dits* (except *L'Orloge amoureus*, which does not have any inserted lyrics) contain the lays: *L'Espinette*, lines 3915–4146; *La Prison*, lines 2142–92 continued in lines 3515–3702; *Le Buisson* has two: lines 3552–3767 and lines 5198–5442.

20. Ed. Hoepffner (above, n. 11) II, lines 43–680.

21. Here, as in all the traditional narratives derived from *Le Roman de la Rose*, Good Welcome is the *dame* (or more precisely is a personification of the lady's welcoming presence). This fact has not always been understood. Scheler (see above, n. 3), complained that "La *dame* apparaît ici un peu brusquement" I, p. 368.

22. See *Le Paradis*, p. 28 for the formal description of this ballade. Like other inserted lyric poems, this ballade was recopied in both

manuscripts of Froissart's poetry, in the section reserved for the lyric poems. McGregor, p. 211 and Baudouin, pp. 13–15 (see above, n. 4) printed the lyric section version of this ballade. Interestingly, it has a different final stanza: the *douce flourete*, like Bel Accueil and the Rose (in *Le Roman de la Rose*), is imprisoned in a *tourelle*, a situation totally unsuited for the happy end of *Le Paradis*.

Sarah Spence

Reg(u)arding the Text: The Role of Vision in the *Chansons* of Charles d'Orléans

Charles d'Orléans has traditionally been viewed as a poet whose lyrics reflect, in their closed forms and intricate allegories, the growing tendency of late medieval Europe to valorize the visual and the spatial.[1] Huizinga ascribes this to a shift in perspective occurring in the early fourteenth century; Wolfzettel allies it with Aristotelian nominalism of the thirteenth century.[2] They, and others, use this argument to suggest that Charles was on the vanguard of a movement which established the self as a separate identity by internalizing the visual.

The advances that many scholars have ascribed to Charles, however, are, in fact, true of texts written centuries earlier, "La découverte du monde extérieur et du plaisir des yeux rend possible la découverte autrement significative d'un monde intérieur,"

Wolfzettel argues in relation to Charles's lyrics.³ But such parallelism between internal and external landscapes describes equally well texts of the twelfth century. Although the lyrics of the troubadours and the contemporary development of Gothic architecture have long been viewed as spiritual, anti-materialist movements—Otto von Simson's view of Suger's renovations as "a veritable orgy of light metaphysics"⁴ or the standard reading of love in the troubadours as essentially Neoplatonic creating and reinforcing such an interpretation—more recent evidence would seem to suggest something quite different. Crosby has argued that the first Gothic structure, Suger's choir at St.-Denis, was organized around a single point at which the Abbot himself may have stood to preside over daily mass.⁵ Radding and Clark have concurred, pointing out that such a plan speaks to a spatial rather than a temporal perception of the self; a seeing body, be it Suger's or that of his architect, served as organizing principle for his choir.⁶ Likewise, it is possible to argue that troubadour lyric is increasingly anchored in the visual world, oriented toward the world it sees, as in the following strophes from a poem of Raimbaut d'Aurenga:

> Ara non siscla in chanta
> Rossigniols, ni crida l'auriols
> En vergier ni dinz forest,
> Ni par flors groja ni blava; . . .
> C'a pauc lo cors no.m n'avanta.
> Q'esquirols non es, ni cabrols,
> Tan lieus com eu sui . . .⁷

> (Now the nightingale does not warble or sing and the oriole does not call in the garden or within the forest, nor does the yellow or blue flower appear. . . . My body almost escapes me; no squirrel or goat exists so nimble as I am . . .)

Subjectivity and the self are, indeed, progressively valorized through the course of the high Middle Ages. Since this valorization would seem to occur as early as the twelfth century, I would argue that it provides the context from which Charles is trying to emerge, not the situation in which he exists and that, at least in the chansons, the poet's efforts are mostly spent trying to escape from or deny any necessary dependence on the world as known through the senses. In addition, such a denial indicates not that Charles himself was of a particular personality type but, rather, that the self in general had reached a certain stage of development by his time.[8] And, finally, the fact that Charles is a poet for whom the world in general and vision in particular are largely negative concepts means that Charles's view of the self, as presented in the chansons, establishes an uncomfortable relationship between the reader and the written text. This, in turn, may account for the fact that Charles is so difficult to write about.

This final comment deserves immediate elucidation since, paradoxically, his lyrics are tantalizingly simple; on first reading they seem to fit easily into established categories of analysis. As a result, many have suggested that the lyrics resist analysis because the work is too plain, because there is nothing there to analyze; and this remains an indictment all readers of his lyrics must contend with; as the Larousse *Littérature française* puts it: "C'est apparemment le plus facile à aborder de tous les poètes de cette époque. . . . L'idée qu'on garde donc du poète est assez défavorable: celle d'un auteur gracieux, mais sans profondeur, d'un ciseleur délicat de choses futile" (60).[9] Nonetheless, critics continue to suggest that, beneath the superficial simplicity lies a very difficult poetry, since despite the facility of his language, he uses the most difficult of literary techniques, allegory, and he introduces one of the darkest concepts in poetry, *nonchaloir*. It is this décalage that has lead recent critics to insist that the simplicity is more a sleight of hand than an indication of simple-mindedness. As Alice Planche writes, Charles invites us to enter "un monde familier et cependant interdit."[10]

I would argue that Charles is difficult to read precisely because his simplicity is rooted in a consistent and systematic denial of a fundamental hermeneutic assumption: that the relationship of reader to text is based on the structure of the self. By undoing that delicate balance—by denying a parallel between these two relationships—Charles undercuts the textual process. In so doing, he threatens the very essence of reading as well as the nature of the reading self and creates literary works that are by definition all but unreadable. For reasons of length I will limit this discussion to his chansons and, within those eighty-seven poems, I will focus on his attitude toward,—and manipulation of—vision.

*****

The chansons are the earliest poems by Charles that we have. While, as we shall see, little topical reference occurs in any of them, critics now think that Charles wrote at least the first fifty-two (for which there exist English translations) during his twenty-five year imprisonment in England following his capture at the Battle of Agincourt. The songs seem to constitute a sort of sequence in which a rough narrative plot develops. With the exception of the first chanson, the poems tell progressively of the persona's infatuation with—and eventual rejection by—a beautiful courtly lady. For a while efforts were made to identify this *belle*. More recently the trend has been to suggest that Charles was trying his hand at writing in the courtly mode. In either case, there is little doubt that the most interesting poems are the last thirty or so in which Charles begins to develop his language of courtly rejection, including his first use of the term *nonchaloir*. It is in these lyrics that he first broaches the area he will cultivate so effectively in the later rondeaux and ballades.

The early chansons, roughly the first fifty-two, suggest a stance of unmediated vision, little hampered by a subjective self. Take, for instance, the following:

> Dieu, qu'il la fait bon regarder
> La gracieuse, bonne, et belle!
> Pour les grans biens qui sont en elle,
> Chassun est prest de la louer
> Qui se pourroit d'elle lasser?
> Toujours sa beauté renouvelle.
>   Dieu, qu'i ...
>   La grac ...
> Par deça, ne delà la mer
> Ne sçay dame, ne damoiselle
> Qui soit en tous biens parfais telle;

C'est un songe que d'y penser.
    Dieu, qu'i . . . (Chanson 6)[11]

(God, what a vision she is,
The gracious one, true and beautiful!
For all the virtues that are hers
Everyone is quick to praise her.
Who could tire of her?
Her beauty constantly renews itself;
    God what a vision she is,
    The gracious one, true and beautiful.
On neither side of the ocean
Do I know any girl or woman
Who is in all virtues so perfect;
It's a dream even to think of her;
    God, what a vision she is!)

The lack of self-consciousness is striking, since even the troubadours, three centuries earlier, suggest the existence of a dual self.[12] There are, however, two factors that keep Charles's chansons from being reduced to the regressively naive: the attitude taken by the persona in the very first chanson and the existence of the English translations. For it is in the first chanson that we encounter a self which denies the power of sight and of love:

Ce May qu'amours pas ne sommeille,
Mais fait amans esliesser,
De riens ne me doy soussier,
Car pas n'ay la pusse en l'oreille.
Ce n'est mie doncques merveille
Se je vueil joye demener,
    Ce May . . .
    Mais fait . . .
Quant je me dors, point ne m'esveille,
Pource que n'ay a quoy penser;
Sy ay vouloir de demourer
En ceste vie nompareille,
    Ce May . . .

(This May when love doesn't sleep.
But instead inspires all lovers,
I needn't worry about a thing,
For I don't have that flea in my ear;

And so it is not the least surprising
If I wish to express some joy
> This May when love doesn't sleep
> But instead inspires all lovers.
When I sleep, nothing wakes me,
For I have nothing to brood about;
And so I wish to remain
In this unparalleled life,
This May when love doesn't sleep.)

While Charles moves on to reject, temporarily, this denying persona—the second chanson begins "Tiengne soy d'amer qui pourra,/ Plus ne m'en pourroye tenir" ("Let him keep from loving, he who can;/ No longer can I hold myself from it")—its introduction in the first chanson is crucial to its reappearance later in the series; when it resurfaces it is not a complete surprise. Its very existence in the first chanson, taken with the fact that it is the first voice we hear, prepares us for its re-emergence and gradual domination later on. In addition, the English versions of the chansons could be seen as a working out of this veiled voice, a way of having it speak without granting it the primary persona. For even as the interiorized voice of the first chanson wears a mask of denial, so the very fact of the French Charles writing in English articulates a comparable masking strategy.[13] Even when the English songs speak of exteriorized concepts, that they do so in two languages at once suggests the inchoate existence of a double self. Before we even reach the second chanson, and the beginning of the courtly poems, then, we are, in effect, granted a double caveat through the voice of the first lyric and the veiled stance of the translations, a caveat that continues throughout the first fifty-two chansons via the translations. The existence of these two voices adds strength to the notion that Charles is not as superficially naive as his songs would make him seem. He is, instead, creating a tissue of externalized life which he does not fully inhabit. Standing behind it, playing with it, he always retains that potential distance into which he can retreat.[14]

Roughly the same moment that the English translations stop, the internalized *moy* re-emerges and the two voices thus

The Role of Vision in the *Chansons* of Charles d'Orléans   299

jockey for position within a single text: "Entre les amoureux fourrez,/ Non pas entre les decoppez/ Suis, car le temps sens refroidy,/ Et le cueur de moy l'est aussi." ("Among the well-dressed lovers,/ Not among those in rags/ Am I, for the weather feels cold/ And my heart is just the same.") (Chanson 60).[15] The last thirty-odd chansons fall into this category; the great majority, indeed, suggest such a double stance, usually split between the *moy* and the *cuer*. Most telling in this regard is Charles's growing interest in watching himself watching:

> Regart, vous prenez trop de paine,
> Tousjours courés et racourés;
> Il semble qu'auz barrez jouez;
> Reprenez ung peu vostre alaine.
> Cuers qu'amours tient en son demaine
> Cuident qu'assaillir les voulez,
>   Regart, vous . . .
>   Tousjours . . .
> Au moins, une fois la sepmaine
> C'est raison que vous reposez;
> Et affin que ne morfondez,
> Il fauldra que l'en vous pourmaine,
>   Regart . . . (Chanson 70)

> (Glance, you work too hard,
> Always running to and fro,
> It's as if you're in a wrestling match,
> Stop and catch your breath.
> Hearts that love holds in his power
> Think you mean to assault them;
>   Glance, you work too hard,
>   Always running to and fro.
> At the very least, once a week
> It is right that you rest;
> And so that you don't get bored,
> It will be necessary for someone to watch you.
>   Glance, you work too hard.)

We are looking at a persona looking. Sight itself becomes quite literally the object of the poem and as a result the poems become increasingly avisual. While the earlier chansons include numerous references to color and actual physical objects, these later songs mention only one color (grey), one place name (Mt. Cenis), and, perhaps most strikingly, offer little sense of spatio-temporal setting. The early songs, for the most part, were set in a particular month—and a particularly evocative one at that, May—and the poems were thus anchored, May songs bringing with them the spatial baggage of the *locus amoenus*. The later chansons have little of this. Space and time both disappear; there is little sense of a definite past or future. Rather, everything is determined by the positioning of an unseen persona:

> Le voulez vous
> Que vostre soye?
> Rendu m'octroye,
> Pris ou recous.
> Ung mot pur tous,
> (Bas qu'on ne l'oye):
> > Le voulez
> > Que vostre
> Maugré jalous
> Foy vous tendroye;
> Or sa, ma joye,
> Accordons nous—
> > Le voulez ... (Chanson 71)

> (Do you want it
> As your own?
> Consider it done,
> By victory or default.
> Just tell me one thing—
> So low it can't be heard—
> > Do you want it As your own?
> In spite of the jealous,
> I will keep my faith,
> Now try, my joy,
> Let us agree,
> > You do want it.)

Or again:

> Cueur endormy en pensee,
> En transes, moitié veillant,
> S'on lui va riens demandant,

Il respont a la volee,
Et parle de vois cassee,
Sans pourpos, ne tant ne quant,
    Cueur endormy . . .
Tout met en galimafree,
Lombart, Anglois, Alemant,
François, Picart, et Normant;
C'est une chose faee,
    Cueur endormy . . . (Chanson 80)

(A heart hypnotized by reverie,
Entranced, half-awake,
If anyone asks it anything,
It answers distractedly
And speaks with a breaking voice,
Unfocussed, neither here nor there,
    A heart hypnotized by reverie.
Everything is a gallimaufry—
Lombard, English, German,
French, Picard, Norman.
It's an enchanted thing:
    A heart hypnotized by reverie.)

Such objects that do appear in these poems are either structures of defense or metonymic fragments within which the persona remains locked.

Que faut il plus a ung cuer amoureux,
Quant assiegé l'a dangier de tristesse,
Qu'avitailler tantost sa forteresse
D'assez vivres de bon espoir eureux? (Chanson 76)

(What more needs a heart in love,
When Suspicion has besieged it with sadness,
Than to stock, right away, its fortress
With enough provisions of fortunate good hope?)

Or again:

Bien viengne, doulz regard qui rit,
Quelque bonne nouvelle porte,
Dont dangier fort se desconforte,
Et de courrous en douleur frit.

Ne peut chaloir de son despit,
Ne de ceulz qui sont de sa sorte) (Chanson 65)

(Welcome, sweet look that laughs,
Bringing some good news
Which makes Suspicion very uncomfortable
And, suffering, tremble with anger.
One cannot concern himself with his spite,
Nor with any of his ilk)

Not only is the internal persona never fully shown; it does not need to see to exist.[16] At first this is presented as a problem, "Fault il aveugle devenir?" ("Must we then blind men be made?") begins Chanson 53 but later, as sight becomes more detached and aggressive, the poet says "Beauté, gardez vous de mez yeulz,/ Car il vous viennent assaillir" ("Beauty, watch out for my eyes, For they're coming to attack you") (Chanson 64); "Retraiez vous, regart mal avisé," ("Back off, ill-directed glance") (Chanson 69) and "Crevez moy les yeulx, Que ne voye goutte," ("Poke out my eyes/ So they don't see at all") (Chanson 72) while announcing that "Mon cueur plus ne volera,/ Il est enchaperonné/ Nonchaloir l'a ordonné." ("My heart will fly no more: / It has been hooded. Indifference has so ordered.") (Chanson 82).

Many of these later chansons suggest, in fact, that sight and vision do not constitute the inner self but merely trap it. Charles is certainly not the first to suggest that pure exteriority is a trap. On the contrary, the later troubadours argue persuasively for the need to mediate such vision, to move beyond the visual into the realm of the unseen. Dante, deriving this from the troubadours, expands this concept most forcefully in the *Vita Nuova* where, first, obsessed with Beatrice's physical presence and a need to remain in direct visual contact with her, he then transcends that need when she dies and in so doing becomes a better poet. Through this Dante suggests that true poetic inspiration is based more on absence than presence and has, ultimately, little to do with seeing.

Charles's reaction to the trap of exteriority is to head in the opposite direction. Moving away from the visual is not, for

Charles, a transcendent act.[17] Rather, it is a regressive one as he backs into his psyche, hiding behind his reified allegory. As Alice Planche argues, he "néglige les bases et les garants philosophiques. Il invente son code et en change selon les besoins. . . . Quand l'exil a fait de lui un introverti, les objets sensibles ne sont pas pour le poète plus nets que l'arrière-plan intérieur, avec lequel il s'identifient."[18] While the visual remains crucial to Charles, it becomes increasingly something from which he is trying to escape; while the lyrics are indeed guided by a spatial perspective, this space has little thickness. The poems do not, in other words, create the illusion of a self that exists in three-dimensional space. Rather, they cut into such an illusion by suggesting that space is constructed of a series of discontinuous planes arranged in a particular order. Behind the last of these planes stands Charles's poetic persona, a self that sees yet is never seen as it remains distanced, separated, alone.

It is significant, I think that the word Charles relies more and more on for the enemy, Dangier, does not in any way suggest its origins as a visual construct. Dangier is a personification of envy, *Invidia*, a desire based, as the Latin makes clear, on sight. Even in the *Lais of Marie de France* the reliance on sight is still there vestigially: the word she uses, *envie*, carries some etymological reminder of the vision that provokes the desire of the jealous. Moreover, Marie very clearly opposes envy to true love which is based on seeing and which transcends or at least mediates the purely visual. For Charles, envy's avatar Dangier bears no direct link with the visual.

Moreover, as Zumthor has noted, Dangier comes increasingly to be replaced by *Nonchaloir*: the word *Nonchaloir* occurs in inverse proportion to the occurrences of the word Dangier.[19] *Nonchaloir*, I would argue, is the name given the textual space where Charles's persona comes to rest. The quality of numbness he ascribes to the term is indicative of his retreat from the world of the senses. One has to be careful not to assign too great a sense of psychological indifference to nonchaloir; it is not, I now believe, a synonym for the abyss. Rather, it is an attempt on Charles's part to mark the existence of a voice that has no direct connection with the world.

In accord with this, Sasaki has observed that Christine de Pisan uses the word *chaloir* in place of *amour*.[20] *Nonchaloir*, then, it could be argued, means the lack of love, the denial of the courtly code. This takes on further significance in the context of vision, for, as Andreas Capellanus argues, courtly love depends on sight; blind people cannot fall in love.[21] This is not, I believe, a trite comment on Andreas's part. By acknowledging and privileging sight, the twelfth century also privileged space but space of a particular kind: enclosed space, volumetric space, systems that are finished off and bound up by the seeing body. The self comes to be an expression of that concept—the self is the third axis that, through sight, completes even as it creates an enclosed space. And love, as expressed in twelfth-century vernacular texts, is the thematization of this space.

Self and love thus meet in reading, meet in the text. The theme of love is played out by the act of reading. Put another way, the written vernacular—and the read vernacular—share with their plots all the constituent elements of the self. The plane that is opened by the page is filled out by the reader; it is his seeing body that gives volume and space to the two-dimensional word. The basic hermeneutic act, then, consists of turning two to three dimensions, even as the basic psychological process consists of perceiving the self as that which connects the three-dimensional body to the two-dimensional soul.

In short, the relationship between self and world is framed in textual terms. The self not only interprets the world; the self engages in the world *just as a text does*. Such an approach to the textual self begins, I would argue, in the twelfth century via such authors as Abbot Suger. Suger, in the *De Administratione*, describes his perspective on both himself and his work in the following way:

> Thus when—out of my delight in the beauty of the house of God—the loveliness of the many-colored gems has called me away from external cares and worthy meditation has induced me to reflect, transferring that which is material to that which is immaterial, on the diversity of the sacred virtues: then it seems to me that I see myself dwelling, as it were, in some strange region of the universe which neither exists entirely in the slime of the earth nor entirely in the purity of heaven.[22]

His description of the process of attaining truth via the visible is both new and crucial to what becomes the Gothic understanding of the self, the first version of the self as we know it. For Suger, this self is that part of man which links the known to the unknown and does so through sight. In this Suger creates a situation which places man at the juncture between the visible and the invisible, and suggests that man's unique qualities are his abilities to mediate between the two. Granting these powers to sight privileges not only seeing; it privileges as well that which can be seen—the external world. The self becomes that which, through participation in the visible world, can also transcend that world. By making that juncture physical, however, Suger is suggesting a shift in paradigm from one based primarily on succession and temporal order to one based on positioning and spatial placement. The hermeneutic space Suger describes is a three-dimensional space in which the seeing self serves as the intersection of the axes of world and word. In granting that self a certain physicality Suger projects it from point to line and so turns a two-dimensional system into a three-dimensional one.

It is by standing in and viewing the hermeneutic space that Suger can transcend his body and the world. Suger is thus not just reader but part of the text as well; one of the results of this hinging via the body is to inscribe the reader into the text. If, previously, it was the ultimately ineffable Word that linked world to truth, it is visual and textualized man who does so now. Unified by vision, man's duality is framed in terms of a part that sees and a part that is seen—reader and text—or, more often, marginalia and central text, in which the seeing part is also textualized as the marginalia.

There is no marginalia in Charles's autograph manuscript.[23] His texts are surrounded by clear margins and by the space at the top of the page, a single voice surrounded by silence. We are given no indication how to read the poems—hence the possibility for later additions that Champion so brilliantly discovered. As a text he is not to be fully read; as a persona he is also consistently undercut.

In fact, the denial of entry into his lyrics becomes almost their trademark. While they are indeed superficially simple, they are intellectually impenetrable, at least in part. The apparent simplicity of Charles's poems arises from two sources: his predilection for short forms and his refusal to make reference to anything that he could not have known first hand. Consequently, the songs appear more as confessional jottings than reflectional poetry. Witness, for instance, the following:

> Au besoing congnoist on l'amy
> Qui loyaument aidier desire;
> Pour vous je puis bien cecy dire,
> Car vous ne m'avez pas failly (Chanson 50)

> (In times of need one knows one's friends—
> Those who loyally wish to help—
> Of you I can safely say that much,
> For you haven't forsaken me)

That Charles does not intend this poetry as "pure" autobiography, however, is made evident through the lack of direct reference to his particular situation—especially in captivity in England—and the thematic connection he makes to the French lyric tradition by relying, at least at the start, on a limited number of standard courtly themes:

> N'est elle de tous biens garnie,
> Celle que j'ayme loyaument?
> Il m'est advis, par mon serement,
> Que sa pareille n'a en vie. (Chanson 4)

> (Isn't she blessed with every virtue,
> She whom I faithfully love?
> It's my opinion, on my oath,
> That no one alive's her rival)

or:

> Se mon propos vient a contraire,
> Certes, je l'ay bien desservy,
> Car je congnois que j'ai failly

Envers ce que devoye plaire. (Chanson 29)

(If my wish finds disapproval
Indeed I have deserved it well,
For I recognize that I have failed
Where I should have pleased)

Yet if Charles intended his poetry not as autobiography but rather as part of the larger French lyric tradition, why does he make no reference to the works of other poets? Charles never quotes from other poets. A large part of Dante's poetics, by contrast, is an evocation of textual memory, as Barolini and others have shown; the *Divine Comedy* is rife with intertextual allusions and quotation.[24] This use of other texts serves as good indicator of Dante's use of the extant to transcend it. Such literary allusions as one finds in the chansons are rather to proverbs and commonplaces, such as *pusse en l'oreille*, and even these are very rare indeed. One result of using commonplaces and proverbs rather than literary quotation is to downplay the specular aspect of poiesis on all levels. Not only do we not have a poet who sees himself in the world, nor a poet who sees the world in his poems; we don't even have a poet who sees the poems as reflections of himself or of other literary texts. This is a strange phenomenon indeed. By negating any form of visual representation in his chansons Charles retreats into a literary space that evades the usual terms of analysts. If, as Gadamer argues, the space of hermeneutics lies between strangeness and familiarity, Charles inhabits an unusual hermeneutic space.[25] While there is no doubt that his lyrics are spatial and that they carve out an area between strangeness and familiarity, they would appear to conflate such a space: what is familiar becomes, through fragmentation and lack of definite setting, alien. Consequently, what is familiar is also strange; the hermeneutic space has been collapsed as neither poet nor reader stands in that space, mediating between the known and the unknown.

In arguing that sight is first dangerous and then unnecessary, Charles opens up the possibility that the self bears, ultimately, a different relationship with the text than reading usually assumes. In this he moves beyond the courtly and, by denying the positive evocative strength of the act of seeing, calls into question the nature of the act of reading text. Charles comes to manipulate the world from a distance as he does to particular effect in the rondeaux and ballades. But this distance is not charged with the tension of desire, as it is for the troubadours and for Dante: and his move away from the visual involves as well a move away from courtly desire. The poems become, rather, a space of pure play, of absolute control.[26]

The construct of the self as shown in the chansons and the relationship between the text and his reader undergo, as a result, a significant change. By denying sight Charles denies the desire—at least the courtly desire—of his persona. But, by reading, we are still engaged in looking, in a textual desire that is strangely out of place. Our relationship with the persona has been subtly but absolutely transformed.

For Charles the text, in the later chansons, becomes a form of writing that first blocks then filters reality. The surface of the text, the actual written words, come to represent the distance from reality behind which the self stands. Using a text to filter the world, one also uses a text to protect the self. Texts, like tears, block vision but they also, in filtering sight, protect the self from being wholly externalized.

In the chansons it can be argued that Charles develops a self that exists in a space behind the text, apart from the world. In denying the power granted the visual he denies as well the ability of a text to express desire.[27] He suggests that the text does not reflect the world, it marks the distance between the self and the world. Images of backing and forthing, to and fro, are common, particularly in the later songs. So, for instance, Chanson 67:

> Mon cuer, il me fault estre mestre
> A ma fois, aussi bien que vous;
> N'en ayés anuy ou courrous;
> Certez, il couvient ainsi estre.
> Trop longuement m'avez pestre,
> Et tous jours tenu au dessous:
> > Mon cuer . . .
> > A ma foiz . . .

Alez a destre ou a senestre,
Pris serez, sans etre recous;
Passer vous fault, mon amis douls,
Ou par la, ou par la fenestre,
    Mon cuer . . .

(My heart, I must be victorious,
In my turn, as well as you.
Don't be annoyed or angered by this;
Surely it has to be so.
For too long you've outfinessed me
And each time I've wound up the loser,
    My heart, I must be victorious
    In my turn, as well as you.
Play to the right or the left
You will be beaten without a comeback
You will have to admit, my good friend,
To either defeat or default;
    My heart, I must be victorious

While such images represent futility in the field of desire, they pave the way for gain in the field of play.

The rhymes of the chansons support this. Most like the rondeaux in their structure, the chansons follow a simple abbaab-ab-abba-ab pattern. Simpler by far than the rhymes of the troubadours they are, consequently, less visually oriented. While the complexity of troubadour rhyme is something that works better on the page than in the ear, Charles's simpler abba rhymes are powerful aurally. Seeing them adds nothing. Similarly, the repetition of the opening line as refrain and final line has more of an aural than a visual effect. The shape of the poem, for Charles, is not the way it appears on the page. Rather, it is the shape it takes in the mind's ear of the reader that matters. It refashions itself after reading from a linear to a circular shape, from a block of lines on the page to a series of echoes in the mind.[28]

What Charles is interested in, it would appear, is the aftershock of the visual. As he moves steadily away from the visual, the constant, from love, and the world, he moves into a space in which fragmentation dominates. The self does not fully reside in a world grounded in or dependent on the visual. It resides instead in a space beyond the visual, a space behind the text.

In this, it would seem that Charles is more closely associated with Montaigne than with the courtly tradition. Courtly texts seem to thematize the interplay of self and text through the vicissitudes of a love based on vision. As such they rely, as we have seen, on the fact that a self based in the world shares many of the same qualities as a text and that that relationship is best described in the terms of desire. Montaigne's relationship with his text would appear to be more cold and calculating, more at a remove, and, as many have noted, to be constantly engaged in a game of *cache-cache*. Moreover, interestingly enough, it is *jugement* that Montaigne associates with the text: he speaks of this faculty as an *estamine*—a filter through which all experiences of the world are to be passed.[29] Yet it is fun to read and write about Montaigne because, even though he shares much in common with Charles, he nevertheless upholds the contract between reader and text. Charles, I would argue, denies it, and as Stanley Corngold argues, in *The Fate of the Self*, when the self is reduced to such a degree the situation becomes intolerable.[30] The act of decoding Charles's chansons becomes an act of undoing the duality of the self. Isolating his persona behind the text causes Charles to isolate his reader before it. While such a rupture may, in fact, reflect the reality of the self, we read in order to gloss that break, not uncover it. When textual desire is reduced to mere play we have entered a realm of anti-hermeneutics and an area that threatens to expose the fragility—even the denial—of our selfhood. For all his apparent simplicity, Charles's message is dark indeed; and while this break has been rediscovered and reasserted at periodic intervals between then and now, he is, I would suggest, among the first to expose it.

NOTES

1. D. Poirion, *Le poète et le prince: L'evolution du lyrisme courtois de Guillaume de Machaut à Charles d'Orléans* (Paris: Presses Universitaires de France, 1965), pp. 466–73; and J. Fox, *The Lyric*

Poetry of Charles d'Orléans (Oxford: Clarendon Press, 1969), pp. 69–76.
2. J. Huizinga, *The Waning of the Middle Ages* (Doubleday Anchor, 1954), p. 254; F. Wolfzettel, "La poésie lyrique en France comme mode d'appréhension de la réalité," *Mélanges Foulon* (Lièges: ARUL, 1980 Vol. 2), pp. 409–19.
3. F. Wolfzettel, "La poésie lyrique," p. 413.
4. O von Simson, *The Gothic Cathedral* (2nd ed. revised: New York: Pantheon 1962), p. 35.
5. S. McK. Crosby, *The Royal Abbey of Saint-Denis* (New Haven: Yale Univ. Press, 1988), pp. 237–38.
6. Charles Radding and William Clark, "Abélard et le batisseur de St.-Denis," *Annales* 6 (1988): 1263–1290.
7. Lines 1–4, 15–17 of "Ara non siscla ni chanta" by Raimbaut d'Aurenga, number 14 in *The Life and Works of Raimbaut d'Orange*, ed. W. T. Pattison (Minneapolis: Univ. of Minnesota Press, 1954).
8. For a detailed psychological study of Charles as an introvert, see R. Cholakian, *Deflection / Reflection in the Lyrics of Charles d'Orléans* (Potomac, MD: Scripta Humanistica, 1984).
9. *Littérature française*, ed. A. Adam et al., (Paris: Larousse, 1967 volume 1); C. H. C. Wright, *A History of French Literature* (New York: Haskell House, 1969) accuses Charles of being an "aristocratic poet who dabbled in verse as an amusement" (122). Slightly more forgiving are descriptions like: "Sa versification est toujours aisée, sa langue facile, légère et colorée comme l'aile d'un papillon," G. Paris, *Esquisse historique de la littérature française au moyen âge* (Paris: Colin, 1907), p. 230; "Une voix délicate modulant avec élégance les thèmes traditionnels de la courtoisie," P. Brunel et al., *Histoire de la littérature française* (Stuttgart: Klett, 1972), p. 64. Even Huizinga, op. cit., talks of Charles's "little songs of disillusion" (308). For a list of further, similar assessments see also the opening pages of Alice Planche's magnum opus, *Charles d'Orléans ou la recherche d'un langage* (Paris: Champion, 1975).
10. A. Planche, *Charles d'Orléans ou la recherche d'un langage* (Paris: Champion, 1975), p. 11. And P. Zumthor calls Charles's use of allegory "un réseau cohérent de signes . . . un langage." *Mélange, offerts à Rita Lejeune* (Gembloux: Duculot, 1969), pp. 1492–93.
11. The texts and translations of the chansons are taken from my *French Chansons of Charles d'Orléans* (New York: Garland Publishing, 1986).

12. See, for instance, "Can la lauzeta mover" of Bernart de Ventadorn.
13. The problem of the authenticity of the English chansons is far from being resolved. I tend to believe that they were indeed written by Charles, for reasons cited here and in the introduction to my edition. The critic most engaged in this problem is Mary-Jo Arn, whose numerous articles give further support for this belief. See, for instance, "*Fortunes Stabilnes*: The English Poems of Charles of Orléans in their English Context." *Fifteenth-Century Studies* 7 (1983): 1–18.
14. A version of this image is given by virtually all critics who work on Charles. Planche, (in "Charles d'Orléans: L'exclusion et ses métaphores," *Exclus et systèmes d'exclusion dans la littérature et la civilisation médiévales* (Sénéfiance 5: Aix: CUERMA, 1978, 401–418) concludes with "Les marques de sa condition, gages de son authenticité, peuvent être un piège pour qui lit au premier degré un texte qu'il faut patiemment pénétrer et décoder. Sans cet effort, le lecteur n'aperçoit que la surface, et la juge mièvre ou manieriste. A sa façon il s'exclut du texte: il n'a pas découvert le secret du tissage." D. Poirion writes: "C'est ainsi que l'allégorie atteint son degré le plus élevé d'épaisseur concrète, l'illusion la plus totale, et conquiert le monde des objets. . . . Dans la situation esquissée passent fugitives des ébauches de personnifications. . . . C'est un univers onirique, un théâtre d'ombres qui se situe 'ailleurs,' dans un espace où les diverses formes de l'expérience humaine (perception, action, pensée, imagination) se confondent, e que le poète contemple de loin, comme le lecteur . . . par la magie du verbe les plans se fondent les uns dans les autres et composent une autre réalité, plus "vraie" et plus éphémère." *Précis de la littérature française du moyen âge* (Paris: Presses Universitaires de France, 1983), p. 269.
15. On the duality *cuer/moy* see Sasaki, *Sur le thème de Nonchaloir* (Paris: Nizet, 1974), p. 55.
16. Or, as Fox remarks, Charles's "exteriorizations were only half formed, never wholly crystallized, so pointing to the inner reality, maintaining an intimate two-way flow between the physical and mental worlds in which he lived," pp. 75–76.
17. As Planche notes, for Charles "l'appel à une transcendance reste exceptionnel," "Exclus," 416.
18. Planche, *La recherche*, p. 729.
19. *Mélanges Lejeune*, vol. 2, p. 1481.
20. Ibid., p. 55.

21. Andreas Capellanus, *The Art of Courtly Love*, trans. by John Jay Parry (New York: Columbia Univ. Press, 1947).
22. Translation from E. Panofsky, *Abbot Suger: On the Abbey Church of St.-Denis and its Art Treasures* (2nd edition, Princeton: Princeton Univ. Press, 1979).
23. On the autograph manuscript (MS O) see Champion, *Le manuscrit autographe des poésies de Charles d'Orléans* (Paris: Champion, 1907).
24. T. Barolini, *Dante's Poets* (Princeton: Princeton Univ. Press, 1984).
25. Hans Georg Gadamer, *Truth and Method* (New York: Seabury Press, 1975), 262–63.
26. Sasaki, in his masterful monograph on "Nonchaloir," concludes: "Nonchaloir est un état dominé par un esprit de jeu: il transfigure la quotidien en une vie symbolique qu'il essaye inlassablement de réaliser" (p. 215). Others have spoken as well of Charles's increasing interest in play: see, e.g., Poirion, *Poète*, pp. 73–84; Planche, *La recherche*, p. 26.
27. On this, see Jean-Charles Payen, "Charles d'Orléans et la poétique de l'essentiel," *Mélange de langue et de littérature offerts à Alice Planche* (Paris: les Belles Lettres, 1984), p. 366.
28. The music metaphor shows up often in discussion of Charles's lyrics. See, e.g., Poirion, *Poète*, pp. 439–47; Planche, *La recherche*, p. 729; Fox, p. 151.
29. "Qu'il luy face tout passer par l'estamine et ne loge rien en sa teste par simple authorité et à credit." *L'education des enfants* in *Oeuvres complètes*, edited by Albert Thibaudet and Maurice Rat (Paris: Gallimard, 1962), pp. 270–300.
30. Stanley Corngold, *The Fate of the Self* (New York: Columbia Univ. Press, 1986).

Cynthia J. Brown

Author, Editor and the Use of Illustrations in the Early Imprints of Villon's Works: "Ung chacun n'est maistre du scien"[1]

In Stanza LXXV of his *Testament*, François Villon voiced his concern about those who wanted to alter the title of his first work from *Lais* to *Testament* without his consent:

Sy me souvient bien, Dieu mercis,
Que je feiz a mon partement
Certains laiz, l'an cinquante six,
Qu'aucuns, sans mon consentement,
Voulurent nommer testament;
Leur plaisir fut, non pas le myen.
Mais quoy! on dit communement
Qu'ung chacun n'est maistre du scien. (vv. 753–60)[2]

In pointing out how an author like himself really had no control over his own words,³ the famous fifteenth-century poet not only put his finger on an issue that would resurface in Parisian law courts some forty years later, namely the ambiguities about literary proprietorship, but anticipated as well the inevitable modifications that would be made in the subsequent versions of his poetry. However, unlike his later counterparts, who challenged the idea that others, printers and booksellers in particular, could tamper with their literary creations,⁴ Villon appears resigned to the fact that no one was the master of his own.⁵ Nevertheless, his voiced opposition to such a turn of events—"Leur plaisir fut, non pas le myen" (v. 758)—suggests a questioning of what we now refer to as *mouvance*, that is, of the conscious or unconscious appropriation and alteration of others' words through oral or textual reproduction.⁶ This form of editorializing, as it were, is implicitly criticized by Villon here.

We do not know of course to whom Villon was specifically referring when he complained about the unsanctioned title change of his *Lais*. Yet we are able to trace more closely similar alterations in the posthumous versions of his works. While one of the more obvious forms of *mouvance*, actual textual changes, has received much attention from scholars, another related area worth investigating is the use of illustrations and accompanying rubrics in some of the early printed editions. As a kind of annotation of Villon's text, they "allowed" an interplay between the editorial and authorial voices, a feature to which the poet might well have objected, for it affected his original design to varying degrees.⁷ And indeed a number of discrepancies between the text and the work's extratextual features can be located. These disparities will be the subject of my investigation here. I shall examine the use of rubrics and illustrations in the early printed editions of Villon's works as a form of editorial intervention. With a focus on Pierre Levet's 1489 edition and a brief comparison with the next major version, edited by Clément Marot in 1533, the following questions will be raised. What is the relationship between these rubrics and illustrations and the literary text? In what way did the editor's arrangement and choice of them correspond to or diverge from the poet's own creation? In other words, what was the relationship between author and editor? By providing an illustration of Villon's raised concern about literary property, I intend to show how the editor's voice did play a part in reshaping the author's.

I should point out that I am using the term "editor" somewhat loosely and anachronistically in order to avoid confusion. The designation "editor" will refer at times to the printer, such as Levet, who, especially in the early years of printing, seems to have wielded primary control over the production of a book. It may also allude to the bookseller, who came to share and even assume some of the functions of a modern editor as the bookmaking process grew more complicated.[8] The term also includes the many other unknown, anonymous contributors to the layout and presentation of books. And finally, even though it was not yet applied to him, the word "editor" will most appropriately describe the role of someone such as Clément Marot, whose main objective was not commercial but rather philological, namely a careful restoration of the poet's text itself. Whatever their title, these figures served as intermediaries between author and public and were often significant shapers of meaning after the text left the writer's hands and before it arrived in the reader's.

None of the extant manuscripts, all of which are posthumous, contains illustrations of Villon's work.[9] It is only in some of the early surviving editions of his poetry that illustrations are found. These images play an important role in the textual organization of the various volumes, and they are related in significant ways to the rubrics, features that typify particularly the extant printed versions of Villon's *Testament*.[10] They provide an example of editorial decision-making in the book production process during the early years of printing in France, and, by extension, insight into late medieval textual interpretation of Villon as well. For the editor's choice of image and rubrics not only reflected his understanding of the poet; it likewise influenced how the reader was going to interpret and remember Villon's words. But the use of illustrations involved above all an economic investment and risk. On the one hand, these extratextual features were presumably adopted by editors in order to attract potential buyers.[11] And yet, as we shall see, the necessary additional financial layout for these woodcuts was subject in ways to constraints that ultimately undermined textual meaning.

All discussion of Villon's editions must begin with the first-known printed volume of his poetry, namely Pierre Levet's version of 1489, since most subsequent editions derived from it in one way or another. As in many *incunabula*, the title page is dominated by the printer's mark [Figure 1].[12] Whereas Villon was greatly preoccupied with signs—literally *enseignes*—in the composition of his numerous bequests, signs which critics have struggled to decode over the years, those who eventually published the complicated legacies Villon constructed around those *enseignes* were themselves very conscious about reproducing their own. As we see in Figure 1, eighty percent of the first folio is filled with Levet's mark, in which the first letters of each of his names are somewhat cryptically reproduced: PIE / LE. The complete reconstruction of the printer's identity depended, therefore, on the reader's recognition of the man behind the mark.[13]

Above the boldly placed printer's sign, the reader discovers the titles of the works contained in the volume:

> Le grant testament villon/ et le petit. / / Son codicille.
> Le iargon & les balades.

It is worth noting that Levet's listing of titles here continued the tradition to which Villon objected, namely that of referring to the *Lais* as a *Testament*; here it is called *le petit*.[14] He has, moreover, reversed the chronological order of the two works in their naming and arrangement, a feature that was imitated up until Marot's 1533 edition (cf. page 332). Thus, all references in the *Testament* to the earlier *Lais*[15] have less value for the reader who does not discover this series of bequests until the end of the collection.

Of interest as well is the fact that Villon's name figures prominently in the title. Although the small size of the letters makes it less obvious than Levet's, it is nonetheless presented in a more directly accessible fashion. The author is once again identified in the colophon at the end of the edition:

Le grant testament villon/et le petit. Son codicille. Le iargon et ses balades

Figure 1

Cy finist le grant testament / / maistre francois villon. Son / /
codicille ses ballades & iargō / / Et le petit testament. Impri
/ / me a paris Lan mil .cccc. qua / / tre vings et neuf.

This is particularly meaningful, since several of the extant fifteenth-century manuscripts of Villon's works present his poetry in an anonymous manner.[16] Since contemporary imprints did not always advertise the author's name on the title page, one must conclude that Villon's name bore a certain amount of authority at the end of the fifteenth century. Levet's decision to publish the poet's works with illustrations and to advertise his authorship was doubtless made with Villon's public appeal in mind so as to attract a significant number of book purchasers.[17]

Villon's presence is reinforced in this first known imprint of his works in another important way. Unlike the surviving manuscript anthologies, all but two of the many early printed editions contain only Villon's poetry.[18] This decision to devote a volume to his works alone distinguishes above all the surviving imprints from the extant manuscripts of his poetry.[19] In this sense, Villon was one of the first vernacular poets to receive such good press.[20]

Although the printer's sign is so boldly advertised on the title page, his apparent presence disappears once the reader begins the *Testament*. It is the author who more obviously dominates both verbally and visually. This concentration on Villon owes in part to the self-reflective and self-centering words of the text, which constantly draw the reader's attention to the narrator's own persona, even through the personalities of other characters. But the choice, use, and arrangement of the illustrations and their accompanying captions reinforce the author's ubiquitous presence as well, for Villon's image and name are repeatedly displayed. When Levet's design coincides with Villon's poetic conception, the former's presence tends to go unnoticed. At other times, however, contradictions between word and image, between editorial and authorial voices, arise, reminding the reader that "ung chacun n'est maistre du scien."[21]

The image and placement of the woodcuts on the first two folios of Villon's so-called *Grant Testament* (ai^v and aii^r) introduce the reader into the poet's world in a very pronounced manner. At the left [Figure 2] one perceives a commonly dressed man, with hand raised;[22] the rubric below reveals that this is the beginning of the "grant codicille & testament" of "maistre francois villon." The Villon woodcut, which occupies the opening space of the work, bridges the gap between the author's name as it is announced in the third person both on the title page and in the rubric below the woodcut—these essentially mark the editor's presence—and the first-person narrator's voice of the opening *huitain* of the *Testament*. At the same time, such an association of text and image creates a convenient confusion between Villon, the extratextually named author, and Villon, the textually identified narrator.[23] In fact, the editor's naming of Villon here in the rubric upstages the narrative voice of the text, which does not directly utter the name Villon until near the very end of the *Testament*.[24] This first illustration, then, depicts an ambiguously defined figure, because he is situated at the threshold of reality and literary creation.

The juxtaposition of image and text here further emphasizes the coexistence of the oral and written traditions in Villon: the pose of the illustrated Villon figure anticipates the numerous first-person voices, in particular the narrator's, that speak directly to the reader in various rhetorical modes throughout the *Testament*,[25] but these, of course, are anchored in a pseudo-legalistic form, which is not only part of a well-established written tradition but which is here essentially fixed in print. This association of author and text, of creator and narrator, of oral and written, is reinforced throughout the edition, for the very same image of Villon reappears four other times.

What is even more telling than this repeated visual immediacy of the author-narrator is the association Levet sets up between Villon and other characters in the text through the use of illustrations. The first such pairing of images, juxtaposed on the opening folios of the work, presents the reader with the most hateful relationship of the entire *Testament*, that of Villon and the bishop Thibault d'Aussigny [Figure 3]. It is because of the bishop's actions against the poet (whose details are provided in the *huitain* below d'Aussigny's image at the right) that the narrator erupts in an anger that sets in motion the *Testament*.

Cy comence le grant codicille & te
ſtamēt maiſtre francois Villon

En lan de mon trentieſme aage
Que toutes mes hontes ieuz beues
Ne du tout fol encor ne ſaige
Nonobſtant maintes peines eues
Leſquelles iay toutes receues
Soubz la main thibault danſſigny
Seueſque il eſt ſeignant les rues
Quil ſoit le mien ie le regny

Figure 2

Leuesque
Monseigneur nest ne mon euesque
Soubz luy ne tiens sil nest en friche
foy ne luy doy nömage auecque
Je ne suis son cerf ne sa bische
Peu ma dugne petite miche
Et de froide eau tout ung este.
Large ou estroit moult me fut chiche
Tel luy soit dieu quil ma este.

a ij.

Figure 3

The terse impersonal rubric "L'evesque," which omits the bishop's name, translates well the disdain of the poet's words as does the visual representation of him as an imposing religious figure with hard-set features. Despite the lack of a bishop's mitre that would have more accurately depicted Villon's nemesis in this woodcut, Levet does comply with authorial design to a large extent by dramatically setting the stage and tone of the *Testament*.[26]

Only four other pairs of illustrations decorate Levet's edition. Significantly three of these groupings present the exact same images, namely the Villon woodcut coupled with that of a woman [Figures 4 and 5]. Rubrics and the context of the illustrations make it possible for the reader to identify the characters represented. Yet the repeated use of the same female illustration for different figures in the text—the Belle Heaulmière, grosse Margot and Beauté—lends a generic quality to their very different personalities and associations with the narrator. Economic considerations on the part of the editor doubtless played a role in this decision that limited a closer alliance between text and image here; it was less costly, after all, not only to use illustrations that had been originally made to decorate other volumes, but also to re-use the same woodcut within the same edition. Yet, this decision essentially undermined Villon's words by blurring the distinctions he had drawn between the different figures.

The first set of these woodcuts (folios biii^v and biiii^r), arranged on facing folios, alerts the reader to the editor's presence. The fact that the printing of the verses on the preceding folio (biii) was halted halfway down the page suggests a conscious strategy on Levet's part to ensure that the illustrations would fall on facing folios and that the related *huitains* would be placed in a logical relationship to them. Not only does his "voice" interrupt the text by referring in the rubric to the narrator in the third person, but, perhaps because of a typesetter error, the original reception of the Belle Heaulmière's speech is modified from hearing to seeing. That is, whereas Villon's words explain "Advis m'est que j'*oy* regretter / La belle qui fut heaulmiere . . ." (vv. 453–54), Levet's rubric reads: "Comment Villon *voit* a son advis la belle heaulmiere soy complaignant." Furthermore, the words of Villon's Belle Heaulmière, characterized by the narrator as those of regretting, are initially described by Levet as words of complaint. Therefore, just as the reader must be aware of the fact that the first-person voice of the text slips almost imperceptibly from the narrator's into that of the Belle Heaulmière, a characteristic feature of Villon's *Testament* throughout, so too one must take into account how the extratextual voice of the editor, present through the rubrics and use of illusrations, seems to coincide with, yet at times diverges from, the textual voice of the narrator.[27] In fact, the editor contradicts himself on the facing folio, where the woodcut of a young woman is mismatched with the rubric, which reads "La vieille en regrettant le temps de sa jeunesse."[28] In these ways, editorial design deviates from poetic intention.[29]

This exact same juxtaposition of the Villon woodcut with that of a woman appears twice more in Levet's edition. We learn, then, that for the editor the relationship between Villon and women was the essence of his *Testament*. Despite the fact that most legacies in the work were accorded to men, Levet nevertheless chose to highlight through illustrations the role of certain women. This focus on female illustrations within the text subsequently gave rise to an edition dating from around 1529 whose only illustration, placed on the title page, depicted the poet and a woman (cf. Tchémerzine, p. 469). In each case, despite the fact that Villon's association with females was particularly complex, as reflected in the various portraits he drew — that of his mother, the Belle Heaulmière, the Virgin Mary, the filles de joie, Margot, Fausse Beauté, the Dames du temps jadis, les femmes de Paris, etc., not to mention the six other specifically named women,[30] the woodcuts do not impart these critical distinctions to the reader.[31] The same illustration is supposed to depict an "old and grizzled" woman[32] (the Belle Heaulmière), a younger, fat prostitute (grosse Margot) and the youthful, abstract idea of Beauty. The reader's awareness of the contradiction between text and image signals in fact the editor's presence and annotation of Villon's words.

Furthermore, whereas the text informs us that the first pairing of Villon with a woman constituted a sympathetic relationship — Villon essentially identifies with and speaks through

Cōment Villon voit a son aduis sa
Belle heaulmiere soy cōplaignant.

Aduis mest que ioy regretter
La Belle qui fut heaulmiere
Soy ieune fille souhaicter
Et parler en ceste maniere
Ha vielllesse felonne et fiere
Pour quoy mas si tost abatue
Qui me tient qui:que ne me fiere
Et que ace coup ie ne me tue

Figure 4

La vieille en regrettant le temps
de sa ieunesse.

Tollu mas la haulte franchise
Que beaulte mauoit ordonne
Sur clercs marchans & gens deglises
Car lors il nestoit homme ne
Qui tout le sien ne meust donne
Quoy quil en fust des repentailles
Mais que luy eusse abandonne
Ce que refusent truandailles

                              b.iiii.

Figure 5

the Belle Heaulmière—as does the third coupling with "grosse Margot," although in a very different manner,[33] the second set of woodcuts presents a very antagonistic relationship, that of Villon (same image as Figure 2) and Fausse Beauté (same image as Figure 5). Not only did the editor take liberties in labelling this illustration "Beauté d'amours," a reference that is not found in Villon's own words,[34] but his re-use of the identical images for this very different relationship clouds the fact that the rhetorical staging of Beauté d'Amours differs entirely from that of the Belle Heaulmière. The poet does not place the woman on stage here as before; he himself launches into an invective against her. In other words, the poet doesn't empower his enemy, Fausse Beaulté, with the right to speak; only those, like the Belle Heaulmière, with whom he identifies or whom he respects, are granted that opportunity.[35] With troubadouresque resonance, the illustration accompanying this *ballade* recalls the traditional lyric image of the silent, supposedly powerful, almost abstract figure of the "belle dame sans merci."

One could argue that the affinity between the female described in these verses—Beauté—and her youthful image in the generic woodcut is closest in this instance. One could likewise maintain that the particular arrangement of these woodcuts back to back on the same folio instead of on facing pages reflects the angry, frustrated tone of the narrative voice in the accompanying *huitains*, thereby signaling Levet's attempt to distinguish this pair from the other two.[36] The female character's posture of defiance can also be seen as a corroboration of the narrator's own experience of rejection at the hands of love, as detailed in the text below. Yet the reader is nonetheless conscious of and perhaps disconcerted at being called upon to accept the juxtaposition of the same image with other female characters in the text. While one might object that in point of fact the late medieval public did not mind whether captions and pictures "told the truth,"[37] it is worth noting that Le Caron's edition of Villon's works, which was printed just a year or so after Levet's (ca. 1490-92), does offer more subtly interpreted female woodcuts. Like Levet's, his illustration of Beaulté d'Amours depicts a young-looking female figure (fol. cvi^v),[38] but another image, one that portrays an older, wrinkled-faced woman with worried expression, serves more appropriately to illustrate the aging Belle Heaulmière (fol. biiii[r]). Unlike his predecessor, who nevertheless served as his model,[39] Le Caron, maintaining the exact same arrangement of text and illustration, did distinguish between the two very different female figures in his use of illustrations; this modification suggests a conscious attempt on his part to relate image and text more closely. There continue to be, however, significant discrepancies. The figure depicted in this woodcut is too well-dressed for the Belle Heaulmière. And, doubtless for financial reasons, the same woodcut was used (fol. evi) to depict "grosse Margot." Yet, at least Villon's relationship with these two women was more similar than that with Fausse Beauté, thereby justifying to some extent the reappearance of the same illustration.

Levet failed to publicize authorial design in another significant way, for he did not emphasize the acrostics generating Villon's denunciation of Fausse Beauté. While such an oversight of authorial intention cannot be blamed on Levet alone, since a number of manuscripts fail to present correctly the acrostics as well,[40] it represents, nonetheless, a serious omission. As another sign of the author's poetic prowess and presence, his signature, which engenders the first stanza—

> Faulce beaulté qui tant me couste cher,
> Rude en effet, ypocrite douleur,
> Amour dure plus que fer a mascher,
> Nommer te puis, de ma defacon seur
> cercher selon la mort d'un povre cueur,
> Orgueil mussé qui gens met au mourir,
> yeulx sans pitié, ne veult droit et rigueur,
> Sans empirer, ung pouvre secourir?

and the name of his addressee, Marthe, at the source of the second—

> Mieulx m'eust valu auoir esté cerchier
> Ailleurs secours ç'eust esté mon honneur.
> Rien ne m'eust sceu lors de ce fait hassier;
> Certes m'en suis en fuite et deshonneur

> Haro, haro, le grant et le mineur!
> et qu'est ce? mourray je sans coup ferir
> Ou pitié veult, selon ceste teneur,
> Sans empirer, ung pouvre secourir?[41]

could be easily missed by the reader, especially since the fourth verse of the second stanza begins with a C rather than a T. It appears, then, that the editor was unaware of the existence of this as well as the other acrostics.[42] Levet's oversight thus fails to reflect the ambiguity of this particular ballad, which is addressed to and attacks the abstract figure of Fausse Beauté, but whose letters spell out the name of a specific girl friend, Marthe.[43]

The final set of woodcuts is the only one in the Levet edition that illustrates poems outside of the *Testament* (fols. gii^v–giii). At the left (Figure 6) the familiar Villon image introduces the quatrain that makes a self-mocking reference to his possible future hanging:

> Je suis Francois dont ce me poise,
> Ne de Paris empres Pontoise,
> Qui d'une corde d'une toise
> Saura mon col que mon cul poise.
>   (Levet, fol. gii^v)

Its dramatic juxtaposition with the woodcut of the three hanging men at the right,[44] [Figure 7] which depicts, on the other hand, a definite finality, completely alters the tone of the quatrain. The sarcastic, distancing first-person singular voice in the verses at the left becomes absorbed into the very sobering first-person plural voice at the right, an association ensured by the presence of Villon's name in both captions. And yet the quatrain and ballad do not appear together in any extant contemporary manuscript version,[45] suggesting that it was Levet who first coupled these poems. By placing some of Villon's miscellaneous verses after the *Testament* in a group that presumably forms a codicil, a term absent from all manuscript versions that appears on the title page of Levet's edition, he was obviously attempting to remain faithful to the pseudo-legalistic framework Villon had adopted as his own narrative strategy.[46] Part of this arrangement involved the association of the quatrain with the two other poems in which Villon specifically mentions hanging, the "Cause d'appel"[47] and the so-called "Epitaphe." But by entitling this four-verse poem "Le rondeau que feist ledit Villon quand il fut jugié,"[48] Levet adds a specific biographical dimension to it which was possibly an incorrect annotation, thereby narrowing their meaning. By the same token, his adoption of the rubric "L'épitaphe dudict Villon" for the ballad at the right was not necessarily appropriate either, given that an epitaph was already located by the poet at the end of the *Testament*.[49] Indeed this very discrepancy was resolved in the Lyon edition of around the same date (1489–92) by a significant caption change: one reads "L'épitaphe Villon" before the *Testament* verses beginning "Cy gist et dort . . . ,"[50] whereas the ballade under discussion here is more aptly announced as the "Epitaphe des penduz." Nevertheless, contemporary editions, including Marot's,[51] continued to follow Levet and, consequently, many modern editions still bear the caption "Epitaphe Villon."

We have seen, then, how Levet's annotation of Villon's words in the form of rubrics and illustrations represents in varying degrees a reappropriation of the author's voice by the editor. One curious consequence of this phenomenon was the adoption of Levet's rubrics in later unillustrated editions. This sometimes resulted not only in a strange disruption of Villon's narrative, but, because captions were not always placed appropriately, in a literal contradiction of the poet's words. For example, in the Denis Meslier edition of ca. 1490–91, the rubrics "Beauté d'amours" (fol. cvi) and "La grosse Margot" (fol. cv^v) seem out of place without the illustrations, because these characters never speak in the text. By the same token, the rubric "L'evesque", which is placed at the beginning of the *Testament* following the caption "Cy commence . . ." in the Le Noir edition of ca. 1505 misleads the reader, because Villon's words are thereby attributed to the very character who is being decried and who is never allowed to utter a word in the text. In these instances, then, the editor's "voice" corrupts the author's through a careless presentation of characters and words.

Le rondeau que feist
ledit Villon quant
il fut iugie

Je suis francois dont ce me poise
Ne de paris empres pontoise
Qui dune corde dune toise
Saura mon col que mon cul poise

Figure 6

Early Imprints of Villon's Works 333

Epitaphe dudit Villon
Freres humains qui apres nous viues
Nayez les cueurs contre nous endurcis
Car se pitie de nous pouurez auez
Dieu en aura pluftoft de vous mercis
Vous nous voies cy ataches cinq six
Quât de la char q trop auôs nourrie
Elle est pieca deuouree et pourrie
et nous les os deuenôs cêdres & pouldre
De nostre mal personne ne sen rie
Mais pries dieu que tous nous vueil
le absouldre   g iii.

Figure 7

A clearer example of editorial intervention is evidenced in Clément Marot's famous edition of 1533. From the initial title page, which prominently advertises Marot's involvement as much as Villon's in the publication (cf. Tchémerzine, p. 476), to the marginal explanations on every single folio, Marot visually shares an extratextual presence with Villon:

> Les Oevvres de / / Françoys Villon / / de Paris, reueues & remises en / / leur entier par Clement Ma- / / rot valet de chambre / / du Roy. / / Distique du dict Marot / / Peu de Villons en bon sauoir / / Trop de Villons pour deceuoir / / On les vend a Paris en la grant salle / / du Palais, en la bouticque de / / Galiot du Pre.[52]

Moreover, whereas Levet had placed a Villon woodcut in the transitional space between title page and text, something more intrusive is done in Marot's edition: he substitutes himself in the form of a dedicatory huitain to François 1er (fol. Aii) and a long letter to his readers in which, to his credit, he explicitly spells out his editorial principles (fols. Aii^v–[Avi]).[53] He further invades Villon's textual space under the guise of helping the reader gain access to his poetic world, for much in the style of Biblical commentaries, Marot's marginal definitions and comments[54] as well as his lengthy explanatory rubrics[55] repeatedly draw the reader away from Villon's words before sending them back to his text. At one point, the editor's marginal comments actually displace the author's centrally-positioned text as Marot literally interrupts Villon's narrative in the middle of the *Testament* in order to provide his readers with a context for understanding the poem he calls the "Contredictz de Franc Gontier." This paragraph, contrasting noticeably with the rest of the narration by its prose form, is prominently announced by a rubric which reads "Clement Marot aux Lecteurs" (p. 79). Such extratextual focus on the editor anticipates the implicit competition between the "je" of Marot's Prologue and marginal notes with the "je" of Villon's narrator throughout the edition, a change that is all the more emphasized by the lack of illustrations that repeatedly reminded the reader of Villon's presence in Levet's edition.

Unlike Levet, then, Marot consciously advertises his editorial presence by informing his readers of the alterations he has made to Villon's text, all the while trying to remain faithful to the writer he edits.[56] For example, deviating from previous printing tradition, Marot consciously places the *Lais* before the *Testament* in his edition and relates how Villon objected to their newly given title;[57] nevertheless, he maintains the inappropriate title himself, thereby revealing that established convention held more authority than the author's own stated wishes. Although insisting that "Je ne suys (certes) en rien son voysin" (fol. Aiii), Marot, an author in his own right, obviously chooses to make his presence known rather than remain ambiguously hidden behind captions and illustrations like Levet and the many previous printers and booksellers. Yet in doing so, Marot consciously takes the side of the author against those producing his works. Already in the Preface to his *Adolescence clémentine* of 1532 he had criticized poorly printed editions which he characterized as "plus au proufict du Libraire qu'à l'honneur de l'Autheur..."[58] and here in the Prologue to Villon's *Oeuvres* he again complains of the corruptness of the earlier editions of the fifteenth-century poet's works and of the ignorance of Parisian printers:

> Entre tous les bons livres imprimez de la langue Françoise ne s'en veoit ung si incorrect ne si lourdement corrompu, que celluy de Villon: et m'esbahy... comment les imprimeurs de Paris, et les enfans de la ville, n'en ont eu plus grant soing.... Tant y ay trouvé de broillerie en l'ordre des coupletz et des vers, en mesure, en langaige, en la ryme, et en la raison, que je ne scay duquel je doy plus avoir pitié, ou de l'oeuvre ainsi oultrement gastee, ou de l'ignorance de ceulx qui l'imprimerent. (fols. Aiii–Aiii^v)

His involvement with the more careful textual re-editing of Villon's works reflected, then, the creation of a new role in the book production industry, that of editor, distinct from printer or bookseller (although it was not yet called such). Indeed, a consciousness of the impossibility of his task, of the inevitable "cicatrice," as he called it, distinguished Marot from his careless predecessors:

> Et si quelq'un d'aventure veult dire que tout ne soit racoustré ainsi qu'il appartient, je luy respons desmaintenant, que s'il estoit autant navré en sa personne, comme j'ay trouvé Villon blessé en ses oeuvres, il n'y a si expert chirurgien qui le sceust penser sans apparence de cicatrice . . ." (fols. Av^v–[Avi]).

And yet, such consciousness also entailed a more active and publicized editorial presence

In conclusion, although printing stabilized texts in a more widespread fashion than earlier reproduction methods, Villon's initial concerns about the title change of his *Lais* proved to be justified even after the advent of print. While Villon's voice and image still dominated most of the early printed editions of his works, there existed at the same time a certain undermining of his authority through the extended use of extratextual features. On one hand, Pierre Levet's advertised presence on the title page of his 1489 edition of Villon's works resurfaces in a subtle but nonetheless intervening fashion within the text through his use of illustrations and rubrics, his poetic arrangement of Villon's verses and his conscious or unconscious oversights. On the other hand, Clément Marot's involvement in his 1533 publication of Villon's poetry was much less subtly presented, for his role as intermediary between poet and public was consciously publicized not only on the first folio and in the Prologue, but throughout the entire edition. Despite the fact that Marot's intentions were honorable in that he sought to rectify previous poor printing and editing practices, he nevertheless ended up at times displacing Villon's own presence and words.

Mouvance, then, didn't entirely disappear with the advent of print. While it was much more controlled at the textual level, because a limitless number of copies of the exact same text could now be reproduced, there nevertheless continued to be a certain reappropriation of an author's words, more conscious perhaps at the textual level, more extensive but less explicit at the extratextual level. One could say that as book production became more and more commercialized, the more conspicuous manifestations of *mouvance* began to shift to the periphery or margins of a printed work. Indeed it was these very spaces that were becoming critical to the publisher, for they initially drew the reader's attention to a book.

NOTES

1. A shorter version of this article was presented at the Twenty-Fifth International Congress on Medieval Studies at Western Michigan University in Kalamazoo, Michigan on May 12, 1990.
2. François Villon, *Le Testament*, ed. Jean Rychner and Albert Henry (Geneva: Droz, 1974), p. 71. Unless otherwise indicated, subsequent citations will be taken from this edition. Although ms. B.N. f.fr. 1661 [=B] most likely dates from after Villon's death (ca. 1480), it provides an example of Villon's objection in these verses. One discovers his *Lais* on fol. 236, but the work is entitled "Le testament de maistre francois villon." In ms. B.N. f.fr. 20041 [=C], dating from the second half of the fifteenth century, the *Lais* are entitled "Le petit testament villon" (fol. 108) and the same work is entitled "Le premier testament maistre francois villon" (fol. 29) in the Stockholm manuscript V.u.27 [=F], copied around 1480. The Arsenal manuscript 3523 [=A], dating from the end of the 15th century, however, "correctly" identifies this work as "Le lais francois villon" (fol. 735). See pp. 332–33 regarding this aspect of the Levet and Marot editions.
3. Cf., however, Giuseppe Di Stefano, "Du 'Lais' au 'Testament,'" *Cahiers de l'Association Internationale des Etudes Françaises*, 32 (1980), p. 43, who suggests that Villon himself may have been responsible for this change.
4. Cf., for example, my discussion about André de la Vigne's lawsuit against the printer Michel Le Noir in *Poets, Patrons and Printers: Crisis of Authority in Late Medieval France* (Ithaca: Cornell Univ. Press, 1995). Cf. also my article "The Confrontation Between Printer and Author in Early Sixteenth-Century France: Another Example of Michel Le Noir's Unethical Printing Practices," *Bibliothèque d'Humanisme et Renaissance*, LIII (1991), 105–19.
5. For a short analysis of this passage, cf. among others, David A. Fein, *François Villon and His Reader* (Detroit: Wayne State Univ. Press, 1989), pp. 71–73.

6. Paul Zumthor is the critic most associated with the theory of *mouvance* (cf., for example, his *Essai de poétique médiévale* [Paris: Seuil, 1972], pp. 43–46, 126, 507). In his *Scandal of the Fabliaux* (Chicago: The Univ. of Chicago Press, 1986), p. 56, R. Howard Bloch refers to this phenomenon by speaking of "the premise underlying the practice of poetry in the High Middle Ages—that is, the circulation of a limited number of texts that, always already stolen, belong to no one, are common property, and in fact, as dead letters, are living proof of the literary text as a system of self-creating value."
7. Of course, it is impossible to determine with any certainty Villon's intentions, since no original or contemporary manuscripts of his works have survived. But the early posthumous versions of his writings provide the only access we have to his poetic world.
8. In certain cases, authors, such as André de la Vigne, Jean Lemaire de Belges and Pierre Gringore, assumed this particular role. Cf. my *Poets, Patrons and Printers*. For a discussion of the various functions involved in the printing process, cf. Henri-Jean Martin and Roger Chartier, eds., *Le livre conquérant: Du Moyen Age au milieu du XVIIe siècle*, Vol. I of the *Histoire de l'Edition Française* (Paris: Promodis, 1982) and Ezio Ornato, "Les Conditions de production et de diffusion du livre médiéval (XIIIe–XVe siècles)," in *Culture et idéologie dans la genèse de l'état moderne* (Actes de la table ronde organisée par le CNRS et l'Ecole française de Rome, Rome, 15–17 octobre 1984) (Rome: Palais Farnèse, 1985), pp. 57–84.
9. It is possible, of course, that illustrated manuscript versions were made during Villon's time, but none survives. Given the poet's apparent poverty and the fact that he did not write the *Testament* for a patron, however, it is more likely that a decorated version was never commissioned or made.
10. In the various manuscripts, rubrics designate the separate poems, but within the *Testament*, the reader finds rubrics that usually designate only generic forms, such as *ballade*. A similar pattern occurs in the printed editions with expanded rubrics associated with the illustrations. The only exceptions in the Levet edition are found on fols. ciii^v ("Cy commence le testament") and eiii^v ("Ballade de la rescripcion des femmes de paris"), which do not bear woodcuts.
11. Cf. Ornato, and Rudolf Hirsch, "Title Pages in French Incunables, 1486–1500," *Gutenberg Jahrbuch* (1978), 63–66.

12. It differs nonetheless from the sign designating the printer's address, which was that of the *Balance d'argent*, located at the end of the rue Saint Jacques near the Petit Pont (cf. the notice of Jacques Guignard in *Facsimilé intégral de l'un des trois exemplaires connus de l'édition princeps du Grand et du petit Testament, du Jargon et des ballades de François Villon* [Paris: Edition d'art Lucien Mazenod, 1975], p. xxii).
13. The colophon does not identify the printer either (cf. p. 318).

As we see here in the Levet edition, the printer often stamped his presence in this critically visible place. On the title page of Jean Trepperel's ca. 1494 illustrated edition, one finds the mark of the bookseller Michel Le Noir (cf. Avenir Tchémerzine, *Bibliographie d'éditions originales et rares d'auteurs français des XVe, XVIe, XVIIe et XVIIIe siècles* [Paris: Plée, 1933], Vol. X, p. 466, for a reproduction of this page), who later became a printer in his own right and published a ca. 1505 edition of Villon's works (without his mark, cf. Tchémerzine, p. 468). Trepperel's name surfaces only in the colophon at the end of his first known edition ("Ci finist le grant testament / / maistre francoys villon ... Imprime / / a paris Par Jehan treperel de / / mourant sur le pont nostre dame."). However, Trepperel places his own mark prominently on the title page of his 1497 and ca. 1501–03 editions (cf. Tchémerzine, pp. 465 and 467), although, as in the case of Levet, the reader must recognize the initials IT as those of Jean Trepperel. The colophon also advertises the printer's name. At the end of the 1497 edition one reads: "Cy fine le grant testament mai / / stre francois villon ... Imprime a paris par: Je= / / han treperel demourant sur le pont. / / nostre dame a lenseigne saīt laurēs: / / Acheves lan mil quattre c̄es quattre / / vingtz:&:xvii le /.viii. iour de Jullet." The colophon of his ca. 1501–03 edition reads: "... Imprime a / / paris par Jehā treperel demourant a la / / rue sainct iaques pres saint yues a lensei= / / gne sainct.Laurens." The title page of the Lyon edition of 1489–92 is unfortunately missing as is that of the Le Caron edition of 1490–92, but Le Caron's mark apparently appeared on the title page of another now lost edition that he published around 1500 (cf. Tchémerzine, p. 466). In many of these early editions, title-page images alone provide the volume's only decoration. In other cases, an elaborately decorated initial letter (L) provides the only illustrative element in the entire volume (cf. Denis Meslier's edition of ca. 1490–92 [Tchémerzine, p. 464]).

The most puzzling and perhaps ironic title-page woodcut is found in Germain Bineaut's 1490 version, for it is the very image of the bishop found in the Levet edition (cf. Tchémerzine, p. 463, and page 319 of this article), even though it is placed below a reference to Villon's authorship. An image of Villon like the ones decorating the Levet edition is found on the verso side of the same folio below the rubric "Ci commence le codicille." How ironic that the illustration of Villon's most detested enemy adorned the title page of this edition of his works and may even have been designed to represent Villon himself. Cf. E. H. Gombrich, *Art and Illusion*, 2nd edition (Kingsport, Tenn.: Kingsport Press, 1965), p. 68, who states: ". . . pictures of people and places changed their captions with sovereign disregard for truth. The print sold on the market as a portrait of a king would be altered to represent his successor or enemy."

In a later series of extant Villon editions dating from the early sixteenth century, the title pages orient the reader's attention in different ways, with images relating to the text, rather than printer or bookseller marks, placed on the title page. The illustration on the title page of Julien Hubert's ca. 1529 edition of Villon has combined the dominant female illustrations found initially in Levet (and subsequently in Le Caron and Trepperel) into one portrait, thus continuing the early printer's focus on Villon and women (cf. Tchémerzine, p. 469, and page 323 of this article). This same woodcut decorates the title page of a later Alain Lotrian edition of ca. 1520–30 (cf. Tchémerzine, p. 470). However, title-page illustrations in other editions, all of which constituted reusable and reused woodcuts, focused on other aspects of Villon's work. A rather crude woodcut underlines its legal testament aspect in Guillaume Nyverd's edition dating from before 1520, for it presents a robed, religious figure (Villon?) standing before (handing something to?) a magistrate, while a scribe records the action. The whole oral testimonial character of the *Testament* is thereby emphasized, recalling the references to a scribe in the *Testament* (vv. 564–68, 779, 787–91). The idea of imminent death is evoked in the illustration of a religious nurse caring for an ailing, abedded man on the title page of the edition of Nyverd's widow and son (?) Jacques dating from before November 1525. The Galiot du Pré edition of 1532 and Clément Marot's edition of 1533 bear no illustrations whatsoever.

14. One finds a similar arrangement in manuscript C (cf. note 2). It is possible that the word "testament" was mistakenly omitted after "petit" here on the title page, especially since it is provided in the colophon. All other editions with title pages up to Marot's 1533 edition imitate Levet's title, except for Michel Le Noir's ca. 1505 version, where the word "son" is also omitted in the title, resulting in a reference to "le petit codicille."

15. For a study of these, cf. Di Stefano, pp. 39–50.
16. In ms. Fr. 78. B. 17 of the Cabinet des Estampes of the National Library in Berlin [=H], dating from ca. 1475, the four Villon poems that are scattered throughout the collection ("La Requeste a Monseigneur de Bourbon," "La Ballade des Langues envieuses," "La Ballade de la grosse Margot" and "Mort j'appelle de ta rigueur") bear no extratextual indication whatsoever of his authorship. While the poet spells out his name in the third line of the "Requeste," the acrostic at the end of the "Ballade de la grosse Margot" is incorrectly presented as VJOLNe instead of VJLLONe. Ms. B.N. f.fr. 1719 [=P] (dating from the end of the 15th, beginning of the 16th centuries), which contains fifteen of Villon's poems, likewise lacks extratextual authorial identification, although the "Requeste" once again provides Villon's name in the third verse, and two poems, the "Ballade de la grosse Margot," and the so-called "Debat du Cuer et du corps" end with his acrostic signature. This, however, is in no way highlighted. In ms. F, Villon is not identified extratextually as the author of a number of poems, some of which contain acrostic signatures, but he is very clearly named as author of some seven others. In mss. A, B, C, O [=B.N. f.fr. 1104] and R [=B.N. f.fr. 12490], Villon is extratextually identified for the reader.
17. Cf. Madeleine Lazard, "Clément Marot Editeur et Lecteur de Villon," *CAIEF*, 32 (1980), p. 7, who states: "Que Villon ait été un succès de libraire au début du XVIe siècle, c'est ce qu'atteste le nombre, considérable pour l'époque, des éditions de son oeuvre." In the Prologue to his 1533 edition, Clément Marot makes it clear that Villon was a highly esteemed writer, when he states: "c'est le meilleur poete Parisien qui se trouve" (Aiii) and ". . . et ne fay doubte qu'il n'eust emporté le chapeau de laurier devant tous les poetes de son temps, s'il eust esté nourry en la court des Roys, et des Princes, la ou les jugemens se amendent, et les langaiges se pollissent [Aiv^v]." In this and subsequent references taken from the original editions, all abbreviations have been expanded, capital letters have been added to mark the beginning of a proper name, the use of i and j, u and v has been modernized, apostrophes have been used to indicate elided vowels, and accents and punctuation have been added or modified when necessary.
18. One early printed verse collection that contains some of his pieces, namely the *Jardin de Plaisance* of 1501, edited by Antoine Vérard, presents them anonymously in a scattered, unrelated manner, just

as many of the surviving manuscripts had (cf. note 16). The 1532 Augereau/Du Pré edition also contains other works ("Le monologue du franc archier de Baignollet" and "Le Dyalogue des seigneurs de Mallepaye et Baillevent").

19. This was not necessarily a characteristic of printing alone, but it does reflect a related focus on authorship typical of late medieval literature. Sylvia Huot has shown how anthologies devoted to a single author were compiled as early as the thirteenth century in *From Song to Book: The Poetics of Writing in Old French Lyric and Lyrical Narrative Poetry* (Ithaca: Cornell Univ. Press, 1987). Cf. also Jacqueline Cerquiglini, "Quand la voix s'est tue: la mise en recueil de la poésie lyrique aux XIVe et XVe siècles," *La Présentation du Livre* (Actes du colloque de Paris X-Nanterre, 4–6 décembre 1985), eds. E. Baumgartner and Nicole Boulestreau (Paris X-Nanterre: Centre de Recherches du Département de Français, 1987), pp. 313–27. In any case, no early printed version ever contained all of Villon's poetry.

20. Other such poets include Alain Chartier, Guillaume Alexis, and Jean Meschinot, author of the *Lunettes des Princes*, which was printed some thirty times (posthumously) between 1493 and 1539. Meschinot has been characterized as "le poète le plus imprimé de son temps" (cf. *Les Lunettes des Princes*, ed. Martineau-Genieys [Genève: Droz, 1972], pp. lxxix–lxxxiv).

21. This discussion will not deal with the numerous textual errors of Levet's edition, which is known to be quite faulty, but rather with its extratextual features.

22. Those later editions that were illustrated made some significant changes in the images they presented of Villon. In his edition of ca. 1490–92, Pierre Le Caron offers two different Villon woodcuts. The reader discovers a more clerkly figure than Levet's, an illustration that was ironically remade from Levet's bishop woodcut by the substitution of a wide-brimmed hat for the cap (fols. biii^v and cvi) (cf. Guignard, p. xx). This was also probably the same woodcut used on the title page of the text, which is now missing in the only known extant copy of this edition, and possibly on fol. ev^v across from the hangmen woodcut, which is likewise missing in this particular edition. However, the woodcut accompanying the "Ballade de la grosse Margot" places on stage another Villon image with a child (cf. Tchémerzine, p. 461). Is this an attempt to distinguish between Villon as poet and narrator or to emphasize the idea that it is a third-person and not a first-person account

of Margot's story? The first extant Trepperel edition (and later Trepperel and Le Noir editions) dating from 1497 (and ca. 1501–1505) depicts a more flamboyant Villon as a kind of *joyeux galant* (cf. Tchémerzine, p. 467). Moreover, the Villon woodcut stands alone on the verso of the last folio, thereby emphasizing the author character of the Villon illustration, juxtaposed as it is with the colophon. These various Villon images, ranging from humble bourgeois to cleric to gallant, reflect differing editorial interpretations of Villon, that were doubtless very contingent on the availability of generic woodcuts. Nevertheless, they must have determined to some degree the public's reception of Villon as a poet.

23. Cf., for example, William Calin, "Observations on Point of View and the Poet's Voice in Villon," *Esprit Créateur*, VII, 3 (1967), 180–87, for a discussion of the different voices in the *Testament*.

24. Cf. vv. 1811 ("Pour l'ame du povre *Villon*"), 1886–1887 ("Ung povre petit escollier / Qui fut nommé *Françoys Villon*") and 1966–97 ("Icy se clost le testament / Et finist du povre *Villon*."). Villon did of course end several of the ballades in the *Testament* with an acrostic signature (the "Ballade pour prier Nostre Dame," the "Ballade a s'amye," and the "Ballade de la grosse Margot), but these were not highlighted in the extant manuscript versions or early editions. Cf. Nancy Regalado, "La Fonction poétique des noms propres dans le *Testament* de François Villon," *CAIEF*, 32 (1980): 66, who points out that:

> Le *je* poétique n'est nommé que lorsque la création du personnage et de son monde s'achève. Le nom *Villon* apparaît en clair dans le texte au CLXVIII[e] huitain, le nom d'un mort qu'on rappelle au souvenir, et toujours au passé et à la troisième personne comme pour marquer la distance par rapport au personnage créé.

25. It is worth noting that Clément Marot still relied on the oral (as well as written) transmission of Villon's verses in preparing his 1533 edition of the poet's works. He explains in his Prologue that he relied in part on "les vieulx imprimez" and in part on "des bons vieillards qui en [=la poésie de Villon] savent par cueur" and in part on his own "jugement naturel" (fol. [Aiv]).

26. The fact that the Villon figure faces left, away from the bishop, intensifies the obstinate hatred he paints in the verses. While

these probably did not constitute woodcuts that were made especially for this edition, their choice and placement is nonetheless quite effective. In the Le Caron illustration of the bishop, which was based on the Levet woodcut, the cap has been replaced by a mitre and the figure now bears a staff, resulting in an image that more closely depicts a bishop (cf. Guignard, p. xx and Tchémerzine, p. 461). The 1497 Trepperel edition portrays a bishop woodcut that imitates in reverse the Levet bishop, but he is now holding a scroll. No other editions bear such woodcuts. Cf. note 13 for details about the Bineaut edition, whose title page bears a bishop woodcut.

27. Just as Villon announces the Belle Heaulmière in the third person, so too Levet announces Villon in the third person. In this sense, Villon plays a role similar to that of an editor as he "selects" what words will be reproduced.

28. Perhaps since she talks about youth, it's a justifiable usage. Here the idea of regret is picked up from Villon's words in v. 453 and contrasts with this rubric on the opposite folio which emphasizes the Belle Heaulmière's complaining. In Denis Meslier's edition of ca. 1490–91, the rubric has been mistakenly changed to read "La vieillesse en regretant . . .".

29. This also corroborates the suggestion that the Levet woodcuts were not made for this edition in particular (but cf. note 44).

30. Cf. the references to Katherine de Vauselles (v. 661), Jehanneton (v. 732), Marthe (vv. 950–55 [acrostic]), Denise (v. 1234), Marion l'Idolle (v. 1628), Jehanne de Bretaigne (v. 1629).

31. I do not completely agree with the connections Rupert T. Pickens establishes between the Belle Heaulmière, the Virgin and Villon's mother (p. 168) nor with the fact that he sees the Belle Heaulmière as "an extension of the 'dames du temps jadis,' most of whom resemble her in one way or another and differ from her, in fact, only in that they are now dead" (p. 170) in "The Concept of Woman in Villon's 'Testament,' " in *Medieval Studies in Honor of Robert White Linker*, eds. B. Dutton, J. W. Hassell, Jr., and J. E. Keller (Editoriale Castalia, 1973), pp. 163–76.

32. Quoted from the Galway Kinnell translation of *The Poems of François Villon* (New York: Signet Classics, 1965), p. 77, v. 486.

33. Margot is not depicted as a pitiful figure, like the Belle Heaulmière, but the image he draws of his association with her and of their bawdy, salacious lovemaking is nonetheless a relatively sympathetic one.

34. Levet seems to have combined the references to "Faulce beauté" and "Amour dure" in vv. 942 and 944, thereby underlining Villon's attack in the ballad itself against an abstraction, even though it is bequeathed to the specific Rose-Marthe (cf. note 43).
35. Villon gives his mother voice in the "Ballade pour priere Nostre Dame" as well. Yet, despite the fact that her presence is illustrated by Levet, "grosse Margot" does not actually speak.
36. Since previously mentioned evidence strongly suggests a conscious design on the part of the printer as regards the placement of woodcuts (cf. p. 322), it is probable that this arrangement (cvi^r/cvi^v) is likewise a sign of editorial intention.
37. Cf. Gombrich, p. 69, who, in speaking about the repeated woodcuts and captions in the fifteenth-century edition of the *Nuremberg Chronicle*, states that "neither the publisher nor the public minded whether the captions told the truth. All they were expected to do was to bring home to the reader that these names stood for cities."
38. He adopts the same caption and back-to-back disposition as Levet. Like the Levet edition, the Trepperel editions use only one woodcut for all three female figures, although it is a different one. But Trepperel is much less careful in his layout and, because he does not maintain the same textual disposition, text, caption and illustration are not always appropriately arranged.
39. According to Pierre Champion in his Notice to *La Plus Ancienne Edition de François Villon* (Paris: Editions des Quatre Chemins, 1924), p. 7, Levet, who supposedly had had connections with the bookseller Antoine Vérard, left his shop on rue Saint Jacques in 1490 and began to work for Le Caron.
40. Only in manuscript C are all of the acrostics presented correctly.
41. These passages are reproduced as they appear in the Levet edition, fols. cvi–cvi^v, with abbreviations expanded and apostrophes, accents and punctuation added when necessary (cf. note 17).
42. In the correct versions this fourth line reads "Trocter m'en fault en fuyte et deshonneur." None of the acrostics in Villon's *Testament* is emphasized in this or any other early editions before Marot's, whose use of indentation for certain lines (cf. pp. 54, 55–54, 75–76, 87) makes the reconstruction of the acrostics even less obvious. A vertical reading of the acrostic FRANCOYS in the first stanza here is, moreover, somewhat thwarted by the fact that two initial letters of his name are not even capitalized.
43. Despite the acrostic that should correctly spell out MARTHE, the verses preceding the ballad allude to a particular girlfriend of

Villon's (Rose?) to whom the ballad-bequest is sent, but explain why he speaks to a more abstract addressee, namely Amours:

> Item, m'amour, ma chiere rose,
> Ne luy laisse ne cueur ne foye;
> Elle ameroit mieulx autre chose...
> Ce non obstant pour [m]'acquiter
> Envers amours plus qu'envers elle...
> Ceste ballade luy envoye... (Levet, fols. [cv–cv^v])

44. Larger in size than all the rest (although symmetrically balanced with its companion woodcut on the facing folio) and different in design because it portrays three figures–hanging men at that–instead of one, the illustration accompanying the so-called "Ballade des pendus" apparently constitutes the only woodcut in the Levet series that was made specially for Villon's edition (cf. Guignard, p. xviii). This doubtless explains the coincidence of editorial and authorial design. In the Le Caron edition the folio with the hangmen woodcut is missing, but the same one appears in the Bineaut edition. The Trepperel edition is the only extant version containing a different hangmen woodcut (fol. Eviii).
45. Except ms. R (B.N. f.fr. 12490), which dates from ca. 1515, that is, after the Levet edition. Marot maintains this coupling in his 1533 edition.
46. Cf. Guignard, p. xv, who states: "Le titre n'est évidemment pas celui que Villon avait donné à son oeuvre, et paraît avoir été inspiré par celui du *Testament* et du *Codicille* de Jean de Meung, dont les éditions circulaient déjà." The so-called codicil consists of the "Cause d'appel dudit Villon," "Le rondeau que feist ledit Villon quant il fut jugié," [=the quatrain], "Epitaphe dudit Villon" [=the so-called "Ballade des pendus"], "Le debat du cueur et du corps dudit Villon," "La requeste que bailla ledit Villon a messeigneurs de Parlement," "La requeste que ledit Villon bailla a monseigneur de Bourbon," and two ballades ("Tant grate chevre que mal gist..." and "Je cognois bien mouches en laict..."). These are followed by "Le jargon et jobellin dudit villon," a series of six ballades so difficult to understand that Marot omitted them in his edition. The *Lais* or "petit testament," as Levet calls it, closes the anthology. Although the particular placement of Villon's miscellaneous poems does seemingly reflect a conscious strategy on the editor's part to relate them to the *Testament,* such an arrangement

is ultimately undermined by the positioning of the *Lais* at the close of the collection, for these bequests offer a less sobering, more open-ended finale than either the *Testament* or the "Ballade des pendus." Nevertheless, this particular arrangement was imitated in all extant editions up to 1533.

47. Cf. vv. 22–24 ("Quant on me dit present notaire / Pendus serés je vous affie / Estoit il lors tant temps de moy taire?"). This ballad immediately preceding the Villon woodcut sets the stage for the theatrical display of these facing folios, for in it Villon appeals his case before one Garnier and implicitly pleads in his own defense, leaving the repeated question of the refrain "Estoit il lors temps de me taire?" unanswered.

48. These verses do not even constitute a rondeau as Marot, himself a poet, implicitly points out in the more appropriately changed rubric of his 1533 edition (my emphasis): "Le *Quatrain* que feit Villon quant il fut jugé a mourir." Cf. also note 49.

49. The same rubric is found in mss. F (which, dating from ca. 1480, could be later than Levet's edition) and R (ca. 1515), but no title precedes this poem in mss. C, P, and B.N. f.fr. 24315. Cf. Calin, p. 184, who states:

> Many scholars think that Villon wrote the poem in 1463 under sentence of death and thus portrayed himself as one of the executed criminals. This belief is stated in the introduction and notes to most editions of the *Oeuvres*. It is also possible, however, that he may have written the *ballade* at some other time and is speaking for his friends or for outcasts in general.

50. This rubric is absent in Levet's edition.
51. Marot expands and elaborates upon Levet's caption: "L'épitaphe en forme de ballade, que feit Villon pour luy et pour ses compaignons s'attendant estre pendu avec eulx" (p. 104).
52. Note the title change from previous editions. The king's role too, described by Marot as the "cause de l'entreprise" [Aii], is well publicized on the title page, as is that of the bookseller, Galiot du Pré. Curiously, the printer's name has dropped out of advertising prominence. This sharing of title-page space is recalled in the colophon, which omits reference to printer and bookseller however (my emphasis):

> Fin des oeuvres de *Françoys Villon* de Paris, reveues et remises en leur entier par *Clement Marot,* valet de chambre du Roy: et furent parachevees de imprimer le dernier jour de Septembre, L'an mil cinq cens trente et troys.

53. Cf. also a copy of the two-year privilege granted to Galiot du Pré on 21 September 1533, which is reproduced in this introductory space (fol. Aii^v) and which emphasizes too the importance of the bookseller in this enterprise.
54. These involve questions of pronunciation, versification, syllabification, vocabulary, etymology, and literary and moralistic interpretation. Cf. Lazard, pp. 16–17.
55. Unlike Levet and subsequent printers, who announced the verses inserted into the *Testament* by means of rubrics such as "Ballade" or "Autre Ballade," Marot devised new titles, which he calls "myeulx attiltrez" in his Prologue (Av^v), such as "Ballade des dames du temps jadis," "Les regretz de la belle Heaulmyere ja parvenue a vieillesse," "Ballade que Villon feit a la requeste de sa mere, pour prier Nostre Dame," "Lay, ou plustost rondeau," "Ballade que Villon donna a ung gentil homme nouvellement marié, pour l'envoyer a son espouse par luy conquise a l'espee," etc. Already in 1532 the Galiot du Pré edition had made slight changes in the rubrics.
56. Marot explains in his Prologue (fol. Aiii): ". . . mais pour l'amour de son gentil entendement, et en recompense de ce que je puys avoir aprins de luy en lisant ses oeuvres, j'ay faict a icelles ce que je vouldroys estre faict aux myennes, si elles estoient tombees en semblable inconvenient." He continues (fol. Av): "Aprés quant il s'est trouvé faulte de vers entiers, j'ay prins peine de les refaire au plus pres (selon mon possible) de l'intencion de l'autheur . . .".
57. "Le petit testament de Villon, ainsi intitulé sans le consentement de l'autheur, comme il dit au second livre" (fol. ai). In his Prologue, Marot states: "Finablement, jay changé l'ordre du livre: et m'a semblé plus raisonnable de le faire commencer par le petit testament, d'autant qu'il fut faict cinq ans avant l'autre" (fol. Av^v).
58. Cited from the edition of Frank Lestringant (Paris: Gallimard, 1987), p. 45.

SELECT BIBLIOGRAPHY

This bibliography includes those works cited in the book which would offer the interested reader more general information about the poets and the literary tradition herein discussed. Studies of a very specialized nature, particularly those in languages other than English or French, have not been noted. This listing also includes a good number of items which have not been referenced by any of the contributors, but which the editor considers accessible and important.

Ainsworth, Peter F. "The Art of Hesitation: Chrétien, Froissart and the Inheritance of Chivalry." In Lacy, Norris J. et al., eds. *The Legacy of Chrétien de Troyes*. Amsterdam: Rodopi, 1988, 187–206.

Altman, Leslie. "Christine de Pisan: Professional Woman of Letters (French, 1364–1430?)." In Brink, J. R., ed. *Female Scholars: A Tradition of Learned Women before 1800*. Montreal: Eden Press, 1980, 7–23.

Altmann, Barbara K. "Diversity and Coherence in Christine de Pisan's *Dit de Poissy*." *French Forum* 12 (Fall 1987): 261–71.

Altmann, Barbara K. "Reopening the Case: Machaut's Judgment Poems as a Source in Christine de Pizan." In Richards, Jeffrey Earl, ed. *Reinterpreting Christine de Pizan*. Athens: Univ. of Georgia Press, 1992, 137–156.

Aron, Mary-Jo. "*Fortunes Stabilnes*: The English Poems of Charles d'Orléans in their English Context." *Fifteenth-Century Studies* 7 (1983): 15–24.

Avril, François. "Les Manuscrits enluminés de Guillaume de Machaut: Essai de chronologie." In Chailley, Jacques et al., eds. *Guillaume de Machaut*. Paris: Klincksieck, 1982, 117–33.

Bakhtin, Mikhail. *Rabelais and His World*. Translated by Helene Iswolsky. Cambridge, MA: MIT Press, 1968.

Bakhtin, Mikhail. *The Dialogic Imagination*. Translated by Caryl Emerson and Michael Holquist. Austin, TX: Univ. of Texas Press, 1981.

Bossuat, Robert. *Le moyen âge*. Paris: Presses de l'imprimerie moderne, 1957.

Bronson, Bertrand H. *In Search of Chaucer*. Toronto: Univ. of Toronto Press, 1960.

Brownlee, Kevin and Stephens, W., eds. *Discourses of Authority in Medieval and Renaissance Literature*. Hanover, NH: Univ. Press of New England, 1989.

Brownlee, Kevin. "Discourses of the Self: Christine de Pizan and the *Rose*." *Romanic Review* 79 (Winter 1988): 199–221.

Brownlee, Kevin. "Metaphoric Love Experience and Poetic Craft: Guillaume de Machaut's *Fonteinne amoureuse*". In Lazar, Moshe and Lacy, Norris J., eds. *Poetics of Love in the Middle Ages: Texts and Contexts*. Fairfax, VA: George Mason Univ. Press, 1989, 147–55.

Brownlee, Kevin. *Poetic Identity in Guillaume de Machaut*. Madison: Univ. of Wisconsin Press, 1984.

Brownlee, Kevin and Scordilis, Marina, eds. *Romance: Generic Transformation from Chrétien de Troyes to Cervantes*. Hanover, NH: Univ. Press of New England, 1985.

Burke, Mary Ann. "A Medieval Experiment in Adaptation: Typology and Courtly Love: Poetry in the Second Rhetoric." *Res Publica Litterarum: Studies in the Classical Tradition* 3 (1980): 165–75.

Calin, William. *A Muse for Heroes: Nine Centuries of Epic in France*. Toronto: Univ. of Toronto Press, 1983.

Calin, William. *A Poet at the Fountain: Essays on the Narrative Verse of Guillaume de Machaut*. Lexington, KY: Univ. Press of Kentucky, 1974.

Calin, William. *In Defense of French Poetry: An Essay in Revaluation*. University Park: Pennsylvania State Univ. Press, 1987.
Calin, William. "Medieval Intertextuality: Lyrical Inserts and Narrative in Guillaume de Machaut." *The French Review* 62 (Fall 1988): 1–10.
Calin, William. "La Fonteinne amoureuse de Machaut: Son or, ses oeuvres-d'art, ses mises en abyme." In *L'or au moyen age: Monnaie, metal, objets, symbole*. Aix-en-Provence: Pubs. du CUER-MA, 1983, 75–87.
Calin, William. "Le moi chez Guillaume de Machaut." In Chailley, Jacques et al., eds. *Guillaume de Machaut*. Paris: Klincksieck, 1982, 241–52.
Cazelles, Raymond. *Société, politique, noblesse et couronne sous Jean le Bon et Charles V*. Geneva: Droz, 1982.
Cerquiglini, Jacqueline. *"Un engin si soutil": Guillaume de Machaut et l'écriture au xive siècle*. Paris: Champion, 1985.
Cholakian, R. *Deflection / Reflection in the Lyrics of Charles d'Orléans*. Potomac, MD: Scripta Humanistica, 1984.
Clemen, Wolfgang. *Chaucer's Early Poetry*. New York: Barnes and Noble, 1964.
Coleman, Janet. *Medieval Readers and Writers*. London: Hutchinson, 1981.
Cosman, Madeleine Pelner and Chandler, Bruce. *Machaut's World: Science and Art in the Fourteenth Century*. New York: New York Academy of Sciences, 1978.
Cropp, Glynnis M. "Fortune and the Poet in the Ballades of Eustace Deschamps, Charles d'Orléans, and François Villon." *Medium Aevum* 58 (1989): 125–32.
De Looze, Laurence. "Guillaume de Machaut and the Writerly Process." *French Forum* 9 (Spring 1984): 145–61.
De Looze, Laurence. "Mon Nom Trouveras: A New Look at the Anagrams of Guillaume de Machaut—the Enigmas, Responses, and Solutions." *Romanic Review* 79 (1988): 378–89.
Dembowski, Peter F. "Chivalry, Ideal and Real, in the Narrative Poetry of Jean Froissart," *Medievalia et Humanistica: Studies in Medieval and Renaissance Culture* 14 (1986): 1–15.

Dembowski, Peter F. *Jean Froissart and his "Meliador": Context, Craft, and Sense.* Lexington, KY: French Forum, 1983.

Dembowski, Peter F. "*Li orloge amoureus* de Froissart." *L'Ésprit Créateur* 18 (1978), 19–31.

Diller, George T. "Froissart: Patrons and Texts." In J. J. N. Palmer, ed. *Froissart: Historian.* Totowa, NJ: Rowan and Littlefield, 1981, 145–60.

Diller, George T. "Froissart's Chroniques: Knightly Adventures and Warrior Forays: 'Que chascun se retire en sa chascuniere.' " *Fifteenth-Century Studies* 12 (1987): 17–26.

Ehrhart, Margaret J. "Machaut's *Dit de la fonteinne amoureuse,* the Choice of Paris, and the Duties of Rulers." *Philological Quarterly* 59 (1980): 119–37.

Ehrhart, Margaret J. "Machaut's *Jugement dou Roy de Navarre* and the Book of Ecclesiastes." *Neuphilologische Mitteilungen* 81 (1980), 318–25.

Ehrhart, Margaret J. *The Judgment of the Trojan Prince Paris in Medieval Literature.* Philadelphia: Univ. of Pennsylvania Press, 1987.

Ferrand, Françoise. "Les Portraits de Guillaume de Machaut à l'entrée du prologue à ses oeuvres, signes iconographiques de la nouvelle fonction de l'artiste, en France, à la fin du xive siècle." In Bailbe, Joseph-Marc, ed. *Le Portrait.* Rouen: Pubs. de l'Univ. de Rouen, 1987, 11–20.

Frank, Robert Worth, Jr. *Chaucer and the Legend of Good Women.* Cambridge, MA: Harvard Univ. Press, 1972.

Gauvard, Claude. "Portrait du prince d'après l'oeuvre de Guillaume de Machaut." in Chailley, Jacques, ed. *Guillaume de Machaut.* Paris: Klincksieck, 1982, 23–39.

Green, Richard Firth. "Chaucer's Victimized Women." *Studies in the Age of Chaucer* 10 (1988), 3–21.

Hieatt, Constance B. "*Un autre fourme*: Guillaume de Machaut and the Dream Vision Form." *Chaucer Review* 14 (1979–80): 97–115.

Hindman, Sandra L. "With Ink and Mortar: Christine de Pizan's *Cité des dames*: An Art Essay." *Feminist Studies* 10 (Fall 1984): 457–84.

Huot, Sylvia. *From Song to Book: The Poetics of Writing in Old French Lyric and Lyrical Narrative Poetry.* Ithaca, NY: Cornell Univ. Press, 1987.

Kells, Kathleen E. "Christine de Pisan's *Le Dit de Poissy*: An Explanation of an Alternate Life-Style for Aristocratic Women in Fifteenth-Century France." In DuBruck, Edelgard E., ed. *New Images of Medieval Women: Essays Toward a Cultural Anthropology.* Lewiston, NY: Edwin Mellen, 1989, 103–19.

Kelly, Douglas. "Les inventions ovidiennes de Froissart: Reflexions intertextuelles comme imagination." *Litterature* 41 (1981), 82–92.

Kelly, Douglas. *Medieval Imagination: Rhetoric and the Poetry of Courtly Love.* Madison: Univ. of Wisconsin Press, 1978.

Kelly, Douglas. "*Translatio Studio*: Translation, Adaptations, and Allegory in Medieval French Literature." *Philological Quarterly* 57 (1978), 287–310.

Kendrick, Laura. "Rhetoric and the Rise of Public Poetry: The Career of Eustache Deschamps." *Studies in Philology* 80 (1983): 1–13.

Kibler, William. "Poet and Patron: Froissart's *Prison amoureuse*." *L'Ésprit Créateur* 18 (Spring 1978): 32–46.

Kibler, William. "Self-Delusion in Froissart's *L'Espinette amoureuse*." *Romania* 97 (1976): 77–98.

Kiser, Lisa J. *Telling Classical Tales: Chaucer and the "Legend of Good Women."* Ithaca, NY: Cornell Univ. Press, 1983.

Langlois, E. *Recueil d'arts de Seconde Rhétorique.* Paris: Imprimerie National, 1902.

Lanoue, David. "History as Apocalypse: The 'Prologue' of Machaut's *Jugement dou Roy de Navarre. Philological Quarterly* 60 (1981), 1–12.

Lanoue, David. "Music Therapy and Guillaume de Machaut: Hope's Chanson Royal in the *Remede de Fortune*." *Romance Quarterly* 31 (1984): 363–70.

Lukitsch, Shirley. "The Poetics of the *Prologue*: Machaut's Conception of the Purpose of his Art." *Medium Aevum* 25 (1983): 258–71.

Morris, Rosemary. "Machaut, Froissart, and the Fictionalization of the Self." *The Modern Language Review* 83 (Summer 1988), 545–55.

Muscatine, Charles. *Chaucer and the French Tradition: A Study in Style and Meaning.* Berkeley: Univ. of California Press, 1957.

Nelson, Jan A. "Guillaume de Machaut as Job: Access to the Poet as Individual through His Source." *Romance Notes* 23 (Winter 1982): 185–90.

Nouvet, Claire. "Pour une economie de la de-limitation; *La Prison amoureuse* de Jean Froissart." *Neophilologus* 76 (Summer 1986): 341–56.

Palmer, R. Barton. "*The Book of the Duchess* and *Fonteinne amoureuse*: Chaucer and Machaut Reconsidered." *Canadian Review of Comparative Literature* 7 (1980): 380–93.

Palmer, R. Barton. "Transtextuality and the Producing-I in Guillaume de Machaut's *Jugement* Series." *Exemplaria* 5 no. 2 (1993): 283–304.

Palmer, R. Barton. "Vision and Experience in Machaut's *Fonteinne amoureuse*." *Journal of the Rocky Mountain Medieval and Renaissance Association* 2 (1981): 79–86.

Patterson, Lee. *Negotiating the Past: The Historical Understanding of Medieval Literature.* Madison, WI: Univ. of Wisconsin Press, 1987.

Picherit, Jean-Louis. "Les Exemples dans *Le Jugement dou Roy de Navarre* de Guillaume de Machaut." *Lettres Romanes* 36 (1982): 103–16.

Planche, Alice. *Charles d'Orléans ou la recherche d'un langage.* Paris: Champion, 1975.

Poirion, Daniel. "Le Monde imaginaire de Guillaume de Machaut." In Chailley, Jacques, et al., eds. *Guillaume de Machaut.* Paris: Klincksieck, 1982, 199–206.

Poirion, Daniel. *Le Poète et le prince: L'évolution du lyrisme courtois de Guillaume de Machaut à Charles d'Orléans.* Paris: Presses Universitaires de France, 1965.

Preston, Raymond. "Chaucer and the *Ballades Notées* of Guillaume de Machaut." *Speculum* 26 (1951): 615–23.

Quilligan, Maureen. "Allegory and the Textual Body: Female Authority in Christine de Pizan's *Livre de la cite des dames.*" *Romanic Review* 79 (Winter 1986): 222–48.
Rowland, Beryl. *Companion to Chaucer Studies.* New York: Oxford Univ. Press, 1979.
Uitti, Karl D. and Freeman, Michelle A. "Christine de Pisan and Chrétien de Troyes: Poetic Fidelity and the *City of Ladies.*" In Lacy, Norris J. et al., eds. *The Legacy of Chrétien de Troyes.* Amsterdam: Rodopi, 1988, 229–53.
Uitti, Karl. "Remarks on Old French Narrative Courtly Love and Poetic Form." *Romance Philology* 26 (1972–3) and 28 (1974–5): 77–93.
Uitti, Karl. "The Clerkly Narrator Figure in Old French Hagiography and Romance." *Medioevo Romanco* 2 (1975), 394–408.
Waugh, Patricia. *Metafiction: The Theory and Practice of Self-Conscious Fiction.* New York: Methuen, 1984.
Wetherbee, Winthrop. *Chaucer and the Poets: An Essay on Troilus and Criseyde.* Ithaca, NY: Cornell Univ. Press, 1984.
Whiting, B. J. "Froissart as Poet." *Medieval Studies* 8 (1946): 203–12.
Williams, Sarah Jane. "An Author's Role in Fourteenth-Century Book Production: Guillaume de Machaut's 'Livre ou je met toutes mes choses.'" *Romania* 90 (1969): 433–54.
Wimsatt, James. *Chaucer and the French Love Poets: The Literary Background of "The Book of the Duchess."* Chapel Hill: Univ. of North Carolina Press, 1968.
Wimsatt, James. "Guillaume de Machaut and Chaucer's *Troilus and Criseyde.*" *Medium Aevum* 45 (1976): 277–93.
Wimsatt, James. "The *Dit dou Bleu Chevalier*: Froissart's Imitation of Chaucer." *Medieval Studies* 34 (1972): 388–400.
Wright, C. H. C. *A History of French Literature.* New York: Haskell House, 1969.
Zink, M. *Roman rose et rose rouge: Le Roman de la Rose ou de Guillaume de Dole.* Paris: Nizet, 1979.
Zumthor, Paul. *Le Masque et la lumière: la Poétique des grands rhétoriqueurs.* Paris: Seuil, 1978.

INDEX OF PROPER NAMES AND TITLES

Only items mentioned in the text are listed. Medieval French names are indexed exclusively under their French spelling. These are presented under the form Christian name/place name, except when convention dictates otherwise (e.g., Christine de Pizan but Machaut, Guillaume de). Authors are listed parenthetically after titles only when necessary to avoid confusion between different works of the same title. Character names from individual works and place names are not indexed.

Adolescence clémentine, L', 335
Aeneid, The, 152
Alain de Lille, 64, 66
Altmann, Barbara, xxvi, xxvii
Amores, 62
Andreas Capellanus, 304
Augustine, 202
Aviarium, 163, 171, 175
Avril, François, xxi, 95–96

Bakhtin, M. M., xviii, 89
"Ballade to Chaucer," xxv, xxvi, 187–209
Ballades notées, Les, 114 122, 127–28
Barolini, T., 307
Benoît de Sainte-Maure, 2
Bernart de Ventadorn, 122
Bestiaire (Pierre de Beauvais), 171
Bestiaire d'amour, 163
Bethurum, Dorothy, 38
Bleu Chevalier, Le, 7
Boccaccio, Giovanni, xvii, 30, 39, 42–43
Bodel, Jean, 122, 128
Boethius, 15, 66
Boniface IX, 204
Book of the Duchess, The, xvii, 30–34, 38, 115, 190

Boucicaut (Maréchal de France), xxvi, 194, 209
Bronson, Bertrand, 38
Brown, Cynthia, xxx, xxxi
Brown, Murray, xxv, xxvi
Brownlee, Kevin, xiii, 4, 76, 77–78, 87–88, 95, 176, 221
Bürger, Peter, 74

Calin, Williams, xiii, xiv, xviii, 86, 95
Canterbury Tales, The, xviii, xviii, 38–42
Capetians, the, xxii
Cent Ballades (Christine de Pizan), xxvi, 218, 221–28, 233, 238, 242–43
Cent Ballades (Jean le Sénechal), 5
Cent Ballades d'amant et de dame, 218, 227–28, 233–35, 239
Cerquiglini, Jacqueline, xiii, 50
Chansons (Charles d'Orléans), 293–310
Charles V, 193
Charles VI, 192, 199–206, 208–09
Charles de Navarre, xvi, xxii, 5, 8, 20, 80–82, 88
Charles d'Orléans, xiv–xv, xxviii–xxix, 5, 293–310

357

358   Chaucer's French Contemporaries

Chartier, Alain, xxiii
Châtelain de Couci, 5
Châtelaine de Vergy, La, 80
Chaucer, Geoffrey, xiii, xiv, xvii, xxv, xxvi, xxx, 20, 29–43, 73, 82, 89, 164–66, 187–209
Chaucer and the French Love Poets, xvii
Chevalier de la Charette, Le, 2, 6, 20
Chrétien de Troyes, 2, 119–23, 128–29
Christine de Pizan, xiv, xv, xxiii, xxvi, xxvi, xxvii, xix, 4, 43, 82, 217–43, 304
Chronicler of Saint-Denys, the, 208
Chroniques (Froissart), 5, 7
Cicero, 37
City of God, The, 202
Clark, William, 294
Clifford, Sir Lewis, xxv, xxvi, 188–89, 194, 197, 209
Cligès, 121
Complaint of Venus, The, 193
Confort d'ami, Le, xxii, 12–14, 16, 97
Conte du graal, Le, 20
Conon de Béthune, 5
Corngold, Stanley, 310

Dante, 42, 302, 307–08
De administratione, 304
De arte venandi cum avibus, 167
De natura rerum, 171
De planctu naturae, 64
Debat de deux amans, Le, 218, 228–30, 232–33, 238
Dembowski, Peter, xxviii, 5
Deschamps, Eustache, xiv, xv, xxiii, xxv, xxvi, 39, 187–209, 219
Dit de la fleur de lis et de la marguerite, Le, 258–60
Dit de la fonteinne amoureuse, Le, xvii, xxiii, xxiv, 1, 2, 13, 14, 16, 19, 31, 33, 37, 40–41, 50, 78, 88, 137–58
Dit de la harpe, Le, 97
Dit de la margherite, Le, 256–61, 263–64, 269
Dit de la marguerite, Le, 11
Dit de la pastoure, Le, 218, 227–28, 232, 234, 236–37
Dit de la rose, Le, 11, 221, 238, 240–43
Dit de l'alerion, Le, xxiv, xxv, 12, 16, 18
Dit du cerf blanc, Le, 11, 12
Dit dou lyon, Le, 18–19, 97
Dit dou vergier, Le, 77, 114, 124, 128
Ditté de Jehanne d'Arc, La, 218
Divine Comedy, The, 307

Donaldson, E. Talbot, 38
Donne, John, 122

Ebles II de Ventadorn, 5
Ehrhart, Margaret, xxiii, xxiv
Epistre au dieu d'amours, L', 238–40
Epistre du roi Richart II, L', 201, 207
Espinette amoureuse, L', 256–58, 264–65, 278

Fate of the Self, The, 310
Fourrier, Anthime, 10
Fowles, John, 75
François, I, xxx, 334
Frank, Robert, 34
Fredegarius, 152
Frederick II, 167, 173
French Lieutenant's Woman, The, 75
Friar's Tale, The, 165
Froissart, Jean, xiii, xiv, xv, xvi, xxvii, xxviii, xix, 4, 6, 7, 10, 11, 143, 16, 18–23, 29–30, 39, 42–43, 219, 252–75, 277–87

Gace de la Buigne, 168, 170–71
Gadamer, Hans Georg, 307
Gaston de Foix, 4
Godefroi de Bouillon, 202
Godefroi de Leigni, 2, 20
Gormont et Isembart, xvii, 115, 117–19, 124–25
Gower, John, 43
Granson, Ot(h)on de, xvi, 5, 193–94, 209
Guichard d'Angle, 194
Guilhem IX, 5
Guillaume de Dole, 123–24
Guillaume de Lorris, 20, 42, 47–66, 77, 81, 278
Guillaume de Poitiers, 122
Guthrie, Steven, xxi

Hardy, Thomas, 75
Henry II, 2
Hieatt, Constance B., xxiv, xxv
Hoepffner, Ernest, xx, 94–95, 97–99, 102, 104
House of Fame, The, 20, 38
Huizinga, J., 293
Humphrey X de Bohun, 10
Huot, Sylvia, xv, xviii, xix

Isabella de France, 191

Jean de Berry, xxii, 3, 5

Index

Jean de Blaisy, 193
Jean de Garencières, 5
Jean de Luxembourg, 3, 8
Jean de Meun, 20, 30, 37, 42, 47–66, 81–82
Jean de Vienne, 199
Jean le Bon, xxiii, 137, 191
Jean le Sénechal, 5
Jeanne d'Armagnac, 3
Jeanne d'Arundel, 10
Jenkins, Atkinson T., 196–97
Joli buisson de jonece, Le, 7, 13, 16, 18–19, 256, 258, 265, 270, 278
Joli mois de mai, Le, 269
Jugement dou Roy de Behaingne, Le, xvi, xix, xxi, 8, 9, 18, 30–31, 34, 37, 71–90, 93–106, 180
Jugement dou Roy de Navarre, Le, xvii, xx, 8, 9, 10, 12, 13, 16, 18, 20, 34, 37, 71–90, 95, 106, 114–15, 118, 124–29, 173

Kane, George, 38
Kelly, Douglas, xiii, xvi, 77, 189
Kiparsky, Paul, 113
Kiser, Lisa, 34
Kittredge, George Lyman, xiv, xvii, 29–30, 42
Klausenberger, Jürgen, 112, 114
Kristeva, Julia, xviii

Lais (François Villon), 315–36
Lais (Marie de France), 303
Lampe, David, 196
Lanval, 121
Lavision-Christine, 237, 242
Le Caron, Pierre, 328–29
Legend of Good Women, The, xvii, xx, 30, 34–36, 165
Letter of Prester John, The, 172
Levet, Pierre, 316, 318, 320, 324–25, 328–31, 334, 336
Livre de la cité des dames, Le, 218, 221
Livre des trois jugemens, Le, 218, 231–32
Livre du dit de Poissy, Le, 218, 228–29, 233, 238–39, 243
Livre des trois vertus, Le, 242
Livre du duc des vrais amans, Le, 218, 227–28, 233–35
Livres du roy Modus et de la royne Ratio, Les, 168
Louange des dames, La, 114, 127–28
Louis de Flandres, xxv, 202–06
Louis de Giac, 193

Louis d'Orléans, 195
Lowes, John Livingston, 29–30, 188, 199
Ludwig, Friedrich, 96
Lukitsch, Shirley, 76

Machaut, Guillaume de, xiii, xiv, xv, xvi, xvii, xviii, xxii, xxiii, xxiv, xxvii, 1–22, 29–43, 47–66, 71–90, 93–106, 111–30, 137–58, 219–21, 223, 243, 251–52, 260–63, 274
Manciple's Tale, The, 39
Manuel, Juan, 43
Marie de Champagne, 2
Marie de France, 120–21, 123, 303
Marot, Clément, 316–18, 331, 334–36
Méliador, 4, 5, 6, 13, 22, 283
Ménagier de Paris, Le, 167, 173
Merchant's Tale, The, 39–42
Miroir de Mariage, Le, 39
Montaigne, Michel de, 31
Muscatine, Charles, 84

Nicole de Margival, 124
Nouvet, Claire, xxvii, xxviii

Orloge amoureus, L', 278
Ovid, 30–31, 37, 42, 62, 274
Ovide moralisé, xiii, xvii, 33, 148, 153–55

Palmer, J. N. N., 206
Panofsky, Erwin, 1
Paradis d'Amour, Le, xxviii, 13–19, 277–87
Paris, Paulin, 49, 60
Parliament of Fowls, The, 164, 195
Parzival, 20
Percy, Thomas, 194
Péronne d'Armentiéres, 6
Petrarch, Francesco, 30, 42
Philippa de Hainaut, 278
Philippe de la Vache, 194
Philippe de Mézières, xxv, 193, 201–02, 206–07, 209
Philippe d'Orléans, 191
Physiologus, 163
Pierre de Beauvais, 171–72
Pierre de Lusignan, xxiii, 193
Picherit, Jean-Louis, 86
Plaidoirie de la rose et da la violette, La, 266
Planche, Alice, 295, 303
Pliny, 169
Poirion, Daniel, xiii, 3
Pope, Alexander, 37

Prise d'Alexandrie, La, xxiii, 7, 13, 193
Prison amoureuse, La, xxvii, xxviii, 251–52, 255, 258, 269, 272, 278
Prologue, Le, 62, 64, 66, 80, 82–83, 86, 219–20, 223

Raimbaut d'Aurenga, 294
Radding, Charles, 294
Remede de Fortune, Le, xxi, 12 ,14, 16, 18, 37, 65, 66, 95, 98, 104–06, 283
Renart, Jean, 123, 129
René d'Anjou, 5
Richard II, 192, 203, 208
Richard de Fournival, 163
Robert d'Alençon, 11
Robert the Hermit, 193, 208
Robertson, D. W., Jr., xix, 72–73
Roman de Brut, Le, 2
Roman de la Rose, Le, xii, xviii, xix, xxv, 30, 39–40, 47–66, 80–82, 164, 189, 195–96, 198, 209, 253–54, 257–59, 262–63, 266–69, 271–72, 274, 281
Roman de Renart, Le, 39
Roman de Troie, Le, 2
Roman des deduits, Le, 168, 170, 173
Romaunt of the Rose, The, 196
Rudel, Jaufré, 5, 122
Ruiz, Juan, 43

Saint John, 42
Scheler, Auguste, 278
Shakespeare, William, xxiv, 73, 166, 180
Solomon, 42
Song of Songs, The, 60
Songe du vieil pélerin, Le, 201–02
Speculum naturale, 169
Spence, Sarah, xviii, xix
Spenser, Edmund, 166
Squire's Tale, The, 164
Sturges, Robert S., xiv
Suger, Abbot, 294, 304–05

Taming of the Shrew, The, 166

Temple d'honneur, Le, 10, 12–13, 16, 268–69
Testament, Le, 315–36
Theory of the Avant-Garde, The, 74
Thibaut d'Aussigny, 319
Thibaut de Champagne, 5, 122, 124
Thomas de Cantimpré, xxiv, 169–71, 175
Troilus and Criseyde, xvii, 20, 30, 165, 195, 198–99

Uitti, Karl, 72, 95
Urban VI, 204

Vergil, 37, 152
Verrier, Paul, 112, 119
Vie de Saint Alexis, La, 112, 129
Villon, François, xv, xxii, xxx, xxxi, 43, 315–36
Vincent de Beauvais, xxiv, 169–71, 175
Virgin Mary, 18
Visconti, Galeas, 191
Visconti, Giangaleazzo, 203
Visconti, Lucchino, 193
Visconti, Valentina, 203
Vita Nuova, La, 302
Voir-Dit, Le, xv, xviii, xix, xx, xxii, xxvii, 6, 12, 16, 18, 37, 47–66, 77, 90, 94
von Simson, Otto, 294
Vox Clamantis, 195

Wace, 2
Wenceslas de Brabant, 5, 11, 15, 22
Whiting, Bartlett J., 277
Willard, Charity Cannon, 239
Williams, Sarah Jane, 94–95
Wimsatt, James I., xiii, xvii
Wolfram von Eschenbach, 20
Wolfzette, F., 293–94

Yvain, 121

Zeeman, Nicole, 221
Zumthor, Paul, xiii, xvi, 303